Napoleon: His Wives, Lovers & Women

Napoleon: His Wives, Lovers & Women

Two Accounts of the Women in Napoleon's Life

The Women Napoleon Loved
Tighe Hopkins

Napoleon, Lover and Husband
Frederic Masson
Translated from the French by J. M. Howell

Napoleon: His Wives, Lovers & Women
Two Accounts of the Women in Napoleon's Life
The Women Napoleon Loved
by Tighe Hopkins
and
Napoleon, Lover and Husband
by Frederic Masson
Translated from the French by J. M. Howell

First published under the titles
The Women Napoleon Loved
and
Napoleon, Lover and Husband

FIRST EDITION

Leonaur is an imprint
of Oakpast Ltd

Copyright in this form © 2013 Oakpast Ltd

ISBN: 978-1-78282-152-6 (hardcover)
ISBN: 978-1-78282-153-3 (softcover)

http://www.leonaur.com

Publisher's Notes

The views expressed in this book are not necessarily those of the publisher.

Contents

The Women Napoleon Loved   7
Napoleon, Lover and Husband   203

Napoleon I

The Women Napoleon Loved

Contents

Prefatory Note	11
Napoleon and the Feminine Tangent	13
Episodes of Youth and Adolescence	26
Josephine	45
'The Queen of the East'	101
The Singer of Milan	109
'Georgina'	114
The Feminine Under the Empire	123
The Women of the Family	131
The Femmes Fortes	145
The Mystery of Madame X——	152
Walewska	158
Marie Louise	171
The 'Tragi-Comedy' of the Rock	192

Prefatory Note

The French themselves have discussed with native candour Napoleon's experiments among the other sex. Their curiosity on the subject overflows in contemporary memoirs by many hands, and our own day has had the expression of it in M. Frédéric Masson's sober and careful essay. *Napoléon et les Femmes*, and in the lively pages—a touch less accurate—of M. Joseph Turquan's *Napoléon Amoureux*. It is a side of Napoleon's life that has not until now been dealt with by an English pen. Through the hard and crude ordeal (one of the least generous, perhaps, that convention has devised for genius) he lives not too badly.

In a very special degree my thanks are due to Mrs. C. M. Patmore,[1] who, when the book was planned but scarcely yet begun, helped me assiduously with research, and more than this, through an illness of four months' duration.

T. H.

---

1. Author of *The Court of Louis XIII*

1
Napoleon and the Feminine Tangent

1

"Sire," said Mme. de Staël to the emperor at an audience, "it is thought that you do not care much for women."

"Pardon me, *madame*," was Napoleon's curt rejoinder, "I love my wife."

The question and the answer stated facts in their degree. "What and how much, after all, have women been to me?" was, as it were, the pulpit query of the exile on the rock of St. Helena. Replies are not wanting, make what we may of them. Here, for instance, is one that reaches us through Gourgaud, at whose pen, says a very recent writer, M. Gonnard, we get Napoleon's real accent:—

> I never was in love, except perhaps with Josephine[1]—a little. And when I first knew her I was twenty-seven years old. For Marie Louise[1] I had a sincere affection.

What belief may we give to the sundry voices that reach us from St. Helena, the works written or inspired by Napoleon at that spot? Upon these rests, in the main, almost the whole of that vast structure known as "the Napoleonic legend;" yet what comes to us from St. Helena has won no universal credence. Lord Acton noted, more than twenty years ago, the "disposition common in France and Germany to reject *Memorial*." Lord Rosebery holds that we have in the private journal or diary of Gourgaud the "one capital and superior record of life at St. Helena." Dr. G. K. Fortescue, in an admirable introduction to an admirable translation of Thibaudeau's *Bonaparte and the Consulate*,

---

1. *Napoleon's Letters to Josephine* by Henry Foljambe Hall and *Marie-Louise and the Invasion of 1814* by Imbert de Saint-Amand also published by Leonaur.

decides that it would have been "more just to the memory of Napoleon himself had the *Memorial of St. Helena* and all the other contemporary records of the petty jealousies and sordid squabbles which took place there, been left unwritten or promptly burnt."

M. Gonnard, in the careful history just glanced at, *The Exile of St. Helena*, is plainly of the opinion that, though we need not swear by every fragment of the "sacred texts," we might not easily dispense with them. Mr. H. A. L. Fisher, in the brilliant final chapter of the Cambridge Modern History volume on *Napoleon*, bids us remember that, if the Napoleonic legend "owes much to the artifice of the exiles," it "has been a force in the politics of Europe." So far as the sayings attributed to Napoleon himself count in the building up of the legend—and they count, of course, for well-nigh everything—we may recall an ungallant word of that gallant worshipper, Stendhal, that a man at the summit of power usually lies when he speaks, and with greater reason when he writes. At St. Helena Napoleon's power extended scarcely to the rabbits that troubled his garden patch; but he had a case to establish for Europe, the world, and posterity.

We may set down, more or less at hazard, a few of the sayings.

Love is the occupation of the idle man, the distraction of the warrior, the rock of the sovereign.

Love is merely a silly infatuation, depend upon it.

Perfect love is ideal happiness.

I believe love to be hurtful to society, and to the individual happiness of men. I believe, in short, that love does more harm than good.

I have something else to think of than love. No man wins triumphs in that way who does not forfeit some palms of glory.

I have conquered hearts as well as countries.

In the Civil Law adultery is a portentous word; in real life it is but gallantry—an episode of a masked ball." (This in a discussion in Council of State on the Civil Code: Thibaudeau is the reporter.)

All the women in the world would not make me lose an hour.

Labour is my element.

It will not do to pretend that we catch in all of these sayings "Napoleon's real accent." Some of them ring true enough; in others we detect the pose of an hour, something idle or disingenuous. What may be said with precision is that at no time was love the "occupation" of Napoleon. In the months in which he was inditing to Josephine the almost hysterical letters that will be read, he was performing prodigies with his half-trained legions in Italy. Love as the "distraction of the warrior" hits the white pretty closely in his case. At the nebulous reference to love as the "rock of the sovereign" we hesitate, doubtful of the interpretation. He can scarcely, in this instance, be thinking of gallantry, which we have seen to be his other name for adultery. "All the women in the world would not make me lose an hour," is far from being totally false, and almost as far from being totally true. Some episodes of the amour with Walewska array themselves against this catholical protest. But the last sentence in our brief imperfect list is one that we can always stand by, always rest in with assurance. Not love, but labour, was Napoleon's element.

And now for an interval let us take wider ground. All but ninety years have fallen since Napoleon died on the rock of his captivity, and more than ever deeply the world is whelmed under the flood of writing in many tongues—writing that struggles to express the minds of many men regarding Bonaparte, regarding the first Emperor of the French; writing that struggles—and for the most part ineffectually—to reduce x to terms of a and b.

Some, with Lord Rosebery, crave an appreciation, yet to be vouchsafed, of the whole being, of his character, of his deeds and their effect upon a hemisphere. But the consummate appreciation, when we get it, will not entirely flatter those readers with whom Napoleon is a cult. As far back as 1887 Lord Acton, the Daniel of a day not poor in literary judgment, was saying, in the *English Historical Review*, that "the produce of recent years . . . will not allow the mighty figure ever again to shine with excessive light." What was said in 1887 may be confidently repeated today. He who was "Puss-in-Boots" to little Mlle. Permon, and to her elders the giant of the seven-leagued stride, and to all incense-burners a celestial in the likeness of Jove, begins to be measurable by standards fetched not from Olympus nor from Brobdingnag.

Rejecting as quite unworthy De Quincey's contemptuous epithet, that Napoleon was a "*sciolist*" (or shallow man) "for any age," we are still unable to pronounce him, as Charlemagne can be easily pronounced, the most accomplished man of his generation. Napoleon was not this. Long (or, at least, some appreciable period) before the cataclysm of Waterloo, his genius for war itself had begun to shrink:

not fate alone disposed that day to Wellington. The admission is Napoleon's own. As Lord Acton observes:

> At Dresden he confessed with magnanimity that the worst blunders of the Russian campaign were his own. Although he despised Massena for his cupidity, he insisted that he possessed military talents '*devant lesquels il faut se prosterner.*' He pronounced himself equal to St. Cyr in attack, but his inferior in the science of defensive war.

Seeley even denied to Napoleon the merit of originality, but this acute and vigorous historian is an enemy avowed. None the less, the question of true and absolute originality is still in argument—and in the near future will be, perhaps, among the questions most debated. .With this is linked the problem of the intrinsic value of his cardinal achievement, the reconstruction of the France from which the Revolution had extruded the Bourbons. For the present, we merely note the direct statement of Professor Pariset in his chapter on the Consulate (Cambridge Modern History: *Napoleon*), that although "it was Bonaparte who created contemporary France," "the history of France during the nineteenth century has been, in many respects, nothing but a long and toilsome reaction against the system" he established.

World-historical, in the strictest Hegelian sense. Napoleon remains: one of those men "who act instinctively as the agent of some change for which the time is ripe." But his shrine is neither of a god nor of a demi-god. It is not even, upon any rigid computation, that of the finished and flawless hero.

But it is with genius that we are dealing after all, and genius still derides our little efforts to docket and define it: we can make of genius no dictionary item. It seems reflexive, independent of the working consciousness. Could there, indeed, be held some nebular theory of that Genius Supreme which we are ever striving to glimpse behind the veil, then might we conceive of genius as one flame of the divine incandescence leaping wide into the void to become, as it were, the nucleus of a Caesar, a Michael Angelo, a Shakespeare, a Newton, a Beethoven, or, finally, a Napoleon. For in such a nucleus we might fancy how sordid particles would get entangled, making the radiance spirtle, making it speckled with dimness; and this conception would at least spare us the futile quest of consistency.

How long were we bidden to look on the invader of England—painted in inky shades—the vulture hovering on Boulogne beach, gluttonously eyeing our shores—we ourselves, in our terror, almost ready to enter the death-agony. "Give me but four hours' lordship of the sea," cried the First Consul, "and I will conquer Britain!"

In drawing-room, tavern, and nursery Apollyon and the Beast of the Apocalypse cohered in this Corsican: Boney! England thought on him for years as, but a while earlier, she had thought on her witches—with that half-animal hatred, flecked with terror, that rises at the vision of the sorceress. Observe him as he is limned in English caricature by Gillray, Rowlandson & Co.: the Chimæra of Christendom.

Then came the turn of fortune, and after the turn of fortune the sheer, irremediable vanquishment, the surrender to England. Did our own government, it has been asked, live in hope that he himself would settle matters with a razor-stroke? The wretched bathos of the poisoning episode at Fontainebleau is known to us. Nausea had intervened, averting death, and the emperor accepted the omen.

From the standpoint of a new century it has been questioned whether, for a man broken to the uttermost, banishment were necessary to the hideous solitude of the Rock. But in what degree was England to blame? Mr. Fisher, in the chapter on St. Helena, has put the facts with perfect clearness.

On July 13 he wrote to the prince regent that he had terminated his political career, and that he came, like Themistocles, to seat himself at the hearth of the British nation and to claim the protection of her laws. Two days later he gave himself into the charge of Captain Maitland of the *Bellerophon*. He knew well that he could expect little mercy from the restored government of France, and that the Prussians would shoot him like a dog. But England was the refuge of the homeless and the asylum of the exile. She had sheltered Paoli, the friend of his youth; she had sheltered the Bourbons, the rivals of his manhood. Out of magnanimity she might shelter him.

But the man whose ambition had wrought such disasters could not expect to be treated with leniency; and the British Government determined that Napoleon was no guest, but a prisoner of war. It was a case of policy, not of precedents; and, even if Lord Liverpool's Cabinet had been accessible to quixotic impulses, it would have been their plain duty to suppress them in the interests of European peace. The Congress of Vienna had declared Napoleon to be an outlaw, and, in virtue of a convention struck on August 2, 1815, the four great powers agreed to regard him as their common prisoner.

Upon us devolved the "ungracious office" of the gaoler. And what of the conduct of Sir Hudson Lowe at St. Helena, the cause of such a terrible amount of acrimonious writing? Readers may make choice between the position of Lord Rosebery on this subject and that of an intelligent opponent, Mr. R. C. Seaton (*Napoleon's Captivity in Relation to Sir Hudson Lowe*), though there is, of course, a mass of other literature on this rather tedious and none too pregnant theme. "Sir Lowe" we may perhaps take leave to dismiss as a worthy and slow-witted English official person, strangely unalloyed by the Irish strain in him. Our prison commissioners at the Home Office would have made of Lowe the pattern governor of one of their finest convict gaols. He might not have been quite up to the standard of Louis XIV's ideal turnkey, Saint-Mars, the gentleman who had charge of the Iron Mask; but his prisoners would have known what rules meant—and what it meant to infringe them. Destiny, not over kind, pitchforked him into the most difficult and delicate of posts, at St. Helena, and for eighty and odd years he has pervaded literature as a type and figure of the historical scapegoat.

As for the general situation at St. Helena, the dreadful repression of captivity doubtless told upon the little band. "Exile is in itself a form of martyrdom; and the exiles of Longwood ate their bread in genuine sorrow." Their life was scarcely normal. Hysteria counts for much; the bickerings, the jealousy of one, the maudlin attentions of another to any feminine creature that came within range. From them poured forth an unexampled stream of literature; Bertrand alone, the most dignified figure of the crowd, abstaining from the quill.

A modern writer begs us not to forget the 11,000 British subjects, prisoners of war, shut up for years in France. Dr. Holland Rose, commenting on the richness of the St. Helena literature, speaks of it as showing:

> The advantage of a memoir-writing nation over one that is but half-articulate. For the dumb Britons not a single tear is ever shed, whereas the voluble inmates of Longwood used their pens to such effect that half the world believes them to have been bullied twice a week by Lowe.

The turn of the tide which seeks to make a demi-god of Napoleon brings us up against absurdities as crude as all the defamation of the past. Then the arguments over his religion. Did he or did he not (at Weimar) launch a question as to the existence of Christ? Did he or did he not aver that Christ was more than man? He did almost certainly say: "Everything proclaims the existence of God; it cannot be doubted." He may have refused, and did probably at heart refuse, belief in the forms of religion; belief in the existence of a God he did not refuse. Personally he would seem to have stood aloof from dogma; yet he could not be persuaded by one of the little coterie of the Rock to abjure all death-bed rites. "Who can say what he will feel in the hour of death?" returned the emperor. Farther, he seems most fully to have recognized the necessity of religions, if only as restrictive and coercive forces on the mass of humanity. But these are vexed and disputable questions.

2

What of his personal appearance? On this point there is less of discord. First, however, does any reader remember the finest fantastical or imaginative portrait of Napoleon ever projected upon paper? It is from the pen of the worshipping Heine, and charms us in the eighth chapter of that delicious fragment, *Book le Grand*. Here in full is the passage (Leland's well-known translation):—

> But what were my feelings when I first saw with highly blest and with my own eyes *him*, Hosannah! the Emperor!
> It was exactly in the avenue of the court garden at Dusseldorf. As I pressed through the gaping crowd, thinking of the doughty deeds and battles which Monsieur le Grand had drummed into me, my heart beat the 'general march' . . . and the emperor with his *cortège* rode directly down the avenue. The trembling trees bowed towards him as he advanced, the sun-rays quivered, frightened, yet curiously through the green leaves, and in the blue heaven above, there swam visibly a golden star. The emperor wore his invisible-green uniform and the little world-renowned hat.
> He rode a white palfrey, which stepped with such calm pride, so confidently, so nobly—had I then been Crown Prince of Prussia I would have envied that horse. The emperor sat carelessly, almost lazily, holding with one hand his rein, and with the other good-naturedly patting the neck of the horse. It was a sunny marble hand, a mighty hand—one of the pair which bound fast the many-headed monster of anarchy, and reduced

to order the war of races—and it good-naturedly patted the neck of the horse. Even the face had that hue which we find in the marble Greek and Roman busts, the traits were as nobly proportioned as in the antiques, and on that countenance was plainly written, '*Thou shalt have no gods before me!*'

A smile, which warmed and tranquilized every heart, flitted over the lips—and yet all knew that those lips needed but to whistle, *et la Prusse n'existait plus*—those lips needed but to whistle, and the entire clergy would have stopped their ringing and singing—those lips needed but to whistle, and the entire Holy Roman realm would have danced. It was an eye clear as heaven; it could read the hearts of men; it saw at a glance all things at once, and as they were in this world, while we ordinary mortals see them only one by one and by their shaded hues.

The brow was not so clear, the phantoms of future battles were nestling there, and there was a quiver which swept over the brow, and those were the creative thoughts, the great seven-mile-boot thoughts wherewith the spirit of the emperor strode invisibly over the world; and I believe that every one of those thoughts would have given to a German author full material wherewith to write all the days of his life.

The emperor rode calmly straight through the avenue; no policeman stopped him; behind his *cortège* rode proudly, loaded with gold and ornaments, on panting horses; the trumpets pealed; near me crazy Aloysius spun round and snarled the names of his generals; not far off growled the tipsy Gumpert, and the multitude cried with a thousand voices, '*Es lebe der Kaiser!*'—'Long live the Emperor!'

Thus and thus the thrice-delightful Heine. And now we may get down out of the cloud-car, and consider more prosaically. We behold this Colossus, who stands not above five feet three or four. Was he not, to his fond cohorts, *le petit Caporal?* Thin—quite obtrusively and painfully so—in the hunger-days of his distressful youth, he wore through life that yellowish dread pallor of the secret cancerous taint that should destroy him, as it had destroyed Charles Bonaparte his father. When, as he grew in years, he gained in weight, he gained thereby also in facial form and colour. His hair, of a dark chestnut, improved immensely in appearance after he had taken to the barber's the lank "dog's-ear" locks of current fashion. The splendid head we know, somewhat large in proportion to the body, the delight of painter and sculptor; the nose so marble-fine; the lips clenched unflinching, yet never losing their half-voluptuous curves.

The eyes pale in tint were of disputed colour; hazel-grey perhaps, taking bluer tone by candlelight: they could be transfused with darker shading under emotional influences—"his eyes would look like velvet"—and betimes like hell. The "sunny marble hand" that Heine draws, the classic hand that blesses alike the tragic actor and the flirt, has "muscle of steel and bone of diamond." The nether limbs took no shame from the tight knee-breeches and the stocking; and the foot (when at last he had the money to fit it with a shoe) matched the shapely leg. On the whole, perhaps, a Caesar in a delicate mould.

From the physical beauty of his prime—when Rome imperial does certainly for a while invest him—there is a gradual and sensible decline. By Waterloo he is getting stout. Is this Lucifer, son of the morning, the adamantine-terrible? After the great defeat he was something of a surprise to those of his conquerors who saw him then for the first time. So much flesh consorted ill with so small a form, and there was a tinge of the grotesque in the redundant outlines. The arch-Terror had come within the range of the pencil of the satirist—the pencil of the satirist without bowels. We can forgive the satirist of the last distressing phase only by remembering that even in this last phase Napoleon's fixed idea was hatred of England and the English. There is no reason why we should quite forget the 'legacy of 10,000 *francs* to the "subaltern officer Cantillon," who did or did not attempt to assassinate Wellington.

One word may fitly here be said on Napoleon's endowment of Personal Ascendency. In what this gift of nature consists, we know not. It baffles us as the definition of genius baffles us; and we are no nearer to knowledge of it when we realize that, though there can be no personal ascendency without genius, there can be genius without personal ascendency. Whatever its essence, we may recognise the virtue in persons whose powers vary often in kind and oftener in degree, as we may miss it in some who have directed or immensely influenced the thought and movement of the world. It resides not wholly in character, for if it shines in Wesley it shines with equal intensity in Mirabeau. In Comte's *Calendar of Great Men*, a list running to some five hundred and fifty names, we have the representatives of the old and the modern civilizations, in theocracy, art, industry, philosophy, and science; but it is only here and there that an instance leaps to the front of sheer personal ascendency in man or woman. Of this enigmatic power of personal ascendency. Napoleon offers us as signal an example as the story of the world contains.

Even in the murk that settles on the closing days at St. Helena, days in which the darkened soul almost relinquishes the hope of glory in the yearning after rest—the penetrable shore of peace—something of the spark imperishable glows within the clay. On the last hours of nullity beneath the quilt, the bouts of torture, the pitiful mistreatment of erring medical attendants, the wail of poison from the people in the death-room, and the yielding of the shaken spirit amid the roar of South Atlantic breakers, what need to dwell? We have heard of these things, and shall hear of them again before the tide of the literature of Napoleon turns for the ebb.

3

We return to the point of departure: Napoleon's outlook upon woman and women. Here, marshalling the episodes of domesticity and of erotic adventure, we have employed to describe them the term tangential, for we discover no such figure as that of the intersecting circles of certain other men's relations with the opposite sex. Sarah Jennings and her lord. Nelson and his Emma have no counterpart in Napoleon's experiments in femininity. There may have lain always in the rearmost chamber of his mind some grudge against the glamour of womenkind, against himself also for any greater thrall to which for the time being he may have been subjected from the Sex. His alleged "hatred" of women—much has been written about this—we do not in the very least believe in. This was a logical man, and at no period in his life had he any reason to hate women. If he was resolved never to be enslaved, he was ready often to be charmed. Youth and a strong joy of life ran long in those glowing veins, and a face of beauty was seldom less than a face of beauty to Napoleon.

But let us next remember that he expressed utilitarian views as to the sphere of woman.

"I hold it an absurdity that a man may not have more than one legal wife. The result is the existence of mistresses, who lead to much greater dissipation of fortune than the concubine of old. In France women are made far too much of; they should not be regarded as men's equals, for after all they are nothing but the machinery for the turning-out of children. The greatest woman is she who has the largest family" (with this last sentence Napoleon had confounded Mme.

de Staël). Absolute social disorder, he declared, would result were women to emerge from the condition of dependence which—to his thinking—was their rightful position. One sex must submit to the other. Should sex-warfare arise between men and women it would, he held, be infinitely more terrible than anything the world had ever known—whether of combat between aristocrat and plebeian or even between the white races and the black. Such a situation arising, pregnancy alone would place women at a disadvantage, for the women of the markets are to the full as robust as many young men.

In the passage just cited there is mention of mistresses. We note at once that in the catalogue of the illicit loves of Napoleon there is no "*maîtresse en titre*," no titular and acknowledged Queen of the Left Hand. If the Countess Walewska be excepted—and the niche that history has found for her is a very tiny one—not a single name in the roll has attained to a high celebrity of dishonour. No really great or striking figure arrests us. There is here no Diane de Poitiers, the brilliant amazonian and intellectual creature that held the heart of Henri II, whose last lance was broken in her honour: Diane, who bathed every day in cold water "filled with crushed gold," rode abroad under all skies, swayed her king's empire, and gave her Venus' form undraped to the immortalizing chisel of Goujon.

There is no such pathetic heroine as poor Louise de la Vallière, the tardy, unwilling, and thrice-repentant victim of Louis XIV, who ended her brief romance in the hair shirt of the Carmelites, and whose story is one of the most poignant in history. There is no resolute and radiant courtesan like the Montespan, who crowed over La Vallière in the day of her disorder, flouted the Church, mocked at society, rode in her coach and six with ten times the pride of the legitimate queen, and had the Black Mass rehearsed over her beautiful naked body by the hideous Abbé Guibourg. There is no sphinx-like Maintenon, devoutest of all adventuresses, whom the scrutiny and persistent inquisitions of more than two centuries have but half revealed to us. There is no Pompadour, a great mistress if ever there were one ("the last king's mistress worthy of the name," Sainte-Beuve says), who had Voltaire for her laureate, and Quesnay, founder of the physiocrats, for her doctor; and who, when told that death had come for her, "dressed herself in her grandest, and met it bravely."

There is no Du Barry, daughter of a Paris "*rôtisseur*," or roasting cook, a veritable *sultana* of the gutter, demirep of very demirep, "with all the cynicism, animation, and refinements" of the trade she exulted in; who plied that royal dotard, Louis XV, with all her harlot's tricks, and made him smother her in gold and jewels; yet was in truth generous and warm-hearted and without malice, who said of a man caught singing ribald songs about her in the streets: "Fill him up in the kitchen, and let him sing it again." Nor, knowing what we know of Napoleon, shall we look to meet in this gallery with a Circe of the strangely-mingled qualities and powers of that Lola Montez of the 'forties—ranker's daughter and dancing-girl—who captured in an hour of delightful impudence the sexagenarian affections of Louis I of Bavaria, routed and smashed his Ultramontanes, ruled his kingdom for a year, liberalizing it from border to border—and in all these amazing months kept her royal slave at the length of the loveliest arms in Europe. For a Lola Montez (in the capacity, at any rate, of political adviser) Napoleon would have had as little use as he found for a Mme. de Staël.

No woman's counsel would he submit to in affairs of State; Josephine on this account had snubbings to put up with. Yet he recognized the conjugal power. "A wife who shares her husband's couch must always possess a certain influence over him." But there must be nothing of potion or pill-box in the influence; the great man would decline on bonbons only. He once writes to Josephine:

> I am used to kind, gentle, persuasive women, these are the women I like.

He writes from Finckenstein in 1807 (campaign against Prussia and Russia):

> But let us come back to these ladies. If I had leisure for any among them, I assure you, my dear, I would have them all pretty little rosebuds.

Le Féminisme he held in horror. The *maîtresse-femme* (our mere "clever woman" is by no means the ideal rendering, but the idea is conveyed), the *esprit fort* as he knew it in the voluminous and assertive person of Mme. de Staël, did more than set his every nerve on edge: this manner of woman filled him in some sort with alarm.

We must go much beyond all this, and say with due and necessary frankness that in the amorous episodes of Napoleon we find neither touch nor hint of transcendentalism; nothing of the loftiness and exaggeration that argue a great and rooted passion. To this immense man who ransacks man, tosses countries to and fro, and rises by distress of nations, no woman is a spiritual beacon! The lava-flow of the earlier letters to Josephine scorches even now, but this is the intensity of passion baulked of satiety by a temporary separation: the volcano is presently stilled, the molten stream cools and hardens. His love affairs were as the entangled particles: they were not of lambent flame.

Not all of the experiences are here recorded. Some among them were as little worthy of preservation as the experimental visits of a tourist to a licensed house in Paris, Vienna, Cairo, or Chicago. In the hour of triumph we see the emperor returning to camp with the cry: "*Une femme! Une femme!*" The outburst was but a momentary expression of the vitality that roared up and foamed in the man's whole being: the caresses of a woman came aptly with the loosing of the tension. He sought, perhaps, no earnest qualities in the woman that he dallied with; but, as far as our searches carry us, he was neither tyrant nor *debauchee* among them. He sought not to reap more than he had sown in Cytherean fields.

From these imperfect strokes of introduction we may go on to the proper pages of Napoleon's *Liber Amoris*. There is no *Confessio Amantis*. Napoleon—and may Heaven be thanked!—lacked Rousseau's presumptuous weakness for that.

2

Episodes of Youth and Adolescence

1

The Napoleon Bonaparte whom we first meet in Paris is a puny, pale, shabby little fellow in his sixteenth year. He was born the 15th of August, 1769 (some four months and a half after the child who was to become Duke of Wellington), and it was on the 19th of October, 1784, that he trudged into Paris at the heels of a Minim friar. He had come with four or five other lads from the preparatory school of Brienne, in Champagne, to the Royal Military School. What the dissolutions of time are! In fifteen years the sallow, undersized collegian had grown into First Consul, at a salary of half-a-million *francs*: master of the Paris he had entered with his clothes in a small handbag.

One of his biographers speaks of the luxury of the young Bonaparte's surroundings in the Royal Military School, but on this point M. Lenôtre has recently enlightened us. In 1785, he says, in the first volume of his *Romances of the French Revolution*, "military cadets were lodged in a wooden dormitory, built in the middle of the first courtyard, each having a small square room, furnished with an iron bedstead with linen curtains, a wooden chair, and a low wardrobe (in which to keep shoes and the powder-bag) on which was a pewter wash-hand basin." To the little Corsican, who at Brienne had been dubbed "the Spartan," this may have seemed luxury; but it is very like the accommodation bestowed on favoured youngsters of the same age in the first class at Borstal Prison.

Not at this period need we look for any *peccadilloes* on the student's part. Youths at the Royal Military would have very few chances of spying out the wickedness of the ill-lighted Paris of that day; and Bonaparte had no mind to spy. He was poor and proud, and probably a good deal isolated. Had there been football, he might and doubtless would have captained a team: he certainly would have hacked the shins of the French, for he hated them;[1] dreaming always and only of his Corsica, which the French were just about to take over. In school, he laboured at mathematics; out of school, he was a rather truculent little demon of a patriot. Woman is still summed up for him in the beautiful, devoted mother whose hand had not always caressed, and the sisters whose frocks he had torn.

He had, besides, another restraint during this his first year in Paris. It was the year of his father's death. The handsome, feckless, shifty man, Carlo Bonaparte, died at a convenient hour. He had, by forsaking Paoli for France, and by climbing every stair in Paris that he could get access to, wrested for Napoleon a place as King's scholar at Brienne. So far as fate went, there was nothing else for him to do: he had placed the child of destiny. Brienne led to Paris; and Paris, simmering itself slowly into the blaze of the Revolution, heralded the not too distant days of purple. Had the father lived, it passes conjecture what Napoleon would have done with him. In the post of Chamberlain in the Palace he would have found excuses to exhaust the treasury six times a year; and to have shifted him anywhere as king would have meant the creation of a new Brobdingnag. He died most opportunely.[2]

In about eleven months, which brings us to September 1785, the Corsican cadet was nominated for a commission as second lieutenant in La Fère regiment of artillery, quartered at Valence on the Rhone. In the following month, at the age of sixteen, he donned his uniform; and his first military boots, they tell us, were so much too big for him that when he strutted off to show himself to those old friends of the

---

1. He said, according to Mme. de Rémusat: "I was educated at a military school, and showed no aptitude for anything but the exact sciences. Everyone said of me, 'That child will never be good for anything but geometry.' I kept aloof from my school-fellows. I had chosen a little corner in the school-grounds, where I would sit and dream at my ease, for I have always liked reverie. When my companions tried to usurp possession of this corner, I defended it with all my might."
2. It was cancer. To Gourgaud Napoleon said: "My father had always been a man of pleasure, but in his last moments he could not draw too many priests and Capuchins around him. On his deathbed' he was so devout that the people in Montpellier insisted he must be a saint." Elsewhere, contrasting his mother's discipline with his father's: "Her tenderness was blended with severity; she punished and rewarded at the same time. She brought to account in us all there was of good and bad. My father, an enlightened man, but too fond of pleasure to concern himself greatly about us, attempted occasionally to excuse our faults. 'Let be,' she would say; 'it is my affair, and not yours, to look to the children.'"

family, the Permons, the two little daughters, *Cécile* and Laure (the second of whom was to become Duchesse d'Abrantès), promptly dubbed him "*Chat botté*," "Puss in Boots."

He arrived at Valence in November 1785. His pay of something less than £45 a year was all he had to live on; he was eager for work, and thought much more of mastering the rudiments of his profession than of amusing himself in the garrison town. At Valence the second lieutenant did, nevertheless, learn to dance! A politely humorous letter survives in which, in 1808, the ex-dancing-master, one Dautel, fallen upon evil times, brings himself to the notice of the emperor. "Sire,—He who taught you to take your first steps in the world commends himself to your generosity." The emperor found a small post for the broken-down professor—as indeed he found posts of greater or less importance for so many of the persons with whom he had rubbed shoulders in his early days.

Except that he was more of a worker and decidedly more of a recluse than the rest of them, the "sombre" sub-lieutenant seems to have lived at Valence in a manner not very different from that of the subalterns of his own age. He did not, as some have said, shun the society that was open to him. Stendhal tells us—with perhaps just a little exaggeration—that he was "immediately taken note of," and that he "pleased the ladies by the freshness and nobility of his sentiments and his audacity in argument." He pleased also at Valence one virginal and simple heart.

The pretty story is known to everyone. Among the families of the neighbourhood to whom Monseigneur de Tardivon, Abbé of Saint-Ruff, had introduced the young officer, was that of Mme. Grégoire du Colombier, a kindly and pleasant lady somewhat past the prime of life. Mme. du Colombier may or may not have been, as M. Turquan suggests, "a sort of mother" to the Bonaparte of this period, but she made him free of her house, and allowed him to be on terms of friendship with her daughter Caroline.

Perhaps there was even some talk of marriage (Mme. d'Abrantès evidently thinks there was), but this is now generally denied. It is denied on Napoleon's own authority in the *Mémorial de Sainte-Hélène*. Whether there was talk of marriage or not, we know of nothing but a dainty and quite innocent flirtation.

Here is how the great man, on his rock in the Atlantic, recalled the little *amourette*:

"No one could have been more innocent than we were. We used

often to arrange little assignations. I remember one in particular, at daybreak, on a midsummer's morning. Will it be believed?—our sole delight on that occasion was in nibbling cherries together."

Just nineteen years later, this idyll of the cherries had a sequel. Mademoiselle Caroline married, in 1792, M. de Bressieux, who had been a captain in the regiment of Lorraine and was a Knight of St. Louis. Probable enough is it that "the cherry-gatherer of Valence" had followed with her woman's heart the career of the war god through Europe; but what probability was there that Napoleon Imperator would remember the Caroline Colombier of Bonaparte? He did remember her.

In the camp at Boulogne, scheming his invasion of England, he received, August 1804, a letter from Mme. de Bressieux. She wrote, not for herself, but "recommending her brother to his notice."

Napoleon replied instantly, and with a gallant grace:

> Your letter was a source of great pleasure to me. I have never ceased to be interested in the memory of your mother and you. I shall avail myself of the earliest opportunity of assisting your brother. I see by your letter that you are living near Lyons, and think it a little unkind that you did not come over while I was there, for it will always be a sincere pleasure to me to see you, Receive this assurance of my desire to assist you.

They met: the Emperor of the French and the wife of the retired captain, who had not seen each other since the days when, at daybreak in the orchard of Mme. du Colombier, they had brushed the dew from the cherries. Years stupendous for Napoleon had sundered them. Here was he now the "day-shining Sun" that men would stand and gape against; whilst with her, the fairy of the orchard, fortune had wheeled in the slow and peaceful sort, and she was something matronly. The emperor found her "*furieusement changée.*" No matter for that. He was imperially good-natured, gracious, and kind to the Caroline his memory fondled, and insisted on appointing her lady-in-waiting to Madame Mère, his mother. Mme. de Bressieux, says the Duchess d'Abrantès, "was both witty and good; her manners were as gentle as they were pleasing." In the history of the loves of Napoleon, the name of Caroline Colombier, who enters his life but for a moment, bears a savour of peculiar sweetness.

We return to Bonaparte—for there are many tugs with fate before we greet him as Napoleon. Towards the close of 1787 we find him again in Paris, Hôtel de Cherbourg, Rue du Four-Saint-Honoré. There is at this day neither a Hôtel de Cherbourg nor a Rue du Four-Saint-Honoré; but the building, No. 33, is still upright in the street which for forty-five years has been called the Rue de Vauvilliers. Here, as M. Lenôtre will tell us, in his *Vieilles Maisons, Vieux Papiers*, Bonaparte occupied a room on the third floor, quitting it only at meal times for one of the little eating-houses in the district where he lunched or dined at threepence the dish. "As though ashamed of the amount he spent, he would fold up his money in the bill, and hand it silently to the cashier."

If he were remarked of anyone in these shy and frowsy restaurants (hard by the quarter where he was so soon to ride abroad as Caesar) it was as a scarecrow man of five feet three or so, pale, with a restless, brilliant eye, whose coat hung loose about his unfilled ribs, and who, when he had dined, looked as if he were saving for a meal. There is, at the date of this second sojourn in Paris, a casual encounter with a young professional street-walker of the Palais-Royal, which is glanced at in another chapter. The episode is as trivial, as commonplace, as it well could be; but to an English reader here and there it will suggest a rather curious comparison: De Quincey's Ann of Oxford Street, another child waif among street-walkers, and Bonaparte's nameless girl of the Palais-Royal.

Bonaparte, a neophyte still so far as women go, takes in hand the first neat-looking young *"fille de joie"* whom he meets on the pavement, questions her politely, in his cool matter-of-fact way, on her profession—and goes home with her. Widely different is De Quincey's treatment of the fragile pariah of Oxford Street, whom in a beautiful passage of the *Preliminary Confessions* he apostrophises as "noble-minded Ann;" and with whom—himself also at that season a hungry, delicate, and homeless walker of the streets—during the nights of many weeks he had paced up and down, "or had rested with her on steps and under the shelter of porticos." But the two experiences, Bonaparte's and De Quincey's, are indeed scarcely to be brought together. To the pure-souled dreamer and idealist De Quincey, learned already in the book of human sorrows, the little outcast of Oxford Street was a creature of infinite afflictions, to whom he, the man, though not much older than she, must play the Christ's part of brother.

Bonaparte, thinking chiefly perhaps that it is full time for the king's officer to have his taste of gallantry, takes the common course—and has even afterwards sufficient interest in the reminiscence to write it out in his diary. Still, this period of Bonaparte's in Paris was in no sense whatever a dissolute one. Had he been so minded, and he was not, it would have asked some ingenuity to act the rake on a purse that restricted him to dinners at threepence the plate.

He had taken a holiday at Ajaccio, had found the family in distress (the irrepressible father "had embarked on questionable speculations, which now threatened the Bonapartes with bankruptcy"), and his anxiety on their account was redoubled. If any woman were in his mind at this date it was Caroline and no other. His care for his mother is revealed in a letter he writes her in 1788 from Auxonne, where he has rejoined his regiment. He has been ill, but makes light of it.

"Work excepted, I have no resources here. I dress but once in eight days. Since my illness I have been sleeping very little; it is incredible. I go to bed at ten, and get up at four. I take but one meal in the day, at three o'clock. This I find good for my health."

He spends another furlough in Corsica; and in 1791 (a disputed date) is again with his regiment at Auxonne. This time he has with him his brother Louis, thirteen years of age. The widowed mother, with eight children and the "questionable speculations" of Carlo, was making a fight for existence in the island home, and Bonaparte had insisted on relieving her of Louis. The pair, of whom one was to be emperor and the other the King of Holland, lived somehow on the subaltern's exiguous pay. They had a couple of miserable rooms in barracks; Bonaparte put the pot on the fire, kept the accounts, and looked after the youngster's lessons.

Obtaining fresh leave, he returned to Corsica in October of this year, taking Louis with him, and remained until May 1792. He had now risen to the rank of captain of artillery (no great gain to his pocket), and in Corsica he was made lieutenant-colonel of the National Guard. To this period belongs a sensational but not too substantial story of an affair with a mistress unnamed. Baron Larrey alludes to it in the first volume of his work on *Madame Mère*, and it is cited by M. Turquan. According to this legend:

> Bonaparte gave his mother a great deal of anxiety in connection with a love-affair with a woman who had conceived a violent passion for him and who was endowed with all the jealousy of her race. Having ascertained that she had been abandoned for another mistress, she resolved on vengeance. Inviting him to dinner she mixed poison with his wine, and caused him to

drink it at a draught. Later in the evening the most alarming symptoms supervened and the young officer's life was in imminent danger. His mother, who had been immediately told of the matter, hastened to his side and prepared the remedies which the doctor had prescribed.

We have not found the story elsewhere. It is not incredible, it is not entirely probable. In the Corsica of that very turbulent epoch a dose of poison might rather easily have been employed to execute the vengeance of a jealous woman; but Bonaparte's days were just then so crowded with intrigues of far other kinds that he could have had but little time or inclination for philandering.

If Bonaparte narrowly escaped poison, did he also somewhat narrowly escape the guillotine? He had overstayed his leave, and took a prominent part in an affray at Ajaccio that has all the appearance of an attempt to capture the town. To Paris he was peremptorily summoned. Professor Seeley and M. Iung, among the historians not too favourably inclined to Bonaparte, have maintained that, had the times been normal, he would in all likelihood have been executed for insubordination. This might have happened; but the Revolution was in full blast, Paris was in a ferment, and the times were not normal in the very least.

We have merely to note the misery of his condition in Paris; disgraced, and destitute. There is mention of the pawning of his watch with one Fauvelet. He and his old schoolmate, Brienne, roamed the tumultuous and cruel streets of Paris in revolution, sat disconsolate in a dingy restaurant, and—having a few *francs* between them—talked of buying up some unfinished houses and sub-letting them! Yet there wanted for Bonaparte but little more than a decade to the *grandiose* days of Empire.

At last, in August 1792, he was righted with the authorities, and restored to his military estate. To Corsica once more, and on this occasion the guardian of his sister Elisa, a schoolgirl of Saint-Cyr, one of the royal houses of education which had just been closed by decree of the Legislative Assembly. They quitted Paris on the morrow of that "wild piping of the whirlwind of the human passions,"[1] which is dreadfully memorable as the September Massacres.

No sooner, however, had the mother Letizia got all her brood about her (for the first time in fifteen years) under the ancient roof in

---

1. Carlyle.

Ajaccio, than she and they were in headlong flight from this immemorial shelter of the family. There was civil war in Corsica, and it drove the Bonapartes from the island. With the romance of this exodus we are concerned only so far forth as it brings before us the heroic figure of the mother in her trouble. She showed the high courage of any of her Roman prototypes.

"In her woman's body," declared her son, "she carried the brain of a man."

At Marseilles we see her grandly taking refuge in a garret, her three girls at her heels; with means straitened to the uttermost, sharing in the ration-bread which was served out to the refugees, she kept up the courage no less than the discipline of her little household. Caroline, then about twelve, had a severe illness to add to the complication of events.

She was already a handsome girl with the delicate hands and feet of the family, and a finely-moulded bust. Her form, which was in days to come so elegant, bore yet the thickness of the hobbledehoy, but her complexion was the delicate rose of youth. And "Paulette," before whose loveliness Europe was to bow, a Medicean Venus of the nineteenth century, she already gave full evidence of her lustrous beauty. A girl friend says:

"For those who only saw her as she returned from the West Indies (after her first marriage to Le Clerc), with her complexion faded by that climate, can form no conception of her first girlish loveliness of colouring."

There in that poor lodging, in the sea-port town, lived the woman who was to be the mother of an emperor to come; there with her daughters, one day to be queens, she sewed and knitted, and nightly knelt in prayer.

Pinched and harassed, she had need of all that thriftiness which in her days of fortune she never put aside, and which Napoleon inherited from her. "For I will gladly give a million as a gift," averred the emperor, "but I hate above all things to see money frittered uselessly away."

We rest our gaze on her who as "Madame Mère" was to sit at the Coronation banquet of her son in 1804, with careful eyes glued on the golden service as the dishes passed before her, and with the bones of her own helping of chicken sedulously picked to the cleanest; rejecting the attempts of the palace attendants to remove her plate until her cautious parsimony had dealt with the last fragment.

2

At Marseilles the days of care, of scantiness, almost of want, dragged on. Corsica, truly, had not always given the Bonapartes the fatness of the earth; but at the old home, in the leanest season, there was garden stuff, there were eggs, and the fruit of the orchard. At Marseilles Letizia's *pot-au-feu* was thin, and there was no garden plot. Pauline, the radiant princess that was to be, had broken shoes, patches to her frock (Letizia would have no raggedness), and "a hat to frighten crows." Bonaparte gave them every *sou* he could out of his pay; he himself had grown used to the half-rations that had so long been his ordinary portion. He was twenty-four, and his thoughts began to dwell on marriage; as much perhaps, at this date, in the interests of the family as for his own comfort or advancement. A girl with a dowry was sorely needed at Marseilles.

Some relief, however, was at hand. In the spring of 1794, for his share in the siege of Toulon, Bonaparte was raised to the rank of general of brigade. Then, being named inspector of the fortifications on the Mediterranean coast, he was able to place his mother and sisters in a snug country villa in the exquisite neighbourhood of Antibes.

Next it was the hap of the eldest brother, Joseph, to do the family a turn. There dwelt at Marseilles a providential soap-boiler, Clary by name, wealthy and benevolent, who had shown a practical pity for the Bonapartes in straits in the town. On Joseph Bonaparte, who also among this amazing family was presently to be fitted with a crown, the soap-boiler bestowed in marriage his elder daughter, Julie. In her lap the bride (an excellent young woman of a seemingly ferocious plainness) brought a fortune of 150,000 *francs*, which, on M. Masson's computation, represented a purchasing power the equivalent of ten times that sum today, (1910). Joseph, in brief, must have been regarded by the rest of the family as having wedded a gold-mine or a customhouse.

Bonaparte felt he could do nothing better than fall in love with the younger daughter, Eugénie-Désirée. "Lucky rascal, Joseph!" was one of his favourite exclamations for some months after Joseph's marriage. M. Turquan is of the opinion that to Bonaparte, "penniless though he then was, it was a matter of indifference whether his bride were rich or poor;" that "marriage for him was summed up in the single word 'woman.'" This opinion we are not quite prepared to acquiesce in. At the period under review, Bonaparte's solicitude for his family and their future seems to us to have equalled (if it did not in some degree surpass) his concern for his own position and prospects; and he had witnessed the pleasure of his mother in the union of Joseph with the heiress of the golden soap boiler. But the soap pans of M. Clary had not ceased to foam, and of their overflowing yield Eugénie-Désirée would receive her due portion. With Désirée also in the family the Bonapartes would have a double grip upon the magic boilers.[2]

The young lady was sixteen years of age, and quite pretty enough to attract the fixed and somewhat melancholy gaze of Bonaparte. Opinions about her are various. One writer hints, as to her behaviour, that it was (in full-bodied Johnsonese) "characterized by unbecoming levity." Not less censorious is Mme. d'Abrantès, who speaks freezingly of her "irresponsive, lifeless heart." We have not discovered in Désirée these ungentle qualities.

No; she unfolds to Bonaparte a heart both tender and impulsive; and we share M. Turquan's belief that she responded promptly yet with delicacy to his earliest addresses. M. Masson also, speaking of her letters, says: "There is a genuine and spontaneous tenderness in these letters of Eugénie's. After the fashion of the day, the young girl, who was known by the name of Désirée, re-christened herself for her lover's benefit, desirous that the name by which he called her should be sacred to him alone. Rough copies of the letters were discovered sixty-five years later among the papers of her who had written them, and preserved them as relics. They are conceived in the very spirit of that age, an age of reaction towards love and life, after a period when death had long been the only spectacle, the only preoccupation."

But, as to its issue, this is another of the early loves of Bonaparte that goes agley. "Amid the ranks of war," the starved-looking boyish general is the wonder of his day; in the jousts of love, with matrimony for the prize, he strikes obliquely every time. He is off the right line.

Precisely how the story ended no one may say with sureness. We are very definitely told that Désirée rejected Bonaparte. We have it, on the other hand, not less precise in detail, that Bonaparte, re-entering Paris, with expectations and ambitions amplified, suddenly or gradually swerved from her. It is to this view that we incline. If we may accept the letter, well vouched for, that Désirée writes to Bonaparte on his marriage with Josephine, our view is confirmed. The first sentence of the letter is sufficient:

---

2. According to one version, M. Clary at this date was dead, and his widow the representative of the house and firm.

You have made my life a misery, and I am yet weak enough to forgive you.

Missing a crown with Napoleon in France, Désirée won another with Bernadotte in Sweden.

3

M. Arthur Lévy[3] perceives in the Napoleon of the first phase a large and serious preoccupation of mind on the subject of women. We are moved, on the whole, to think that his preoccupation of mind on this subject was inconsiderable. "Labour is my element," he said at St. Helena; "I have never found the limit of my capacity for work." And have we not just conned one of his letters to his mother—"I have no resources but work"? Bonaparte at school, at college, and climbing painfully and eagerly in his military career, is the most strenuous creature in France. It is not, indeed, the case that there was no stuff of woman in his heart or thoughts; but it is the case that he found his best satisfaction not in pleasure but in toil. He could live with little food, little sleep—and very little dalliance. The one thing he could *not* dispense with was work, and work in prodigious quantities. Had not work been invented some years before Bonaparte's time, he would have invented it.

The young man, civil or military, who has a large preoccupation of mind on the subject of women, usually displays some wantonness in clothes. In the case of the Bonaparte of the first phase, we may not talk, with Herrick, of—

A sweet disorder in the dress,

—for he seems to have been as slovenly a dresser in his youth as was Mr. Gladstone in his maturity. He was, in truth, a great deal worse than Mr. Gladstone, who, at his untidiest, did visibly "keep clean." Bonaparte was not scrupulously washed. The Duchesse d'Abrantès, at the Paris house of whose parents, the Permons, the young officer was a regular visitor, observes that his hands were not merely ungloved but "dirty;" that he slouched along the streets with a careless and rather clownish gait, and that his boots were as badly cared for as they were badly fitting. Another lady gave Stendhal a long description of the Bonaparte of this same period. His lank hair floated uncombed over his shoulders, his overcoat was threadbare, his whole appearance unkempt. "He was far and away the thinnest and the most curious-

---

3. *Napoléon Intime.*

looking creature I had ever met," so desperately thin, in fact, "as to give one the notion that he was the victim of some wasting disease." The slovenliness seems to have been very generally remarked upon.

Now this is hardly the style in apparel of a man who has a large and serious preoccupation about women. It may be affirmed with very little hesitation that Bonaparte had not this preoccupation; though he was not at this date cynically inclined where the other sex was in question. It may be asserted, too, as we think, that the Bonaparte of the first phase was not a man especially attractive to women. He did not look the lover, he did not look the man of gallantry. He would always, we fancy, have been noticed; for, as unkempt as he might be, he could never have lacked personal distinction. Says the fair correspondent of Stendhal:

> I saw at once that he was a person of genius, or at the least a person very far above the common level.

But in a numerous or strange company, at any rate until he rose into fame, Bonaparte (conscious perchance that he was not exactly the most presentable young man in Paris) must a little have resembled Hood's Eugène Aram, in his remoteness and silent melancholy. Mme. de Bourrienne, watching him as he sat alone one evening in a box high up in the theatre, remarked "a look of ferocious boredom" on his pallid countenance.

Still, if he were neither a hunter of women nor, in these days, a man hunted of them, Bonaparte—Italian, and deep imaginer, with dreadful fires slumbering behind that weary mask—had even now some spells, some mastery of charm. The abrupt, incisive tones could be softly thrilling; the falcon's eyes were now and then as velvet; and the expression which could smite and terrify could also, as one of the French biographers puts it, *"melt into a caress that made the receiver blessëd."* Genius, at its youngest and its most uncouth, is usually genius. The Cartwright of the seventeenth century, who has dowered British poetry with a piously flamboyant ode on the recovery of Charles II from smallpox (to quote it were to grieve the poet's ghost), might have turned some facile lines in celebration of the early loves of Bonaparte. But the lyrical note, if we do not altogether miss it in these passages, is within a touch of the imperceptible. Nothing of the pretty innocence of children's love is wanting to the scene in the orchard of Mme. du Colombier; but the Bonaparte who sheers off from Désirée Clary (if this version of the episode is the true one) begins to open his eyes upon a world in the management of which the plain affections hold little sway.

With this period of early manhood is associated one other pleasing image or vignette. For an instant indeed we seem here to be at the opening pages of a veritable love-affair, but we turn a leaf, and the place beyond is blank. Bonaparte was with his captain of artillery, Marmont, on a brief visit to Marmont's father at Châtillon-sur-Seine. Junot, one of Bonaparte's *aide-de-camps* (who was to marry Laure Permon, conquer Portugal, receive the title of Duc d'Abrantès, and die insane), was of the party; and both he and Marmont had praised their young general to the skies. The seedy-looking general of the Republic did not, however, impress himself too favourably on the county magnates; and he for his part was not less taciturn than usual. The visit might have turned out poorly but for Mlle. Victorine Chastenay.

Bonaparte had been taken by his hosts to be presented to the de Chastenay family. Mlle. Victorine treated the company to an Italian ballad, and timidly inquired of Bonaparte if her pronunciation were correct. He with unsocial brevity assured her it was not. The start was unpromising; but on the following evening, when the de Chastenays dined at the de Marmonts, Bonaparte made amends. Mlle. Victorine, her curiosity piqued by the long-haired, monosyllabic, military person with the devouring eyes, approached him deliberately and insisted on his talking to her. She drew him out on Corsica and, fortunately for her, Bonaparte at this date would discourse Corsica "from morn till noon, from noon till dewy eve."

It was not from want of words that he was ever mute, and ideas rose naturally and with rapidity in his mind. Mlle. Victorine was astonished, electrified, enchanted. They met again, and on one occasion at least went flower-gathering in the fields—though not at daybreak. Mlle. Victorine was perhaps more heedful than Mlle. Caroline. At this point alarming news (that his command had been taken from him) reached Bonaparte, and he must hasten from Arcady to Paris. His idyllic interludes were destined to discouragement.

Bonaparte returned no more to Châtillon-sur-Seine. Later, amid the radiant days of the Consulate, Mlle. de Chastenay was once a visitor at the Luxembourg. She had a favour to solicit in the interests of an *émigré*, and for some reason she elected to ask it not of the First Consul himself but of Josephine. Josephine had heard of the young lady, and from the lips of her husband, who had forgotten neither the summer holiday nor its genius. While the suit was being explained he entered the room, and at once began a cordial conversation. Josephine, as we are informed, betrayed not only nervousness but even some degree of agitation. What was her mind working on? Bonaparte at one period of his married life, tiring of an amour, would sometimes make a jest of it to Josephine, and wheedle or bribe her into helping him to send the lady packing.

But with this interesting young noblewoman there was not and there had not been the very suspicion of a liaison. It must have been that Josephine suspected or imagined the possibility of one. Bonaparte gave Mlle. de Chastenay a general invitation to spend an evening with them at the Luxembourg, and Josephine promised to procure her a formal interview for the presentation of her petition. She, who so seldom forgot a promise, seems carefully to have forgotten this one, and Mlle. de Chastenay did not pass an evening at the Luxembourg.

Of the sparse idylls of Bonaparte, this is the last recorded.

4

Whom have we next?

With the next lady we return to the matrimonial schemes of Bonaparte, which were growing insistent. In an hour of illusion, pathetically droll, he cast himself at the feet of Mme. Permon. This estimable lady, mother of a family, was Corsican by birth; she had known the Bonapartes at Ajaccio, and was on very kindly terms with Letizia. It was in the house of the Permons at Montpellier in Languedoc that Carlo Bonaparte, the father, had died; and at their house in Paris Napoleon Bonaparte was an intimate. To Mme. Permon he made an audacious offer of marriage.

In her spirited way the Duchesse d'Abrantès (the little Laure Permon of the days in question) narrates the story in the first volume of those rather romantic but entirely delightful *Memoirs*. Mme. Permon was not only a widow but in weeds. Etiquette imposed on her a rigorous seclusion from society, but her health had suffered, and the family doctor prescribed a course of mild distraction. Mme. Permon must take a private box, hide herself at the back of it, and watch the play discreetly every evening. This counsel the widow adopted, and with a guard of her friends went nightly to the theatre, Bonaparte being usually of the party. The drama proved a capital tonic, and Mme. Permon's wasting spirits were refreshed. For Bonaparte was it reserved still farther to exhilarate them.

He called one morning on the lady with a proposal to unite the two families by no fewer than three marriages. Pauline Bonaparte, praised even then as *"la jolie Paulette,"* should marry Mme. Permon's son. This young man, as we meet him in the fervent pages of his sister's *Memoirs*, was a paragon of twenty-five, who painted as well as Vernet, played the harp better than Kromphultz, spoke English, Italian, and modern Greek, made verses "like an angel," worked like a horse, had a talent unsurpassed for the conduct of affairs, and stood five feet nine in his boots.

In the second place, Mme. Permon's daughter Laure should be given in marriage to Louis or Jérôme Bonaparte.

"My dear friend," smiled the widow, "you are a perfect high priest this morning. You are for marrying every one, children and all!"

But Bonaparte had not finished. Bending over the plump white hand of the widow, he gravely assured her that he had that morning resolved to entreat her to begin the union of the Bonapartes with the Permons by accompanying him to the nearest altar.

For a period of seconds she regarded her suitor with an astonishment which, says Mme. d'Abrantès, *"tenait de la stupéfaction,"* and then—shook with laughter. Bonaparte looked graver than before. Mme. Permon made an effort to recover herself:

> My dear Napoleon, pray don't think that I am laughing at you; I am laughing at myself for the ridiculous role you are assigning me. Perhaps you think that you know my age? Well, you don't, and I am not going to tell it to you. What I *will* tell you is that I am old enough to be your mother, and not only yours but Joseph's to boot. And now let us bring this afflicting joke to an end.

Bonaparte continued to beseech her, declaring that never had he spoken more seriously. But if he was importunate the widow Permon was obdurate. Her refusal was as definite as refusal could be, nor was she ever again persuaded to bestow another thought upon the matter. A good-natured, sensible, matronly woman of the world, who shall say or think that she had not acted wisely?

If in the foregoing there is some smack of comedy, the story that succeeds it treads very close to farce. This mellow siren, Montansier! Actress, manageress, adventuress and woman of pleasure, sedate history knows nothing of La Montansier; but, commonplace as she is to the hard core of her, her career, extending through nine-tenths of a century, discloses France or Paris to us under five separate aspects. She is, as far as French annals go, the old world and the new. With an energy flaming, beaming, and indestructible she goes through the greater part of the long reign of Louis XV, through the reign of Louis XVI, the Revolution, the seven years of the Republic, the years of the Consulate and the Empire, the wreck of Waterloo, and the first years of the reign of Louis XVIII.

Strange that Carlyle, who makes so brave a figure of Théroigne de Méricourt, never once glimpsed Montansier in the Revolution; we miss thereby one brief chapter of his *History* that would have been, in Meredith's phrase, "a cataract of laughter!" When, during or after the September Massacres, her Paris establishments were closed, she gathered her company about her, from the actors to the scene-shifters, and marched them through the streets to the Assembly in congress at the Riding School. Her lover and chief performer, Neuville, harangued the Assembly in a written speech, in which he stated that the Demoiselle Montansier, manageress, begged that her whole company might be allowed to join the army of the Republic as volunteers for the defence of the nation.

A few days later they marched out amid the cheers of Paris. In the neighbourhood of Rheims they "played a farce between two battles;" and Neuville, reviewing his company for the benefit of the townspeople, was pitched from an unfamiliar saddle clean over his charger's head. The organizer of this Thespian corps for the relief of France was an elderly actress, who, if we could accept an unacceptable chronicle, might have been Empress of the French. But no, emphatically no!

Who Montansier was no one seems positively to know. She herself would have had it believed that her father was an advocate. The Vicomte de Reiset, in a very recent volume, *Belles du Vieux Temps*, says that he held "*un petit emploi dans la marine.*" M. Lenôtre, in his *Vieilles Maisons, Vieux Papiers*, brings documentary evidence to show that he was a pin-maker at Bayonne, where, undoubtedly, in December 1730, the heroine was born. She escaped from a convent school at Bordeaux, joined a *troupe* of strollers, sailed with them to America, and after some years returned to France.

During the old *régime* Montansier (whose domestic name, if M. Lenôtre is correct, was Brunet) seems first to have achieved notoriety as a woman of the town, visited by such gallants as the young Duc de la Trémoille, the Marquis de Jonsac, the Comte d'Esparbès, "and many others." At no period was she really distinguished as an actress, but in some comic piece that she played in at a little theatre in Versailles, her broad southern accent tickled the fancy of Marie Antoinette,[4] who, it is said, shared a bowl of soup with her behind the scenes. The young queen, in those days before the Terror, had high spirits, and could enjoy a romp, and was fond of flouting etiquette.

Then Montansier began to be famous. The playhouse in the Rue de Satory at Versailles she had opened by special leave; and court favour, won by characteristic effort on her part, procured for her somehow "the management of all the theatres in the three districts of Rouen, Alençon, and Caen." According to M. Lenôtre:

> Through Marie Antoinette she obtained the exclusive privilege of managing all the theatrical entertainments, balls, and *fêtes* of Versailles. She took advantage of this to construct at the end of the *château*, opposite the prettiest part of the park, the grand theatre which still exists.

In no long time, if faith may be placed in sundry chroniclers of the period. Mlle. Montansier was in some sort manager-general of the French theatrical world. The female Frohman of her day seems altogether too small a title for this all-conquering woman who moved and had her being in an orbit almost Napoleonic.

But Montansier was always for Montansier; a keen, self-centred, calculating lady, with splendid eyes, tip-tilted nose, and universal smile, whose motto was: "*The winning side for me.*" An invincible royalist under royalty, the Revolution found her very democrat of very democrat.

Out of her profits reaped in Normandy and Versailles she bought and rebuilt the Palais Royal marionette-show, called the Beaujolais. Here she had both a theatre and a "*salon!*" Common Paris crowded to the theatre, and in the *salon* were seen of an evening a "fantastic pell-mell of all sorts and conditions of men," from "*Egalité*" Orléans and the Duc de Lauzun to Danton, Robespierre and Barras. After the play there was a very free-and-easy supper; and:

> At one end of the torn and faded old sofa sat the mistress of the establishment arranging with her stage-manager, Verteuil, the programme for the week; while at the other end the player Grammont planned with Hébert the riots that should take place the next day at the Cordeliers.

---

4. *Marie Antoinette and the Downfall of the French Monarchy* by Imbert de Saint-Amand also published by Leonaur.

On her re-entry into the capital, after the excursion with her volunteers to Rheims, in the very midst of this disastrous epoch when men and women trembled for their heads, the undefeated and irrepressible Montansier, now well toward in years, built in the Rue de Richelieu the biggest and grandest playhouse ever seen, the Théâtre National. When the Terror was at its height she planned an opening in Montansieresque style. Down on her at this moment came the Commune of Paris, with an order for the confiscation of the building. But what to do with the manageress, who was not in the habit of playing the bystander when property of hers was in danger? Up rose Chaumette in the Convention, and accused Montansier of having erected a theatre for the express purpose of setting fire to the National Library! The denunciation was good enough, and to the prison of La Force she went. Here, however, the undaunted woman made so terrific a to-do that the Commune was fairly afraid of guillotining her; and Thermidor set her at liberty. She claimed from the Convention seven million *francs* in compensation. "Pooh!" said Bourdon de l'Oise, "we could build a fleet for that."

Montansier returned to her quarters in the Palais Royal. A part of these, as the story runs, she shared with Barras; and, says M. Lenôtre, "it casts an instructive light on the manners of the Revolution, when we find the most influential man in the government living in the house of an actress."

To Bonaparte at this period the "most influential man" rendered a variety of services; and Barras himself it is who tells us that he brought together the ill-dressed, cadaverous soldier of fortune and the now rather ancient charmer of Paris, and arranged a match between them. What a spectacle were it to have seen Napoleon, a few years later, crowning the Empress Montansier at the altar of Notre Dame! Barras dwells with infinite gusto on the fictitious history of their "engagement."

> I betrothed the future spouses that very day, and they both agreed with equal willingness. I thought I must have exploded with laughter, but was compelled to keep serious. At table, I placed Mlle. Montansier beside me, telling Bonaparte to take a seat opposite. Throughout dinner they sat with their eyes fixed on one another, etc., etc.

Page after page of this stuff does Barras regale us with, and all of it is dull and futile fiction. The history is unsupportable by any testimony save the word of Barras; and this, whenever Bonaparte is concerned, is generally worse than worthless. He would, when Bonaparte was in power, fabricate any lie to injure him; but of Barras's efforts and achievements in mendacity this may be stamped as the silliest. Bonaparte made no proposal of marriage to Mlle. Montansier. If Mme. Permon were old enough to be his mother, this Circe might have been his grandmother. "She could not have been less than seventy," says Barras. This was a final touch of malice; but, to be exact, the lady was turning sixty-five. A most wonderful woman, none the less, and she lived to be ninety; bequeathing "all her creditors to the King of France," who was then Louis XVIII.

Has any reader of this generation ever chanced upon Mrs. or Lady Elliott's [5] *Journal of My Life during the French Revolution*? It is, if not of the highest interest, extremely well worth reading. The lady's anonymous editor informs us that she had received an offer of marriage from Bonaparte, "which, however, she rejected." But for the curiously abrupt termination of the *Journal*, which seems to have been hurriedly set down one day and never resumed, we might have had from the author herself a statement on this important point. Perhaps His Majesty, who read the work piecemeal, as the successive sheets were carried to him by Dr. Dundas, forgot to send it back. It remains that we do not really know whether Bonaparte proposed marriage to the most beautiful and fascinating young English lady in the Paris of his adolescence.

---

5. Grace Dalrymple. When a mere girl she was married to Sir John Elliott, a man older than her father, and by him was shortly afterwards divorced. She bore a daughter to the young Prince of Wales, and it is said to have been "at the express desire" of George III that the *Journal* was composed.

3

Josephine

1

There are domestic legends, as there is a political legend, of Napoleon Bonaparte. The political legend relates chiefly to the career of the emperor, and to the objects, real and professed, of that career. The domestic legends belong for the most part to the various phases of the young, struggling, rising, and ambitious Bonaparte. To many readers, one among these legends is doubtless quite familiar. It describes the romantic first encounter and interview of Bonaparte and Josephine. Scarcely one of the biographers omits it.

After *Vendémiaire* (October 5, 1795), Bonaparte, transformed into general-in-chief of the army of the interior, was in command at Paris. The disarmament of the sections had been carried out. The widow Josephine had preserved the sword of her husband, Alexandre de Beauharnais, and resisted the demand of the agents for its delivery. Another version of the story says that the weapon had been given up, and that Josephine sent her son Eugène to beg it back from the general-in-chief. Bonaparte, charmed by the lad's address, and touched by his appeal, at once acceded to it; and Josephine hastened to the bureau with her compliments and thanks. The gallant young general, smitten at sight, made equal haste to return the visit—and fell in love.

This is the legend. There would be no great harm in accepting it, but the pretty tale has been invalidated. It is denied in the main by Barras, but that is unimportant. It is affirmed in the main in the *Memorial of St. Helena*, but that celebrated document, on which so much has been founded, is not pure gospel. What seems incontestable is, that Bonaparte and Josephine were acquainted before the date of the disarmament of the Paris sections. Had they not met in the *salons* of the

JOSEPHINE

Directory, where the graceful, elegant, and captivating widow was in some degree a celebrity, and where Bonaparte, at one time the shabbiest and least observed among the guests, was, a little later, received and most intently scrutinized as the hero of *Vendémiaire*, the hope of the Republic whose fortunes he was held to have restored?

In Ouvrard's *Memoirs* we have a glimpse of Bonaparte, "shortly before the 13th *Vendémiaire*," in the drawing-room of that conspicuous beauty, Mme. Tallien, "Our Lady of Thermidor." Ouvrard says that the Bonaparte of this period was the least noticeable and the least regarded by fortune of all the persons who composed Mme. Tallien's *salon*. Sitting aloof, as a rule, from the knots of gossipers, he would on rare occasions join them, jesting then with the merriest. In one of these moods he pretended to be a fortune-teller, and taking the hostess's hand, "*débita mille folies*." Among the ladies of the circle on this evening was Mme. de Beauharnais, languorous and nonchalant in her light-flowing draperies. What destiny the fortune-teller read in the plump palm of Mme. Tallien, we know not. The company would have thought but poorly of his powers had he turned from her to Josephine with the remark: "And you, *madame*, in nine years or so, will be seated on the throne with me as empress."

It was not until the 26th of October, 1795, that Bonaparte was definitively named general-in-chief of the army of the interior, and installed at the *quartier général* of the Rue des Capucines. But we have a letter to him from Josephine, dated October 28, which, if not precisely a love-epistle, is little like the formal note of a mere acquaintance. In this, indeed, the lady complains, with scarcely a pretence of reserve, that Bonaparte no longer visits one who is "tenderly attached" to him, and ends with a "*Bonsoir, mon ami; je vous embrasse.*" Clearly, their relations were not of the day before.

Bonaparte, waiting upon fate, distracted with anxiety for his own future and that of his family, had taken his part now and then in the very lively society of the day, less for the amusement it offered than for the chance of finding there some patron who would help him to a profitable place. Of this society Josephine de Beauharnais—at one fashionable house tonight, at another tomorrow—was an assiduous frequenter; and Josephine also, with two growing children, and no income to speak of, had her future to make. The pair of fortune-hunters had found themselves together at Mme. Tallien's, at Barras's, and elsewhere.

At what place, on what particular evening, they first exchanged a word, it is idle to inquire. We do not know by whom they were introduced. Perhaps no one introduced them; introductions could be dispensed with at those curiously mixed reunions of the Directory. But the poetic legend of "the sword of my father" is most probably a fairy-tale. It seems not to have been known at this period to the friends either of the lady or of the youthful general himself; and is perhaps to be classed with the other and more famous legend of the prediction to Josephine that she would one day wear a crown.

What is here to the purpose is that Bonaparte was very soon and utterly in bonds of love to Josephine; and it has now to be shown that if the Bonaparte of these days was in sore want of a patron or protector, not less sore was Josephine's want of a man to make good her very dubious future.

2

The Josephine of our earliest knowledge is a rather gawky and long-legged girl running wild with little niggers on a sugar plantation of the West Indies. She was through and through a Creole; the Creole offspring of Creole parents. Her father, Joseph-Gaspard Tascher de la Pagerie, was the son of an emigrant, Gaspard-Joseph, who had quitted France for the West Indies in 1726. The family belonged to the small provincial nobility of the Orléanais district. Josephine, the eldest child of her parents, was born at Trois-Islets, Martinique, in 1763, a few months after the signing of the Treaty of Paris which ended the Seven Years' War. Her early years were passed in the sugar-refinery which was the only building left standing on the Tascher estate after the hurricane of 1766; and at the age of sixteen she sailed with her father for France to be married to Alexandre de Beauharnais.

The match had been adroitly arranged by Josephine's strong-minded and not over-scrupulous aunt, Mme. Renaudin, who was living as the mistress of Alexandre's father. This gentleman, the Marquis de Beauharnais, had held the appointment of Governor and Lieutenant-General of the Antilles, a command in which he was undistinguished. Relieved of it, he returned to France; and with the family went Mme. Renaudin, who, during the sojourn of the Beauharnais in the West Indies, had obtained a situation as companion to the governor's wife.

The marriage in 1779 of Josephine and Alexandre, coldly contrived on the part of Aunt Renaudin (who had long thrown over her own husband), turned out a most unblest affair. Beauharnais the younger, an odious compound of libertine and prig, was but two years ahead of the schoolgirl from Martinique on whom he tried the airs of a *dominie*. Josephine was for no *dominie*. A little later she might have won him by the wiles that Paris talked of, but these were still untried. She knew scarcely more of life than the slave children she had romped with in Martinique; and for the conquest of a husband (*vicomte* to boot) who was at least in touch with the elegance of Paris, she lacked all but the slender accomplishments of a West Indian convent.

Josephine's best gift from nature was a figure of surpassing grace; and, for all her Creole origin, her figure at the era of her marriage had barely touched the stage of spring. She had never any smack of native wit; the arts defensive and offensive were equally and entirely unknown to her; and her one consummate power, the power of pleasing, seems not to have developed till she felt the hard need of using it. A wife of sixteen, she was neglected and brutally victimized by a hidebound and pedantic rake of a husband two years her senior.

Within a few months of their marriage Alexandre had practically deserted her. He had entered the army as a lad, and early in 1780 he rejoined his regiment. On September 3rd of this year, Josephine gave birth to Eugène, who was to be Viceroy of Italy. Alexandre, who had returned for this event, left France again immediately afterwards for Italy, where he remained until July 1782. In France once more, he drifted between Paris and Verdun, bestowed a week or more of his tediousness upon Josephine, and at the end of two months sailed for Martinique. Wedded life was as good as over. In Martinique he picked up a new mistress (his habit under every sky), who, feigning an intimate and infinite knowledge of the Taschers, crammed him with horrid tales of Josephine.

To Josephine, a girl-wife not yet twenty years of age, against whom he had nothing to produce but the slanders of a woman of ill-fame, his mistress, Alexandre wrote a letter of superlative malignity. He called her "the vilest of creatures;" renounced and cast her off. At about the time that the husband was sharpening his pen for this effort, the wife was bringing into the world (April 10, 1783) a daughter, Hortense, who was to be Queen of Holland and mother of Napoleon III. Alexandre returned to France and Paris, Josephine took refuge in a convent. This was in the autumn of 1783. They had been man and wife not quite four years, and had dwelt together in all some nine or ten months.

The husband's family were wholly with Josephine. Alexandre set on foot proceedings for a separation; Josephine, handsomely backed by Aunt Renaudin, did the same. Alexandre, manifestly, had no case, and he it was who had finally to yield. In a lawyer's office, on March 3, 1785, he retracted everything, and agreed to a separation, the conditions of which were entirely to Josephine's advantage. It was one of the few satisfactory days of her married life.

Three years later, in 1788, *Mme. la Vicomtesse* made a voyage to Martinique. She may have tripped in some love-affair (though of this there is no evidence); she may have been in the toils of the money-lenders; she may simply have thought it would be nice to be called "my Lady" by the dusky playfellows of her childhood. All we know is that she went for two years to the West Indian home. Before she sailed on her return to France the Revolution had burst.

Of the new, anarchic order in France, Alexandre was making the most; and after the death of Mirabeau, in April 1791, he was no less a character than President of the Assembly. That Assembly towered for a while above France, and ceased. Alexandre received orders to betake himself again to his regiment; and in 1793, we behold him commander-in-chief of the Army of the Rhine—an inexplicable promotion. From this altitude his fall was swift. For all the fluent liberalism of his talk, Alexandre was an aristocrat, and every aristocrat had enemies by the score. Failing to relieve Mayence, he resigned his command, and was presently under arrest in the prison of Les Carmes. This, the dreadfully transformed abode of the energetic Carmelites, was one of the emergency prisons of the Revolution. Paris abounded in temporary gaols, from palaces to convents, and all of them were packed full. The Reign of Terror had set in.

Josephine herself was now in danger; so also were her children. Hortense she apprenticed to a dressmaker, Eugène to a carpenter. Although there had been no reconciliation between husband and wife, Josephine did undoubtedly exert herself for Alexandre; but in six weeks or so she followed him to prison. The suspects in these places were not isolated; and, with death confronting or threatening both of them, Josephine made her peace with the man who had so grossly used her. In July 1794 Alexandre died under the guillotine.

Josephine looked for the same fate, and it came very near to her. She was, it is said, expecting her summons one night. All who lay in the revolutionary prisons knew what that meant. It meant removal to the *conciergerie*, and the journey thence by tumbril to the scaffold. In what is now the vestibule or entrance to the Buvette du Palais, a little restaurant for lawyers frequenting the Palais de Justice, the victims of the day met to take their places in the death-cart. Clients hang up their hats within a yard or two of the spot where Samson's assistants performed the "toilet" of the condemned. Samson himself, in his long-skirted brown *surtout*, went every morning, as a tradesman on his rounds, to the public accuser for "orders." The public accuser could usually tell, before judgment had been delivered, what the tale would be for the day: so many victims, so many tumbrils, at twenty *francs* the tumbril.

But the tide of blood on a sudden fell. It fell with the head of the elder Robespierre on the 9th *Thermidor* (July 28, 1794). A tradition runs that on the 10th *Thermidor* Josephine was to have been brought before the Tribunal, but that she had fallen ill and was in the hands of a Polish physician at the Carmes. It was less her own malady than the death of Robespierre that saved her. She was released on the 6th of August, 1794, after having spent in prison rather more than one hundred days.

Josephine was a widow, she had two children, and she must have been almost penniless. She was thirty-one years of age, and a Creole in the seventh lustrum is clean past her youth. Pleasure she may meet, youth she will meet no more. This, in the autumn of 1794, was the Vicomtesse de Beauharnais's situation in Paris.

For charms of person and of manner, however, the widow of thirty-one carried it over the bride of sixteen. It is whispered that in prison itself, in the very shadow of the guillotine, some captives of note had sighed for her—and certain it is that love did very strangely flame in the prisons of the Terror. Briefly, Josephine at thirty-one, with her soft auburn hair, her southern pallor that was more beautiful than colour, her tender grace and suppleness of form—

Straight, but as lissom as a hazel wand,

—was a woman rarely planned to fascinate. And from the "very border of destruction" her feet were once again upon the slopes of life. That for the moment was the thing.

From the black and fetid Carmes she was launched upon a Paris intoxicated with a new sense of liberty. To the Reign of Terror succeeded the reign of woman, woman emancipated anew, and resolved—as the French say—*to fling her bonnet over the mill*.

> She became the wanton sovereign of a panting, fevered, restless, tossing kingdom, a fair-green where appetite and vile passions, petty gains, sordid amours, and every merchandise from which

good feeling shrinks, were exposed for sale and barter.

Marriage, according to Cambaceres, was nothing but "the action of nature," and the civil compact was dissolved at the pleasure of either party. The De Goncourts point to the woman of the period passing "from one husband to another, unbinding and refastening her girdle" as the fancy seized her.

> They marry and divorce, destroy marriage to marry again, without a touch of retrospective jealousy on the man's side, of modesty on the woman's; and the unions of those days would appear to have been fashioned after the practice at a horse-breeder's, where first one mate and then another is tried.

In *salons*, in public gardens, at every street corner, all Paris danced madly, frantically. It was less carnival than Saturnalia, for everything, or almost everything, was permitted. There were balls in graveyards, the dancers whirling in and out among the gravestones. Stranger than these were the "*Bals des Victimes*," which represented for a time the highest efforts of fashion gone crazy. To a "*Bal des Victimes*" none were admitted who could not prove the loss of a relative on the scaffold. Guests arriving at this ball, says Octave Uzanne, "bowed *à la victime*, with a sharp jerk of the head, imitating the movement of the condemned when the executioner lays him on the plank and pushes his head through the lunette.

Much studied grace was given to this mode of greeting, and every one sought to excel. So great a degree of elegance did some of the young dandies impart to their performance, that the members of the female Areopagus did them special honour. Each gentleman approached his partner, and quitted her, with a bow *à la victime*. Some of the most polished among the cavaliers had their hair cropped close at the back of the neck, copying the style of Samson in the toilette of the condemned. The ladies followed suit, and the *coiffure à la victime* spread throughout France. To crown this ghastly jest, the daughters of persons who had died under the guillotine sometimes wore a red shawl, in memory of the one that the executioner cast over the shoulders of Charlotte Corday, and Mesdames de St. Amarante, before they ascended the scaffold;" and sometimes a thin red ribbon was worn around the neck, to imitate the knife-mark. The waltz had but recently come in, and they claimed it at the *Bal des Victimes*.

Thermidor, followed by the Directory, had shifted the clock for everything: manners, morals, customs, and clothes. Manners returned to the barbaric simplicity of the nursery; morals slept; customs veered to the pagan; and clothes, for ladies, were abolished. The fierce Mercier asks of a lady surrounded by a crowd of admirers:

> Is she naked? I can scarcely tell. Come a little nearer; here's a subject fit for my pencil. Look at her thin pantaloons! Are they not like the celebrated skin breeches of his Highness the Comte d'Artois? This lady's under-garment, tight as you see it, seems a kind of silk in texture, and is set off with a bracelet. Her dress above it, slit open to a nicety, shows the full bosom swelling beneath a finely-painted gauze. The chemise of transparent cambric shows both legs and thighs, and these, you see, have golden circlets set with diamonds. . . . So slight is the veil over all, that I think modesty might gain by the removal of it. . . . Splendid, indeed, the days that have succeeded to Robespierre's

Octave Uzanne observes:—

> The ladies insisted that their dresses should show every contour, and be of transparent fabrics. In vain the doctors spent their breath in assertions that the French climate, temperate as it was, did not admit of clothing as light as that of ancient Greece. The counsels of the disciples of Hippocrates fell on deaf ears, and, at the close of the year VI, Delessart found himself in a position to assert that he had seen more young girls die during the reign of nakedness veiled in gauze, than during the forty years preceding it. A few daring women—among them the fair Mme. Hamelin—ventured to show themselves without any covering save a straight garment of gauze. Others displayed their naked bosoms. But these indecencies were not repeated. The good sense of the populace, and its rough jests, nipped them in the bud, and, when the yells and insults of the passers-by drove them back to their own homes, the profligate women, who were dead to any sentiment of shame, realized, at least, the danger of their own impudence.

The same writer says, in his comments on the close of the eighteenth century:—

> It is fair to confess that the ladies of the Directory period possessed none of the delicacy and languid grace with which our fancy has endowed them, nor any of those ultra-polished and die-away charms which in later times were held to constitute

refinement. Without exception, almost, they were buxom, healthy, loud-voiced beings, masculine in their ways, broad in their talk, opulent of charm, with the appetites of nursing mothers, greedy and dainty too, ruled solely by their senses, in spite of their sudden simulated fainting-fits and sham headaches. It was a sight to behold them, when the concert was over, falling on the supper, demolishing turkey and cold partridge, truffles and anchovy pates, in mighty mouthfuls, pouring down wine and liqueurs; eating, in fact, as one pamphleteer put it, 'for every fundholder, and soldier, and clerk and *employé* in the Republic' And, indeed, these half-naked nymphs were bound to provide themselves a solid framework to resist the chest attacks that lay in wait for them at every door. The winter draughts would soon have triumphed over those cambric gowns and tunics *à l'aurore*, if a course of high feeding had not preserved their wearers.

The frightful reaction which was called the Terror produced, of necessity, another reaction in *Thermidor*; and society, even where it pretended to some degree of regulation, was a scramble, a hurly-burly, and a riot. By contractors, by speculators in corn and land, and by other adventurers, fortunes had been magically made. The vulgar rich, with their vulgar rich wives, thrust their way to the front, and were envied. As to the means by which great sums of money had been gathered, questions were not openly asked. The business in chief, now that the Terror was overpast and there seemed a prospect of retaining what one held or might acquire, was to follow the example of the clever few who had turned to their own profit the season that had been the ruin of the many.

The rage for pleasure notwithstanding, there were anxious souls in the medley of guests astonishingly garbed at every festival, semi-public, or private, in the newly-constituted Paris. The *salon* of Mme. Tallien, the most beautiful and influential woman of the Directory, and the woman who lent an ear to all requests, was haunted nightly by petitioners of both sexes. Bonaparte, in his stained and rusty regimentals and broken boots, might have been overheard one evening soliciting her interest with Barras for a length of cloth to make him a new uniform. Women had places to seek for a husband, a son, or a lover; other women were seeking something for themselves. The hunt was prosecuted in every *salon* of Paris.

Josephine was seen at Mme. Tallien's, Josephine was seen at the voluptuous and all-powerful Barras's, Josephine was seen elsewhere, and Josephine was as needy a lady as any in the town at this glittering and pleasure-ridden but not too salutary epoch. It is probable that no two persons were more concerned than she and Bonaparte about the days that loomed from *Thermidor*. Every hour of the first phase of Bonaparte is strenuous, beset with care, harassed with forebodings of the future. The Creole Josephine bends much more easily to circumstance, and acquiesces rather than opposes; but under the Directory she is, by pressure and without choice, an adventuress with a very limited horizon, and for her children and herself she schemes with an eye to safety.

In the first weeks of her freedom she risked a country residence at Croissy, near Paris. It was no doubt a calculated venture, a draft upon the destiny that as yet was undisclosed. Fashionable Paris, flowing excitedly between the capital and the pleasant rural parts beyond it, might come to Croissy. The handsome, dissolute Barras, who, for the sins of the Directory, personified that brief *régime*, and was almost as completely its dictator as Bonaparte was the dictator of the Consulate, did certainly go there. He was, on the occasion of his every visit, the supreme guest at Croissy, and Josephine was at shifts to entertain him. Game and fruit furnished a table the plates and service of which were procured by loan. Josephine, it may be supposed, was quietly playing for the end of her own security, but no woman could be hostess to Barras and keep a name unspoiled. That raffish patron of the sex was accustomed to exact for his patronage a payment in kind which the morals of the Directory allowed, and which was perhaps not always or often disputed.

It is generally taken that Mme. Tallien was one of the mistresses of Barras, and he himself has hinted in terms the plainest that Mme. de Beauharnais was another. This is not proved, and, good evidence from other sources failing, the "cankered hate" of Barras's references to Josephine and Bonaparte quite puts him out of court. Barras is both liar and villain. Where envy moves him he deals wholesale in detraction, and the reputation of the woman exposed to his tainted and tainting breath asks the mercy of historian and critic. Barras lied of set purpose, and with a gusto like that with which he bounced about his intrigues and *amours*. He is probably a liar at this day in whatever circle of the Inferno has the evil luck to possess him. So far as Barras is concerned, Josephine receives the full benefit of the doubt.

But she wanted a husband at her side; a husband to protect and a husband to support her. Her children, Eugène and Hortense, mounting in years, had need of the guiding and controlling hand of a father. Josephine required money. Throughout her life, indeed, she demanded money more than love, albeit she was not what we call a mercenary woman. Her appetite for money was that of the born spendthrift. When she has cash she scatters it with both hands, and when it is gone she scatters rather more on credit. But she bestows on others as readily as she disburses for herself; and on her prodigious charities—unscientific and indiscriminate as they were—rests the legend of Josephine the good. But, for Josephine, the blessed days of credit without limit were not yet arrived, and wherever she went debts rose around her like a rampart. She suffered eternally from Falstaff's malady of galloping consumption of the purse, the malady that knows no remedy.

Here, then, in *Thermidor*, or somewhat later, was the hour; and the man, as we have seen, had presented himself. It is to be remembered that the Bonaparte of this hour was a far more promising person than the sallow, long-haired soldier of fortune who had whispered Mme. Tallien his want of a roll of cloth for new clothes. The general had got his new clothes. He had got other things besides. He was installed in quarters, he went abroad now in a carriage (*"en superbe equipage,"* says Lévy), he who but a little while before had wetted himself to the skin on a night of rain, seeking a doctor for a sick man. In a word, the Bonaparte of the hour of Josephine's necessities was something more than the hero of Paris; he must have been regarded by all who were in touch with the government as a person whose future was illimitable. And Bonaparte was in love, abjectly, with Josephine.

On the lady's side, the story of the courtship is sadly shorn of romance. Art did not lack her to persuade Bonaparte that his passion was returned; but passion, in truth, she had none, and we should perhaps flatter her memory by suggesting that even her affections were engaged. She was not in the least in love with Bonaparte, and her friends were well aware that she was not. Circumstances of the newest had made him the most eligible person she had met since her return to the world she had so nearly quitted. Her fancy, no doubt, was smitten. The lean, pale-faced, half-starved Bonaparte, with the perfect mouth and the glow of his falcon's eyes, had slain no hearts as yet; but some among the few women he had ventured to approach had been magnetized a little by that woebegone face, thrilled a little by the quick, vibrating voice that could be velvety enough, and drawn and cowed a little by the half-command of a youth's inarticulate genius. The youth of genius, changed in an hour into the victorious man who embodied the hopes of a struggling State, might have weakened a nature less facile than Josephine's.

There are tales that their courtship was partly a *liaison*. We may believe of this what we please. Marriage under the Directory was sometimes not more than an excuse for a flying *liaison*; a *liaison* was sometimes cemented into an enduring marriage. There would have been nothing unusual or unfashionable in an amour before marriage, but in Josephine's situation it is permissible to think that prudence would have stepped between concupiscence and interest. Her whole interest lay in fastening through matrimony to a man who could give her the assurance or the promise of maintenance for the children and a reasonable future for herself. It was in this expectation that she married Bonaparte.

Josephine might be lukewarm; Napoleon, for his part, was under an absolute possession; he had, as the phrase goes, a demon upon him. One letter of his, written during the progress of their brief courtship, and celebrated as a witness of his passion, must be quoted once again.[1]

> I awake filled with you. Your picture and yesterday's intoxicating evening have given my senses no repose. Amazing indeed, sweet and incomparable Josephine, is the effect that you have wrought within my heart. Are you angry, do I see you sad, are you uneasy—my very soul is bruised, and for this poor friend of yours there is no rest. But is there more when, abandoning myself to that emotion which subdues me utterly, I drink a flame of fire from your lips and from your heart! Well indeed did I prove this night how different from you is your mere picture. You start at midday; in three hours I shall see you. Meanwhile, *mio dolce amor*, a million kisses; but give me none, for they are a consuming fire in my veins.

At this height of passion, as we shall see, Bonaparte sustains himself for a long time. The conduct of a vast and difficult campaign, victory in the field of arms, increase of personal glory, have no power to qualify his overmastering love for Josephine.

Through the winter of 1795 the courtship went on; Josephine evidently playing her part with skill; for Bonaparte, notwithstanding that his days are given to the preparation of a plan of attack for the

---

1. *Napoleon's Letters to Josephine* by Henry Foljambe Hall also published by Leonaur.

army of Italy, is more and more the devout and ardent lover. His formal demand was made in January 1796. Josephine, who had been living with an aunt, Fanny de Beauharnais, in the Rue de l'Université, moved in January into a small "hotel," 6, Rue Chantereine, bought or rented from the wife of the actor Talma. Of this "Hôtel Chantereine" nothing now remains.

Bonaparte, once accepted, paraded the lady proudly among his friends in Paris; but Josephine, even yet, had not quite made up her mind! There is a story, often given in the French, and pretty well authenticated, of a visit which she paid, on the very eve of marriage, to her notary Raguideau. Bonaparte, whom she took with her, sat in an ante-room, and listened to the criticisms of the lawyer.

> What! Marry a general who has nothing but his cloak and sword! Why, he lives in a den or a hovel, doesn't he? A little bit of a general without a name or a future, under the feet of all the generals in the Republic! You'd much better marry a contractor.

Bonaparte passed these compliments without a word; and it is said that, eight years later, on the eve of his coronation, he summoned Raguideau to the Tuileries, and gave him a ticket for a good place in the cathedral, that the man of law might see how far the "little general without a future" had brought his client on her way.

The marriage was really a little like an elopement, an elopement without its hazard. There was no need, of course, for the young people to run away, and run away they did not; but they were married, with the scantest ceremony, at a rather late hour of the night. It was what Maître Raguideau might have called (and he it was, perhaps, who did so call it) a "cloak and sword wedding."

No. 3, Rue d'Antin is one of the few houses upstanding at this day in Paris that claim a place in the true history of Bonaparte. Dating only from the Regency, it was then the property of the Marquis de Mondragon, who, among other high or ornamental offices, held that of private secretary to *Madame*, a lady of strong, humorous, and pungent memory. The Revolution confiscated this mansion as the "estate "of an aristocrat, and it was converted to the use of the *Mairie* of the 2nd *arrondissement* of Paris. In 1815, after the upheaval of Waterloo, the Hôtel de Mondragon reverted to the representatives of the family who had been its first owners. Rented from them by the City of Paris, it still served, says M. Lenôtre, as the *Mairie* of the 2nd *arrondissement*, until very early in the reign of Louis Philippe.

The house is now, (1910), in the possession of the Paris and Netherlands Bank, and the chamber that was formerly the Salle des Manages is the office of one of the directors. In this chamber, on the night of the 9th of March, 1796, was celebrated the civil marriage of Napoleon Bonaparte and Josephine de Beauharnais.

Me. Raguideau had drawn up the civil contract the day before. Bonaparte's declaration was as simple as might be. He owned, he said, "neither real nor personal estate;" was indeed possessed of nothing "except his wardrobe and his military accoutrements." The estimated value of these he was on the point of stating, when he suddenly broke off, unwilling to lay bare his poverty. Then, in a spasm of faith, he settled on his future wife "a dowry of an annuity of fifteen hundred *francs*." Josephine's contribution was nothing at all, and had she ventured into particulars of her wardrobe there would have been little but underwear in the list.

M. Lenôtre says:

> The original of this contract is preserved among the records of Me. Mahot de la Quérantonnais, the present owner of Me. Raguideau's office. Its only interest lies in its signatures. That of 'Napolione Buonaparte,' hastily written and already illegible, is distorted, passionate, and underlined by a broad stroke, and forms a contrast to that of Josephine—'M. J. R. Tascher,' traced with an indifferent hand. We can imagine the honest scrivener casting a protecting look at the poor devil of an officer, 'without either real or personal estate of any kind,' whose paltry possessions he had just set down on paper.

At eight in the evening of March 9th, at the *Mairie* in the Rue d'Antin, the marriage certificate was signed.

> The reception-room where this ceremony was performed has preserved its pompous decoration of the beginning of the eighteenth century: a broad frieze in two shades of gold, on which divinities, mingled with cupids, sport in grottoes, wainscotings, doors, shutters, mirror-frames with their borders of reeds and roses, garlands, and old gold; frieze panels on which mythological heroes are enthroned in Olympian heavens after the style of Natoire.

It has more than once been said that on the wedding night Bonaparte had to rouse the mayor in his bed for the due performance of the ceremony. This was not the case. The mayor, who could not possibly suppose that this was a wedding for history (it must in truth have been one of the dullest little affairs he had ever presided at), had indeed gone to sleep, but not beneath his counterpane. The fact is that Bonaparte was late, and kept the company waiting. A small company it was, and with one, or at the most two exceptions, very undistinguished.

No member of the bride's family was present, no member of the bridegroom's. Josephine's children (and it was good of her that she had not told them what manner of man he had been to her) cherished a romantic memory of their father, and had opposed the second marriage. As for the Bonapartes, not one among them had a notion of what was happening at the *Mairie* in the Rue d'Antin. Madame Mère's consent to the match had never been asked. The eldest brother Joseph had not an inkling of it. Madame Mère, the brothers, and the sisters were none of them privy to the secret which must have been shared by a good many people in and about Paris. Bonaparte, aware that the whole family would be terribly jealous of the widow of the ex-aristocrat, had astutely resolved to marry her without their knowledge.

So, while the clock ticked in the gilded office of the *Mairie*, there were assembled, besides Josephine in her flowing and semi-transparent tunic, only Barras and Tallien, who were to sign for Bonaparte, Camelet, the confidential man of the bride, and mayor Leclerc. The clock ticked on, and the mayor went to sleep in his armchair. Suddenly, at about ten o'clock, there was a clatter of swords on the stairs, the door was thrown open, and Bonaparte, accompanied by his *aide-de-camp*, Lemarois, entered the room. Scarcely waiting to salute his guests, he shook the mayor into consciousness.

"Wake up, *Monsieur le Maire!* Come, marry us, marry us!"

The mayor, restored from dreams, was doubtless only too glad to marry and to speed them. Everything was dispatched in a hurry, and the marriage certificate is a wonder of irregularity. Bonaparte added eighteen months to his age, Josephine took four years from hers; and both produced certificates of birth which had been fabricated for the occasion. Bonaparte's stated that he was born in Paris on the 8th of February, 1768! Lemarois, it may be added, had no right at all to sign as a witness, inasmuch as he was under age. The mayor was probably the sole person present who did not know that the documents put in were farcical, and that the whole ceremony was legal only in a qualified degree. To the possible inquisitions of history no one gave a thought.

There was no wedding supper. It was growing late; the mayor saw the party off his premises, and no doubt went to bed. Barras's coach took him back to the Luxembourg, and the rest of the witnesses went their several ways. The luxury of a coach was Josephine's also, a *barouche* and two black horses. She had obtained them from the Committee of Public Safety, and as that body was not indiscriminate in gifts of *barouches* to ladies of the aristocracy who had escaped the guillotine, we may perhaps surmise that Barras had helped her to so useful a present. In the *barouche* with the two black horses Bonaparte and Josephine drove to the modest hotel in the Rue Chantereine. Thus was solemnized, with such sparse solemnity, one of the most curious marriages in history.

Two days later, March 9th, Bonaparte set forth to take command of the army in Italy.

3

Bonaparte stayed two days at Marseilles on a visit to his mother, that handsome, shrewd, anxious, and very capable Corsican, who had known how to discipline her children, and of whom her children stood not a little in awe. To his mother Bonaparte gave the news of his marriage. Madame Bonaparte the elder made the best of it, but was only persuaded that Joseph her firstborn was the wiser man in having taken to wife the daughter of Clary the soap-boiler. From this time to the end, the Bonapartes, mother and brothers and sisters, were the foes of Josephine. Sound Corsicans all, they were no strangers to hereditary hatred, and this domestic feud was never healed.

Still, the mother of the family was in duty bound to write to her daughter-in-law, who, by the way, had written first. As Mme. Letizia Bonaparte had almost no French, "and could scarcely write more than her own name," someone must have drawn up the letter for her.

> I am in receipt of your letter, *madame*, and it could but heighten the estimate I had formed of you. My son had told me of his happy marriage, and from that moment I could not but esteem and approve you. When I have seen you my happiness will be complete. I beg you to know that I have a mother's tenderness for you, and shall cherish you as one of my own children. I understood from my son, and this is confirmed in your letter, that you would pass through Marseilles on your way to join him. I

look forward, *madame*, to the pleasure which your visit to this place will afford me, and this anticipation my daughters share. Pray believe that my children, following my example, will show you all the friendship and tenderness which they give to their brother. Believe, *madame*, in the regard and affection of
Letizia Buonaparte Mère.

A letter from Joseph followed the mother's.

Madame, It was with the liveliest interest that I heard of your marriage with my brother. The friendship which binds me to him forbids me to question the happiness you will bring him. From the idea that I have formed of you, I am not less sure of it than he is. Receive, I beg of you, this expression of the fraternal sentiments of your brother-in-law.

For a daughter-in-law and sister-in-law the reception was frigid enough. But "malice domestic" scarcely wounded Josephine, who was never malicious towards anyone. Bonaparte's own letters, had she cared for them, would have yielded balm, if balm had been her need. They contain as much passionate love in headlong indifferent prose as could be crammed up into large sheets of paper. A very brief selection must be made from them.

On March 14th (three days after leaving Paris) he sat down to write to her at Chanceaux.

I wrote you at Chatillon, sending you a power of attorney.... Each moment sunders us more widely, my beloved; each moment finds me less able to endure the separation from you. You are eternally in my thoughts, my imagination exhausts itself in guessing what you are doing. If I picture you sad, my heart is rent, my grief redoubles. If you are gay among your friends, I reproach you for having so soon forgotten the wretched parting three days agone.... May my good genius, which has ever held me safe in the midst of danger, enfold you. Ah! be not gay, be a little melancholy....Write me, dear one, at full length, and take from your devoted and true friend these thousand kisses and another.

In the oblivion of passion, Bonaparte addressed this letter to "The Citizeness Beauharnais"!

Soon after this he receives letters from her (very few of Josephine's letters have come down to us), which fire his heart anew.

> What eloquence, what feelings you discover! (One is tempted here to think that Josephine, like Mme. Letizia, must have found an amanuensis.)

> They are of fire, you set my poor heart ablaze! My sole Josephine, away from you there is no more happiness, away from you the whole world is a desert, wherein I stand alone.... You have taken from me more than my soul; you are the central and only thought of my existence.... To live for Josephine: that sums up my life.

From Albenga, in the first week of April:—

> Your last letter does not satisfy me; it is cold as friendship.... But oh! how I am infatuated.... It is impossible you should have inspired a boundless love without partaking of it.

Towards the end of April he begins impatiently to call her to him from Paris.

> Come soon. I warn you that if you delay you will find me ill; fatigue and your absence are more than I can endure together. Your letters make up my daily pleasure, and my happy days are not many. Junot is the bearer of twenty-two standards to Paris. You should return with him—do you hear me? ... You will soon be beside me, on my breast, in my arms. Get wings and come quickly!

But Josephine got no wings. Paris was not a place she was in haste to fly from. She was amusing herself very well; Barras's mimic but luxurious court was more attractive than the camp. Josephine was gadding to and fro with Mme. Tallien; spending all the money her husband could afford her, and going a-borrowing. The two children were temporarily off her hands; Eugène at the Collège Irlandais, Hortense at the fashionable academy of Mme. Campan; not a cloud at present overcast the gay purposes of Josephine.

Arnault, in his very entertaining *Souvenirs d'un Sexagénaire*, tells us concerning the Josephine of these days that, though not the most beautiful, she was decidedly the most pleasing and good-natured woman to be seen at Barras's. Beautiful Josephine was not, and that term is very rarely met with in descriptions of her. A pretty mouth was spoiled by indifferent teeth, and to this defect was owing the "close-lipped smile" we read about in all the memoirs that are kind to her. With the smile went an amiable play of very pleasant eyes; and the light that visited those gems was as soft as it was dangerous to men. She had a voice that was seduction in itself; not thrilling, but murmurous and velvety, a lure and snare for the ear.

Though she never sought to rival in wantonness of dress the Juno-like Tallien, who exhibited in public her modish legs to the modish knee, the Greek things that Josephine swayed and swam in—by day as by night—revealed every line of a form which kept almost through life the virgin graces of a nymph. Has not Napoleon himself left it on record that she was graceful even in going to bed?

With her arts of captivation perfected all at once, Josephine, who scarcely even simulated a love for her husband, knew that in Paris they would be at least as potent as in Italy; and Paris was home, and Italy was not. To Paris she clung desperately. Bonaparte, abasing himself in his devotion, wrote frantically in the midst of the battles he was winning for the Republic; and his letters amused Josephine when she was bored, and bored her when she was amused. Her comment on them, when she showed the letters to her friends, was: "*Il est drôle, Bonaparte!*" Paris began to shout the victories of Bonaparte in Italy, and Josephine was pleased; but his letters, entreating, imploring, commanding her to join him, gave her now the blues and now a fit of merriment. She piled excuse upon excuse for remaining at the Rue Chantereine: she even invented a pregnancy—she who, during her second marriage, was never once pregnant.

There is pathos in the situation. Turquan says, not inaptly, that Bonaparte worships Josephine less like a man than like a youth at college, a "*collégien*." The officers on his staff in Italy, through all the earlier stages of the "miraculous campaign," not only beheld but heard from the general's own lips the passion that at once inspired and tormented him. Marmont relates in his *Memoirs* that, the novel greatness of the young Bonaparte's position notwithstanding, his daily and hourly engrossment in the interests confided to him, his thoughts about his own future, he was seldom too much occupied to talk of Josephine. "Of her and of his love he often spoke to me, in the effusive manner and with all the illusions of a very young man." One day he accidentally broke the glass of the miniature of Josephine which was always worn next his heart. "See what has happened!" he exclaimed to Marmont. "My wife is either very ill or unfaithful."

Ill she was not, for all her pretences that way; nor, at this period, so far forth as is known, was she unfaithful. She was dancing, picnicking, flirting, at the Luxembourg, at Mme. Tallien's, at Mme. Récamier's, at Saint-Germain-en-Laye, at Saint-Cloud, at Sèvres, at Passy, at the Tivoli. Assuredly she was not thinking very much of Bonaparte, except—as on occasion of a letter from Italy—that he was "really too droll." Yet, as Turquan observes, what woman should not have been happy in knowing herself the source and fount of such a love? What woman should not have been proud as the newly-wedded wife of a man whose genius in the field was just beginning to focus the gaze of Europe? But the language of adoration that Bonaparte addressed to her, almost in tears, almost upon his knees, was unintelligible to the "*légère Créole.*" Certain favoured members of the staff in Italy were not the only persons who received at this season the outpourings of that overflowing heart.

He even wrote to Carnot, one of the Directors:

> I owe you my particular thanks for the attention you have been good enough to show my wife. She is a sincere patriot, and I love her to madness.

There could be no testimony more striking or more strange of an infatuation the most strange and striking in history. France at this moment was gaining more than was the wife herself by the intensity of Bonaparte's passion for Josephine; if we may accept the view of one historian, that, under the daily stimulus of this passion, his genius for war itself expanded to the utmost and rose to the highest. Josephine herself came to be saluted in public as "Our Lady of Victory." She liked the flattery, but went on making jokes about Bonaparte's love-letters.

But, in the course of time, having fibbed herself to the end of her resources, Josephine must needs pack up for Italy. Not for a moment did it occur to her that she might shine in Italy as she was now shining in Paris: Arnault tells us that at her last supper at the Luxembourg she "melted in a flood of tears, sobbed as if she were going to torture." She had comported herself better in Les Carmes, envisaging the guillotine! Junot and Murat had come to Paris with the flags and were to go back to Italy with Josephine. Joseph completed the escort.

The splendid Serbelloni palace at Milan had been prepared for her reception. She would have exchanged, says Arnault, the palace at Milan, "and all the palaces in the world," for the nest in the Rue Chantereine which she was locking up behind her. *Adieu* to Paris; and now for a miserable journey into benighted Italy! But the journey, as it turned out, was not wholly barren of episode. The paraphernalia of Josephine included her maid, Louise Compoint, "a fine strapping girl," and the poodle dog, Fortuné, that had bitten Bonaparte in the leg on his wedding night. One big coach, it seems, sheltered all the travellers. Josephine disposed herself to flirt with Junot, a gallant and handsome young man. Junot, however, was soul and body for Bonaparte, and disregarded the bait. Instead, he regarded Louise, who was indiscreet enough to be complacent. Here was a comedy of imbroglio for the rest of the inside passengers! It was a situation, to be brief, which ultimately cost another to Louise; for scarcely had Josephine set foot in Milan when her handmaid, bereft of a character, was setting foot from out it. Her subsequent fate, according to rumour, was an English jockey. She might have been a duchess, for Junot became Duc d'Abrantès.

Received as a queen in Italy, Josephine had soon put Paris from her variable mind. The Palazzo Serbelloni, in itself a treasure-house, was now forthwith the centre of an elegant, effusive, and obsequious society; and for the amiable and bewitching hostess there was the copious homage that she loved. There was also, of course, the husband, whose *"collégian's"* transports of delight were the alloy of Josephine's Italian happiness; she consoled herself in reflecting that he had a war as well as a wife upon his hands. Naturally he was much from her. At Roverbella he wrote in the first week of July:—

> I have defeated the enemy. Kilmaine will send you a copy of the dispatch. I am tired out. I beg of you to come at once to Verona; I want you, for I believe I am going to be very ill. From bed I send you a thousand kisses.

But for a Juliet at Milan it was a long step to a Romeo at Verona, and Josephine did not go. She was ill herself, she said. Bonaparte replied, urging her strongly to ride for the sake of her health: "it cannot fail to do you good." He has apparently forgotten his own illness. "I thought I loved you some days past," he says in the same letter, "but seeing you I feel that I love you more a thousand times. My worship of you increases every day." Again, from Marmirolo, on July 19, he writes:

> For two days I have been without a letter from you—the thirtieth time today that I have told myself so. You think this very wearisome, but you cannot doubt the tender and unique anxiety I feel for you.

There might have been less of tenderness in Bonaparte's anxiety had he known, what was now beginning to be a theme of gossip at Milan, that his wife was taking steps to provide herself with a lover. This was a young dandy of the army, Hippolyte Charles by name; a little black-haired person with a tanned complexion, and pretty little hands and feet; incurably given to puns. He had, however, a very taking air in his hussar's uniform, and had unquestionably found favour in the eyes of *Mme. la Générale*. He haunted the Palazzo Serbelloni, and the scandal of the town had already linked his name with Josephine's. Mme. d'Abrantès says :

> He lunched at the Serbelloni as often as Napoleon was called elsewhere. It was known to everyone in the army, and to everyone in the town of Milan.

The scandal of the town could scarcely miss the camp, for officers of the staff were passing to and fro; but it had not yet attained the ear of Bonaparte. At about this time, nevertheless, a vague jealousy begins to stir in him. From Verona, under date September 17, he writes:

> I write very often, my dear, and you very seldom. You are a bad and ugly girl, very ugly, as ugly as you are frivolous. It is shocking to deceive a poor husband, a devoted lover. Is he to lose his rights because he is far away, loaded with business, overcome with fatigue and worry? Without his Josephine, without the assurance of her love, what does the world hold for him? What shall he do?

M. Turquan comments:

> Poor Bonaparte, who does not know that no more must be demanded of a woman's heart than it is capable of giving! He believes his Josephine good because he sees her as he would have her be, not as she is. His eyes are not yet opened to her careless and perhaps unconscious strayings. He fondly fancies that she loves him, because the eyes with which he looks on her are themselves full of love. But have a care, *madame!* Those eyes, I think, begin to see more clearly, despite the love which until now has blinded them. Jealousy begins to find a corner in that heart which until now has been so *naïvely* trustful.

But Bonaparte's letter, sounding a doubt, winds up thus:—

> *Adieu*, adorable Josephine: one of these nights will see your

door flung open as by a jealous lover, and in a moment you will find me in your arms.

The shelter, alas! that Josephine was not too eager to extend.

She remains indifferent, totally apathetic. Caresses, menaces, the half-timid note of jealousy, leave her quite unmoved. Bonaparte grows indignant, tries a bolder tone.

> I don't love you one bit (this from Verona on November 23rd); on the contrary, I detest you. You're a good-for-nothing, a tomboy, a silly and a slut. You never write to me, you don't care an atom for your husband. You know the delight your letters are to me, and you fling me a bare half-dozen lines when the fancy takes you. What, then, do you do with yourself the livelong day, *madame*? What is the absorbing business that gives you no time to write to him who loves you? What interest is it that stifles and thrusts aside the love you once showed me? Who can this wonder of wonders be, this new lover, who engrosses your every moment, tyrannizes over your days, and forbids all concern for your own husband? Josephine, take care! One fine night your doors will be forced, and you will behold me.

But he ends on the customary note:—

> I hope that before long I shall enfold you in these arms, and cover you with a million kisses burning as the sun of the equator.

The beauties of Italy, women of rank, women of the world, women of the opera were intriguing for a word or token of gallantry from the victorious young soldier who was fighting their battles against Austria. Neither word nor token did he vouchsafe them; every hour he could rob from war was given to these frantic epistles in which he grovelled before the one woman in Italy who treated him as naught.

After the triumph of Arcoli he coursed back to Milan. Josephine was not there. She had gone to Genoa, in the company, there is little doubt, of Charles. To her at Genoa the husband dispatched this:—

> I reach Milan; I hurry to your room. I have left all that I might see you and press you in my arms. And you? You were not there. You are off to the towns and their merry-makings. You fly from me when I come; your dear Napoleon is dear to you no longer. You loved him for a caprice; your love or your caprice is turned

> to fickleness; you are all inconstancy..... I shall be here until the 9th. Do not put yourself out; have your fling of gaiety; pleasure was invented for you. The whole world is but too happy if it can amuse you; your husband is the one unhappy man in it.

And on the day following:—

> You have not, I feel sure, had time to write to me.... Berthier has been good enough to show me the letter you sent him. My intention is that you make no change whatever in your plans, nor with respect to the pleasure-parties that are arranged for you. I am worth no trouble on your part, and the happiness or unhappiness of a man you do not love can scarcely be expected to engage your interest.... Farewell, beloved wife; farewell, my Josephine!

He seals the letter, and tears it open again.

> I reopen my letter to give you a kiss.... Oh! Josephine!... Josephine!

Is not this pitiful?

Isn't Bonaparte droll?

Who was his first informant as to the intimacy of Josephine with the pretty captain of hussars is not precisely known. Such a matter could not long be hidden from him, and the lady herself had no especial skill in intrigue. It is said that the pair were betrayed by Bonaparte's sister Pauline, and any Bonaparte woman would cheerfully have done that much for Josephine. The sisters and their formidable mother had just made her acquaintance at Montebello, Bonaparte's headquarters during the summer heats; and a curious party it was that he gathered about him at that delightful spot. The ladies seem not to have been more than outwardly polite to Josephine; and Pauline, when her sister-in-law's back was turned, put out her tongue and made faces.

Perhaps it was Pauline who told tales, perhaps it was another; the affair, as was inevitable, was somehow blown. The Duchesse d'Abrantès is responsible for the statement that Bonaparte wished to have his rival shot. The entertaining duchess is not the most trustworthy gossip when Josephine is concerned, and this tale must be rejected. Not even in an army of the French Republic could a commander-in-chief court-martial a brother in arms, and procure him to be shot, for the offence of having made love to his wife. It would have been a proper Corsican vengeance, but an awkward theme for a report to the Directors in Paris.

Still, a commander-in-chief can do much, and Captain Hippolyte Charles vanished on a sudden from the army. Bonaparte dismissed and broke him. The young man had been found playing tricks among the contractors, and this was excuse enough for getting rid of him.

Josephine paid a double debt of tears. She wept first for the loss of Hippolyte Charles, and wept again to be restored to her husband's favour. The sea does not more easily resolve "the moon into salt tears" than she could cause her own to flow. She is one of the best, most abundant, and most successful weepers in history. She could at almost any time weep Bonaparte into contrition for things that he had said or not said, done or not done. She almost wept him from the great divorce. She wept him into weeping a little himself for having caused Josephine to weep for Charles. The reconciliation was made—the first of many, many reconciliations due to those "pure messengers" from the eyes, if not the heart, of Josephine.

But from this date we note a certain difference. Not only did Bonaparte make no effort to detach himself from Josephine, he did not desire to make such an effort, could not possibly have succeeded in such an effort. She was the star both of his heart and of his will. He loved and continued to love her. From this date, nevertheless, the passion begins to melt from his letters; it is affection rather than passion that will now breathe from them. We may say, no doubt, that his own feelings begin to be in some slight measure qualified; but, with more assurance perhaps, we may say that he begins to realize a little of what is missing in his wife, and ceases—half involuntarily—to demand what it is absolutely not in her nature to bestow. He ceases to be the "*collégien*" in love.

In December 1797, summoned or invited by the Directors, Bonaparte returned to Paris. In January Josephine followed him. Hailed in Paris as the "liberator" of Italy (a title given with greater propriety some fifty years later to Garibaldi), Bonaparte was officially feasted in the style that was as trying to him as it was grateful to "*la Générale*." The banquet that shines with the best lustre in the memoirs was Talleyrand's, at which Bonaparte and Mme. Staël (the "*Begum* of Letters," whose white arms were presently "waving through the drawing-rooms of Europe") had their historic first encounter.

Bonaparte and his wife were once again installed in the Rue Chantereine, where Josephine, with her incurable propensity to luxury, was for queening it in a style that her husband declined to support her in. She had, however, the joy of embellishing the house with her Italian spoils, the gifts—lavishly if not always too cordially heaped on her—of Pope, princes, and lesser notabilities. As the street, in Bonaparte's honour, had just been rechristened Rue des Victoires, Josephine's trophies had found a not inappropriate resting-place.

But Bonaparte's stay in Paris was short. His martial destiny was now fairly impelling him. He was named commander of the army for the invasion of England; this was soon converted into the Army of the East; and the change of policy made Egypt the next objective. For Egypt Bonaparte set his face in the spring of 1798. Josephine, who might have gone, and made a show of going, remained behind. What should she do in Egypt? Italy, which she had entered with distaste, had in the end amused her; but what could the spoliation of Egypt yield in pictures, statues, or cameos? She may never have heard of the Pyramids, and she did not want an obelisk.

She said goodbye to Bonaparte at Toulon; went to Plombières, for the waters; had an accident there, by the fall of a balcony, which might have been far more serious than it was; returned to Paris; and plunged into debt on the scale that never ceased to fascinate her by purchasing Malmaison for two hundred and ninety thousand *francs*.

Malmaison is the scene of the interlude that was so nearly fatal to her. Charles the *beau* and bold, eliminated from the army, was upon the bounty of his country, without visible means of subsistence. Was it not the *beaux yeux* of Josephine that had laid him low? She, the ever amiable, whose friends' afflictions were her own, took on her to be Charles's providence. Her influence sufficed to achieve for him a partnership in the firm of Bodin, contractors; and as the young man seems to have been genuinely talented in adulteries of all kinds, he was soon making a very nice income—somewhat, suggests Turquan, *"au détriment de la nourriture du soldat,"* to the detriment of rations for the army. To make money at the expense of the service one has been cashiered from cannot but be an agreeable manner of revenge.

But Captain Charles's good fortune was not restricted to the sale of inferior victuals at splendid profits to the comrades he had ceased to bear arms with. By the providence of Josephine he was enabled to deal another stroke at the happiness of the commander who had broken him. In one and the same hour, to spoil a man's dinner in Egypt and his bed in France: Was this not a consummation of the rarest?

For it is barely open to doubt that from a privileged and habitual visitor at Malmaison, Charles became an inmate of that hospitable seat. The pleasant walks of the *château* were perhaps inadequately screened; certain it is, at all events, that by many of the neighbours the hostess and her dapper favourite were beheld strolling together of an evening, in the conversable way that spoke of friendship well matured: Josephine in her adorable Greek draperies, with a light veil about her temples; the rising contractor in civilian wear of black or dark blue. Evening by evening they were seen in this sociable proximity.

One would think that Malmaison had been an eyrie in the Alps, instead of a country house against the Saint-Germain road. Simple persons attached to those parts spoke of *madame's* "brother," and her manifest affection for him; others remarked on her tenderness for her "son." Paris, which was just at hand, was ignorant of any brother of *madame's*, and knew that her son was with Bonaparte in Egypt. Paris also knew that the companion of *madame's* evening walks was an ex-captain of hussars named Hippolyte Charles.

The unfaithful wife could scarcely have gone farther in imprudence. The Bonapartes, all the family, were an ever-present danger to her; and, although the least aggressive woman that ever lived, she had other enemies in the capital. What was her hope, flaunting a lover at Malmaison, to cheat the *quidnuncs* in Paris?

She had, however, bethought her of the possible support of a respectable friend or two in town, and had been sedulously cultivating the Gohiers, husband and wife. Gohier was the starched and elderly President of the Directory, and Mme. Gohier had been Gohier's cook. These harmonious hearts opened to Josephine, who was pleased to make herself at home beneath their roof. But Gohier knew both what was doing and what was saying, and his hard sense counselled Josephine to divorce. Scandalized or not at the *liaison*, he saw the tremendous danger of it.

> Get a divorce. Your feelings for M. Charles, you say, and his for you, are merely those of friendship; but, if this friendship is of a kind so exclusive as to compel you to outrage the proprieties, I must talk to you as I should in a case of love: get a divorce! If you don't, this is the sort of friendship that will land you in an awkward place.

But this, as one easily divines, is not the advice that would go down with Josephine. If her duties as Bonaparte's wife were irksome, the benefits of the situation were no longer despicable. Divorced from him, she might be cast upon the hands of Charles; and a partner in Bodin's, even with prospects of wealth unlimited from the sale of tainted meat and paper boots to the soldiers of the fatherland, was in no way yet the peer of the thrice-victorious general at their head. Besides, the lover might be in no burning haste to exchange that office for the husband's. No; divorce was not the most delectable solution.

Then, in an hour, the situation underwent a fateful change; and it was Josephine herself, in the character of prospective victim, whom the terrors of divorce confronted. Dining in Paris one night at Barras's, she had Talleyrand beside her; and that accomplished trimmer devoted himself entirely to Mme. Tallien. So flagrant an example of disdain on his part was in itself a signal of alarm for Josephine. Had sudden death in Egypt swept Bonaparte from the theatre of politics? In that event, the common social correspondences would have restrained even a Barras from spreading his cloth for company. But Bonaparte alive was worse than Bonaparte dead for the wife who had once again openly betrayed his honour. It must be, then, that the haplessly transparent secret of Malmaison had revealed itself in Egypt. Talleyrand, convinced that Josephine's disgrace was imminent, had turned his supple back on her.

Next came the clap of news that Bonaparte was returning from Egypt, had returned; was approaching Paris, had all but reached it. These tidings overtook Josephine at the tranquil board of the Gohiers, where and when she was discussing with the president her precautionary measures. Gohier tells us, or gives us to think, that she was seized with a frantic anxiety for her safety, in the persuasive fear that the Bonaparte brothers and sisters had fortified the jealous husband with a battery of proofs against her.

In effect, Bonaparte's knowledge went deeper than the suspicions of Josephine on the subject. We have a letter of his to his brother Joseph (one among other letters found in a French vessel captured by English warships at the mouth of the Nile), dated July 25, 1798, in which he says:—

> I may reach France in two months or so, and to you I commit my affairs. I have grievous domestic trouble; the veil has been completely torn away. What a wretched condition is this, to feel in one's heart so many conflicting emotions in respect of one and the same individual. You know my meaning. I must have a

house in the country on my arrival, somewhere near Paris or in Burgundy. I shall most likely pass the winter there, and immure myself. I am weary of human nature; solitude and isolation are a necessity to me. Fame oppresses me, feeling is exhausted, glory has become meaningless. . . . I intend to keep my house; I will give it up to no one.

At the date this was written Bonaparte was but twenty-nine years of age, and had been married little more than two years to Josephine de Beauharnais.

Few passages in the *Memoirs* of Bourrienne [2] (at this time secretary to Bonaparte) have been oftener referred to than the dramatic one which discloses the furious grief of the dishonoured husband. Bourrienne observes a strange conversation between his master and Junot at the springs of Messoudiah.

I saw Bonaparte walking alone with Junot, as indeed he often does. I was at a little distance from them, and—I know not why—my eyes were fixed on him as they talked. The face of the general, always very pale, was paler now than ordinary. There was something convulsive in it, something wild in his air, and more than once he smote himself on the head. After a quarter of an hour's conversation, he left Junot and came towards me. I had never seen him more distraught, more preoccupied. I advanced to him, and the moment we met he said, with a sudden harshness: 'You never cared for me. . . . These women! . . . Josephine! . . . Had you been in the least attached to me, you would have told me all that I have just learned from Junot. Junot is a friend indeed. . . . Josephine! . . . And I six hundred leagues away! . . . You should have told me of it. . . . Josephine! . . . To have played thus with me! . . . She! . . . Ruin on them! . . . I will exterminate this race of fops and dandies! . . . As for her, divorce! . . . Yes, divorce! . . . Divorce public and scandalous! . . . I must write! . . . I know all. . . . This is your fault; you should have told me.'

But was it indeed the fault of Bourrienne? He was, it is true, something more than Bonaparte's hired secretary; but he had had kind treatment from Josephine. He sought to appease the infuriated man,

---

2. *Memoirs of Napoleon Bonaparte*: Volume 1—1769-1802, Volume 2—1802-1813 and Volume 3—1813-1821 by Louis Antoine Fauvelet de Bourrienne also published by Leonaur.

tried to make him think he had been hearing old wives' tales, and sounded the note of his augmenting fame in Europe.

Bonaparte cried:

> My fame! Oh, what would not I give to be assured that what Junot has just told me is false! . . . If Josephine is guilty, divorce must separate us forever. I'm not going to be the laughing-stock of all the sots of Paris. I shall write to Joseph. He will see to the divorce.

In a while, and for a while, this wrath died down in Bonaparte; ready to whiten again. In a measure he took into his confidence young Eugène de Beauharnais, his *aide-de-camp*, though the youth was but just seventeen; and Eugène had some very difficult letters to write to his mother on the situation. But Bonaparte did not satisfy himself with the doubtful consolations of Eugène, who of course must defend his mother. He sought distraction in the first *amour* he had known since his marriage; and made poor M. Fourès unhappy, to blot from his mind for a time the infidelities of Josephine.

That lady, however, had reason enough for the tumult that filled her heart when the news ran that Bonaparte was returning from the East. His journey up through France to Paris was a taste of the progresses of triumph that custom was by and by to make a property of tediousness. The country was sick of the Directory; and with the coming of Bonaparte out of Egypt was associated in the popular imagination the idea of some immediate great awakening.

Mr. H. A. L. Fisher says:

> From the olive groves of Provence to the *boulevards* of Paris the enthusiasm was indescribable. France had experienced no such thrill of emotion since the fall of the Bastille ten years before. Her greatest general, the aureole of victory on his brow, and invested with the glamour of an eastern crusade . . . had returned to save the Republic, to clear out all that was sordid and corrupt, to quell the hideous menace of the Jacobins, and above all to finish the war by an honourable peace.

Bonaparte was a whole week, from October 9 to October 16, in traversing France from Fréjus. Josephine, on the morning after her dinner with the Gohiers, eager above everything to forestall her husband's family, had flown to meet him. Chance decreed that she should take the wrong road—and miss him. Says her son:—

At Lyon Bonaparte left his fellow travellers, and started alone in a light carriage, to get the quicker to Paris. By an unhappy accident, my mother, who, the instant she heard of our landing, had set out to meet him at Lyon, took the Burgundian route, while he was hastening by the Bourbonnais. We therefore reached Paris forty-eight hours in advance of her. The field was thus left open to her enemies, who lost not a moment in the effort to inflame the husband's mind against her.

By "enemies," Eugène intends the brothers of Bonaparte, two of whom—Joseph and Lucien, with Pauline's husband, Leclerc—more fortunate than Josephine, had fallen in with him upon the road. In what manner they primed him it is not difficult to guess. Bonaparte, in the light post-chaise, sped glowering to Paris.

There, in the Rue Chantereine, he alighted at six on an October morning—a chill hour at which to find one's door fast and nobody at home.

No; this is not the strict truth. The general's house was not barred against him. He was expected; there was a little crowd to welcome him; the clan Bonaparte had filled the house. His mother was there, his brothers—save those whom he had left upon the road—and his ardent, vociferous sisters. They were there to prove to him what family love did truly mean, the love of the Bonapartes. Those loving hearts were all assembled to greet him—with the sole disastrous exception of the one he looked for.

The mental state of Josephine also we may faintly realize when she learned, at some stage along her route, the trick that chance had played her. Instantly her horses were turned about, and at main speed she posted back to Paris. Bonaparte would think that she had fled from him; her fond relatives would assure him that she had. What more infernal jaunt could her malignant star have sent her on! She re-entered Paris feeble, wan, distracted, and desperate.

There had been no wife to extend her arms to the husband, there was no husband to extend his arms to the wife. Bourrienne informs us that Bonaparte "*était exaspéré au dernier point.*" Three awful days elapsed, each minute of them a separate century of despair for Josephine. Three days he would not see her.

*Aloof he sits
And sullen, and has pitched his tents apart.*

Three days he would neither see her nor hold communication

with her. He scouted the explanation of her misadventure on the road; declared, raving, that he knew she had eloped with Charles, and, thinking better of it, had returned to throw herself upon his pity. Pity in him she should find none. He would abandon her, and no one should put him from his purpose.

The friendly Collot, friend to both sides, tried to play the go-between. "All France is watching you," said Collot. "What! Are you going to make of yourself one of Molière's husbands? You!"

"Well, then," said Bonaparte at last, "Josephine might betake herself to Malmaison. Under no roof of his should she set foot again."

"Pooh!" said the peacemaker gently. "Your very rage tells me that you love her still. She will come with her little excuses to you, and you will forgive her."

"I? I forgive her! "clamoured Bonaparte. "Never! Did I not know myself resolved in this, I would tear out my heart here, and fling it in the fire!"

"Well, well," persisted Collot, in his smooth, pacific way, "send her off, if you must—but not now. This is not the moment. You have first of all to set the State upright again. When that is done, you may find—or not—a thousand reasons to justify your anger. France knows nothing of your private affair, but you understand our ways sufficiently to appreciate this fact, that you cannot afford to begin by making yourself ridiculous."

But Bonaparte sat obdurate. At that moment he cared nothing for the ridicule of France; he was willing to be the butt and jest of Paris as "one of Molière's husbands;" his fixed idea was to send his wife packing, to whistle her down the wind with a divorce. He would give Collot no other answer.

We are to remember that Josephine herself, who had arrived late at night, was in the house all this while. The clan had decamped; satisfied, no doubt, that they had wrought the heart of Bonaparte to the right temper. He sat insulated in his study, the door locked, and would entertain no parley.

Josephine, all tears, contrite and shaken, approached and tapped on the door. Not a sound in response. "Open to me," she wailed; "open the door, my friend, my kind friend: I will explain everything. Oh! he won't open the door.... What have you against me? Tell me! ... Oh! my friend, if you but knew the agony you are. causing me."

Bonaparte, paler now than ever, we may think, behind that unyielding door, is said to have hissed out some inarticulate rageful words. The sobs of Josephine echoed through the house. What was this inarticulate fury that opposed her? Never before had Bonaparte resisted her like this. Never until now had her tears failed to weaken him. She sank mute, some tell us, full length on the stairs outside the door, at the end of her strength and her resources.

No; not yet quite at the end of her resources: one hope remained. There were the children, Eugène and Hortense: he had always been so kind to the children. Speedily someone was dispatched to fetch them. They, well knowing, we may fancy, what a storm was tearing the home, ran to their mother's aid. What a sight! Poor Josephine, half-clad, outstretched upon the stairs, tear-stained and moaning, waving her hands feebly at the unrelenting door.

The two young ones now raised their voices for her, protesting her innocence, imploring the stepfather that he abandon not her or them. Their mother would die of grief, they said; and had not they themselves lost a father on the scaffold, and were they not now dependent on that father whom Heaven had sent them? Would he desert them all?

The door was opened, and the children were allowed in.

"Well," said Bonaparte presently, "go and fetch your mother."

The siege was ended. The peace was struck.

Bourrienne adds that Collot came to lunch the next day, and was received by Bonaparte, who looked a little sheepish. He gave Collot his own version of the reconciliation. "Well," said he, "she's here after all! ... How could I help it, Collot?" for Collot had made haste to assure the general that he had done emphatically the right thing.

"As she was going down the stairs crying, I saw Eugène, and there was Hortense in tears too. I can't stand too many tears, Collot, and that's the truth. Eugène was with me in Egypt, you know: a brave and good boy, and I had grown to look on him as my adopted son. Hortense is just making her entry into the world, and everyone who knows her speaks well of her. I declare to you, Collot, I was profoundly moved. The sobs of those poor young things were too much. for me. I said to myself: 'Ought they to be victimized for the fault of their mother?' I kept Eugène with me, and Hortense came back with her mother."

"They will be grateful to you, be sure of that," said Collot.

"They ought to be, Collot, they ought to be: they have cost me enough!"

Not forgetting that Bonaparte had been unfaithful to his wife with

Mme. Fourès, we may admit that he behaved with generosity. He made only one condition with Josephine, the not unreasonable one that she should see no more of the ex-captain of hussars. Bonaparte himself, if we may trust a curious story, beheld him once again. He was going one day with Duroc to examine the Austerlitz Bridge. A carriage overtook them, and as it passed, Bonaparte gripped his companion by the arm and turned very white. The occupant of the carriage was Hippolyte Charles.

It may be asked, was the reconciliation complete between Bonaparte and Josephine? We have had, through Bourrienne, the testimony of the peacemaker Collot. An earlier and more important witness was Lucien Bonaparte. Calling at the Rue Chantereine, at seven in the morning, he had found husband and wife in bed.

4

From this date we hear no more of the infidelities of Josephine. It is the infidelities of Bonaparte with which, in the main, we shall henceforth be occupied. We may scarcely, in the case of Josephine, speak of "that fierce thing they call a conscience," for Josephine's was made in Martinique; and, wherever made, conscience, as Sheridan says, "has no more to do with gallantry than it has with politics." But she had felt a shock that had come very near to sinking her. She had only just escaped the public repudiation at her husband's hands which would have left open to her scarcely any other career than the courtesan's. And Josephine, though not a model woman, or a very wise, was a passing clever one. She could, at least, "perceive the sun at noonday;" and the mode of adventure that might spell divorce lost its peculiar savour. Bonaparte, less easily divorced (the facile, iniquitous pull of the man over the woman!) was just breaking ground in this direction.

For the clan Bonaparte, the reconciliation was a reverse. From Mme. Bonaparte, Mère, to Jérôme, who was turning fifteen, they were furious. Josephine, who had as little skill as liking for the pure offensive, essayed the truce that might conduct to peace. She thought of marrying Hortense to the truculent little Jérôme. She fancied, says M. Turquan, that she had perceived the beginning of sympathy between them. She had seen them playing together in the diminutive garden of the Rue Chantereine. To link them now by betrothal, were this possible, would be a consummate stroke. It would be the breaking of the feud. At best, the peace of the families up to this had been an armed one; here was hope of converting it into an enduring amity.

But Josephine's conspiracy for union came to nothing. The Bonapartes were not prepared to treat with her. So sure had they made of expelling her from among them, that, when they realised that she was still the wife of Bonaparte, their malevolence built against her a stiffer barrier than before. In the end it was Louis who fell to the violet eyes and golden tresses of Hortense—and the marriage was a tragedy of the commonplace.

5

As this is a history neither of war nor of politics, the *coup d'état* of *Brumaire* (November 1799) concerns us only from the personal standpoint. It is *Brumaire* that overthrows the Directory, and this signal revolution within a revolution makes Bonaparte for the first time a political character in France. Henceforward he is as important in politics as in war.

In the chapter on *Brumaire*, in the eighth volume of the *Cambridge Modern History*, Mr. H. A. L. Fisher says:

> By the spring of 1799 the government of the Directory had become completely discredited.... Amid the disorder, the misery, and the vices of the time, there was one all-pervading passion—the craving for peace abroad and methodical government at home. Everyone was disgusted with the Revolution; but no one save the priest and the *émigré* wished to recall the *ancien régime*.

Dr. Fortescue, in the admirable introduction to his admirable version of Thibaudeau's work on the Consulate, cites a pregnant passage from the *Souvenirs* of the Duc de Broglie.

> Those who have not lived through the epoch of which I speak can form no idea of the profound misery into which France fell during the period between the 18 *Fructidor* (September 1797) and the 18 *Brumaire* (November 1799). We were plunging under full sail back to the abyss of the Terror, without a gleam of consolation or of hope. The glory of our arms was tarnished, our conquests lost, our territory threatened with invasion. The *régime* of the Terror no longer appeared as an appalling but temporary paroxysm, conducting of necessity through a salutary reaction to a more settled order of things. The reaction had failed utterly, the government, which owed to it its existence, was transporting its founders to perish at Sinamary. All the ef-

forts made by honest statesmen to secure the legal enjoyment of their rights had been crushed by violence.

There seemed to be nothing before us but to return to a bloodthirsty anarchy, the duration of which it was as impossible to foresee as it was to find any remedy. The remedy was found on the 18 *Brumaire*. Not that the 18 *Brumaire* was alone sufficient. We had gone through plenty of *coups d'état* during the last ten years, but we had found hitherto none of the qualities which can alone excuse a *coup d'état*: the genius, wisdom, and vigour which could enable its author to turn his victory to the benefit of society and save us from further danger of violent revolution. The 18 *Brumaire* was, as its author intended it to be, the opposite of the 18 *Fructidor*. It restored all that the 18 *Fructidor* had destroyed. It founded the order of civilization under which we still live, in spite of all the changes of half a century.

The vibrant story of the *coup d'état* of *Brumaire* (November 1799), of first importance in a biography of Napoleon Bonaparte, possesses for us only a secondary interest. More than once Bonaparte had snubbed Josephine for an interference in politics which, as he conceived, displayed her inconspicuous intellect at its least conspicuous; but he was fain to admit that the part she played under him in the plots and counter-plots of *Brumaire* was neither maladroit nor valueless. Josephine had no greater genius for conspiracy than she had for any other mode of intellectual exercise, but such designs of State as could be pushed in flirtation by a pretty woman in her own drawing-room were eminently to her liking. And the *salon* in the Rue des Victoires (as the Rue Chantereine, in Bonaparte's honour, had just been rechristened), magnetically drawing in these days of perplexing expectancy the representatives of all parties in Paris, was a fair stage for her talents.

She did the honours there with native grace to a nondescript crowd of "generals, deputies, royalists, Jacobins, *abbés*, a minister, and the president himself of the Directory." Bonaparte aired the diplomatic arts he was learning, "discoursing to his colleagues of the Institute on the state of the ancient monuments of Egypt and the prospects of a Suez Canal." Due allowance made for the anxieties that wait on all attempts to change the settled order, the march of affairs to the revolution of *Brumaire* was comparatively easy. Not a drop of blood was spilled. Bonaparte, opposed by the Jacobins, and fearing poison, might carry his own bread and wine to the banquet offered him by the councils; and might even, for a night or two, sleep with pistols under his pillow. For the most part, however, as the German historian Lenz observes, everything in the tragi-comedy of the 18 *Brumaire* "went as if by clockwork."

When the curtain had finally dropped upon the scene Bonaparte was First Consul and the practical Dictator of France. In his proclamation to the nation on the eve of the new century, December 15, 1799, he said

> Citizens! The Revolution has returned to those first principles from which it started. It has reached its end.

Josephine, as *consulesse*, found herself luxuriously nested in the Petit Luxembourg. Thus far had the cloak and sword marriage brought the sugar planter's daughter from Martinique. The Petit Luxembourg already had something of the air of a court, and we note that the courtly title of "*Madame*" began to displace the *sans-culottic* one of "*Citizeness*."

Bonaparte and his wife, as we know, had started on the adventures of matrimony with scarcely a shot in the locker. Josephine, as we also know, had returned from Italy with much useful plunder; but ready money in satisfying quantities had not heretofore been hers to command. The credit, however, that was wanting to the wife of the general still carving his way to fortune would scarcely be refused to the wife of the First Consul; and Josephine had very soon begun the practices that were to cost her husband such enormous sums.

Bonaparte, to whom fame and power had brought as yet no wealth, had taken one of his wife's necklaces for a wedding present to his sister Caroline, just married to Murat. Josephine ought not to have been very angry, for had not Bonaparte recently paid off her debts he would have had money enough for the gift to Caroline. Angry or not, she meant to replace the necklace.

It happened that Foncier, that very fashionable jeweller, had a lovely set of pearls to dispose of. The price was a little daunting; two hundred and fifty thousand *francs*, says Bourrienne, five hundred thousand, says Mme. d'Abrantès. It was a case for courage, and Josephine, with no money at all, went to Foncier's and bought the pearls. Then she summoned to her confidence and aid Berthier, the war minister. "You see," she said to Berthier, "I meant to pay Foncier out of my savings, but as the poor man seems rather in want of the money you must . . .

well, you know what, Berthier."

Berthier of course knew what. Also, he knew how. Some monies on their way to, or intended for, the hospitals in Italy, did not reach that destination; but Foncier ceased to present his bill.

Having secured the pearls, Josephine's next difficulty was how to wear them. Bonaparte would hardly fail to recognize that they were none of his offering. "I really don't know how I shall ever put the things on," the *consulesse* said one day to Mme. de Rémusat, to whom she was showing them. "Bonaparte would be sure to make a fuss, though after all they are only a little present from a father whose son I had got out of a scrape." Mme. de Rémusat, who did not believe in the father or his peccant son, was unable to cut the knot.

Josephine's best help was usually drawn from the other sex. She betook herself to Bourrienne, the confidential secretary. "You know, Bourrienne," she said, "there is going to be a great reception tomorrow, and at any cost I must wear my pearls. But you know *he* will begin to scold when he sees them. Now you must keep near me; and if he asks where the pearls came from, I shall say I have had them ever so long."

Bourrienne could do nothing but promise his assistance, and the next evening Josephine figured in the pearls of great price. Bonaparte stopped before her.

"Well, what have you been doing to yourself? You look very fine. What pearls are these, eh? I don't remember them."

"*Mon Dieu!* This is the necklace the Cisalpine Republic gave me. I have turned it about and put it in my hair."

"Well, but, it seems to me—"

"Ask Bourrienne. He can tell you."

"Well, what do you say, Bourrienne? Do you remember them?"

"Oh, yes, general! I remember very well having seen them before."

The pearls had in fact been seen before by Bourrienne, and he informs us further that Josephine had received a collar of pearls from the Cisalpine Republic, "but they were incomparably less beautiful than Foncier's."

In a sordid little comedy of this sort Josephine was, as the French say, "*de première force*;" and, as Mme. d'Abrantès says, she "could tell just what lies she pleased." With this side of her character Bonaparte grew better acquainted as the years of their married life revolved. When money was in question, Josephine had the morals of a fox in a henroost. *Fouché* bribed her (to the tune, it was said, of a thousand *francs* a day) to keep him posted on affairs at the Tuileries; and M. Turquan reproduces from the memoirs of Thiébault the story that:

> She pocketed a commission of half a million *francs* for arranging in the interests of the Compagnie Flachat the contract for supplies to the army in Italy—those Flachats to whose barefaced robberies were traceable the misery and famine of our troops at the siege of Genoa, and the pact with Mélas that was forced upon Masséna.

From the Luxembourg Bonaparte removed himself, with sagacious audacity, to the Tuileries. He knew, even at this date, that he was indispensable to France. In many ears the Tuileries must have sounded as a name of omen, but Bonaparte was far too clever to quarter himself alone in that ancient abode of royalty. He caused the *"pavilion de Flore."* to be assigned to the third consul, Lebrun; Cambacérès preferred to stay in his old residence.

Josephine passed her first night at the Tuileries in the bedroom of Marie Antoinette. "You little Creole! "Bonaparte is reported to have exclaimed. "Tumble into the bed of your masters! "

Life at the Tuileries, on all occasions of parade, began to be stiff and stylish. The First Consul had a power of assimilation that is not always found in the parvenu of genius; and, though his taste had no depth, and naturally inclined a little to the simple and the vulgar, he was an actor of the very best. At the Tuileries he began to have visions tinged with purple, and his policy was one of levelling up. Josephine had to accommodate herself to a new social set. The sculptured calves and knees of Mme. Tallien were not on view at the Tuileries, where they might have offended such a guest as Mme. de la Rochefoucauld. There were receptions of ambassadors; etiquette was once again "in the air;" and there were those who said that Bonaparte was playing at being king.

But if, in the *entourage* of the First Consul at the Tuileries, the dawn of a new court may be descried, it is a more seemly prospect, as regards both dress and manners, than could have been seen late or early in the days of the Directory. Government itself was in some degree restored to dignity when its supporters laid aside the garments of *opéra bouffe* and the conversational style of the flash-house. Society had not all at once grown modest in dress and decorous in the externals of behaviour, but it no longer chuckled over its wantonness, and was a good deal better than it had been.

Bonaparte himself, though he was now not without mistresses, gave no public example of licence in conduct; worked without ceasing, and lived frugally enough. There is no burking the fact that Josephine was never again to be free from cause of jealousy; but at least she had never to endure the daily insult of her husband's avowed and overt preference for a concubine. No leman of Bonaparte's rode abroad with him, or was set up in a great establishment, or enjoyed a tittle of authority in the State, or any warrant to boast the favouritism she could temporarily claim.

Josephine had given cause of jealousy, and was now in her turn to feel the smart. As *consulesse*, nevertheless, she was leading a life that she relished; and from Bonaparte she received a thousand proofs that, let him wander as he would, she it was who held the worthier part of his affections. After the dazzling triumph of Marengo, while he was listening to the continuous acclamations of the crowd, Bonaparte turned to Bourrienne and said, "You hear these plaudits? There seems no end to them. The sound is as sweet to me as the voice of Josephine."

The First Consul must have half-effaced from memory the sufferings of Bonaparte on account of Hippolyte Charles, for he greatly favoured Malmaison as a residence. Josephine, too, had a particular fondness for Malmaison, notwithstanding that, when she and Bonaparte were more or less alone at the *château*, there must have been many hours of tedium. During the days when Bonaparte worked incessantly, life at Malmaison was humdrum.

> The First Consul gave to his wife all the time he could spare from toil, but this was only when they met at meals, and the general seldom sat long at table.

The capacity and passion of Bonaparte for work are a theme too trite to enlarge upon. Lévy overstates it scarcely at all when he says:

> This man, one perceives, is invariable in his habits. Take Napoleon where one will, in the hour of triumph or defeat, of splendour or distress, at the moment of pompous entry into an enemy's capital or humiliating return to his own palace, his first thoughts go out to the work that awaits him, the work that must be done.

At Malmaison, when bedtime came:

> Mme. Bonaparte followed her husband to their chamber. The

general got promptly into bed, and Mme. Bonaparte seated herself at the foot and read to him for a while. She was a good reader, and Bonaparte preferred her to any other. But during the daytime, what idleness was hers! Doing nothing occupied the greater portion of her time. Vainly did she change her chemise three times a day, make three separate *toilettes* in the day, receive visitors, go for walks in the park: she still had time upon her hands. Often she left the park, whose tranquil beauty wearied her, and—though Bonaparte objected—took Hortense with her (whose tastes agreed with her mother's) for a stroll along the dusty highroad, where they could see people and watch the carriages.

Then she did a little tapestry, and tired of that. Then she took up her harp; but as she had only one tune, and played and replayed it as often as she touched the instrument, her musical exercises did not long enliven either the performer or the audience. Josephine had few real tastes, no real talents, and nothing whatever of application. Her three chief sources of amusement at Malmaison—all ministering alike to her weakness for spilling money—were the remaking of the park and gardens, the private theatre, and the replenishment of her wardrobe. At these occupations she was happy.

In the park and gardens she did wonderful things on a wonderful scale. She made great fishponds and filled them with strange fishes, and set swans, geese, and ducks of all kinds to swim on them. She made great glass-houses and loaded them with exotic plants and flowers. Bonaparte amused himself sometimes by firing with a carbine from his study window on the rare birds that flew over the ornamental waters. Josephine cared little what damage he did among them, provided she could go on buying more. Of the *château* itself she made a picture gallery, a museum, and a *bric-à-brac* shop. The thoughts of Bonaparte, as he sauntered here and there with her in his brief intermediate hours, must have reverted to his first lodgings in Paris and his meals in the shy restaurant at a few pence the dish. As for Josephine, disagreeables of the past had no import for her while there was money to scatter in the present.

For the evenings of the theatre at Malmaison there was usually good or sufficient company. The evenings of Sunday and Wednesday were given to this diversion; a strictly private one, when pieces were played "*en famille*." On Sunday there was a small dance, on Wednesday a dinner of some ceremony, and a light dramatic representation to follow.

Bonaparte and the *consulesse* greatly enjoyed these little performances. There was no lack of company; choice and varied refreshments were served in abundance; and Mme. Bonaparte did the honours of these private parties with a tact, grace, and amiability that made each guest in turn think that he or she was the favourite of the evening: everyone went home pleased.

Malmaison cannot have been quite so dull as Josephine pretended to Hortense, and she herself was perhaps thrice as good a hostess as she fancied.

But the extravagant pleasures of laying out Malmaison, the legitimate pleasures of gratifying her husband's guests, were trifling in comparison with the secret or semi-secret pleasures of running into debt for raiment, and anything and everything else that could be bought. This was a permanent joy, qualified by the alarms that heightened it. "*Surchargée de dettes*," as M. Turquan says, there was no inducing her to keep down her expenditure—and this notwithstanding her very real dread of a "scene" with Bonaparte. Her allowance might be, and usually was, exhausted: she made no account whatever of that. Tradespeople came to tempt her with all sorts of, finery, and gewgaws; and she would go on eternally buying things of which she could never properly use the half.

Pictures, bonnets, trifles for the toilet-table, curios, yards upon yards of lace, trinkets of the costliest and most useless description: Josephine could deny herself none of them. Very seldom were they paid for on the spot, but this of course was a mere postponement of the inevitable day of reckoning; and as Bonaparte had a rooted horror of debt, his wife's devices to keep her extravagance as long as possible a secret from him were often comical enough. But tradesmen would not be put off for ever; the universal indebtedness of the *consulesse* was both a joke and a scandal in Paris; and Bonaparte must needs hear of it.

Despite his wrath, he acted delicately in the matter, as he so often did when Josephine was concerned. To Bourrienne, and not to his wife, he went first. She must, he said, make a clean breast of it, and let him have notes in full of everything she owed. "These tradespeople were a pack of robbers; he must see all their accounts."

Bourrienne presented the request to Josephine, who was at first vastly relieved to hear that the burden of debt was to be lifted from her shoulders. No sooner, however, had she arrived at the total than her terror rose above her joy. "No!" said she to Bourrienne. "It is impossible. I can't tell him the whole amount. There will be a frightful scene. I shall halve it." Bourrienne urged the prudence and propriety of telling all. Since the general was prepared to pay, why not profit at once by his generosity? As for the "scene," that would probably have to be gone through—"for the half as for the whole."

"But see," whimpered Josephine; "it is a matter of twelve hundred thousand *francs*, there or thereabouts. No; I shall tell him six. That will be quite enough for the present. I shall pay the rest out of my savings." Those savings of Josephine's!

Bourrienne at last gave in. Six hundred thousand *francs* should be the inculpatory whole.

But Bonaparte paid the bill in handsome style, and poor reckless Josephine was redeemed. The picture dealers were satisfied, and the curio merchants, and the *modistes*, and the milliners, and the carriage-makers, and the saddlers, and the jewellers, and all of them. In one bill was an item of thirty-eight hats or bonnets supplied in a month, a number that seems either too many or too few. She is said sometimes to have bought six hundred dresses at a time; a laying out which recalls the words attributed to a *courtesan* of the Second Empire, that her wardrobe was a saving for her decent burial. She bought, by report, a tulip bulb for four thousand *francs*. For tulips, Josephine had no livelier an affection than for tomatoes or transcripts from the Chaldean; it was the awful charm residing in the notion that for a single bulb you could pay four thousand *francs*.

Bonaparte's case reversed a widespread tradition. His wife cost him more than his mistresses.

6

But now, as Bonaparte's star ascended, Josephine began gradually to apprehend a calamity the worst that can befall a married woman. She was thirty-eight, and had borne her husband no child. He, increasing steadily in greatness, was asking himself (as he was asked by his family) who should succeed him. This question grew in urgency when, in December of 1800, on his way to the opera one night, he had a very narrow escape of assassination. A barrel of gunpowder placed in a cart exploded, and it is a wonder that the two carriages containing the Consular party were not hurled in pieces. More than ever vital now became the question of heredity, and with this was closely linked the question of divorce.

The first of the two questions Was mooted in semi-privacy long before the second had begun to be generally discussed. Among the Bonapartes, who never wavered in their hostility to Josephine, it was a favourite topic; and scarcely did they hesitate to tell her to her face that she could give no heir to their brother. When she replied that she had already had children, Elisa observed: "But you were young then, my sister." Josephine, nearing thirty-nine, wept helplessly—and went again to try the virtue of the waters of Plombières. Her physician assured her that she need not yet despair, but she felt the danger thickening.

Added to this danger were the sharp pains of jealousy. It was no secret in these days to Josephine that her husband played the truant and the gallant; and though the day comes when we may almost accuse her of lending countenance to certain of his amours, it is not yet. Did she not one evening insist on Mme. de Rémusat's accompanying her upstairs in order that they might surprise Bonaparte with the actress George? It was after this that he in turn insisted on occupying a room apart from his wife's. One of the ugly sides of Bonaparte's nature is occasionally displayed to us when he tries, quite in vain, to defend himself against Josephine's complaints of infidelity. He turns upon her roughly enough, acts the despot and the tyrant, and finally braves the situation out by declaring himself "a man apart from all the world," whose conduct must be measured by no common standard of behaviour. It must also, however, be remarked that these rude and cynical outbursts were of exceptional occurrence. In ordinary, Bonaparte's attitude towards Josephine was that of the affectionate, if not the doting, husband; and this attitude—his liaisons notwithstanding—contained very little of hypocrisy. Here is a letter he wrote to her at this period, while she was on one of her visits to Plombières:

> I am without news of you, but I suppose you must have begun to take the waters. We are rather dull here, but your amiable daughter does the honours of the house wonderfully. For the past two days I have had something of my pain. Your big Eugène arrived yesterday, marvellously well. I love you as on the first day; you are above all things good and amiable. Hortense tells me that she has written to you many times. A thousand kind messages and a kiss of love.—Ever yours, Bonaparte.

It was not exactly true that Bonaparte loved Josephine "as on the first day;" the fire and fury had passed out of his love, and constancy and continency had ceased; but his wife was still nearer to that strange heart than any of the light creatures he had dallied with, and he half believed that his amours did not touch his conscience. In any case he was pleased to view himself "a man apart from all the world;" and Josephine could always be reminded that the apple was bitten first by her.

But the jealousies of Josephine, at their most acute, could never expel from her mind the constant menace of divorce. Was there any force on her part by which this prevailing peril might be met? At thirty-nine, her age when Bonaparte by plebiscite was elected First Consul for life, she could have had but slender hopes of giving him a child. What if the child, the daughter, she already possessed could indirectly aid her? To heal the spirit of faction in the family, she had devised a marriage of Hortense with Lucien; in the hope that Hortense would bear a son whom Bonaparte might adopt as heir, she now arranged the marriage of Hortense and Louis.

Perhaps this is putting the matter a little brusquely. Josephine, for all we can produce against her, was as fond a mother as a woman so irresponsible could be; and Louis seemed and for a while imagined that he was in love with her daughter. But, in the straits she was being daily reduced to, Josephine must have thought of this union as a very possible salvation for herself. Hortense's son, chosen by Bonaparte as his successor, might save Josephine from divorce. Hortense de Beauharnais and Louis Bonaparte were married; and on October 10, 1802, the son was born to them that Josephine had so greatly desired. But, although greatly favoured of Bonaparte, the child of Hortense and Louis, baptized Napoleon-Charles, was not to live to be Josephine's deliverer.

The Cadoudal conspiracy (followed by the execution—more properly called murder—of the Duc d'Enghien) thrust Bonaparte nearer to the steps of the throne. The great schemer, "mirror of all martial men," whose fame was beginning to fill the world with its report, was about to bind upon his brow "the golden circlet of sovereignty."

The Senate said:

> You have raised us up out of the past. Through you we feel and bless the benefits of the present; give us now a guarantee for the future. Finish your work, great man, and make it immortal like your glory!

The plebiscite to which was submitted the proposal for an Imperium "by an overwhelming majority gave expression to the assent of France to Napoleon's policy;" and on the 18th of May, 1804 (28th *Floréal*, year *xii*). Napoleon Bonaparte was the first man in the realm. Cambacérès, president and spokesman of the senators, proclaimed him "Emperor of the French." Then the Senate proceeded to the apartment of Josephine, who in her turn was proclaimed empress.

Cambacérès said to her:

> Fame sends abroad the tidings of your good works, which are without end. She publishes that you, ever accessible to the wretched, employ your influence with the chief of the State only to relieve their misery; she tells how to the pleasure of conferring an obligation you add a sweet delicacy that makes gratitude the more grateful, a good deed the more precious. The Senate is happy in being the first to greet your Imperial Majesty, and he who has the honour to speak for it ventures to hope that you will reckon him among your most faithful servitors.

The Imperial dignity "was declared hereditary in the direct, natural, legitimate, and adoptive descent of Napoleon, and in the direct, natural, and legitimate descent of Joseph Bonaparte and Louis Bonaparte." It was, of course, the childlessness of Josephine that placed Napoleon under the necessity of naming his brothers Joseph and Louis. To them he looked as the hope of the new dynasty. On the emperor was lavished a civil list of a million sterling (exactly the same sum, Lenz observes, as the Constituent Assembly had fixed for the reformed monarchy); new dignities and offices of State were created, and an Imperial court. The coronation completed the famous work. Here also:

> A harmony with the traditions of Carlovingian times was preserved, by the invitation which Napoleon sent to the Pope, asking him to come across the Alps and give him consecration with the holy oil. Pius VII came. Like Pope Stephen of old, his successor crossed the Alps to consecrate this new Frankish dynasty with the solemn words of the Church.

Napoleon himself, as we know, took from the altar the crown of golden laurel leaves, "fit symbol of a power based upon victory," and with his own hands placed it on his head, and then with his own hands set her crown on the head of Josephine.

Two days before this august ceremony the emperor and Josephine were married—for the second time. The first marriage had been a mere civil contract; the Church's sanction of the union had never been obtained. The Pope, learning this, learning that Josephine in the eyes of the Church was not a legitimate wife at all, had promptly declared that he would take no part in the service of the coronation. This was a hint amounting to a papal mandate, and Napoleon had not the least choice but to obey it. The religious marriage, therefore, took place in the chapel of the Tuileries on the night of November 30th. Cardinal Fesch, Napoleon's uncle, performed the ceremony, which was witnessed only by Talleyrand and Marshal Berthier. "A profound secrecy was observed; but the requirements of Pope Pius were satisfied."

And now at last Josephine might surely think that she had shot beyond the danger zone! She had been solemnly wedded at the altar. She had been crowned in Notre Dame with Napoleon. The coronation was, beyond question, a signal and most significant honour for her. M. Masson has dwelt upon the fact that the coronation (joined with the consecration) had no connection whatever with politics. It was an act dictated by sentiment on the part of the emperor; it expressed all his regard for the wife who had journeyed with him from the Rue Chantereine to the Luxembourg and the Tuileries. Since Marie de' Medici, second wife of Henri IV, no Queen of France had received the combined honour of coronation and consecration; "and not even she at the same time as her husband." As Mr. Sergeant says:

> This fine piece of sentiment was manifested in little more than a year after the period when he was supposed to be growing tired of her, and might well have been taken to prove the falsity of such suggestions.

On the whole, the empress must have entered on the splendours of her new existence with a feeling of confidence such as the *consulesse* had seldom known.

To be sure, the splendours of the new existence were not indefectible. A court is a court, and tedium will dwell there; it is a court, and suffers from restraints. When a great public show was to be organized, Napoleon could do perfectly all that was necessary for the dazzlement of a crowd; but in the art of amusing his guests he was a very indifferent hand. As for the restraints of his court, it was often said that he himself was the only person who enjoyed any freedom there.

At Malmaison, Josephine, in the lazy way that was her natural way, could always make some lazy pastimes; but during the five years and a half that she shared the throne with Napoleon she spent at this retreat not more than seven or eight months. She was at the Tuileries, off and on, for about a year. She visited Saint-Cloud, Fontainebleau, and Rambouillet. She had, in a word, during her reign as empress, no real home. At Malmaison she could always provide herself with amusement of some kind, but she breathed her happiest in Paris, and from the summer solstice she must have turned eagerly to the winter season there.

No doubt at first she derived some entertainment from her position as mistress of a numerous and very ornamental staff of attendants: her lady of honour, her lady of the bedchamber, her palace ladies, her chamberlains, her equerries, her grand almoner, and her secretary (the working staff was probably thrice as numerous); and she still had the daily cheer of a toilet three hours long; dressing and rougeing and powdering herself. More than occasionally, however, Her Majesty was "dull as a beetle"—who is perhaps never dull. It is little surprising. Josephine was a woman poor in intellect and imagination, and with no remarkable endowment of vitality. Her mental resources were of the slenderest kind; a well-filled purse of which the strings were ever open was her chief pleasure during the middle period of life.

She writes from Saint-Cloud to her daughter Hortense:

> Since your departure I have been constantly ill, melancholy, wretched. I have even had to keep my bed, with some feverish attack. The illness has left me, but the grief remains. How could I help grieving, separated from a sweet and loving daughter who makes the joy of my life!

To be occasionally bored is one thing; to be perpetually suspicious of the gallantries of a husband is another and a worse thing. From the very beginning of the Imperial era the empress was made jealous with good cause. Her rivals lurked in many places; at the court, in society, on the stage. At the Tuileries the emperor had what may be called a bachelor's den, approached by a secret staircase; and one can fancy how the Imperial consort would regard this lair of Bluebeard.

Curiously, it was in these very days that she first began to display what looks like warm affection for the intriguing gallant of a husband. Napoleon starts for the campaign against Prussia and Russia, and at Mayence takes leave of Josephine. Scarcely will she be parted from him, falls weeping on his breast, clings to him, until Napoleon himself is sobbing with her. She might almost have had some prescient feeling of a certain happening of this campaign; for was it not to cast Napoleon into the arms of Walewska? Small wonder that by and by we find him inventing manifold excuses to stay her from coming to the seat of war!

The letters of Napoleon during this campaign are in marked contrast with the Italian series. Now and then we get an ardent phrase, and the tone is seldom other than affectionate; but there is no rage of love or jealousy in them, the lava-flow of the epistles from Italy has chilled. Some breath of the *amour* with the siren Pole—in which all the erotic Corsican suddenly flames again in Napoleon—must have been wafted to Josephine, for we read by implication in his answers to her that she is restlessly anxious to be where he is.

Napoleon writes (from Posen, December 2, 1806);

> All these pretty Poles are French at heart, but there is only one woman for me. Do you know who she is? I could paint a very good picture of her, but I should have to flatter it too much for you to recognize her.... How long these nights are, all alone.

Eight days later:

> I love you and long for you greatly.

January 3, 1807:

> Your grief oppresses me, but one must submit to events. It is too wide a country for you to travel between Mayence and Warsaw.

The same week:

> Think that it costs me more than you to put off for a few weeks the happiness of seeing you: events and the success of my enterprise will have it so.

The week following:

> The distance is too great for me to allow you to come so far at this time of year. I am in splendid health, rather wearied sometimes by the length of the nights.

January 18:

> I am very well, and I love you much; but if you are always crying I shall think you have neither courage nor character. I do

not love cowards, and an empress should be brave.

January 23:

> It is out of the question for women to make such a journey as this.... Return to Paris; be happy and contented there. I myself may be there before very long. I was amused at your saying that you had taken a husband in order to be with him. In my ignorance I fancied that the wife was made for the husband, the husband for his country, his family and glory. Forgive my ignorance; one is always learning something from the fair sex. Goodbye, dear. Think what it costs me not to send for you. Say to yourself, 'This proves to me how precious I am to him.'

All this would be pretty enough did we not remember that it was but a few days since he had written to the young Countess Walewska:

> I saw only you, I admired only you, I desire only you. Answer immediately, and calm the impatient ardour of—N

But a few evenings since he had said to her:

> You need not fear the eagle; he claims over you no power but that of a passionate love, a love that will content itself with nothing less than your whole heart.

The last letter but one of this series to Josephine was written from Tilsit in July, just after the conclusion of that treaty which was so humbling to Prussia.

> The Queen of Prussia is truly charming; she overflows with *coquetry* for me, but you need not be jealous. I am an oil-cloth— it all glides over me. It would be too costly to me to play the lover.

He had played it easily enough in seducing the girlish Marie Walewska!

Meanwhile there had been a domestic tragedy, and one which for Josephine was full of dreadful omen. On May 5, 1807, died the first child of Hortense and Louis Bonaparte. An attack of croup had carried off the little Napoleon-Charles. Grief turned the poor mother almost to flint, Josephine was distracted, and the emperor deeply moved. He wrote:

> I realise to the full the sorrow which the death of our poor

Napoleon must cause you. You can guess what I, too, am suffering. I wish I were with you, that I might try to keep your grief within moderate bounds. You have had the happiness never to lose a child, but it is among the conditions and trials inseparable from our lot in this world. I beg you to let me hear that you have been reasonable and are keeping well. Would you add to my sorrow?

Alas! Josephine could not but feel that for her the death of the boy prince was or might be something more than a bereavement. It brought nearer to her the possibility of divorce. Napoleon had wished to adopt his brother's child, had built on this child his plans for the succession; the ever-jealous Louis had refused the offer. Plans for the succession had now become more than ever difficult, inasmuch as Napoleon had bestowed on his brothers Joseph and Louis the crowns of foreign countries; and, as Lenz says:

> It was hardly conceivable that either of them could unite in his person a foreign crown and that of the French Empire. . . . And the brothers of Napoleon counted for less in this matter of the succession, because they had disappointed the hopes he had raised of their co-operation in his work.

There was something besides all this for Josephine to brood over. A few months before the death of Napoleon-Charles, there had been born to the emperor (December 13, 1806) a child to whom the name of Léon had been given, the fruit of a liaison with the beautiful girl Eléonore Denuelle. The birth of this child was known to Josephine, who knew also that Napoleon could now say to her, "You see, it is your fault that I have no legitimate heir!"

But the unfaithful husband did not cease to love the wife he had now so many times betrayed; the emperor, conscious of the advantages of divorce from the standpoint of the reason of State, clung to the consort he had crowned, the woman who had wound herself about his heart. Again and again we read that "his passion for Madame Walewska had shaken his affection for Josephine." This in a measure is true enough; but for a long while before this date Napoleon had merely pretended to be the lover of his wife—in the sense, that is to say, in which the poet speaks of "sublunary lovers' love."

What is significant is, that although Napoleon himself began seriously to ponder the question of divorce, and to take counsel on it, immediately after his return from Tilsit, he was two full years in accomplishing the step. Not for nothing did that swift, decisive man dally for two years with a scheme of any sort. What kept the scheme of divorce two years upon its course was Napoleon's profound sentimental reluctance to part from Josephine. Two curious years these are. The graceful tears of Josephine bedew them plentifully; the *"funerall teares"* of a divining heart. She weeps, pleads, protests, and is sometimes as nearly defiant as a soft, indolent, and yielding nature will let her be. She shows by turns a plaintive dignity in answering Napoleon and a pathetic want of it in her readiness to go behind his back and abuse him to the people of her household, to ministers, to anyone. Napoleon, on his part, mixes tears with argument, caresses with reasons of State, cajoleries with appeals to the needs of France and the imperious calls of his destiny. Ministers ply the unfortunate woman with motives for self-sacrifice, are sent packing by her, and are then trounced by Napoleon—who had given them their cue.

But Josephine's battle—doubtful as the issue repeatedly seemed—was in truth from the first a lost one. We behold it finally spent at the family council held at the Tuileries on the night of December 15, 1809. Josephine's eyes were tear-swollen, but it is agreed that the poor lady had schooled herself to a very queen-like composure. Napoleon's emotion was plain to all within the circle. In the course of the brief speech which he substituted for the one that had been prepared for him, the emperor said of the wife he was divorcing from him:

> She has adorned fifteen years of my life, and the memory of these years will never quit my heart. She was crowned by my own hand. I desire that she retain the rank and title of crowned empress, but above all that she never doubt my feelings and that she retain me always as her best and dearest friend.

For Josephine, too, a set speech had been prepared, but we incline to think that the words she used (they were in her own handwriting and on her own paper) had either been penned by herself or adapted by her from the document she had received.

> With the leave of our august and dear spouse I declare that, since I am without the hope of bearing children to satisfy the requirements of his policy and the interests of France, it is my pleasure to afford him the highest proof ever yet given of my attachment and devotion.

This brief exordium reached, the unhappy woman gave way, sobbing audibly. Regnauld de Saint-Jean d'Angély, Secretary of State to the Imperial Household, took the paper from her, and read it to the end.

> To his bounty I owe everything. His was the hand that crowned me, and while on the throne I have received from the French people nothing but testimonies of affection. I recognize this, I think, in agreeing to the dissolution of a marriage which has now become a hindrance to the welfare of France. . . . But the dissolution of my marriage will not change my heart. The emperor will always find in me his truest friend. I know how sorely this act, which his policy and great interests render necessary, has hurt his heart; but we shall both win glory from the sacrifice we consent to for our country's sake.

These words, if they were Josephine's own, became her well. The whole circle was visibly distressed. During the reading by Regnauld the empress, outwardly calm, carried her handkerchief several times to her eyes; the grief of Hortense, seated behind her mother, was more audible; and the son Eugène, Viceroy of Italy, supporting himself with difficulty from the opening of the scene, fell in a swoon when the speech was ended. The termination of the ceremony was a huge relief for everyone. But before the night was over. Napoleon had yet another shock. He had retired to his room and to bed. Suddenly at the door of the chamber appeared Josephine, dishevelled, weeping, "her eyes strangely fixed." After a moment's pause, "she advanced towards Napoleon's bed, moving like an automaton. At the bedside she sank forward, and folding the emperor in her arms, let her loud lamentations take their course." Napoleon was an hour in bringing her round. After what had just passed at the family council he could give her no promise but that of friendship, and with this she was at last persuaded to leave him.

On the following morning it was announced to the Senate that the emperor and empress were jointly agreed to sever their bonds of wedlock. The resolutions of the family council were presented by Count Lacépède, who said:

> Today more than ever the emperor has shown that he desires to reign solely that he may serve his subjects, and has shown, too, how well the empress deserves that posterity should associate her name with Napoleon's.

Lacépède bade the Senate remember that no fewer than thirteen of the predecessors of Napoleon had broken the chains of matrimony the better to discharge the duties of sovereign, and that "among these were the most admired and beloved of French monarchs—Charlemagne, Philip Augustus, Louis XII, and Henri IV."

By Committee of the Senate it was decreed that:—

(1) The marriage contracted between the Emperor Napoleon and the Empress Josephine is dissolved.

(2) The Empress Josephine will retain the titles and rank of a crowned Empress-Queen.[3]

(3) Her jointure is fixed at an annual revenue of £80,000 from the public treasury.

(4) Every provision which may be made by the emperor in favour of the Empress Josephine, out of the funds of the Civil List, shall be obligatory on his successors."

In their address to the empress the Senate said:

Your Imperial and Royal Majesty is about to make for France the greatest of sacrifices. History will forever preserve the memory of it. The august spouse of the greatest of monarchs cannot by more heroic devotion be joined to his immortal memory. The French people, *Madame*, has long revered your virtues. It holds dear that loving kindness which inspires your every word, as it directs your every action. It will admire your sublime devotion. It will forever award to your Majesty, Empress and Queen, the homage of gratitude, respect, and love.

In the very hour of parting from her, Napoleon was once again to be reminded that his enchantress had cost him dear. Once again had he to lift from those fond shoulders a crushing weight of debt. One hundred and twenty "creditors severe" presented themselves, with claims in the neighbourhood of two million *francs*. And once again Napoleon sealed up this avenue of woes, giving Josephine to know that he would

Pay every debt, as if God wrote the bill.

Not that he paid every debt in full. He knew Josephine's trades-

---

3. It has been noted: "This clause gives considerable trouble to Lacépède and Regnauld. They cannot even find a precedent whether, if they met, Josephine or Marie Louise would take precedence."

men, the large simplicity of their ways with her, and the large simplicity of her confidence in them. In cheating these tradesmen somewhat he probably gave them somewhat above their due. This at least shall be hoped, for a fair half-million was knocked off the total. There were one hundred and twenty thousand *francs* to a lace dealer, and above five hundred thousand *francs* to jewellers. Josephine could have rubbed the virtue out of Aladdin's lamp!

4

'The Queen of the East'

Who, after his marriage with Josephine, was the first woman to share an amorous episode with Bonaparte? Her time was not in those early days of glamour; of this, conviction seems to come unhalting. There could have been no room for inroads, on his lightest emotions even, during his first separation from the wife, older than himself, with whom he had spent an ardent honeymoon of two days, before the military necessities of Italy called him to the camp. The *aura* of the new existence clung to him, it pervaded the lines of battle.

The portrait of Josephine was in his hand, it was thrust upon the attention of every comer; in any lesser man *niaiserie* would have been discovered by the officers whom he buttonholed and into whose ears he poured the glowing stream of description of the new wife; there could have been no corner in his existence for any other *voyageuse à Cythère*. While every spare moment was filled with the writing of letters in burning strain to the absent bride, no other could have had the chance of being even the accomplice of those merely sensual flares which rose and died out in a few days, or even in as many hours, in the later life of Napoleon, First Consul and Emperor.

"I kiss you on the lips—I kiss you on the heart;" such outpourings and many more were lavished on the absent one. Poverty had combined with military discipline to avert most episodes of the merely venal kind. Bonaparte was only twenty-seven when he became a husband, and the feminine desire to throw itself at the feet of the conqueror and the sovereign could only beat unheeded on the barriers guarded by another image.

Thus there seems to be a gap of some three years before any affair of importance in the feminine cosmos is recorded. Bonaparte had gone down into Egypt, on a mission regarded by certain of the Powers as vague and somewhat suspicious. To humble England was the aim alleged of him by some. Egypt was doubtless the keyhole of the East and of the Indies; Bonaparte may well have hankered for the turning of the key; it was, besides, or so ran fable, a land of treasure, treasure lying loose for the picking. We have heard the same legend of the streets of London the Relentless, and of many an Eldorado. "Egypt is a very different country in reality from the written descriptions of it," said the general-in-chief himself.

Josephine, as we have seen, did not go down into Egypt.

Bonaparte, meanwhile, had there fallen in with one who was to provide him with a feminine experiment of some standing. He was, we may think, on the scent of an adventure in the intervals of his admiration of the Pyramids, to him one of the most stupendous impressions of his life; for he had caused a bevy of Asiatic beauties to be brought to his quarters at Cairo, that he might inspect for himself their loudly-vaunted charms. But their figures and their corpulence, so esteemed by the Oriental male, had no value for the European general. He soon bundled them off. Not long, however, had he to wait for a more delectable specimen of femininity. Riding one day with his staff in the neighbourhood of Cairo, Bonaparte had to draw rein to allow of the passage of a party of travellers mounted upon the Arab donkeys of those parts. His ready eye picked out among the riders a young woman with a piquant and vivacious expression.

This was Pauline Fourès, wife of an officer of reserves, then on service in Egypt. This young traveller, a native of provincial France, the offspring of a *mésalliance*, had lived her quiet life blameless as a work-girl in a little country town. Pretty from her childhood, "Bélilotte," as she was nicknamed, had attracted the notice of a worthy man of the middle class, the son of a retired tradesman of the same neighbourhood. He married her, and at the call for reserves for duty in the Egyptian campaign, he took his wife with him to that country. Fair, with the fresh rose colouring of a school-girl, and sparkling with vivacity, the young wife met the party of the general. Light-heartedly enjoying her donkey-ride, she happened on the fateful hour. Bonaparte said nothing of his impressions at the moment, but at once contrived a plan for seeing something more of the gay rider.

There was, however, nothing indicative of his connivance in the invitation received next day by Madame Fourès to dine with General Dupuy, the military commandant of Cairo. Some lady, either a relative or a useful friend, was accustomed to play hostess for the general when he entertained ladies of correctitude. So the young wife took things as being *en règle*, when the commandant and this *"manière de* Madame Dupuy "requested her company. Fourès, alone, was puzzled that his wife should be invited without him.

"For, after all, I am certainly an officer," remarked the lieutenant of *chasseurs* with some huffiness. However, he allowed his wife to go, only, with a vague sentiment of jealousy, enjoining her to let everyone know that she was a married woman.

The little dinner went off very well. The lieutenant's young wife was offered every attention. There was, says the chronicler, nothing that could have given her the slightest suspicion as to coming events. Dinner was over, the guests were at the stage of dessert, and the coffee was just arriving, when sounds were heard in the house, the folding doors were thrown open with energy, and between them appeared the commander-in-chief. Dupuy, apologizing for being still at table, asked General Bonaparte to take at least a cup of coffee with them. The general accepted and sat down, and before us arises the picture of the scene.

Silently sipping the cup, the man of whom a world had begun to talk, fixed a steady gaze on the young guest, who, blushing at the obvious attention of the great man, cast down her eyes in silent confusion. She had not even the relief of passing off her embarrassment in light chatter. Bonaparte ate an orange and drank his coffee, but spoke not a single word to Madame Fourès all the while that his eyes, suffused perhaps with that velvet mist which visited them when bent upon an object of desire, swept every line of her form. Then he rose and took his leave. We are told of a ruse by which Napoleon contrived an immediate assignation with Pauline—the intentional overturning of a cup of coffee (or, according to another account, of iced water) upon the lady's dress.

In the days of the second king of Israel a certain warrior-husband had been found *de trop*. To him, by royal mandate, was assigned the fearful glory of fighting in the front ranks of the Chosen People against their enemies. The simple savagery of Israel was, on the eve of the nineteenth century, replaced by a far finer and more subtle scheme. Fourès must be removed, that he might not interfere with his commander's gallantries. General Berthier stands for Joab in the tale. He was chief-of-staff in Egypt during the campaign.

A few days after the momentous dinner, Fourès was summoned before him. "My dear fellow," said Berthier, "you are the luckiest of the lot; you are to see France once more! Such is the confidence reposed in you by the commander-in-chief that he is sending you to Europe to carry dispatches for the Directory; you are to leave in an hour's time. I only wish I were in your shoes!"

With these words he handed to the astonished Fourès a bulky package.

"I must go ... and warn my wife ... to pack up," stammered Fourès, at length finding his tongue after the stunning effect of a favour which instinct whispered to him was of a very dubious quality.

"Your wife!" exclaimed Berthier; "your wife! Why, you must be crazy! For one thing, she would be horribly ill on a small vessel, badly victualled, and which may have to face some risks—besides, it would never be allowed. To be sure, I can quite understand, my friend, that you must feel the separation from a wife whom you love."

And here, says the story-teller, a little imaginatively, Berthier fell to sighing and to gnawing such fragments of his nails as the habit had left him.

Human vanity triumphed at length over astonishment and distrust. After all, reflected the lieutenant, he did possess qualifications which fitted him for the honour of selection, and these were explanation enough of the commander's choice of him. But Pauline, who had divined Bonaparte's reasons a good deal better than her husband, bade him farewell "with a tear in one eye and a smile in the other." And Fourès sailed away.

But there was many a slip in those days 'twixt setting sail and landing in France; for the English scoured the Mediterranean, and many vessels fell into their hands. The *Pomona*, in which Josephine had once journeyed from Martinique to France, was one of the prizes—the little craft in which Fourès had embarked was another. The contingency was one not unforeseen by those at headquarters. Stripped to the very shirt in the search for secret dispatches, Fourès stood before the English naval commander. Nothing was found on him but some documents which, as the Englishman recalled, had already done service—they had indeed been reproduced in an official print in Paris some time before. But now, how to dispose of Fourès? Let us hear the Duchesse d'Abrantès's own account, for its piquancy is inimitable.

> The English captain, a man, be it said, most polished and urbane, asked the ambassador-lieutenant where he would like to be put ashore. They were sailing, he explained, for Mahon, thence to

the Moluccas, and after that for a pretty big cruise in the Pacific; towards the Pole even it might be; everything depended upon what sailing orders were awaiting him at Macao; after all this they would probably be returning to the Nile. If then the lieutenant cared to accept a lodging on board during their little expedition, he, a captain in H.B.M.'s service, was entirely at his orders. Poor Fourès, who thought as he listened to all these geographical names that they were talking of the realms of savagery unexplored and awful, asked hesitatingly if it would not be feasible for him to return whence he came. For he preferred to tackle all the serpents of old Nile to facing Chinamen and the Spice Islands.

'Observe, too,' he suggested discreetly, 'now that I am nothing but an empty dispatch-box, what is the use of dragging me about the world, far from my wife? Let us put back to Cairo.'

Unlucky fellow! for at Cairo he was fated to discover that it is not only in the Nile that crocodiles are to be found!

Now the English commander was, as it happened, just as well posted in the internal affairs of Egypt as if he had himself been stationed in Cairo and Alexandria.

He knew quite enough of the episode of the commander-in-chief and Madame Fourès to feel overjoyed at being able to engineer such a striking effect in the little comedy which was being enacted, and in which the husband who had been sent a-travelling was now about to perform a role which had not appeared on the programme nor figured in the *mise-en-scène*. And so with the utmost courtesy and with apparent cordiality he landed the worthy lieutenant upon Egyptian territory—and wished him good luck.

Poor Fourès hastened to the arms of the lively Pauline, only to find the nest empty, the bird flown. It was not long before he discovered her whereabouts in a lodging close to the quarters of the commander-in-chief. Bonaparte and Pauline had spent the time of Fourès' absence very satisfactorily from their own point of view. The young Frenchwoman's natural gifts, aided by acquired embellishments, had rendered her a delightful companion to the general, a man in the fullness of his vitality and separated at the time from women of any charm or brilliancy. Her beauty and her ingenuous surrender of herself to his desires made Pauline an accomplice after his own heart in the hours of pleasure which were spared from his conduct of military affairs.

Upon this glowing picture was cast the shadow of the unexpected husband. Anger and embarrassment must certainly have seized upon the pair. Upon the unhappy Fourès the blow fell heavily; he cried his wrongs and his distress for all to hear. A few of the onlookers were touched, it is true, by his misery, but they could not interfere. His turbulence did not retrieve for him the erring "Bélilotte;" he got merely a divorce, valid under the local administration, which led, as we shall see, to further complications at a later date.

Pauline's daydream was soon to finish. The intimacy she must have enjoyed with Napoleon is evidenced by the fact that she was the one outsider to whom he confided his approaching departure from Egypt. This, no doubt, was one of those weaknesses which are in the experience of Samson, and for which Napoleon would lash himself in retrospect. Still, he went no farther; Pauline was made to understand that she could not be his travelling companion. Tearfully, she declared herself prepared to face all danger in her hero's company. It was not, however, of her, but of his own reputation, that the general in the hour of parting thought first. The English might capture him: think of the scandal were she found aboard! Mrs. Grundy doubtless was a power to be reckoned with even by a Bonaparte.

Besides, Pauline had not fulfilled her mission—the greatest of all feminine accomplishments. Josephine, stung by the reflections upon her sterility, had retaliated with counter-charges; the failure might be on the other side, she retorted, and the waspish words had stabbed Bonaparte almost into conviction. Pauline might have made the accusation void, but she failed. "*La petite sotte!* she could not even bear a child," was his conviction in an outburst of irritation.

With sad fortitude, Madame Fourès accepted the situation. It was indeed a sore one. Here was she left in Egypt, now to her a boundless waste, poignantly remarks Madame d'Abrantès. There was her husband, still raving with jealousy and undestroyed devotion; while General Kléber, who had been commanded by Bonaparte to arrange as soon as possible for her departure with others who were returning to France, showed towards her traits inconceivably paltry in a man of such stature and such a fine appearance. He gave his energies to heckling the mistress of his general, and spared no pains to cut her off from such acquaintances as remained to her in the hour of disorder.

When General Junot returned to Paris, Napoleon, white with rage, listened to his account of Kléber's persecution. Moved he was by anger, and by a half-born fear that Kléber might have gained for himself the place of his master. At last, however, Madame Fourès secured the necessary passport, and got to Paris. Here she found her idol as First Consul, more than ever glorious and desirable. But the glamorous days of Egypt were gone by forever. The differences with his wife had just been patched up, and Bonaparte was in a cautious mood. He would not allow Pauline Fourès to establish herself in the capital, but indicated to her a retreat in the neighbourhood, and to this the saddened woman retired. From time to time she showed herself in public, and it was at the opera that the Duchesse d'Abrantès, then a young married woman, first saw the "Queen of the East," for so the generals of Napoleon had named Pauline. Fair-haired and rosy as a schoolgirl of sixteen, Madame Fourès, in a splendid shawl of white embroidered cashmere, dawned on the sight of her chronicler.

Poor Pauline! if she had strayed she suffered sorely for it; a fresh chapter of harassment opened for her when her husband returned at length from Egypt. He was still infatuated with the woman he had married. Profiting by irregularity in the divorce, which had not been confirmed in France as was obligatory, he beset Pauline with the utmost urgency, begging, threatening, moving things high and low in his efforts to obtain her return. The clamour of the affair was intensely irksome to Bonaparte, for whom Madame Fourès was becoming an affair of the past, and who was, moreover, at the time in the culminating moment of his life-consulship. With some asperity, he pointed out to the young woman that the divorce had been pronounced; in spite of quibbles of the law, Fourès and Pauline had been unmated. The simplest way out of the difficulty, he declared, would be the marriage of Pauline to a fresh husband. He indicated the worthy holder of a post in the consular service, and Pauline immolated herself.

She regarded as paramount the wishes and the convenience of the lover who had grown cold; married the consular gentleman, and retired into oblivion. Yet she did riot forget, and in the days of the captivity of St. Helena her love displayed itself once more in pathetic efforts to sever the shackles of the lion. Such is the charming sentimentality of the Duchesse d'Abrantès's story. M. Frederic Masson pours a little cold water over it. "Bélilotte," he says, went to Brazil in company with a retired officer of the Guards named Ballard, and scrupulously denied all interest in the emperor, lest she should fall a victim to the suspicion of the police who were already keeping an eye upon her as "an old friend of Bonaparte." The lady even assumed another name that she might more certainly retire into oblivion. She lived to be old, but kept her relations with the "Man of Destiny" in the secret hoard of her possessions. He had written her many letters, which a world would gloat over today. She afforded no chance to the one or to the other: the unknown outpourings of the hero, whatever they may have been, were muted by the flames.

5

The Singer of Milan

"Italians," said Napoleon dictatorially, "are the only people that can produce opera." In other words, it was Italy that gave to the conqueror the music he delighted in. English music he declared vile, the worst in the world; the melody of "*Ye Banks and Braes*" could not have been so charming had it been English, he declared to the little islander of St. Helena, who with her childish pipe sang to him in the land of his captivity. The music of France was little better.

Italy gave all things: the melody and the composer, as well as the singer whose utterance, "yearning like a god in pain," was to hold the ear of Europe—Giuseppina Grassini, who, not least of all, was to be mistress to the deliverer of Italy.

Grassini may well have had the lark for her earliest rival, for the father of the singer was *un simple cultivateur*, a Lombard peasant. The daughter of the soil early displayed a golden voice, and having attracted the notice of a certain General Belgioso, received professional training at his expense. Giuseppina (she called herself Josephine during her operatic reign in France) was under thirty at the time of Marengo, and was, with the tenor Marchesi, chosen to hymn the paean of victory at Milan in the spring of 1800. She presented to her generation the bundle of contradictions which are the artistic temperament. Her personal appearance formed an astonishing contrast to her style of dress and to her speech.

Her features, cast in a grand and tragic mould, reminded an English *raconteur* of those of her relative Giulia Grisi. Dark-haired, with strongly-marked eyebrows, and the opulent lines of the cantatrice, she turned on all men a gaze which seemed fraught with deeps of amorous inclination. Yet her attentions were most unflatteringly evanescent, her emotions cooled within the hour. We must not even take too seriously Grassini's own rhapsodies poured out to Bonaparte himself. The singer, in her earliest bloom at La Scala, had thrown herself at the young Corsican general, then first dawning in Italy.

Grassini said:

> Then I was in the full splendour of my beauty and my talents. There was no talk of any but myself in the *Vergine del Sole*. I alone drew every eye, inflamed all hearts. The youthful general alone was cold, yet he alone enthralled me. How strange, how seldom found! When I really was worth something, when all Italy was at my feet, and I was spurning her in high-flown fashion for one of your glances, I failed to win one, and now behold! you bend them on me who am unworthy of your pains; no longer do I merit your condescension.

All this may be a little histrionic; in any case Grassini had her triumph, if a deferred one. But when? There is confusion on the point, arising from the discrepancy between the reminiscences of Napoleon himself and of the other witnesses of his relations with the great contralto. Bourrienne falls foul of Napoleon's own reminiscences, believing that he wilfully misrepresented the date of the liaison. Yet to what end could Napoleon have wilfully perverted dates in a matter of such small historical import? Bourrienne himself is by no means faultless on points of exactitude. Napoleon's blunder in placing the beginning of his intimacy with Grassini at the Italian coronation of 1805 was probably quite innocent. To begin with, the allusion to the incident was in one of his St. Helena retrospects.

Even before the final breakdown of his health there were preliminary stages in which his memory had taken on the senile characteristic of recalling best the substance stored earliest in the brain-cells. Then we know not how much was due to the editing of the little band who wrote at his dictation. Indeed to Napoleon, in a retrospect so thick with event, so dazzling with glory, a few of the films of the biograph may well have been misplaced. The keen edge of triumph, had it not rather been in the day of Marengo than in the apex of sovereignty, after all? As for Grassini's hankering for a glance from the hero, is it not much more likely that when she yearned in vain it was in those days of '96 when young Bonaparte had eyes for Josephine alone? There is evidence enough to place the *amour* in 1800.

At the *fêtes* at Milan which celebrated the triumph of Marengo Napoleon heard with enthusiasm that thrilling voice. The soft fullness of the glorious contralto tones enthralled him; they transported him to the very peak of emotional ferment, and sending for the singer "he found her in no way cruel; in a few hours' time the victor of Marengo had added to his conquests." Next morning the lady breakfasted with Napoleon and General Berthier, and Napoleon was fixed in his intention of securing her for the national fetes in Paris on July 14. Bourrienne recalls the orders he received to attend to the financial side of the affair, and to arrange the transit of the star, and of a fellow artiste, Bianchi, to the French capital. And there is a still more detailed touch in reference to the question of chronology.

When Napoleon was awakened with the news of the capitulation of Genoa, in the same year, the slumbers of Madame Grassini were disturbed at the same time.

And now Grassini sang to France as she had sung to Italy. There, on the anniversary of the republic on the 25th *Messidor, an viii*, did the Italian singers at the Invalides hail the victor, and hymn the liberation of Italy, in a poem specially composed for the event by Bonaparte's commands. Three orchestras united to make the musical occasion a peerless one. Berlioz himself scarcely surpassed an undertaking so colossal. Italian music had her triumph in the great acclaim.

Grassini had her reign in Paris. As to her adventure with Napoleon, the artistic temperament and feminine imperiousness conspired together to cut it short. The First Consul had no idea of languishing at the singer's feet. He soon made her understand that at the best she was to consider herself as placed within a niche indeed, but one in which she was not to expect too frequent adoration. Captious and exacting, like other of the "daughters of musick," Giuseppina pouted and rebelled, then launched on open treason. For Rode the violinist understood better than the First Consul how to play upon the strings of temperament; he failed not to burn incense and to lavish the *petits soins*, which, after all, tell with many women far more than the occasional instance of a hero's softness.

As a queen of song, Grassini triumphed too in England and in Russia. At her *début* at the Royal Opera House in the Haymarket she did, it is true, meet with some obstacles. Popular devotion at the time was with the soprano Mrs. Billington, the favourite of a royal duke. Grassini's opportunity came with one great duet in the opera *Il Ratio di Proserpina*, specially composed to give full opportunity to the glorious notes of her register. Together she and Mrs. Billington sang in the duet, and together they received an ovation.

Over the real merits of Grassini's voice and style there has been much dispute. Fétis, the French composer and critic, heard her with rapture. The writer of the Grassini article in Grove's *Dictionary of Music* directs attention to the opinion of Lord Mount-Edgcumbe, a musical *dilettante* of the time. Referring to this amateur's own writings we find him speaking of Grassini in somewhat disparaging terms. "She had but one good octave," he avers. Others dilate upon the *sopranic* flexibility which she added to her gift of *contralto* quality.

For a conviction of the wondrous quality of Grassini's voice and powers let us hear De Quincey. The Opium-Eater declares:

> Her voice, (the richest of *contraltos*) was delightful to me beyond all that I had ever heard. Yes; .or have since heard; or ever shall hear . . . thrilling was the pleasure with which almost always I heard this angelic Grassini. Shivering with expectation I sat, when the time drew near for her golden epiphany; shivering I rose from my seat, incapable of rest, when that heavenly and harp-like voice sang its own victorious welcome in its *Threttánelo*. . . . This same Grassini, whom once I adored, afterwards when gorged with English gold, went off to Paris; and when I heard on what terms she lived with a man so unmagnanimous as Napoleon, I came to hate her.

Grassini's social triumphs were considerable, though gossip again depicts her *allure* as somewhat *bizarre*. With her tragic grandeur of feature was allied a freedom of speech absolutely grotesque in association. Her sayings had not the fineness of wit, they provoked laughter simply by their astounding baldness and the strong Italian accent with which the speaker rolled out both French and broken English. Her *mot* on the decoration of the *alto* singer Crescentini need not be repeated here.

In her dress, Grassini had the tastes of a gipsy. Every colour of the rainbow appeared together without the slightest taste in blending; her appearance was indeed "that of a strolling actress equipped in Ragfair."

She was a fine actress, thinks Lord Mount-Edgcumbe. He, too, is kinder with regard to her outward demeanour than is the *viveur* quoted above.

She was *fêted*, caressed and introduced as a regular guest in most of the fashionable assemblies; of her *private* claims to that distinction it is best to be silent, but her manners and exterior behaviour were proper and *genteel*.

Perhaps Grassini, in Lord Mount-Edgcumbe's company, was in a more reticent mood than usual, for others speak of her alarming frankness on many occasions. Lord Londonderry was astonished to the pitch of dumbness by her account of her tender friendship with his father, Sir C. Stewart, when minister at Paris. Of Napoleon and Wellington she spoke with equal disregard of blushes.

See this snuff-box; Napoleon gave it me one morning at the Tuileries where I had paid him a visit. 'This is for you, you are a fine creature,' he would say. Ah! why would he not listen to me and patch things up with *ce cher Villainton?*

The Iron Duke himself had a tender episode with the singer, or so it is related. Neither of them knew one word of the other's tongue; but they contrived, says gossip, to understand each other well enough.

Some of the aroma of the imperial past clung to the singer. She was again in Paris when the city was in the hands of the allies; and there Wellington's niece, Lady Burghersh, met her at the British ambassador's, and speaks of the interest which Grassini excited on account of her having been a favourite of the deposed emperor.[1]

As years went on the grand *contralto* tones were lost, and Grassini's voice was transformed into a somewhat rasping soprano. She contrived to have somewhere in her a vein of carefulness, not always kin to the artistic temperament, and saved money in a manner not common with her sisters of song. She retired a wealthy woman, and died in Italy in 1850 at the good age of seventy-seven.

---

1. *Reminiscences of Lady Burghersh*. Edited by Lady Rose Weigall.

6
'Georgina'

The varied splendours of this career have lain in the dust some forty years or so—scarce more than forty. Mlle. George is within a little of our own ebullient generation. Born (1787) two years before the great Revolution, she died (1867) three years before the great destruction of Sedan. Victor and vanquished, Napoleon droops and sinks at St. Helena, travels to his home among the dead; forty years later his "beautiful Georgina," his "ever kind and good Georgina," in mere glimmering and decay, but still with gold in her heart, creeps neglected and unknown amid the by-ways of suburban Paris. Burdened with an obesity that made strangers turn and stare at her, she shuffles along in the half-provincial solitudes of Passy, not forgetting and not repining, keeping warm those memories invested with "puerperal gleams" of the Consulate and Empire.

In the curious gallery we are wandering through hers is certainly one of the most sympathetic figures. What a mixture of childishness, good-nature, and simple vanity we find in her *Memoirs*, which have but recently been given to the world! She writes these with an untutored pen at seventy years of age; a poor old unwieldy thing, unheeded and obscure in the mad Paris of the Second Empire; she who had been Clytemnestra, Mérope, Lucretia Borgia,[1] Marie Tudor—and the lover of Napoleon. Her gaze is on the past; she sees herself treading the stage with Talma, moving as a goddess and looking as a queen; she breathes the air of an October morning at the hunting-lodge of Butar, walking the misty woods, a radiant girl half-fearful of her dubious glories, her arm trembling in the arm of Napoleon.

---

1. *Lucretia Borgia An Exceptional and Notorious Woman of the Renaissance Papacy* by Ferdinand Gregorovius also published by Leonaur.

Georgina (Mlle. George)

Her pen stops for a moment, and as she tries one spelling after another for the word she wants to put on paper, her old bleared eyes (not those that flame upwards from the canvas of Lagrenée!) take in the wretchedness of her lodging, and she remembers how frightened her girlish modesty was (or pretended to be) at the great blazing chandelier in the great bedroom at Saint-Cloud, on the night that Constant slipped her in there to meet face to face for the first time the foremost man of Europe. All these things she brings to mind without bitterness; all these triumphs of a life that revolved betwixt the noblest theatres and the most splendid and potent courts in the world; all the people who applauded and showered gifts on her, and those who fought and caballed against her; and when she thinks she has found the right way to spell the word (which is generally the wrong way), she takes up her palsied kind old pen again:

> All these remembrances are very dear to me, and I have the sweet consolation of knowing that I have never varied in my affections. I am poor; what does that matter? I am rich in heart, I think, and above all in my devotion to that *immense* family which befriended my youth. I shall have the honour of carrying my first sentiments to the grave with me. Perhaps I shall not have enough money to bury me. It is quite possible; I was not born to heap up riches. But I shall have a spadeful of earth and a few flowers from my friends. What more does one want?

2

In the winter of 1802, the year in which Bonaparte was named First Consul for life, Paris was rather excited about a *début* that was to come at the Comédie Française. That distinguished tragic actress. Mlle. Raucourt ("Sappho" Raucourt), had picked up at Amiens a lovely little stroller by whose precocious talent she had been so much impressed that she had insisted on carrying the neophyte to Paris as her pupil. "Mlle. George" was the little stroller's name before the public. Her father, George Weymer, was the manager and *chef d'orchestre* of a nomad *troupe*, in which the mother played the parts of *soubrettes*. To Paris they went, George and the careful mother, under the wing of Mlle. Raucourt.

The resplendent Raucourt, waited on by princes and other high origins (for the Terror was overpast), and occasionally shooting rabbits and giving water-parties at Orleans, was a very lazy teacher. Happily for Georgie there was at hand good Mme. de Ponty, Raucourt's companion and *duenna*, daughter of a former maid of honour to Marie Antoinette. "You must get on with the child's lessons," said Mme. de Ponty; "you are neglecting her shockingly. See, there is that Duchesnois girl, our rival, has already made her first appearance, and George was to have been before her." So the lessons were pushed on, and in November of 1802 Mlle. George obtained her "*ordre de début.*"

"Play Clytemnestra, Racine's Clytemnestra, at sixteen? It is ridiculous and impossible!" Probably this was the general and genuine opinion in Paris, an opinion that was certainly voiced with some loudness by the partisans of Mlle. Duchesnois, who was eight-and-twenty. But let us come to the *début*, merely noting that, on her way home from rehearsal the night before, the *debutante* had amused herself by knocking and ringing at every door in the Rue des Colonnes.

Clytemnestra in *Iphigénie en Aulide.*

Georgina tells us, and emphasizes the fact that she is "not lying," that "at midday the crowd thronged all the doors of the theatre." Mlle. Raucourt had sprained her ankle, and had to be carried in to her pupil's dressing-room. "The pit was filled with actors and people of distinction." On the side of the debutante, "my brother in the pit, and my sister in the stalls, put on all my mother's old gloves to make the utmost possible noise in applauding." Georgina informs us that she faced her audience with scarcely any fear. Mlle. Vanhove was the Iphigenia, and Talma the Achilles.

There was some growling and even some hissing from the faction of Duchesnois, but as the play advanced the plaudits grew hot and wild. The audience sat amazed before this imperial girl, the stroller's child from Amiens, who took the stage like a splendid creature in her prime. We have Geoffroy's article on this historic first performance.

After remarking on the "most terrible siege" at the doors of the theatre (Georgina, as she said, was "not lying"), he goes on:

> The councillors of Priam, on seeing Helen pass, cried, 'A princess so beautiful deserves to be battled for; but, let her beauty be never so marvellous, peace is before all things.' And I, seeing Mlle. George, said to myself, 'What surprise that people are suffocated for so superb a woman? But were she, if possible, more beautiful still, it is better that we should not be suffocated, even in her own interests; for spectators, when the sight costs them so dear, are more apt to be severe upon a debutante.' Preceded on the stage by an extraordinary reputation for beauty, Mlle.

George has not belied her fame. In her face are blended the graces of France with the regularity and nobility of Greece. In figure she is sister to Apollo as she moves on the banks of Eurotas, surrounded by her nymphs, and lifting her head above them. Her whole person might be offered as a model to the chisel of Guérin.

When her opening lines were heard, the ear was less inclined to her than the eye; the nervousness inevitably due to such a moment had altered her voice, naturally flexible, sonorous and of wide compass. Some defects which could be perceived in the acting and diction must be ascribed to the same cause—defects quite easy of correction. A girl of sixteen, appearing for the first time before so vast and imposing an assembly, could scarcely have the full use of her faculties; it suffices that she showed at her debut the possibilities of greatness as an actress. Her very faults have a noble origin; they spring from impetuosity and an ardour that at present she knows not how to regulate, for in that lovely body is a soul eager to gush forth. This is no statue of Parian marble; it is Pygmalion's Galatea, live and warm, but overwhelmed as yet by the legion of her new sensations.

Among the audience was the First Consul, who marked his disapproval of the malcontents by the vigour of his own applause.

3

The nomad from Amiens, still in her teens, blazed among the stars of Paris. She was a frolicsome star, given to playing hide-and-seek in the streets at night when she was not playing tragedy in the theatre. She was a runaway star, and there were brave attempts to capture her. Lucien Bonaparte wanted to set her up in his house, Prince Sapieha did set her up: "I had my bedroom in lilac and embroidered muslin." Enterprising suitors elbowed one another in her dressing-room. There was a "M. Papillotes" (Mr. Curling Papers) who "assumed the air of a kind papa"—and did up Clytemnestra's hair with 500-*franc* notes.

Almost imploringly does she whisper us that not one among these fribbles, old or young, had tasted love with her. Though we have but her word for it, we dare be known to think that she speaks the truth. The destiny that was to plant the name of George on the edge or in the appendices of history had not yet got its grip on her. We remark, however, that the First Consul was almost always in his box when she performed, and that in the midst of the scene her eye was caught by the "sunny hand" playing nervously upon the cushion.

"My dear, you are crazed about your First Consul," said Prince Sapieha.

"No, I am not a bit crazed about him. I like him and admire him as everybody else does. Don't all the women rise and applaud him when he appears in his box?"

One night—

> On returning home I found the consul's chief valet. Constant, who came to beg me, in the consul's behalf, to allow myself to be taken, at eight o'clock next evening, to Saint-Cloud. The consul wished to compliment me on my success.

A night of tremors, succeeded by a day of tremors. She means, of course, to go, but plays prettily enough upon the reader's expectations. In the day she strays to the Bois, visits her perfumer and milliner, and towards evening wanders to the theatre, where she is teased by Talma about her air of conquest. At eight—

> I found Constant at the foot of the staircase at the stage door. We got into the carriage, driven by the celebrated César, who was rather too fond of the bottle.... What passed within me on the road it is impossible to describe.

Arrived at Saint-Cloud—

> There was I alone in that huge room. An immense bed somewhere in the background had green silk curtains, and a big sofa was stretched before the fire. There were large candelabra filled with lighted candles.... Not even a little mysterious corner where one can undress.

It is thus, of course, that a young lady of the theatres prepares to receive the felicitations of Caesar. But Caesar, it seems, was not that evening in the forceful or compelling humour. If we may believe the *Memoirs*—and the *naïve* style of the narrative at this point stirs no suspicion—this first encounter passed in very temperate endearments. "He was very tender and delicate. He did not wound my modesty by excess of fervour." "Not today; wait, and I will return. I promise you." "He yielded—this man to whom all the world yielded.... We went on so till five o'clock in the morning." At which hour the jolly-faced Constant was standing, very sleepy, at the carriage door, waiting to drive Cinderella back to the lilac chamber in the Rue Saint-Honoré.

"He fell fast asleep, and snored all the way." Cinderella tells us that she did not sleep a wink; but she was young, and had something to think about.

She was to return to Saint-Cloud on the morrow, and did so, after pretending to her confidante Talma that she would disobey the command. On the following night she played in *Cinna*, and the First Consul was in his box. A significant line that she spoke in the fifth act—

Si j'ai séduit Cinna, j'en séduirai bien d'autres,

—was thrice applauded. Georgina was frightened in her soul. Was the liaison out already, and would the consul think that she, Georgina herself, had published it? That night she was again at Saint-Cloud. There were no questions and no reproaches; the lover was bent this evening upon conquest. Is it strange or not strange that time should disclose to us, through the half-literate pen of a girl of the theatre, a portrait of Napoleon Bonaparte in the role of lady's-maid?

> With such gaiety, with such grace and seemliness, did he enact the part, that in spite of myself I was compelled to yield. How was it possible not to be fascinated by and attracted to such a man? He became simple and childish to please me. No longer was he the consul; he was, perhaps, a man in love, but whose love was neither violent nor rude. How gentle was his embrace, how tender and how modest were his words! (and so forth.)

M. Constant, it may be hoped, enjoyed his rest; for the cue did not come to him till seven in the morning.

Concerning this third interview we are told that it was the "definite" one. The meaning may be divined.

> Here I am launched upon a lively existence, sweet for the moment, but which will occasion me plenty of grief. . . . Yes, it is sad, it is heart-rending; it is slavery in golden chains.

It may be questioned whether George ever really thought in this way. The First Consul was distinctly the first man in France, and, as manners and morals went, a young actress in the position of Georgina was rather distinguished than degraded by his choice of her. "See what a place it is for you!" cried Talma, who took the shrewd conventional view, and probably thought the girl was quibbling when she talked of shame, virtue, servitude, and golden chains. In a measure she probably was quibbling.

We decline to be sentimental over Georgie's situation. She did not honestly feel that she had disgraced herself; nor, in the estimation of a world much wider than her own small theatrical one, had she in reality done so. She did not believe herself to be in a state of slavery—neither, of course, was she. There was no *harem* at Saint-Cloud or the Tuileries. The man in power had flung her the handkerchief, and she had picked it up. Was she in love with Bonaparte? Yes, there is scarcely question of it. A young girl, a young girl of the plebs, a young girl of the stage suddenly risen into fame among the very peers of her calling—and the First Consul of France, the "morning star of war," at her feet. And she pretends to talk of servitude and chains! We read between the lines, and know that she is playing with us. We know, too, that not for a moment does she mean us to believe her.

It is with a lively affection and an infinite loyalty that she dwells (at seventy years of age) on these passages which were for her the greatest in her life. In the dim and hoary days in which the *Memoirs* are written she is Napoleon's still, and the poor little efforts at saving and pretence in them are of no consequence whatever. If we may credit Dumas, who knew her closely, Georgina would have followed the exile to St. Helena.

With his "good and kind" Georgina, Bonaparte threw off his years (which were not so many) and played the boy again. All those stories of his rudeness and violence with women, she says, were a calumny; and towards her, at any rate, he would seem to have been almost uniformly gentle, considerate, affectionate. He was "gay and even childish." Often they played and romped together like children.

> I arrived. Constant said to me:—
> 'The consul has gone up and is waiting for you.'
> I entered. No one was there, and I made a hunt in all the rooms. I called out. No answer. Then I rang.
> "Constant, has the consul gone down again?'
> 'No, *madame*; search well!'
> He winked, and pointed to the door of the *boudoir*, where I had never thought of looking. The consul was there, hidden under cushions, and laughing like a schoolboy.

One chilly evening in the library at Saint Cloud the consul sits on the rug before the fire and pulls Georgina beside him.

> We both sat on the carpet. Then he climbed the small library ladder. He wanted to take *Phèdre* and make me read her decla-

ration, which bored me horribly, so much so that whenever he was about to take down the volume, I wheeled the ladder into the middle of the library. He laughed and climbed down, and boxed my ears just as softly as it could be done.

The evening's frolic over, they retired for the night. She suggests to her friend Mme. Valmore, that the sleep of Caesar:

Was as calm as a child's, and his breathing soft; that his awakening, with a sweet smile on his lips; that he rested his noble and handsome head on my bosom, and nearly always slept so; and that I, young as I was, made some almost philosophical reflections on seeing the man who commanded the world abandon himself completely in the arms of a young girl. Oh! he knew well that I would let myself be killed for him.

If there is no question of Georgina's love for Caesar, we can as readily believe that she was to him much more than the passing fancy of an autocrat. This intercourse lasted six years. On her return from her travels and conquests abroad—had she not received the homage of Alexander I and King Jérôme?—the beautiful woman, still in the bloom of youth, was restored by Imperial decree to all her rights as a member of the Comédie Française. Napoleon never forgot her. Georgina's name was on his lips at Saint-Helena.

7

The Feminine Under the Empire

The proclamation of the Empire in 1804 was the touchstone of Napoleon's plan, his *système de fusion* of the *ancien régime* with the mushroom aristocracy of his own creation. His generals and statesmen, rewarded, it may be allowed, in many instances for no inadequate return of merit, were now to measure themselves off as courtiers against the Faubourg with whom courtliness was an instinct, a tinge in the blood. Their women, and this was still more crucial, were to join in the *entourage* with the haughty *grandes dames* left over from the Terror. Except in cases where it had appeared a menace to internal peace. Napoleon had granted to the *émigrés* leave to re-enter France.

The ladies of the new order were not ill-pleased to figure in the Court picture. Republican simplicity, however much it may be vaunted as an abstract gain in ethic scheme, has a want of glamour for the feminine imagination; something dreary wraps it round.

Now, Court dress and gems and feminine emulation were to have their field in the new order of things at the Tuileries. The Faubourg even may have felt that there was here some attempt at dignity, some imitation of the picturesque which in the former century had reigned at Versailles. They might scorn the upstarts with whom they must rub shoulders, though the terrible object lesson of the bloody head, the ensanguined retrospect of the *fin-de-siècle* would stifle any larger protest against the new development of social affairs.

Some drew the line as tightly as they dared. Mme. de Narbonne, for instance, would put in an appearance at Court only twice a year or so, on such occasions as were more or less compulsory.

"I fear your mother does not like me," said the emperor to the Comte de Narbonne in tones of pique.

"Sire, she has not as yet advanced beyond admiration," rejoined the *comte*, splitting the difference between truth and rudeness with a *finesse* which left the newer courtiers empty-mouthed.

This hobnobbing with the plutocrat and the new *noblesse* seemed strange also to the foreigner.

"It is certainly very odd and difficult to think of these people as princes and princesses," says young Lady Burghersh of Princesse de Talleyrand Périgord, her neighbour at a great imperial function.

There must have been relief that the refinements of every-day habit need no longer be dreaded as indicative of the accursed aristocrat. For, when the empress changed three times a day, a marked attachment to clean linen could hardly ban a *citoyenne*; and "*citoyenne*," indeed, she was no longer, for "*Madame*" had returned to usage. The apostles of Fraternity preserved, it is true, among the returning tide of courtliness, some unlovely marks of Liberty. English ladies, visiting the theatre in Paris, beheld, with amazement, the *parvenu* seated near them in the dress circle, and, indifferent to their presence, spitting with equality both around himself and on the neighbouring seats.

Beethoven, it is true, might rend the score of his Eroica Symphony, and throw it to the ground, when he heard that his idol had the clay feet which had led to the assumption of an imperial diadem, but, on the whole, the new development pleased the crowd, the feminine half of it especially. For what was a fairy tale without a palace and a prince? The emperor, too, had gifts as a stage-manager. He was less concerned, doubtless, than the hanger-on at the possibilities for sumptuous raiment and imperial ceremony, but he had a master's knowledge of their influence on the crowd.

"Don't imagine for a moment," he explained to one of his brothers, "that I care for these things myself, but the public is impressed by them," and with an eye to the gallery he used his state coach with all its magnificence of trapping and its eight horses of *couleur Isabelle*. The velvet and gold lace of the imperial robes sat less impressively on him than the unobtrusive *redingote grise* and the plain beaver hat which had carried him through his truer triumphs, and he was always pleased to get rid of them; but he let them play their part in the *mise-en-scène*.

Again the empress's *entourage* was now to be regulated in accordance with the new order. To her relative, Madame de la Rochefoucauld, was given the appointment of Dame d'Honneur with an annual stipend of 40,000 *francs*. She was hardly an impressive Mistress of the Robes, being deformed, and obliged to have a cushion placed on the seat of her chair to raise her to a suitable height at table. Madame de la Valette was the lady-in-waiting. Twelve *dames du palais* replaced the lady companions who had been enough for the wife of the First Consul. Josephine, as is frequently the case with her sex, showed far more adaptability to the throne than did the emperor. Her deportment at the coronation was admirable, say several observers, in spite of the difficulties of the regal train which her Bonaparte sisters-in-law maliciously neglected to carry properly, and which, dragging from her shoulders, nearly caused the empress to stumble.

At the smaller audiences she had a more felicitous manner of address, and in her few words to the *presentees* did not fall into the blunders made by Napoleon, whose small talk was not ready and who, in absence of mind or indifference, often said awkward things to the ladies present. He would inquire after the nursery of a lady already a grandmother—this, indeed, might have passed as a subtle implication of compliment. But the blunder was irreparable when he inquired of young unmarried people whether they had any children, or when, on hearing the name of a lady newly come to court, he exclaimed: "You! Why, they told me you were quite good-looking!" Yet there was a simplicity in his manner which favourably impressed some foreign ladies, even while he was saying what were palpably "royal nothings."

The scheme of entertainment was developed with the coming of the Empire. Large dinners of two hundred guests were given at the Tuileries every fortnight in the Salon des Maréchaux, after, which the guests would retire to the Galerie de Diane. Here also a concert, listened to with some boredom, was sometimes given, followed by a much more attractive entertainment by *danseuses* from the opera.

If the code of morals was somewhat improved by the purging of the Terror, the standard of luxury soon rose as high as ever. The women of the new *régime* were as sumptuously decked with gems and clothed in garments quite as costly as their forerunners at Versailles. At first Greek styles prevailed, merging in later years into a more gorgeous Orientalism congenial to the emperor. Sumptuous Turkish fabrics became the vogue, and gold and silver thread and spangles were used as trimmings for India muslins and for tulle, then newly introduced. Short or trained dresses were worn according to degree of ceremony. Blonde and other Belgian laces, or *point d'Angleterre* trimmed dresses, caps and underwear.

Of the Empress Josephine's personal extravagance we have already heard enough. She would throw money in the gutter, yet did not pay her debts. In a few short years she had spent on dress over six million *francs*. Her successor kept within her allowance of a half million yearly. Napoleon was urgent with Josephine to appear well dressed, but he deprecated *le gaspillage* in which she revelled. He was forcible in his disapproval. Yet once at Brussels he thought her attire less splendid than that of the ladies of that capital, and was only reassured when one of his Cabinet ministers artfully reckoned up the cost of the outfit to the empress's advantage. Another time a pink and silver gown displeased his taste, and he threw an ink-pot at his consort to emphasize his disapproval.

Powder and the enormous hair-constructions with which we associate Marie Antoinette, had vanished years before. Ladies now were *coiffées en cheveux*, wore their own hair, in short. Gems and artificial flowers or feathers were worn at night, and by day a hat with strings tied under the chin. Josephine wore such a hat all the earlier part of the day, and received in the same in her *salon* at the Tuileries. On dressing in the morning, however, she would tie her head up in a bright *bandanna*, and this was always becoming to her Spanish colouring. The toilet in her case held secrets, and part of it was performed in complete seclusion. *Blanc de perle* and *rouge* were called into the service.

Mme. Martin, a celebrated manufacturer of *rouge*, had survived the Terror. When this part of her dressing was over, Josephine, in a light dressing-gown, would submit herself to the *coiffeur*. Herbault and Duplan held this office, but waited also on ladies outside the palace. Napoleon, gauging rightly the opportunities for gossiping that the plan involved, paid Duplan a large salary and retained him for the exclusive service of the young Empress Marie Louise. Napoleon was in the habit of visiting both his empresses at their *toilette*, and here would take place some of that horse-play of which we hear so much: ear-pinching, teasing of the empress and her ladies; sometimes clumsy treading on the toes of one of the latter.

There were good looks enough among the palace ladies, but it is a vexed question as to which had the advantage, the *ancienne noblesse* or the new "smart set." Most contradictory views were held. One *viveur* says that smartness was out of fashion in the Faubourg on account of the display of that quality by the upstarts of the Tuileries. The aristocrats entrenched themselves in dowdiness. But again, an Englishwoman avers that the former ladies showed still to great advantage beside the latter. However a lady of Georgian times might have no use for smartness any more than had the *émigrés*, we may infer Paris fashions were the standard which London tried, sometimes rather clumsily, to live up to.

The general style of the Empire dress has been rendered so familiar by recent revivals as to render exact description superfluous. We know of the long clinging skirts, the waist line raised to the arm-pits and the heel-less and, generally, sandaled shoe. A low-necked dress was worn for morning as well as evening toilet, a kind of frilled *guimpe* being sometimes used to cover the neck early in the day. The *cherusque*, suggested by the Medicean collar of two centuries before, but narrower and setting closer to the form, gave scope for the display of delicate transparencies in lace or cambric.

The muff and boa of fur were in use, though the latter seems to have been less in fashion than under the Consulate. Swansdown was a favourite material for muffs and trimmings.

Sleeves were either of the puffed variety, covering the top of the arm, or were long, transparent and close-fitting, reaching to the wrist, and fastened through their length with loops and buttons. We have seen their originals on many a classic goddess.

A smaller ruff, a modified version of the Valois or Elizabethan kind, sometimes helped to cover the bare neck by day time. Even more does it suggest to us the "Toby frill" of the 'eighties.

In the latter years of the Empire there was more restraint in head-gear; toques, close and neat with a small plume clinging to the curve of the brim, take one's mind back to fourteenth-century masculine head covering. Again, a frilled cap sometimes appears as outdoor wear, more like the Transatlantic "fascinator" than anything else we can recall, though made of fabric and not of knitting or crotchet.

The hair was sometimes cut short and curled all over. Sometimes, classic loops or knot were arranged at the back and curls over the forehead, such as Anne of Austria might have worn. More severe was the Chinoise style, when the hair was strained tightly to the top of the head and imprisoned in a band.

Gloves were very long as worn with the short sleeve which they met at the shoulder. White and tan seem to have been the best worn tints, while grey appears in mourning garb. Shoes often matched them. Children appear in mittens.

As we have already said, Paris then, as well as later, set the wear of the day, and sent coloured prints to England to enlighten her neighbours across the Straits of Dover. There were items not approved sometimes. "I don't know what you will say to the stripes," says Lady Burghersh, "but everything is worn so large just now in Paris." She decries the hats, just as one of her compatriots had decried a little earlier the bonnets of which he wrote as "deeply slovenly, confused-looking things."

Lady Burghersh thinks the hats "worse and worse, they make them now with very narrow small pokes (brims) and crowns two feet high, and the front covered with enormous bows and bunches of flowers, and these are worn by every creature."

A precursor of the coal-scuttle of the mid-century these appear to have been. Then there were military shapes *à la Prussienne*, almost as high as a Welsh peasant's hat and decked with wildly-waving cock's plumes.

In the royal meals the simplicity of Napoleon's personal taste was combined with the stateliness which he regarded as indispensable to the staging of imperialism. His own meal might be dispatched in ten minutes and be quitted hastily for labours in the *cabinet de travail*. His tastes were satisfied with a grill of mutton, a *poulet* Marengo, the chicken stewed with oil and a dash of garlic, which was endeared to him by sentiment perhaps as much as gastronomy. Beans, peas or lentils would make another course if time allowed, but it was not uncommon for him in his haste or abstraction to eat indiscriminately of roast and sweet *entremets* in turn. Chambertin and water was his common drink, and except for some gossip about drunkenness after his Russian disaster, we hear of no excess in this direction. Gossip, too, crediting him with a dozen cups of black coffee daily, may be disregarded. Sometimes an early morning cup of tea, or infusion of orange flowers, would be taken on rising.

The irregularity of meals was met by a standing order to keep a roast chicken always ready. Thus, at regular intervals, the palace scullions must have spitted poultry to keep in touch with the exaction.

The menu for the ladies and the suite was not prodigal. Napoleon himself went into details of the commissariat as any hotel proprietor might have done. By giving an allowance in lieu of coffee he saved largely on the palace exchequer. His economies were nothing to those of Madame Mère, who banished melon from the board because her ladies ate sugar (a serious item) with the fruit.

The fusion of ostentation and parsimony is seen again in the Princess Pauline, whose servants had orders to put out the candles in her reception-rooms when any lull in the stream of visitors occurred, and to relight them on necessity.

Napoleon apprised himself of the current price of the most trivial article.

Some curtain-fastener or what-not was required. He went *incognito* to the dealers' and, having learnt the usual price, was ready to beat down the extortions of the royal purveyor.

"How much," he asked one of the great officers of the Household, "do you suppose this *vol-au-vent* would cost?"

"Twelve *francs* to you, Sire, six to a private person," was the reply.

"That's how I'm rooked!" cogitated the emperor.

Marie-Louise was, in the manner of a schoolgirl, something of a gourmet. She enjoyed the creams, the pastry and cakes of her new capital, which could have held no disappointment even after Vienna.

If the state dinners at the Tuileries kept up the pitch of splendour and ceremony, it would seem that a greater simplicity was making its way in general society in the latter part of the reign. Indeed at one house of average *ton*, the services were reduced to a minimum, except for fish and meat courses the whole *déjeûner* was put on the table at once.

The palace gave no lead to the *dévote*. Mass was celebrated on Sundays—that was all. Napoleon, while recognizing that religious form was a social necessity, would ill have brooked interference from spiritual directors. The wise direction of the Bishop of Nantes, who was confessor to Marie Louise, receives his approbation.

When the empress consulted him as to the Friday abstinence from meat, he inquired what was the custom of her husband.

"Then, as you sit at his table, do as he does in public. You will find plenty of ways in which to mortify yourself secretly in the sight of God alone."

Again, when there was a question of her receiving the Holy Communion in public, he dissuaded her, saying it would only draw attention to the absence of the emperor at the Holy Feast.

Again, court ritual recalls the old dispensation.

Ladies-in-waiting, it is true, had benches and did not kneel or crouch upon the floor, as under the early Bourbon kings, but there is a flavour of old time in the regulations laid down for the imperial worship. The *fauteuil* was restricted to the emperor and his consort. The sisters Bonaparte found themselves debarred and not a little ill-tempered in consequence, but Madame Mère preached docility to imperial decrees in the great day of her son's glory.

The general standard of elegance and luxury in furnishing was going up. Every lady of fashion had a bathroom and used it as often as two or three times a week (a lavish use indeed!). Mme. Récamier's bath, when not in use, was covered with a scarlet cushion. Her bed must have outshone the imperial couch; *la haute finance* does not lag behind today in its household appointments.

The suite occupied by the emperor and empress at the Tuileries was on the ground floor and was the same that later formed the apartments of Marie Louise. First came an ante-chamber, from which opened a *salon* hung with a violet blue shade patterned with maroon. Here was Domenichino's "St. Cecilia." The second salon opening out of this was the object of admiration on the part of Parisians and foreign visitors alike. It was hung with yellow silk with fringe of brown and red. The mahogany furniture was upholstered with Indian silk of similar colouring or with superb tapestry. From the ceiling hung an English chandelier of crystal lustres mounted with ormolu. The mirrors were not framed, but draped with silken fabrics, and at their base console tables of fine marble held specimen pieces of *Sèvres*, vases of granite, and finely designed candelabra. Here Napoleon and Josephine gave their private audiences, entering it from the bedroom which opened out of it. In the latter room a double bed of mahogany with gilded ornaments stood in an alcove, curtained with the prevailing colouring of blue, with gold and white fringes. Pictures by old masters hung upon the walls.

Next was a simple bathroom from which, by a of grandeur to the Parisian eye, but made a different impression on visitors from England, whose more sombre reception- and sleeping-rooms caused the bright tints and costly fringes to appear sumptuous beyond description.

In their early days at the Tuileries, the Bonaparte couple observed a *bourgeois* communism in their sleeping arrangements. "They actually slept together!" exclaims surprised Miss Berry. In the more formal days of the Empire, Napoleon frequently visited the empress, sometimes because she persuaded him that her lighter slumbers were a security to him. Roustan, the faithful Mamelouk, could snore, as we shall hear, through nocturnal invasions of his master's chamber. Napoleon, too, was a chilly being, and would arrive in the middle of the night, explaining to the empress that he needed to be warmed. Marie Louise, however, found much warmth unsuited to her. Her bright colouring increased to petunia intensity before the large fires demanded by the emperor. Napoleon rarely remained with his second consort for the whole night. Here, again, old Bourbon days returned to oust Republican family habits.

8

The Women of the Family

In the estimates of witnesses of Letizia Bonaparte's own day we find expected inconsistencies and confusions, yet there is concord on the subject of her appearance. Even in her fifth decade she faces our contemplation with noble outlines and grand austerity of feature. Her form, a little bent with time, has not the full advantage of its height of five feet four, a measurement rather above the average of her generation. Her hands, those beautiful hands which Napoleon inherited, are marred a trifle by an accident to the first finger of one, which remains rigid when the other fingers have assumed a curve. Of her feet there is no word but praise; rounded, high-instepped, and of perfect shape and size, they inspire the laudatory pen of the Duchesse d'Abrantès.

Her style of dress is perfect, its tones and stuffs accordant with the balance between her age and the voice of fashion.

The *valetaille* gossip of that streak of miserliness which showed itself amid the glories of the Tuileries, there jangling more discordant than in the straitened days of yore. Yet Madame Mère could loose her purse-strings to relieve the misery of Paris; in a winter of distress she gave most liberally, and was a substantial patroness of the sisters-of-mercy who cared for the sick poor of the city. Of course the most engrossing speculation lies with the question of how Napoleon's mother judged of him in her secret soul. Always he had been the leader in the family conclave, and in the main she would seem, as did so many others, to have believed that the king can do no wrong. If Eugène de Beauharnais could bend his judgment to conformity with Napoleon's project of divorcing the Empress Josephine, his mother, it need give us no surprise that Mme. Letizia was satisfied that the hero-son must shape destiny and be approved by the feminine contingent of his blood.

Behind the fence of her strong soul, cares for her daughters must have fretted her mother-nature. The intoxicant of such an upward flight as theirs in so small a space of time may well have swept them off their feet. For her it was to question their adaptability, the future outcome of their progress on that *viâ regia* to which no known associations of ancestry or of habitude could serve as finger-posts. She, on the brink, watched their essay in royal waters, for her creation as princess-mother was later than her daughters' royalty.

Between the mother and the son there was a certain cloud in the early days of empire, for she had taken sides with Lucien in the quarrel between him and the emperor relating to his marriage with the divorced Mme. Jouberthon. Jérôme's marriage, too, had been a fresh sore. Madame Mère bore her son's neglect in silence, but, mother-like, she had sad hours in her own soul. Yet in the main Napoleon felt for his mother a respect which he held for no other woman.

Then came the final years when all the glory of her Napoleon had blackened into the storm-cloud, and when he had been led away captive to the Southern seas; and then all that there was of her remained pure mother. Had the journey meant death, she would have braved it to be with the son who had ruled all nations, and who must now pace the cage barred by the distrustful caution of the Powers. In those days, when Napoleon gave so many of his pent-in hours to retrospect, he spoke to the little company who shared the rock with their lost leader of his mother with words which, if tinged with a *soupçon* of the rostrum, were yet extended beyond any *imprimatur* he had vouchsafed to womankind.

The eldest of the Bonaparte sisters who grew to womanhood, although she has been set in the background by the tale of beauty and of feminine dazzlement told of the younger women of the family, is to some thinkers the one who most piques contemplation. For she was, they tell us, the one most like Napoleon in temperament, and by this very likeness was most surely destined to arouse his enmity. She was less plastic than pretty Caroline, and light-living Paulette, with her wilful moods and alternating amenability. Marianne, as she was in her schooldays, or Elise, as in her imperial ones, had the outlines of the *femme forte* in her mental frame. Educated in the royal foundation of St. Cyr, we come upon her there in one of those hours in which, as Victor Hugo says, the sorrows of the child make nothingness of those of men or even women. Elise, struggling with tears, confessed at length to the kindly friend Madame Permon, who had accompanied Bonaparte to the school, that, a picnic-tea having been arranged as a farewell feast for one of the royal pensioners, she had not a sum large enough, even if she gave the whole six *francs* of her possession, to contribute to the fund. The bitterness of the family poverty is here revealed.

When we see Elise again, she is the masterful spirit that must of necessity fall foul of the brother-autocrat. Not a pleasant person either to the general acquaintance; the Napoleon-in-petticoats style is not ingratiating. As princess, dowered with one of the Italian territories, we find her living with her brother Lucien in Paris, less intimate with the Faubourg than with the "consort of geometry." Mme. Laplace replaced in her *entourage* the dames of the old *régime* who had been installed by Napoleon in his sisters' households. Elise was disposed to mental cultivation of the most aggressive kind. She would have grounded herself on the model of a learned aristocrat, but Napoleon, with a sneer, decried alike her model and her own replica. Elise, descanting with a Voltairean flavour on admirations of her own which ran amok of all her brother's estimates, drew forth at length the acrid "You! you're just a caricature of the Duchesse du Maine!" and so Napoleon flung himself out of her reception-room. General Bacciochi seems to have been principally Princess Elise's husband. He was a general officer with his wife as commander-in-chief. Married to him in 1798, Elise and her husband played less illustrious roles in the royal show than the more malleable Caroline or Pauline, or than the step-daughter Hortense de Beauharnais.

Caroline, though not next in the family chronology, seems to claim attention before her more resplendent elder sister, Pauline. After the loveliest woman of her day, as Napoleon and others of her contemporaries thought Pauline to be, Caroline may fall a little flat perhaps in the story. Yet she had her own dower of physical attraction. A little thick-set and awkward in her movements she is in her early teens, as we first see her, and, owing to the family vicissitudes, much neglected in her education. But with dawning womanhood her points developed, her bright-coloured hair, her white and shapely bust, and her complexion tinted as the rose-petal or as the inner shell. "Her features could not compare with those of Pauline," says the Duchesse d'Abrantès, "but her skin resembled *un satin blanc glacé de rose*"—we despair of finding English for this delightful pen-painting. Caroline had a rustic charm; the magnificence of regal robes overwhelmed her; her bloom seemed to fade, says the acute lady of the memoirs, beneath the weight of diamonds and of rubies.

About her betrothal to Murat there is much clashing of evidence among contemporary witnesses. It was perhaps at Milan that Murat first saw the young sister of his commander, while his request for her hand was made at the Luxembourg, where the consular court was established.

Caroline was about sixteen, and was still known by the name of her childhood, Annonciata. Bonaparte was much opposed to his demand. He had other plans for Caroline, in the first place, and a personal objection to the suitor.

"I cannot give my sister to the son of an inn-keeper," he pronounced. One tavern-keeper was enough among the Bonapartes-in-law. Mme. Lucien's father was one, we must remember. It took a week to melt the resolution of the consular head of the family. Then Bonaparte came round. "Well, I believe they suit each other." (Josephine and the rest had taken the lover's side.) "It shall not be said that I was one to aim at great alliances for my sisters." (Here one eye must have been upon the gallery.)

So they married, and Caroline reigned. Together, they were sovereigns in Naples, where Murat revolted traitorously, it must be feared, against his *suzerain*. The sister who had received all from him was to turn against the family autocrat and the family benefactor. It is a sordid spectacle; let us leave it, and turn to that elder sister who redeemed a thousand faults by an ultimate loyalty.

Pauline the renowned, the historic, the one *véritable princesse* of the family (said the Faubourg); the loveliest woman in Europe, said her brother. In childhood she played mischievous tricks on the miserly uncle of the family. We know that she was considered by the friend and chronicler, Mme. d'Abrantès, to have been far more beautiful in the days of her earliest girlhood, when yet unknown to the ears and eyes of Europe, than in her pride of later years as the sister of a Napoleon and the wife of a Roman prince.

Pauline was, above all, a woman, says one; this was her truest, her most eminent charm. She had the inconsistencies, the incongruities, the blending of attributes out of which the spell of woman is woven. Behind her languorous gaze scintillated suggestive fire. Her petty caprices, her childish *bouderie* were forgiven for one gleam of her mist-veiled eyes. Napoleon winced at her easy loves for the undistinguished; he was deeply displeased at her behaviour to his second empress, to whom at times she would not offer even decent civility. Yet the streak of gold shone out in the days of downfall. It was Pauline who sent her jewels to her brother in the last evil days, jewels which were taken from his carriage after the catastrophe of Waterloo, and which, they tell us, were exhibited and gloated over by the curious Londoner, though by no shadow of pretence could they have been claimed as lawful spoil of the conquering Allies.

Of course among the clatter of a thousand tongues are many false reports about Pauline, or again many tales which we must set against the custom of today. When she bared her lovely limbs to Canova for the reclining figure chiselled by the sculptor, it would not appear that modesty received the shattering it might expect in our own day. The plaster cast was moulded on her very person, and Mme. d'Abrantès, who appears as champion on the point, says that it had been stated that Canova rectified certain defects which existed in the princess's limbs.

"I, like many others, have seen the legs of the Princess Borghese, and . . ." in short, her friend could award her a *testannur*.

An almost morbid vanity and delight in her own beauty seemed to possess Pauline. Between the bath and the handing of the chemise (which was carried out after the royal precedent of France) she would pace her dressing-room . . . there are tales indeed . . . relates the emperor's valet. Constant, but. . . . Then chimes in a third conclusively: "She was perhaps a demon, but oh! what a lovely demon!"

Leclerc did not live to become a sovereign. Like the husbands of other beauties his path had thorns. Pauline's lightness (to call it nothing worse) distressed the general. She worried him by capricious tricks of every description, and, although she had married him of her own free-will, never ceased to remind him a hundred times a day of his overwhelming good-fortune in having gained for his wife a sister of the First Consul.

Pauline's little ways were not a little disturbing to her brother. Caesar's womenkind should not be talked about. Napoleon might wish that he had not been so easily persuaded to let his sisters marry mere soldiers, when a year or two was to make so great a difference in the status of the family. As things were, however, he intended that Pauline should be hedged about by proper marital proximity from damaging her own and the family lustre. Leclerc was ordered to San Domingo. Pauline thought only of remaining in joyous Paris, but "if not absolutely forced, was most strenuously invited by Napoleon to accompany her husband." This plan, it is said, put a discreet closure on a pleasant little *amourette* with an actor of the Théâtre Française.

Marie Pauline, Princess Borghesse

Pauline might struggle, but none could long resist the giant's behest. Towards the end of 1801 she sailed with her husband and her young son for San Domingo, accompanied by a perfect flotilla of bandboxes and Paris finery. *Adieu, France!* Pauline probably gave her general a bad quarter of an hour or so while the coast receded.

Her exile, however, came suddenly to an end; for Leclerc died, and she returned to France. "Lovely as an angel "in her weeds, she remained in decorous seclusion at the house of Joseph Bonaparte and his wife in the Rue du Faubourg St. Honoré. "But oh! how bored she was! how hideously bored!"

Pauline had flies in her amber. She could hide those *plaques* of gristle, her ears, the one defect in her lovely person, with her abundant hair, but the tropics had taken their toll, and one of her beautiful hands was for some time disfigured by a dreadful sore. However, *tout passe*; she was still the reigning beauty of Europe; and Napoleon, consul of France, was arranging her second marriage with Prince Camille Borghese, a worthy nonentity, brought up without education by a Roman father who, with a touching simplicity, considered that his children had all learning enough to be good subjects of the Papal Sovereign.

Pauline was sufficiently good-natured, on the whole, to her young women friends, though "I have heard that in after years she was very spiteful," says Mme. d'Abrantès.

She made her Camille dance. She quarrelled with her Roman prince on the question of precedence when they were making a tour of Piedmont. He was but the husband of an emperor's sister. Poor Borghese! he and his wife were incompatibles. They appear to have led a politely separate existence in the papal capital.

As we watch Pauline, with her subtle and illogical charm, there dawns on us the consciousness of her likeness to another unforgettable figure, that of Mary of Scotland. Both with the temperament of the *amoureuse*, both with that faculty for inspiring devotion and fidelity which is so often linked with an incapacity for a reciprocative measure of constancy; both wedded, in a glamour of passion, to husbands soon despised and wearisome, both, in years of sorrow and chastening, levelling the balance of the earthly aggregate with the burden of patience and contrition. And both again, with sudden bursts of the fierce courage of the *bête fauve*, when calamity assailed their kin or their cause, standing by the threatened. If "*Madame* and Dear Sister," in the insolent splendour of her youth, drew from Napoleon condemnatory warnings, all were forgotten in his downfall, when she even sought from his gaolers the right to be his nurse on the desolate rock of his captivity.

Hortense de Beauharnais, Napoleon's stepdaughter, later his sister-in-law, was, in the course of events, the most important woman connected with the Bonapartes, for she was mother to the Third Napoleon; he who, almost as an adventurer, came to rule over France, until the foe of 1870 crossed her borders. "What dear children are Eugène and Hortense!" wrote the young stepfather in the early days of his marriage to the widow Beauharnais.

Hortense had a merry wit, and would join with her mother in practical jokes played perhaps on the harmless valet Carrat, who attended the Bonaparte ladies at Plombières while Napoleon was absent on the Egyptian campaign. Now, it would be a ghost *à l'Anglaise* with sheet and signs of portent, before which the timorous valet fell half-fainting; again, a booby trap contrived by passing a string through a hole made in the partition between the valet's sleeping-room and an adjacent ante-room. The collapse of his bed-tester and a drenching from the suspended jar of water, unnoticed in the darkness, were not enough calamity for the ill-used valet. To his cries of woe, his mischievous young mistress responded by a stage-aside to her mother and the ladies on her side of the partition. "Oh, mamma! the frogs and toads in the water will be falling on his face!" The damp valet dried with his own anger at his young mistress's too far-reaching pleasantry.

Hortense and her mother were tenderly devoted to each other. Together they often rode out in the country round La Malmaison. Once the horse ridden by the young girl ran away and, failing to disengage herself from the stirrup, she was dragged along for some feet, but was rescued unhurt by some of the cavaliers of the party.

In the theatrical entertainments of La Malmaison Hortense was able to play a successful part. Girl-like, too, she revelled in *bonbons* and good things. At every halting-place on her journeys the carriage would be filled with *friandises* for the merry traveller, who, it must be noted, could not even then refrain from playing tricks on her drowsy companions. They, scared from slumber by the explosion of a bomb, discovered by the bouquet of a foaming douche which burst upon them that the infernal machine was in reality a bottle of champagne which, provoked by the jolting, by the heat, and, finally, by the selfish fingers of Miss Hortense, had projected its cork with a furious report.

We linger over the scenes of happy girlhood, for womanhood brought tragedy into the life of Hortense de Beauharnais. "The Queen of Holland was born for sorrows." A throne was merely one among the number.

Napoleon had formed some idea of marrying his stepdaughter to Duroc, one of his generals; and Duroc, though he had no great personal inclination for the marriage on its own account, would have accepted Hortense at the instigation of the chief. Later, "when crowns began to rain upon the august family with which he had needed but his own decision to ally himself," the general began to feel regret at having lost such an opportunity. Hortense herself seems to have given her heart to one "M. Carolus," who was speedily chased off the scene; and she was not, it is said, unfavourable to Duroc, but the chief opponent of development in this direction was her own mother.

Josephine, anxious—as we have already seen—to gain a champion in her husband's family, in which she had so many enemies, was pressing for a match between her daughter and Louis Bonaparte, Napoleon's younger brother, then twenty-four years of age, a neurotic, in a feeble state of health, who was himself not ardently desirous of wedding Hortense, since his affections were already given to some other, a shadowy form, says the raconteur, whose identity has never been established. The marriage, in spite of the unwillingness of both parties, was concluded. Hortense, a very pretty girl, of lively wit, yet of greater strength of character than Josephine, was tied to the melancholic Louis, who, in spite of his attenuated temperament, yet most closely resembled his wondrous elder brother in outward feature.

The marriage, we have stated, took place on January 7, 1802, in a private house.

At the same time was solemnized the marriage of Caroline Bonaparte and General Murat, which had previously been a civil contract only.

Poor Hortense could not conceal her sorrow, and wept during the ceremony, and the bridegroom's feelings were too hurt for him to attempt any endearments. It was a melancholy business. More than melancholy was the horrid gossip, taking its rise, so it was said, in scurrilous English prints, regarding the relations between Napoleon and his young stepdaughter, with whom, said these foul tongues, he had been intimate before handing her over as a bride to his younger brother. "No man is a hero to his own valet," but it is the valet Constant who indignantly disclaims for his imperial master any association of so sinister a kind with the young girl who looked up to him with the respectful fear of a daughter of her times.

Here we may dismiss with a word or two of infinite contempt the other loathsome tales which brought Napoleon into horrible association with his sisters Caroline and Pauline. None who had the right to judge can we find to confirm such incommensurable vileness. Indeed, we may affirm that in the history of Napoleon no trace the very faintest has been found of any of the hideous abnormalities which were laid at his door—whether manufactured in England, or concocted, as M. Lévy says many tales were, for the amusement of Louis XVIII.

Hortense we have seen again in the depths of her tragedy, a *Mater Dolorosa* set in stone, when her eldest son, Napoleon-Charles, lay dead; and the queen, his mother, could not let loose her anguish even in tears till her Chamberlain, by a terrible experiment, set the dead boy in her arms and her weeping came to save her reason. Hortense, as the mother of Napoleon III, is set about with tales of intervention in paternity; but these are not for us.

There are minor feminine personalities as well in the family group. Stéphanie de Beauharnais, a niece of Josephine, who strikes our vision in the entrance hall of the Tuileries, youthful, glowing with girlish freshness and warm-heartedness. What a picture she makes as she stops to caress a little white-frocked *bébé* who is paying a visit to her godmother the empress! For her was arranged a match with a worthy princeling, Ferdinand of Baden, rather a wooden being, but good of core.

After the marriage, however, poor Ferdinand was driven to despair by the vehement refusal of his bride to allow him access. It is even said that she made use of a young friend, one Nelly Bourjoly, as a sleeping companion to bar the way for the disconsolate Ferdinand. In vain he coaxed and threatened, the *impasse* seemed complete, till Napoleon himself gave the recalcitrant bride a talking-to. In time, the real goodness of the ill-used bridegroom prevailed with Stephanie, and, barring one episode of jealousy, their matrimonial affairs seem to have settled down to smooth working.

Another relative of Josephine was Emilie de Beauharnais, a school-fellow of Caroline, and perhaps the object of admiration of Louis Bonaparte.

There is a touch of the patriarchal in Napoleon's dealings with the Princess Amélie of Bavaria, who had become the wife of Eugène de Beauharnais. Step-papa-in-law writes to her, when her health is flagging a little, to tell her to take for her infirmities a little wine without water with quite a Pauline-like solicitude. Indeed, with all, when they behaved themselves and fell into his scheme of things, the world-wonder Napoleon was ready to be benevolent, and often, with all his obduracy, was he cajoled into a lavishness which must have strained his own austerity of principle, when his womankind with kittenish greed knew where to get at his susceptibility.

But if Elise and Pauline and the Queen of Naples were importunate, and obtained largesse on many occasions, Hortense, we are told, received nothing from the stepfather with whom her fair young name was coupled so atrociously by the rags of English journalism, Joseph had been a "lucky fellow" in marrying Julie Clary—a match, which, when it took place, had seemed a glowing financial accomplishment to the impoverished Bonaparte family. Even when a few short years had converted them into sovereigns, or consorts of kings, Julie, gentle, unpretentious and full of charitable deeds, maintained a hold, not only on the members of Napoleon's family, but on the subjects of her husband, the unassuming Joseph. "She was adored by the poor; we need not tell of her good deeds, for they are known to all."

Madame Mère felt always secure as she looked on Joseph's wife, who, while not dazzled, nor even elated by her queendom, yet set herself steadfastly to fulfil the duties of her great condition.

With Lucien and Jérôme it was another story. Their marriages had provoked a series of deadly feuds between Napoleon and the younger men. Here his autocracy displayed itself in its unpleasant aspect; it became an ugly thing. There was not in Christine Boyer, Lucien's first wife, any intrinsic ill, but she was out of the picture of the family development. Even the impoverished refugees of Corsica might look for something better in alliance than the daughter of an inn-keeper. Napoleon's procedure was, none the less, arbitrary and irrelevant. He was not as yet a potentate who could claim direction over subjects, and his arrogation of power over the head of Joseph, the eldest of the family, and of the Signora Letizia, the bridegroom's mother, was a piece of illogical dealing quite lacking in that dazzlement which could disguise the crudity of other promulgations, upon which, fresh-minted from his genius, Napoleon made men fix their blinded eyes.

Christine Boyer was a daughter of the South; her dark skin and graceful carriage alike were the dower of her native air. Simple, yet with a heart of gold; without ambition, and tremulous before her new dignities of the 18th *Brumaire*, she yet, with the adaptability of women, and with the ardour of affection towards her husband, rose to the occasion. Her outward embellishment was taken into the hands of the first *modistes* of Paris. We find Mme. Lucien entertaining in the capital. Her affectionate nature was rejoiced by the relenting of the First Consul. Joyfully she ran to a sympathetic elder friend, that Mme. Permon who knew so much of the inner life of the Bonapartes.

She lived in tender family affection with her husband and their daughters in their country house of Plessis-Charmant. Her kindly gentle life was cut short by premature maternity and medical mismanagement. After a trying illness, she left the little family whom she had loved so dearly. The unhappy Lucien scarcely preserved his reason. He erected a mausoleum for her on the estate at Plessis-Charmant, and at this final resting-place the sad father would kneel with the motherless daughters. There were onlookers, says Mme. d'Abrantès, who found these visits an absurdity, but the warm-hearted *duchesse* herself was not among them.

If Lucien's first marriage had evoked dissatisfaction, his second produced a perfect tornado of discord. The conqueror was more than ever keen on rendering the family fortunes accordant with the glory of the most illustrious of the Bonapartes. Mme. Lucien the second was a divorced person, and for such Napoleon had a distaste of the most extreme kind. He was, therefore, absolutely implacable towards the culprit and towards the mother who sympathized with Lucien. For her maternal partisanship, Letizia Bonaparte was under the cloud of her son's displeasure for some time. She was absent from the coronation, though things were afterwards patched up to a sufficient extent to allow of the introduction of her figure into the command picture of the event painted by Gerard. Poor Signora Letizia! her name had a sad incompatibility with her many sorrows. Torn between her maternal love and pride in her sons—she must in her inner soul have known the sword. Napoleon was not satisfied with displaying his resentment within the family circle—he made the matter an affair of state—so quickly had the new dynasty rooted itself. "Never," said he at a Cabinet Council, "will I give countenance to or receive the wife of my brother Lucien."

Lucien resisted every effort made to part him from the widow Jouberthon. She made him a tender and unselfish wife, even ready to sacrifice herself that he might gain a crown from his brother, but Lucien stood firm. Perhaps it was their best fortune that they fell into the hands of the English as they fled from France by sea, and were for some years prisoners of war in this country.

Jérôme, no less than Lucien, had incurred the anger of the o'ermastering brother. As a mere stripling of nineteen, he had married the daughter of a New York banker, one Mr. Patterson.

The Pattersons were not, it appears, in ignorance of Jérôme's position as a minor in making a marriage without leave under French domestic law. They took their risk. Elizabeth Bonaparte was soon to know herself under the description of "the person calling herself the wife of my brother Jérôme Bonaparte." She was, under the law of France, nonexistent as a wife, though expecting to be a mother. Jérôme had always been a tiresome coxcomb, and over this latest act of his insubordination Napoleon was implacable.

Napoleon, too, hated foreigners; possibly *l'Américaine* was detestable to him for the cause of her nativity. The English, again, were a special aversion; the little grey island, lashed by the rodent seas, withstood him when Continental peoples had succumbed. He would himself have alleged that there was exaggeration in the tale of his animosity, and so there may have been; still, there was a core of truth, and the revolted colonists of the New World were still too closely akin to the mother people to be acceptable to the First Consul of the French. Today, (1910), it is a little hard to believe that we are of such close kin to our Transatlantic neighbours, but a century ago they were less remote.

Yet, in the very land of the unacceptable Elizabeth, Napoleon's own brothers and nephews were to find a domicile. And, most absorbing reflection of all—did Napoleon himself but live today, where would he find his nearest kind in many of his salient points: his pervading energy, his intimacy with detail and the intense activity of cerebration which have made him a figure without counterpart.? It would be among the children of the great republic which numbered among its earliest immigrants the family of Elizabeth Patterson. Napoleon's genius had for its chief display the field and the erection of Imperialism; who can say that, in this day of ours, he who sought to run Europe as a vast department-store might not, as a despot of finance, have made "the Street" to tremble?

The marriage was not annulled without some opposition from the clericals; the situation bore some likeness to that of Mrs. Fitzherbert and the Prince of Wales, valid in religion if not in law. It was civilly a nullity, and young Jérôme Napoleon, born at Camberwell, had no status of French legitimacy. Later, Napoleon thawed, felt that he had been harsh towards Elizabeth, and Jérôme, being now King of Westphalia and safely married to the Princess Catherine of Würtemburg, Napoleon granted a pension to the ex-Madame Jérôme. From her valid spouse, Elizabeth had declined an offer of alimony; contempt for his easy surrender of her had bitten into her soul. Jérôme somewhat pettishly complained that she accepted his brother's offer yet declined his own. The bitter tongue darted its quick reply: "I would rather take refuge beneath the wings of the eagle than dangle from the bill of a goose!"

Jérôme's queen was a great contrast to his first partner. We see her, a girl of nineteen, arriving in France as a bride, having been previously married by procuration. A little dowdy in comparison with the brilliant French court ladies who received her, the *nuance* of her white moire dress out of date among Parisians, battling with her timidity and with the consciousness that Jérôme was so far nothing to her but *un homme dont la première femme était vivante et investie de ses droits d'épouse et de mère*. Her German *entourage* had been dismissed two days before. Jérôme arrives to conduct her to the emperor and empress, from whom she received a kindly and almost paternal reception. With a splendid heart she stood by her husband, and even when her father sought to separate her, in the days of the Napoleonic downfall, from Jérôme, Catherine clung to the husband she loved in his misfortune as deeply as in his days of splendour. She is, we think, the truest woman-soul among them all.

As we look backward through the intervening century to the family group of the Bonapartes themselves, we are startled by a sudden revelation of their likeness to a company of Pagan deities. Rome dreamed her gods into being in form much the same as those of these Corsican descendants of ancient Italy. The beauty, the autocracy, the martial clangour, the streaks of *naïveté* and childish petulance, and the erotic adventurousness are all in the picture. Juno, Venus, Minerva, Mars, and the Father of Olympus, the concepts of a classical mythology, seem personified in these island-dwellers sprung from the bosom of an Italy which, even to this day, is tinct with Pagan heritage.

Subman and superman, said Nietzsche of Napoleon. He the centre, the incandescent core of the nebula which flamed through Europe, is not his figure kindred to those heroic incarnations which the classic *muthos* evolved from the conjunction of "gods made in their own image" with daughters of men for whose loveliness they had condescended to gird themselves with mortal envelope of flesh?

9

The Femmes Fortes

Madame de Staël, whom he disliked, whom he feared, with a fear strange to witness in such a temperament, was for Napoleon an influence far more troublous and pervasive than were the greater number of the women with whom he had relations. With his wives he could deal as the domestic autocrat; of the ephemerals he could make short shrift; but Madame de Staël, decried as a woman, odious as a *Féministe*, fretted the conqueror for many a year and in a multitude of ways. From the beginning she was obnoxious to him; towards her he was for long a tyrant and a persecutor. Upon him, she, on her part, turned with wrathful retaliation. Yet was there a great gulf fixed between their respective methods of hatred. For Mme. de Staël did not begin at all by hating the young general, the rising star of the *Directoire*. Quite otherwise. One of the most acutely-driven points in M. Paul Gautier's valuable and interesting study on Mme. de Staël's relations with Napoleon [1] is that of insistence upon the early admiration, the romantic ardour even, of the baroness for the apostle of liberty.

At the time of Bonaparte's marriage in 1796, Mme. de Staël was thirty years of age. Estranged from a spendthrift husband, she had thrown her emotional force into a *liaison* with Benjamin Constant, whom at times she rendered dizzy by her strenuous mentality. She was, indeed, we gather, rather a tiring friend. The confusing hubbub of effervescence must have been felt overwhelmingly in her vicinity. Her temperament was a misfortune to herself. As with other women of unusual calibre, her tragedy lay in the introduction into the feminine constitution, with its necessities of romantic aspiration, of those quasi-masculine faculties which reduced her charm for the more strenuous

---

1. *Madame de Staël et Napoléon.* P. Gautier.

type of the male being. It was Rocca, the amiable and somewhat invertebrate Rocca, who loved her with sentimental and romantic ardour. For the man of more vigorous mentality, or harder temperament, she was deficient in attractive power.

It was but a short time before the vehement mentality of the baroness brought her to clashing-point. While she was soaring in the atmosphere of liberal reform, the First Consul was beginning to reveal the cloven foot of autocracy; her disillusionment lashed furiously upon the rock of his imperturbable dictatorship. Yet Bonaparte, in the earlier stages at all events, was disposed to conciliation. "What is it she wants, repayment of her father's security?" for Necker had deposited two million *francs* in the Treasury as surety-money upon the candidature of Benjamin Constant as tribune. "Well then, I will pay it." "What is it then? A permit for domicile in Paris? She shall have it." But no, the baroness is restive. Yet, as M. Gautier clearly indicates, she had no supporters among the other parties of the moment. Neither to royalist nor to Jacobin was she *persona grata*. Nevertheless, with Bonaparte virtually her only standby, she seizes upon this moment of all others in which to attack the dictator "*et elle s'étonne que Bonaparte s'irrite!*"

The century opened with thunder. Paris herself was rumbling, in some quarters, against Bonaparte. The man "who had never loved opposition" was soon in a white squall of resentful anger. Tongue and pen, his own and those of his agents, were on fire with recrimination; with resentful self-justification. With these generalities, however, we have not to deal. Mme. de Staël was between the fires of journalistic and social obloquy. The public prints were staring with her name and with ribald anecdote. Infinitely more harrowing—for a woman and a hostess—ten of the guests invited to a dinner given by her in honour of Constant made excuses. The dogs of war were loosed upon her.

She might, with discretion, have saved the situation; now, all the rancour of the First Consul, risen to a head, foamed out upon her. Through Bonaparte's intervention she found herself deserted by the *habitués* of her social entertainments; daily, things became worse; "*le vide peu à peu, se faisait autour d'elle.*" As she sat neglected in a corner, at an evening party, one heart more compassionate than the rest was moved at the spectacle of her isolation. One of the guests, Mme. Custine, moved over to her, with kindly words. In after years the authoress gave to her heroine Delphine the Christian name of the tender-hearted fellow-guest.

Having thus involved herself in the toils of hostility, the baroness turned for succour to the very hand she had wounded. She waylaid the First Consul, beheld him with proud *insouciance* entering into official residence at the Tuileries. "Beholden to none," he ascended the steps of the palace amid the plaudits of the crowd. "He did not even see her as he passed; she remained stunned, scarcely able to draw breath."

Then Napoleon gave a final stab to the adversary,: "Let her be judged as a man! "

Here was his ultimatum of distaste, for in woman the ultra-feminine alone was tolerated by Napoleon.

At this crisis, Necker himself came forward. His millions might give him confidence in many emergencies; his prestige was fully exploited by his daughter. "What an odd set were those Neckers!" said Napoleon once in retrospect—forever floundering in mutual admiration, each burning incense at the other's shrine!"

At this critical moment, when already it seemed doubtful if Necker's intervention could yield anything, it came about that his daughter poured her ultimate oil upon the flames by plunging into literature. "Writers had a difficult time of it under Bonaparte," says the author herself. Yet her own eyes must have been filled with dust, or she must, with complete perversity, have worn a glass eye to turn towards the signal, when she started in her work *On Literature* to tilt on the printed page with an already exasperated enemy. What did she expect from it? asks M. Gautier, and he tells us how Napoleon, recalling an attempt to read the work, scathed it by a memory of its verbiage, its "big words indeed, but I could not grind any meaning whatever out of these ideas, credited with such profundity." It was a far more crushing dictum than all the outcry as to its revolutionary propaganda which flushed the channels of the press.

The book was, in short, a *résumé* of everything antipathetic to the Dictator. "It hurled the glove at the First Consul in the name of the Revolution."

Within a short time of the appearance of the work, Necker and Bonaparte met at Geneva. M. Gautier gives in Chapter VI a graphic and entertaining account of the interview and the respective impressions produced by "Necker, corpulent, *énorme*," and "*le maigre et ardent Bonaparte*:" but we are concerned with the daughter, not the father. No sooner had Bonaparte left Paris than the Baroness was hotfoot on the enemy's track. Watching from Coppet, she gives evidence of the warring forces within her. Her own assertiveness, her quasi-sibylline pose as high-priestess of liberty, and her obsession by the all-conquering egoism of the hero tear her being. The suave retreat by the lakeside calms her to some extent. With effervescence much allayed, she returns to Paris in the winter of 1800.

She keeps up a vigorous correspondence with Mme. Récamier, and drags Constant at her heels through the maze of social dissipation in the capital. So it goes on—she passes between her Swiss retreat and Paris. The thunder growls along the months. In 1802 Bonaparte is shining out in the culminating radiance of his splendour, and Mme. de Staël is widowed. Her husband, a matrimonial figure-head, dies, almost suddenly. All through, there seems to have been in Mme. de Staël a visionary confidence that she would compel Bonaparte to admiration, even, it might happen, to conviction. Grotesque delusion! He sent a warning that it would be as well for her not to return to Paris after her summer outing in Switzerland. He only wanted to be quit of her, and she cried still upon the housetop to invite his attention. We might almost, in a ribald aside, declare that she laid herself out for a black eye. We have been loosely prone to over-pity for her wrongs at the hands of the dictator, but careful scrutiny compels the admission that her buzzing had resounded to distraction in his ears before Bonaparte smashed the aggressive queen-insect.

The baroness says:

> During the autumn [of 1803] I believed myself forgotten by Bonaparte. . . . I arrived at a little country-seat I owned ten leagues from Paris . . . I only wished to see my friends there and to go now and then to the theatre.

Would she indeed have contented herself with so mild a programme? Bonaparte was not going to give her the chance of an experiment; he and she could not share the atmosphere within so small an area. So *Madame* receives an intimation that she is to retire to a greater distance, and that a military guard will be sent shortly to convey a formal warrant. Yet in the face of this, breathlessly listening, as she herself owns, for the trot of a mounted messenger, the baroness accepted the invitation of Mme. Récamier to visit her at her country *château* at St. Brice, within two leagues of Paris. Having thus incensed the enemy by eight leagues of increased proximity, the baroness still believes that the edict may be annulled, in virtue of her plaints; and she continues to urge Joseph and Lucien Bonaparte to smooth down the irate god of the machinery. Her fervent imagination has stunned all logical faculty. With her friend Juliet, then, she spent a few days of calm. Ominous tranquillity!—it was the airless silence before the thunder.

Yet for all her self-deception, the aggressive lady trembled, in a corner of her consciousness, even after her return to her own more distant residence. There, seated one afternoon at a meal with some friends in a room which looked out on the entrance-gates, she saw a man on horseback draw rein, heard him ring the bell. She is convinced of his errand, though led to await an escort in uniform, while this man wears a harmless russet suit. In the garden, radiant with sunshine and fragrant with flowers, she went to meet this ill-omened Hermes, who introduced himself as military commandant of the Versailles guards. He produced a letter signed by the First Consul ordering the banishment of Mme. de Staël to a distance of forty leagues from Paris—and that within twenty-four hours.

In the boundaries of a chapter we are not going to follow Mme. de Staël through the years of banishment, with their vexed, resentful outbursts on her part, and the disdainful relentlessness on the part of Napoleon. It was not banishment nor political misfortune which held the true essence of the victim's woe. No, we are again forced back on the earlier deductions.

There was ever with Mme. de Staël a sense of abortion, of falling short. Her intellect and her amative temperament desired alike an equal mate. Napoleon, however, was the last to whom a Corinne should have looked for an admiring glance; yet, because the feminine does not appear to be at ease unless looking upwards, Madame de Staël was unsatisfied by the devotion of the lesser man. The delicate attentions of Rocca could not enthral in her waking hours her whose dreams had been of the eagle.

We turn from this robust personality to that delicate Julie whom she loved with such an ardour of friendship, and from whom she, in turn, received such steadfast, though undemonstrative, attachment. There is none among us but is familiar with Mme. Récamier from one or another representation in pictorial art. She looks upon us from the walls of the Louvre, resting with such a tenderness of simple modesty on her straight, classic couch, that she makes the voluptuous beauty of Canova's Pauline Bonaparte seem even vulgar—though she reclines in marble in Eternal Rome, and Mme. Récamier in the civic galleries of the French republic.

She, down to the tapering foot, is the white lily "or ever the soil has smutched it," plucked and laid unsoiled and dewy-fresh on David's canvas.

She loved white raiment and pearls, we are told, and never wore the diamonds which were the property of the wealthy banker's wife. Yet, for all her quasi-maidenly reserve, there was a resolute fibre beneath the exterior softness of Mme. Récamier. When the crash came upon the banking-house which meant for her husband and herself almost total ruin, she sat that night at her table entertaining friends, with never an indication of the stroke which had befallen them. When the luxury, the refinement in every detail which had surrounded her from birth, were suddenly shorn from her existence, she kept the unimpaired fineness of her exquisite exterior. No wonder that Madame de Staël, writing to pour out sympathy, should wind up with the rhapsodic *envoi*: "It is with the utmost reverence that I kiss your enchanting face!"

It was this woman whom, in the dawning of his Empire, Napoleon wished to include in his *système de fusion*, by giving her a place about the palace; and she it was who, quite modestly and courteously, yet quite determinedly, refused the advances made through Fouché. Did she fear a snare? Fouché had affronted her delicacy with his presentment of the emperor's need for a pure and noble attachment.

When Caroline Murat gave Mme. Récamier a pass for her box at the Théâtre Français, it is said that the terms in which it ran occasioned some uneasiness to the recipient. She did not use the box, says one; another chronicler shows her occupying it on two occasions, and submitting to prolonged scrutiny through the emperor's opera-glasses. Mme. Récamier did not pass under the emperor's influence. Whatever form of dominance he may have contemplated, she kept herself beyond the boundary, yet with the same serenity as marked her course in general life.

Lucien Bonaparte's romantics she disposed of shortly; she played no Juliet to his Romeo. A delicate smile may have played about her lips, there was no bitterness to curl them in that gentle breast. She was to be loved by a Prince of Prussia, who would have paid her the ultimate honour and devotion of legal marriage, for even the Catholic Church might have been approached for a declaration of nullity of marriage in the case of the *pro formâ* association of the elderly Récamier and his girl-bride. But the gentle hand would not inflict a wound so deep on the friend of a lifetime. Récamier appealed not vainly to her mild soul. She turned from the vision which, for a moment, had allured her contemplation, and fell back once more into the even tide of her virginal existence.

With regard to Napoleon's attitude towards the delicate Juliet, speculation is somewhat baffled. Did the masterful desire of ruling everywhere prompt his advances to the young wife? Did he resent exclusion from the favour she bestowed so charmingly both on the men and on the women of Paris? Did he merely consider her as a useful instrument for his *système de fusion?* Why did he devise such special wiles by the agency of Fouché to win over the fair young citizen? Vulgar sex intrigue was, of course, an impossible suggestion to this stainless creature: yet how entirely incompatible with his general trend was the proffered intellectual fellowship; an Egeria for Napoleon;—it is a mere grotesque.

Beside her it is that Napoleon's texture shows up at its worst, with every coarser fibre grinding itself against our vision.

10

The Mystery of Madame X——

It is in the early days of the Empire that we light upon this puzzle. Who was Madame X——? Chroniclers, a few, have spoken as if they knew all about the lady and her liaison with Napoleon; others have displayed a curious anxiety to keep her name, if not the amour itself, a secret. Why this tenderness? So great a solicitude, or the show of it, for a lady's reputation is not exactly the rule at the date of the First Empire.

Let us study this heroine and the episode from the points of view of several observers. We shall meet with diversity enough to puzzle us. First we may hear the story from one of Josephine's ladies. Madame de Rémusat calls her Madame X—— , and tells us of the infatuation of Prince Eugène for her. Fair of hair and complexion, she was, at the time of her first appearance at court, about twenty-five years of age. "Her blue eyes were expressive of everything save candour." Her aquiline nose was rather long. (Josephine said contemptuously that, with a nose of that length, one shouldn't play the part of Roxalana.) Her form was slight, almost too slight indeed, but elegant and of medium height. With no special gifts of intellect, she yet was not deficient in a certain craftiness; her temperament was placid and her emotions not easily aroused.

Married to a husband much older than herself, Madame X—— appeared at court about 1805, and soon attracted the notice of Napoleon. The emperor took the opportunity of visits to the play, which he made in Josephine's company, to chat with Madame X——. She, with cold complacency, preserved an aspect of indifference, yet used every art of dress, of glance and gesture to give encouragement to her imperial admirer.

The empress, taking notice of the emperor's abstraction, and divining an *affaire*, had at first suspected the Maréchale Ney of being the favoured beauty. She was early cured of her error.

Josephine took the matter greatly to heart, and did not conceal her feelings. She openly reproached her husband, who received her expostulations in very bad part, saying that she grudged him the least amusement. By way of temporizing at this juncture, the emperor indulged in a spell of rather noisy fun with all the court ladies—"he lavished on us the speeches of his *sauvage galanterie*." Madame X——, meanwhile, restrained herself from any response that might betray her to the watchful eyes of Madame de Rémusat or others; she uttered an occasional monosyllable, but no more.

Josephine, at the other end of the salon, alone and sad, looked on from a distance at the card-players, listening to their badinage. Her grief was intensified by her knowledge of the suffering which her son Eugène was undergoing in consequence of his stepfather's attraction towards Madame X——.

The lady had perhaps—so hazards Madame de Rémusat—boasted jestingly to Napoleon of the prince's infatuation. Wishing to draw a herring across the trail, the emperor contrived that his brother-in-law, Murat, should feign an *empressement* in connection with the lady. The empress was not deceived. She even went the length of suborning *employés* of some of the Paris shopkeepers in order to secure information by their medium. Poor Josephine, indeed, gave herself away like any shop-girl—her son did contrive to maintain an appearance of calm on the surface of his tribulation.

We can find nothing whatever distinctive about the quarrels of the emperor and empress over Madame X——. They have been heard in the shop-parlour a thousand times. At length—*Iunonis ob iram*—the final shaft was hurled. Josephine announced her intention of denying to the offending goddess the *entrée* to her own apartments.

The emperor, heckled and angry, was quick to bring the intrigue to a head. The court was suddenly ordered from the Tuileries to La Malmaison, where greater facilities were afforded for the climax. It was a sudden transit; two hours only, declares one narrator, were given for preparation. It was in the depth of winter . . . and there was not even time to warn the caretaker to light fires in the royal apartments. "So we left the Tuileries, where we were in an oven, to go to La Malmaison, which was a perfect icehouse."

And here Josephine played the spy like any jealous shop-woman. With an attendant who had sat up, trembling with cold and wrapped in a counterpane, the empress watched through a glazed door to see her husband steal to the midnight interview. When her bitter doubts had been only too well confirmed, she returned to bed and, we may well believe, to a sleepless night. She was, poor woman, not the light-hearted and light-mannered bride of '96. Now years were beginning to tell on her; there had been already whispers of divorce; Napoleon was irked by her confirmed sterility.

The actresses, dancers, opera singers might have been reckoned with, but here was a court lady who might become the *maîtresse-en-titre* and a far greater disturber of her peace than all the fleeting femininities who had gone before. Napoleon, too, was now resplendent with a lustre which she had not foreseen in the ardent young Corsican of ten years earlier. She had seen her son suffer for love of the court *intrigante*; she had seen him dispatched by his stepfather on a foreign mission in order that his presence should be no bar to the affair; still more, perhaps, to testify to the emperor's displeasure at his having presumed to raise his eyes to the same lady as he had himself found desirable. But Josephine was, although she did not know it, already about to see light through the forest.

Probably, desire being assuaged, Napoleon became the victim of the ordinary reaction. He soon, at all events, began to find Madame X—— a nuisance, and his own infatuation contemptible. And then came a revolution, a turning of the tables, which was almost comic in its childishness. Napoleon, in a moment of softness, returned to his kindlier attitude towards the empress, and before long he had confided to her his weariness of the episode, and engaged her to rid him of Madame X——. It must have been a moment of triumph for the empress. She readily agreed to overlook the affair, stipulated merely that she should have a personal interview with the erring lady. Her method provided the most complete humiliation for the offender, while preserving for the empress herself an attitude of dignity. She represented to Madame X—— the dangers she had brought on herself by her "frisky" behaviour, and, enjoining her to be more cautious in future, she promised for her own part to overlook the matter.

Madame X—— had need of all her resources of *finesse* and calmness of demeanour. She succeeded in disclaiming the necessity for the empress's warning, and in hiding her sorely-wounded vanity (for from love, says one contemporary, she had no impulse). Napoleon himself did not refrain from allusion to the affair and its passing. The indelicacy of his comment doubtless filtered through to the object of it. The bitter sediment of this adventure of gallantry must have flavoured the lady's cup for some time to come.

Now we may ask—Is Madame X—— to be identified with the Madame of eight asterisks to whom the Duchesse d'Abrantès refers in a story connected with olives? There is certainly a connecting-link in the fact that the heroine in each case is the object of attention on the part of Murat. But what a different complexion is put upon the heroine and her story by these two memoir-writing court ladies! Madame de Rémusat, it is clear, regarded Madame X—— as "a cat" (there is no term so succinct), while Madame d'Abrantès saw in the lady of eight stars a woman of tone, charm, and the object of an almost ethereal love on the part of a man not given to the softer emotions. Here is her story of the olives. The emperor had manoeuvred all the evening at the Tuileries to get near to the eight-starred attraction.

At the supper-table she was seated next to the Duchesse d'Abrantès (Madame Junot she then was), when the emperor came behind the pair and, leaning on the backs of their chairs, began to talk with much urbanity to the *duchesse*, in order, says that lady, to cover the real aim of his proximity. ("It is astonishing," declares one lady of the time, "how quickly the emperor assumed the demeanour of the past monarchy; it was as a very Bourbon that he lounged behind the ladies' chairs!")

In a little dish, such as would be used for radishes and *hors-'d'œuvres* generally, were some olives. The lady beside Madame d'Abrantès stretching out her hand to reach this dish, the emperor placed it before her.

"But," said he, "you do wrong to eat olives at night—they will make you ill."

Madame d'Abrantès listened with all her ears. The emperor concerning himself about a lady's health—here indeed was something new!

"And you, Madame Junot," continued the imperial host, "are you not eating olives.?—you are wise not to imitate Madame X——, wise indeed in every sense, for is she not inimitable?"

The tone of the emperor's voice betrayed his feeling. The lady of the olives cast down her eyes, and sat blushing with the excitement and the embarrassment of a compliment so moving. The episode had been marked by other eyes. A few days later, the empress, in her own private room, sounded Madame d'Abrantès upon the subject, covering her real design by allusions to the attentions of Murat to the lady under discussion. Madame d'Abrantès met the situation with *aplomb*.

With an ingenuous air she answered the empress's questions, and expressed her admiration for the beauty and good style of the lady under discussion. Josephine was seething with distress and resentment, and picking up a book, she said that all the women had got it into their heads that they were like the heroine. This was the story of Louise de la Vallière, a romance then at the height of fashion.

Madame d'Abrantès was "taking notes." Visiting the rooms of several of the court ladies, she was moved to laughter, for; on the little table beside each bed, the flagrant novel displayed itself. Penetrating into the room of Madame ********, there again behold the inflammatory work! It was all childish, schoolgirlish, indeed; yet the *duchesse* still expands upon the fresh and glowing sentiment of the emperor for the heroine of the episode of the olives.

Again, are we to identify Madame X—— with that Madame D—— so vaguely remembered by Napoleon's valet that he puts the affair back into the Consulship, and on whose account he was commissioned by the emperor to take a house in the *Allée des Veuves* where the pair might meet in secret? It seems that the first to give her a name was the compiler of a *chronique scandaleuse* of later years.[1] Here she is identified with Madame Duchâtel, one of the court ladies, and later memoir editors have given her the same description. The *chronique scandaleuse* must always be handled with suspicion.

However, let us assume that, though viewed by very different eyes, Madame X—— and the lady of eight stars are identical, and that she also is rightly Madame Duchâtel. (M. Turquan does not hesitate to name her, though M. Frédéric Masson contents himself with reducing her asterisks to three.) If we do this, there is a very big question in the way. It is this. When Napoleon, in 1810, formed the household of his young Austrian bride, he did so with an almost paternal solicitude and caution. Yet Madame Duchâtel appears on the list of her ladies. Is it conceivable that a being so autocratic, and at the same time so particularly bent on a special weeding-out, would have retained the services of a lady whose presence might have roused inconvenient reminiscences and gossip in the court; a woman, too, of whom, if she were indeed Madame X——, he had years before sickened, and who would be for him an irksome reminder of a passage which in his own retrospect he visited with self-contempt? It is curious also to find Madame Duchâtel calling on the Empress Josephine at La Malmaison after the divorce.

---

1. See on this point Lévy's *Napoléon Intime.*

No! we still feel that we would rather not accept the identification, in spite of the eight stars of the Duchesse d'Abrantès and the rest. Nor is it a gracious task to pass in review the other ladies who might be made to fit in one way or the other into the pattern of Madame X——, alias Madame ★★★★★★★★ (if these are identical), or rather into the widely differing moulds cast respectively by Mesdames de Rémusat and d'Abrantès. We prefer to leave the unimportant mystery where it stands.

11

Walewska

November 27, 1806, 2 a.m., Napoleon at Meseritz writes to the Empress Josephine at Mayence:—

I am about to make a tour through Poland. This is the first town there. Tonight I shall be at Posen, and shall then send for you to come to Berlin, so that you may arrive there the same day as I. ... My affairs prosper. The Russians are in flight.

Two days later he writes at noon from Posen:—

I am at Posen, capital of Great Poland. ... I am about to take a circuit round Poland. My troops are at the gates of Warsaw.

The Polish Countess Potocka (pronounce Pototska) tells in her *Memoirs* how high through all Warsaw excitement ran at the prospect of the coming of Napoleon: the Liberator, as Polish hopes depicted him. When the first French regiment marched in through the gates of the city, Warsaw went crazy with joy. "The whole town was lit up as if by magic." People fought for the new arrivals, the soldiers of the emperor, "carried them off, vied with each other in treating them best," offered them their houses, "the cellar included." Tables were laid in the streets and squares—in a Polish winter—and the brave army and the young, fiery Polacks got drunk together. The great man had not yet appeared, but Murat had ridden in amid roars of welcome.

By and by came the conqueror himself, riding a screw he had hired at the last relay station, and seemingly not in the best of humours. His first harangue took the Poles somewhat aback. Slapping his breeches' pockets, he told them he had the Frenchmen there. "A sort of silent surprise depicted itself on the faces of his hearers."

But this mood vanished. Napoleon had to yield to the almost furious enthusiasm which his mere presence worked in stricken Poland. Let Mme. Potocka portray for us the emotion she experienced at her first sight of him. The passage is worth citation for its historic value. The scene is one of the first receptions held by Napoleon at the palace in Warsaw. Talleyrand, as Grand Chamberlain, advances—

> With a loud and intelligible voice uttering the magic word that made the world tremble: *The Emperor!* Immediately Napoleon made his appearance, and halted for a minute as if to challenge admiration.
>
> So many portraits exist of this astonishing man, his history has been so much written about, all the stories told by the children of his old soldiers will live so long, that the generations to come will know him almost as well as ourselves. But what will be difficult to grasp is how deep and unexpected the impression was which those felt who saw him for the first time. As for me, I experienced a sort of stupor, a mute surprise, like that which seizes one at the aspect of any prodigy. It seemed to me that he wore an aureole. The only thought I could frame when I had recovered from this first shock was that such a being could not possibly die, that such a mighty organization, such a stupendous genius could never perish. I inwardly awarded him *double immortality*.

In the same magnetic thraldom as the Countess Potocka all Warsaw lay. In the eyes of the Poles, passionately yearning for freedom, hoping and expecting it at his hands, the emperor shone with a splendour more than imperial. Like some enchanter he moved among them. Never before perhaps had his glamour been so potent.

It is well known that all the ladies of Poland are beautiful; it is said that all their hearts are kind. Napoleon, seated on top of fortune's wheel, was in the full vigour of thirty-seven. It was not the affair of the Polacks that he had come to them without his wife; it was eminently their affair that he should not abide a widowed man within their borders. A liberating emperor . . . in Poland the hospitable . . . and no care-charmer at his side. The duty of the Poles was plainer, a great deal plainer, than their sun at noonday. They took the case to their bosoms.

Did the gracious and beautiful young Marie Walewska, wife of the aged Count Anastase Colonna de Walewice-Walewski, receive from the unseen any signal or premonishment of the fate that was silently weaving for her?

Again, where and in what circumstances did Napoleon first view this Iphigenia of the North?

M. Masson has regaled us with a pleasingly romantic history. On the first day of January, 1807, the emperor, journeying from Pultusk to Warsaw, stayed for a change of horses at the little town of Bronia. A crowd had gathered to welcome him. Duroc, the general officer in attendance, was politely jostling his way to the posting-house when "clasped hands were raised to him in supplication, and a voice exclaimed in French: 'Ah, *monsieur!* help us to get away from here, and let me see him, if but for a moment!"

The suppliants were two ladies, wedged in the throng of peasants and workmen.

"The one who had addressed him seemed hardly more than a child. She was dazzlingly fair, with large blue eyes, peculiarly sweet and candid in expression, and sparkling with a fire as of some sacred frenzy. Her delicate skin, pink and fresh as a rose, was flushed with nervous excitement. Somewhat small of stature, her figure was so exquisitely moulded, so supple and undulating, that she was grace itself. She was very simply dressed, and wore a long black veil."

Duroc, of course, "took in all these details at a glance." They are the details that are so easily taken in at a glance—and that no one ever takes in at a glance. Twenty men in Duroc's hurry would have given us twenty different descriptions, and not one of them would have answered to a photographic picture of the scene. M. Masson's Duroc is too precise; he speaks too closely by the card.

But M. Masson goes on unflinchingly.

> Extricating the two ladies from the crowd, he gave his hand to the beautiful blonde, and led her to the door of the carriage. 'Sire,' said he to Napoleon, 'here is one who has braved all the dangers of the crowd for your sake.'
>
> The emperor took off his hat, and bending towards the lady, began to address her. But she, beside herself with excitement, agitated almost to the verge of delirium by her emotions, cut short his speech, and greeted him in a kind of transport. 'Welcome, thrice welcome to our land!' she cried. 'Nothing we say or do can adequately express our attachment to your person, and our delight at seeing you tread the soil of that country which looks to you for deliverance!'

Napoleon gazed at her attentively as she uttered these words. He took a bouquet which was in the carriage and presented it to her. 'Take it,' he said, 'as an earnest of my goodwill. We shall meet again, I hope at Warsaw, when I shall look forward to thanks from your beautiful lips.'

Duroc took his place by the emperor's side. The carriage drove off rapidly. Napoleon waving his hat from the door by way of farewell.

The young woman was Marie Walewska.

Seldom does M. Masson, the judicious and sedate, lift us so near as this to the level of Dumas! It might be history, but the authorities are missing; it is at least a fine romantic story. The young wife, we are further told, had skipped off to Bronia, keeping the adventure a secret from her venerable husband: perhaps! The whole affair is something closer to the latitude of the Arabia of the *Nights* than M. Masson is in the habit of luring us. Briefly, the tale wants confirmation.

We must turn again to the Countess Potocka. This lady, however, it should be premised, is a witness not quite free from prejudice. The fair and gentle Walewska, she tells us, was dull: as if a dull woman could have taken this leviathan. She does far worse in writing that Napoleon had a predecessor in her affections: this, as far as may be known on any hand, is calumny.

Napoleon himself is reported to have stated that the Countess Walewska (who, at this date about twenty-two years of age, found herself yoked to a husband older by nearly half a century) was secured for him by Talleyrand. This is in a manner confirmed by Potocka. It was at Talleyrand's (Grand Chamberlain and Minister of Foreign Affairs) that the first of the Moscow balls in the emperor's honour was given. Napoleon took part in a square dance—

> Which paved the way for his affair with Mme. Walewska. . . . We learnt afterwards that M. de Talleyrand had extended his labours as far as managing this first interview, and smoothing the preliminary obstacles. Napoleon, having expressed a wish to count a Pole among his conquests, one of the right kind was chosen—lovely and dull. Some pretended to have noticed that, after the *quadrille*, the emperor had shaken hands with her, which was equivalent, they said, to an appointment.
> It was rumoured that a great dignitary had gone to fetch the fair one. . . . People said a great many things they perhaps did

not know, and invented at pleasure. They even went so far as to assert that Rustan, the Mameluke, had acted as lady's-maid! What is certain, however, is that we were all distressed that a person admitted to society had shown such facility, and had defended herself as little as the fortress of Ulm.

Poor Walewska! But the sparkling Potocka is signally unfair to her. Walewska's is not at all the case of a Montespan or a Du Barry strenuously scheming for the honours of *courtesan*-in-chief. We have other records in which a larger justice is done to the girl who, with her aged husband in the background, seems to have had a position not unlike that of a youthful widow in the society of her day. Far from springing into the net, she seems inclined at first to spurn it. If M. Masson's tale, sentimental and bordering on the lachrymose, is acceptable, we have in Walewska—with her Greuze-like and semi-virginal beauty—the victim, half terrified and wholly reluctant, of a singular clique of patriots who insist on thrusting her to the altar in the name and for the sake of Poland-about-to-be-liberated-by-Napoleon. Walewska's virtue is the price of Poland's liberty.

We reject this notion, as we reject the notion of Mme. Potocka that Walewska capitulated without a protest.

All credible and fair record goes to show that the girlish wife of old Walewska was full of eagerness, as her whole people were, for the freedom of the Polish fatherland. Ostensibly to give this boon to Poland, Napoleon had come. Every Polish woman must have had a heart for him that pregnant winter; and not for a moment need we doubt that a deep love of country was first among the chords to throb in the bosom of Marie Walewska at her earliest sight of Napoleon. But this consideration can be urged without the least extravagance. To conceive of the heroine as immolated, slain as a sacrificial victim, is unnecessary.

Do the fascinations of Napoleon count for nothing? A kind of passion sweeps him at the vision of this Greuze girl of Moscow, married to a snuffy septuagenarian noble—the husband of a French comedy. Without a moment of respectable delay he dives into courtship. If any trust may be reposed in the printed letters to Walewska (there are admissions, confessions, protestations which disturb our belief in them), we can but say that he flings himself into this amour with an abandonment that recalls the honeymoon by post or courier with Josephine.

Napoleon, autocrat at this hour of an empire to which he adds

Madame Walewska

an arch or so daily as a breakfast egg, writes or does not write these insensately effusive *billets-doux*. But over the Walewska of twenty-two he gains an absolute ascendency, crushes down all her scruples; and the devoted young patriot, never for a moment abandoning her country's cause, is presently also the enchanted and enamoured mistress.

Napoleon, on his part, has the air of a man not smitten merely, but utterly engrossed. Constant shows him to us on the morning after the ball "unusually agitated." The master—so the valet feigned to think—would never have done with his toilet that day: he rose up, paced the room, sat down and jumped up again continually. Luncheon over, a person of importance was commissioned to carry to Mme. Walewska the respects, vows, and entreaties of the emperor. Concerning this person of importance the valet is silent; it was either Duroc or Prince Poniatowski. The brusque, imperious advances, we gather, were not too smilingly received; the person of importance retired, embarrassed and surprised. Next day Napoleon was "absolutely silent" at his toilet: conduct unprecedented. Unprecedented also, in his view, the behaviour of the lady must have seemed, for he had already twice or thrice importuned her by letter. We are asked, for example, to believe that the emperor addressed himself in these terms to the girl of twenty-two:—

> There are seasons when all splendours grow oppressive, as at this instant I but too deeply feel. How may I satisfy the desires of a heart that yearns to lay itself at your feet, when at every point its impulses are checked by considerations of the highest moment? Oh! if you would . . . you alone might overcome the obstacles that keep us apart. My friend Duroc will smooth everything for you.
> Come! oh! come. Your every wish shall be gratified. Your country will be dearer to me when you take pity on my poor heart.

If such letters as these were really written or received (and we may be certain they were received if written), it is pretty clear that the conqueror must shortly have his way. One narrative tells us that the young countess was handed over to Mme. de Vauban, Poniatowski's mistress and "the moving spirit of the whole intrigue," who was finally to convince her that where the hearts of monarchs were concerned there were limits to the nonsense Providence would stand. But perhaps the intervention of Mme. de Vauban (who had lived at Versailles under the old *régime*, and knew the duty of a court madam) was not necessary.

Walewska at last consented—consented to an interview. Between the hours of ten and eleven at night she would see the emperor privately. She was shaken with emotion, and in one report we read that early on the evening of the appointment someone turned the key in her door, that there might be no escape by flight. Towards 10.30 she was summoned. Muffling her fair head in a cloak, she resigned herself to the person of importance (Duroc this time almost certainly), who had one of the imperial carriages in waiting, and was swiftly driven to a privy gate of the Great Palace.

For an instant the indiscreet, obliging Constant pulls aside the curtain, that we may observe the emperor striding to and fro in his impatience. "He scarcely left off asking me the time."

Constant, seeing the condition of the lady whom he was to introduce, must have felt some perturbation. Was this a morsel for an emperor? She was wasted with tears; sobs choked her utterance. Even thus we may suppose some childish prey of Louis XV to have been brought to his *Parc aux Cerfs!* Trembling she clung to the valet's arm—and he in his valet's soul may for once have rendered thanks that fortune; had not made of him an emperor. The valet and the great personage withdrew.

May not the scene as well end here at its very opening? for, as we know,

Venus smiles not in a house of tears.

Constant, on guard without (how many nights of slumber did this Constant lose!), is our witness that *madame* "could be heard sobbing and moaning in heart-rending manner, even at a considerable distance."

This *tête-à-tête* must a little have staggered Napoleon himself; for after all the lady had not been exactly kidnapped. Cajoled into the assignation she in some degree had been; but to a lover at the altitude of Napoleon this must have seemed the behaviour of a nun abducted by brigands. Still, although probably she knew it not, the young Walewska had taken a very safe course. Tears—as Josephine had divined even before the era of the Jews—found Napoleon weaponless. He could see no woman crying. Tact and gentleness, moreover, he had at natural command; and this interview without a rapturous moment was in equal manner without an offensive one. At least, when, at two the next morning, the curious meeting broke, Walewska was the "Marie" of her lover—and had faintly promised to return; though it seems that

Constant ushered her out with the handkerchief still to her eyes.[1]

What memories she summoned up that day to the sessions of her silent thought we know not; but she kept her promise to return. Constant fancied "she would never come again"—and mere want of sleep must often by now have fed this simple hope in him. What a procession of ladies had Constant led at dawn to one postern or another! On the whole, perhaps, his *Memoirs* are a not unfair revenge for all the sleep he missed.

But Walewska returned. There was an interval of "two or three days," and then she reappeared: the beautiful little blonde, with her blue eyes and skin of dazzling fairness. Emotion, we read, was still "depicted on her entrancing features;" but she was now at least dry-eyed and moderately calm. This second *intermezzo* was presumably more satisfying than the first. The midnight visits were repeated: Walewska was vanquished.

And what of the husband? We are not in a complete degree assured as to his part. His wife, it is said, separated from him in the first days of the liaison; it is also said that the count himself "refused ever to see her again." Nevertheless some doubt remains. It is apparently beyond question that the son borne by Walewska to Napoleon (Alexander-Florian-Joseph-Colonna: May 4, 1810) was brought into the world in Count Walewski's castle of Walewice. It was at Schönbrunn that the unfaithful wife became enceinte: why did she return to her husband's home for the birth of a child that was not his? Without some renewal of interrupted relations she could scarcely have done this; yet it were strange there should be any healing of the breach in circumstances that gave new dishonour to the outraged husband. It is incredible that Walewski accepts paternity of Walewska's [2] son by Napoleon.

Now begins the series of double-tongued letters to Josephine

---

1. The secondhand account of this interview ("doubtless," as M. Turquan says, "the version current at the Tuileries"), in Vol. 1 of Mme. de Rémusat's *Memoirs*, may be set aside as lacking every element of the plausible. In this, the elegant young countess is offered "a bath and some supper" (as if they had just fetched her in tights from the reeking coulisses of a music-hall), and told that she may afterwards if she pleases "go to bed;" while the Napoleon whom we have seen in a fury of amorous impatience for her coming "went on working till a rather late hour." No: this won't do at all!

2. The briefest note here on what the translator of the Potocka *Memoirs* calls "this buzz of *yska's*, *owski's* and *wicz's*." It is but necessary to say that Marie Laczinska (her maiden name), conferring her hand upon Count Walewski, becomes Countess Walewska.

glanced at in an earlier chapter. Josephine at Mayence had already no doubt been put upon the scent. Napoleon perhaps knew of or perhaps suspected this. He exhausts himself in excuses to keep the empress at the safe distance of Mayence.

> I am touched by all that you tell me; but in this cold season, with roads very bad and not too secure, I cannot consent to expose you to such dangers and fatigue. Return to Paris for the winter.
>
> It would take you at least a month to come. You would arrive ill, and by the time you were here it might perhaps be necessary to start back again: what folly this would be! ... I am more vexed about it than you. I should have liked to spend the long nights of this season with you, but we must obey circumstances.
>
> I fear you are greatly grieved at our separation and at your return to Paris (he has at last got her back to Paris) but I insist on your having more fortitude. I hear you are always weeping. Fie! how unbecoming is this.... Be worthy of me; show a little more character. Cut a good figure at Paris; and, above all, do be contented!

There are above eighty of these ingenuous epistles. The kindest interpretation of them is that with which the ever-faithful M. Lévy consoles himself. Napoleon is lying—but in how considerate a spirit! He has a new mistress, but his wife must suffer no jealousy on her account, and deceit is so easily compassed. We may admit at any rate that on the subject of his marital infidelities Napoleon has scruples to which a self-ridden and flint-hearted *Grand* Monarque is at all times superior. He is the first man of his exalted rank in France who goes about to hoodwink a wife in the interests of a mistress.

From Warsaw Napoleon sets forth on his campaign against the Russians. The fierce, indecisive Battle of Eylau is fought (February 7-8, 1807): "the bloodiest battle fought in Europe since Malplaquet," says Dr. Rose.

"What a massacre, and without any issue!" exclaimed Ney. The carnage of Eylau seems but to have whetted Napoleon's appetite for love.

> Notwithstanding the thought of so many thousands lying dead or dying in the snow, his heart was with his beautiful paramour.

He who had said or was to say:

All the women in the world would not make me lose an hour.

The longing to have her with him again "outweighed all his regrets for the horrible slaughter at Eylau."

He established his headquarters at Finckenstein, and thither Walewska hastened to him. It is from this place that Napoleon writes to Josephine:

"I know not what you tell me about ladies in correspondence with me. I love only my little Josephine, sweet, pouting, and capricious."

At Finckenstein for three weeks Walewska kept her lover company. They took all their meals together, and from Constant we have it that on Napoleon's part the conversation was always bright, amiable, and attentive; tender, passionate, and melancholy on hers. What did the army make of it, the brave and suffering army? M. Turquan is perhaps not very far wrong in these reflections:

> The rank and file, when they saw her taking drives with the emperor and returning with him to the *château*, thought, with their national matter-of-fact way of looking at things, that he ought not to have had his mind occupied with such distractions, seeing how cruelly the army had been decimated at Eylau, and what privations they were then enduring from cold and hunger. They knew well enough it was not to share their sufferings that she had come to Finckenstein, and they regarded her in a light anything but favourable.

Still one may feel that had she known a way to cheer the drooping ranks of the French, this gentle, warm-breathing creature would not have sat idly at her lover's knee. Hers was hardly the responsibility for Eylau.

Poland, meanwhile, had not been restored (was Napoleon ever more than lukewarm on this subject?), and we divine something sore and sad in the heart of Walewska. It is even conjectured that she at first refused to follow him to Paris. Possibly she did refuse—but not for long. She was in Paris early in 1808, circled again by those constraining arms.

And now to Schönbrunn. After Wagram (July 1809), Napoleon went into residence in the palace of Schönbrunn, and hard by in a *faubourg* of Vienna he prepared a charming nest for his love. Evening by evening Constant fetched her "in a plain carriage with a coachman out of livery." The road to be traversed was indifferent, or worse, and Constant received all manner of minute instructions. "Be very careful tonight. Constant. It has rained today and the road will be frightful. Are you sure of your coachman, and is the carriage sound?" One night, seeking to avoid a rut, the coachman upset his fares; *madame*, falling on Constant, was unhurt: "She thanked me with her own peculiar charm," says the valet.

When she becomes *enceinte*, Constant cannot relate to us the half of Napoleon's care for her, and she herself makes little confidences to the valet in this strain:

> *Toutes mes pensées, toutes mes inspirations viennent de lui et retournent à lui: il est tout mon bien, mon avenir, ma vie.*

The child that came to her bore, we are told, a striking resemblance to his imperial sire.

To Paris, with the infant son, the happy mother returned in 1810. She was first in "a pretty house in Rue du Houssaye, later in Rue de la Victoire; the summer months she spent at the Château de Bretigny, Mons-sur-Orge; and it is of some interest to note that her husband's two sisters. Princess Jablonowska and Princess Birginska, constantly chaperoned her. So far as prettiness went, Walewska was well worthy of *duennas*, but she needed none. No *femme entretenue* ever lived a simpler, more secluded life. As in Warsaw she had scorned the place that society would have granted her as the conqueror's Sultana, so in Paris she hid herself almost as closely as poor pent-up La Vallière had done. "None save a few Poles among the society of the day seem to have had the slightest suspicion" of her relations with the emperor.

Here indeed we have our own suspicion that M. Masson is not speaking by the card; for Josephine (albeit she was now divorced) was ignorant neither of the liaison nor of its fruit, and Josephine kept no secrets but her own. Paris, the Paris of the court, of society, and of scandal, could not have lain in utter darkness on a subject so deliciously improper. But may we not write it a little to the credit of Walewska that she esteemed her love so highly as to vaunt it in Paris no more than she had done in Poland? And open scandal there was none. Napoleon, on his side, does not seem to have bound her in any way to secrecy. Boxes are to be reserved for her at all theatres, every place of interest in Paris is to be open to her, Corvisart is to care for her health, Duroc is to see that she has whatever she may want—and at every chance Napoleon slips from the Tuileries, like a clerk surreptitiously married, to kiss the baby after he has kissed the mother.

The baby, by the way, he loses no time in creating count. Recipient of favours not grudgingly bestowed (we are thinking still of the wretched state in Paris of Louis XIV's La Vallière), Walewska lives remote in the Paris where her lover gazes on his own splendour, as the world gazes on it. Even in the matter of expenses—wherein a mistress is traditionally bound to shine—she takes on the whole so little heed to herself that we are rather glad of the £5 to Leroy for a lace pocket-handkerchief. Such seems Walewska in Paris.

"*Do not forsake me at my end*," runs a line of the *Dies Iræ*. On that black night [3] in April 1814, at Fontainebleau, when, half-demented by the "maddening tumults" of mind that followed on the signing of the first abdication, the dethroned and deserted emperor poured out the opium he had carried in a phial from Moscow, Walewska was keeping vigil in an ante-chamber. Not so the wife, Marie Louise!

Also what visitor to Elba is this, whom, on a moonlit night of September, Marshal Bertrand assists out of a rowing-boat at the pier of Porto Ferrajo: a lady unknown, with a little boy at her side? Along the Mariana Road, bathed in moon-rays, comes Napoleon "riding on a white charger"—but not the emperor beheld of Heine in the avenue of the court garden at Düsseldorf. For the lady too there is a horse led by a mameluke, and she mounts and rides with the emperor. The moon drops among the clouds, and in the darkness the lady and the emperor ride on alone to the hermitage, where in the garden a tent stands beneath a chestnut-tree.

"The unknown remained two days and two nights, making no appearance, and the emperor showed himself twice only, to give some orders. The child went for walks with one of the men composing his suite. He appeared to be about four or five years old, and was dressed in the Polish fashion."

The lady went away, and the islanders said: "It was kind of the Empress Marie Louise to come and see the emperor." But the fallen emperor had no visit from Marie Louise.

---

3. What *was* the precise night of this attempted suicide? Thiers and Constant agree in assigning it to the night of 11th or 12th. Dr. Holland Rose, following Fain and Macdonald, refers us to the next night. It is a pity we have no memoirs of Mme. Walewska.

12

Marie Louise

"The amazing marriage," were not this title Mr. Meredith's, would fitly describe the match between Napoleon and the Archduchess Marie Louise of Austria. "It was his ruin," says Lord Acton. The emperor himself is reported to have alluded to it at St. Helena as "an abyss covered with flowers." The abyss, of course, was Russia. But for this Austrian match there would probably have been no Moscow to record—and through the flames of Moscow we may dimly descry the wreck of the First Empire.

As great as he was at the time of the divorce of Josephine, Napoleon found it not the easiest matter to replace her. "He would not think," observes Dr. Lenz, "of choosing a wife among his vassals," of whom at this epoch he had rather an embarrassing number. "For him there was question only of some princess from one of the reigning families of the Great Powers." Daru had respectfully advised his master to marry a Frenchwoman, a Frenchwoman not burdened with relatives who would want crowns or *baksheesh*. Napoleon had replied sagaciously enough that his immediate business was to establish his influence "outside," and that a successful marriage in the right quarter would be the best help to that. He had, however, to remember that, far from being a king-born king, he was a monarch without ancestors.

Hope seemed to offer of a family alliance with Russia. The Czar Alexander had two sisters to dispose of Grand Duchess Catherine and Grand Duchess Anne. Catherine was in Napoleon's mind up to the interview at Erfurt; but she, as we know, was presently given to Prince George of Mecklenburg. Anne at this date was extremely young for marriage, but Napoleon persevered. These *pour-parlers* were in progress while Josephine was still undivorced; couriers hastening slowly between Paris and St. Petersburg.

Not in France only, but in Europe, the general opinion began to give it out as settled that Josephine's successor was the younger sister of the *czar*. But St. Petersburg was dallying with the great question. Alexander made every show of amiability, but . . . the Grand Duchess Anne was so very young . . . her mother's consent was difficult to obtain . . . there was the question of the young lady's religion . . . there was also the Polish question. In the end. Napoleon grew tired. A sovereign without a pedigree, he was none the less at this hour the arbiter and umpire of Europe. It was given to the Emperor Alexander to understand that the Emperor Napoleon was no longer a candidate for his sister's hand. But before this message went to Russia, Napoleon had made sure of Austria.

In a volume published at the end of last (1909) year, (*The Austrian Court in the Nineteenth Century*), Sir Horace Rumbold says concerning this matrimonial pact:

> Of many questionable transactions held to have been justified by reasons of State, this one seems in many ways exceptionally odious.

Yet, once accomplished, it was regarded by both sides as a masterstroke of policy. One important person in the bargain counted for almost nothing; the victim herself, Marie Louise. Lord Castlereagh had given it as his opinion that "to propitiate the Minotaur, an Austrian maiden should be offered up." According to Meneval (*Napoléon et Marie Louise*), the maiden herself, when first the scheme was submitted to her, uttered very nearly the same words:

> *Se regarda presque comme une victime devouée au Minotaure.*

Odious or not, the affair was certainly amazing. Had France, since the outbreak of the Revolution, been on the most devoted terms with Austria, it would still have seemed well-nigh incredible that a Bonaparte should become a son-in-law of the thrice-proud House of Hapsburg, the heirs of the Germanic Caesars. But, in fact, what had been the relations between the two countries? In 1809 Marie Louise's father, the Emperor Francis—now just forty-one—had occupied his throne for seventeen years. During all but four of these years (since 1796, that is to say) he had been fighting against Napoleon—fighting and losing all the time. To the young Marie Louise, France was the country that had guillotined her aunt (she was the great-grandchild of Marie Thérèse and grandniece of Marie Antoinette), robbed Austria of Italy, and abolished God. And to Marie Louise, France was Napoleon Bonaparte.

In 1805 Napoleon's victory of Austerlitz had cost Austria 28,000 square miles of territory, a population of nearly 3,000,000, and a revenue of over 14,000,000 florins. Up to this date Francis had been revered as the august overlord of the Holy Roman Empire. In 1806, "under the rude impact of the Corsican Caesar," this historic empire vanished. A great region of Germany was become the mere vassal of Napoleon, and under the Confederation of the Rhine! Francis had to declare himself simply the first of the emperors of Austria. Austerlitz in 1S05; Wagram in 1809. Once again Austria saw her capital in Napoleon's hands, and from this fresh campaign—which historians are agreed in describing as the most memorable and splendid in her annals—she emerged with a loss of 42,000 square miles of territory, 3,500,000 inhabitants, and some 11,000,000 florins of revenue. Scarcely had the cannon of Wagram ceased when the conqueror reappeared as the most amiable of suitors. The hand of Marie Louise, the eldest born of her father and his favourite child, was asked in marriage.

What did the girlish archduchess know of this momentous offer? She knew nothing whatever. It was but a little while that she had left off playing at soldiers with her brother, when the ugliest waxen figure on the board was christened Bonaparte, horribly wounded with pins, and heaped with maledictions. Not until within six or seven weeks of her betrothal had Marie Louise an inkling of the project.

Marie Louise Léopoldine Caroline Lucie, born in Vienna the 12th of December, 1791, was just eighteen at the end of 1809. All the daughters of her House were strictly and dully reared in sequestered chambers remote in some degree from the Court. They had their ladies and their domestics, among whom they lived, says Meneval, "*avec une bienveillante familiarité.*" Their whole existence, up to the day of marriage, was passed "*dans une retraite absolue.*" Practically, indeed, the young archduchesses were cloistered. When a master gave lessons, the governess-in-chief was always present.

If in some respects the education of Marie Louise was below the standard of a modern High School, it was in some other respects above this standard. An Austrian archduchess of the period, traditionally supposed to be capable of speaking to or greeting everyone in the "great Babel" of the Empire—and destined to she knew not what marriage of convenience—was quite necessarily a linguist; and Marie Louise, with some schoolgirl's Latin and at least a phrase or two of

Turkish, was firmly grounded, as Masson says (*L'Impératrice Marie Louise*), in German, English, Czech, Spanish, Italian and French. She was crammed with history, logic, and chronology; made some progress in drawing; could touch the piano agreeably; and on the harp had a tune or two beyond the solitary air upon which Josephine erected her pretensions to this instrument.

Some simple and pretty letters have come down to us from her childhood and girlhood. The most interesting of these are letters to her favourite governess, Mme. de Colloredo, and the governess's daughter, Victoire. In the severe and almost nun like opening of her life the little archduchess throws herself into the arms of this beloved governess. The Mme. de Colloredo of this correspondence is "*maman;*" the archduchess's mother, when she alludes to that lady, is "*ma mère.*" For her imperial father Marie Louise has a deep, half-fearful, half-romantic, and half-reverential affection. When, scarcely admitted to the scene, her eyes behold "Papa on his Throne," her very elbows shake.

By and by her girlish pen is spluttering its way into politics. She receives as a present *Plutarque de la jeunesse*—the lives of illustrious men from Homer to Bonaparte.

> This last name spoils the book, and I would much rather the author had left off at the Emperor Francis (her father), who also has done some remarkable things . . . while the other person has simply committed injustices in depriving people of their country.

Again, to Victoire, she writes:

> I have just heard such a funny thing; that M. Bonaparte, when he was in Egypt and his army was completely ruined, escaped with only two or three of his soldiers, and became a Turk. He said to the people, 'Yes, I am a Mussulman, and the great Mahomet is my prophet.' Afterwards, when he got back to France, he pretended he was a Catholic, and it was only then they made him Consul.

In 1805, when Francis was brought almost to his knees, and the Imperial family was flying hither and thither, Marie Louise thought Providence should be getting ready to intervene:

> Papa must win in the end, and then will come the moment of the usurper's discouragement. I should not wonder if God had allowed him to go as far as this, so that when He abandoned

him his ruin might be all the more complete.

In April 1807 her mother died, and in January of the following year the Emperor Francis took for third wife his youthful cousin, Marie Louise Beatrice of Este, who was but four years older than her stepdaughter, Marie Louise.

No one in Austria more cordially detested the French Revolution and its heir. Napoleon. The family of Marie Louise Beatrice had lost the Duchy of Modena, and she herself seems to have been animated with a kind of fury against "*le Corsicain*." To the easy-going Francis, when the blasts of war again began to blow, the third wife was both whip and spur.

The standards of the newly-formed *Landwehr* were solemnly blest, Marie Louise assisting at the ceremony. Presently there are tidings in Vienna of an Austrian victory (Eckmühl), and the archduchess dashes off a letter to her father in camp:

> We have heard with joy that Napoleon was present at the great battle which he lost. May he lose his head too! Everyone here is prophesying about his coming end, and saying that the Apocalypse is meant for him. They declare that he is to die this year, at Cologne, in an inn called the Red Crab. I don't think too much of all these predictions, but how happy I should be to see them realised!

As M. de Saint-Amand [1] remarks, these sentiments "are a singular preparation for the next year's wedding."

Wagram finished the campaign, and the last gun fired there was Josephine's warning to pack. When Napoleon "reappeared crowned with victory at Fontainebleau, October 26th, 1809, Josephine felt that her fate was sealed. The immediate result of the Battle of Wagram was the divorce."

Marie Louise's piano-master, Kozeluch, was among the persons who talked of it. She writes:

> I hear that Kozeluch has been speaking about Napoleon's separation from his wife, and also that he mentions *me* as her successor! He is certainly mistaken there. He is too much afraid of being refused, and too anxious to do us still more harm, to risk a demand of that sort; and papa is too good to use any con-

---

1. *Marie-Louise and the Invasion of 1814* by Imbert de Saint-Amand also published by Leonaur.

straint with me in so important a matter.

This is early in January 1810, and she writes at the same time to Mme. de Colloredo, to whom she still addressed herself as an affectionate and truthful daughter to an understanding mother:

> I let everybody talk; it doesn't trouble me in the least (*Je laisse purler tout le monde, et ne m' en inquiète pas du tout*). I am sorry only for the poor princess whom he chooses; I'm certain *I* shall not be the political victim.

Then in a flash it seems to be revealed to her that she, after all, is the lamb for whom they are building the sacrificial altar.

> I commit my fate to Providence. Providence alone knows where our happiness lies. If misfortune wills it, I am ready to give myself up for the State.... I don't want to think about it, but my mind is made up.... Pray that it mayn't be!

When this letter was written Marie Louise's fate was sealed. Her father had decided for the marriage. We have it on almost every hand that the Austrian princesses were to marry where and when the policy of Austria decided for them. They lived under a private coercion law. Paternal authority in this very ancient family was practically as absolute as in Israel. Metternich was deputed to submit the case to Marie Louise. He knew very well what his commission amounted to.

"What are really the wishes of my father?" Marie Louise asked him.

"Do not ask what the emperor wishes," was Metternich's nice evasion: "tell me what you yourself wish."

Marie Louise knew what she wished, and Metternich knew what she wished, and her father knew what she wished. She wished Napoleon dead. But she replied:

> I wish only what I am commanded by my duty to wish. It is the interests of the Empire that must be consulted, not my feelings. Ask my father to consider nothing but his duty as a sovereign."

This was precisely the answer that had been looked for. Marie Louise, at eighteen, was old enough to know that it was the only answer she could venture on. Had not Metternich just written privately to his wife?

> Our princesses are little accustomed to choose their husbands according to their own inclinations, and the respect which a daughter so devoted and so well brought up feels for her father gives me confidence that she will not oppose us

Metternich reports to the Emperor Francis the issue of his interview with Marie Louise, and the emperor replies:

> I am in no way surprised at what you tell me. Knowing my daughter as I do, this is just the answer I expected.

So the most desperate marriage in history was arranged at a diplomatic gasp. In fewer than six weeks from the proper opening of negotiations the match was whirled through, and Napoleon—who danced as ill as he rode—was learning the Vienna waltz, and sending for tailors "to fit him properly," and inquiring for the lady's portrait.

Pen-portraits of Marie Louise are numerous, and some of the most elaborate are the least to be trusted. Lamartine describes her as a comely maiden of the Tyrol (she was no more of the Tyrol than of the Tiber):

> Blue-eyed and fair-haired, her complexion tinted by the whiteness of its snows and the roses of its valleys, slender and supple, and with that languorous attitude of the German woman who seems to need a man's heart to lean on.

Her lips this painter finds a little full, "*la poitrine pleine de soupirs et de fécondité*," the arms long and admirably sculptured. Her great-grandmother, Maria Theresa, was famed for the beauty of her arms and hands.

Lamartine's picture is over-limned. Metternich's, less flattering, comes nearer to historic canvases. He writes to his wife:

> Her face is rather plain than pretty, but she has a beautiful figure; and when properly dressed and made the most of, she will do well.

There was a wide space between the eyes, which were rather curiously placed. Masson remarks on the want of proportion in the lower lip ("*cette lèvre démesurée*"), which was rather heavy and pendulous, though it lacks the complete foolishness of the under-lip of Velasquez's Charles II. Sir Horace Rumbold imagines Marie Louise as "the perfect embodiment of German girlish beauty and freshness . . . in short, as sweet and dainty a maiden as could be." The quality of "freshness" we may accept without the least reserve. Marie Louise was fresh, sound, and winsome.

To the public announcement of the betrothal, Vienna's first response was a blank amaze.

> The sudden outburst of a volcano would not have been more startling than this piece of news from a clear sky. The impression made upon the populace was one of surprise which merged in disbelief. People stopped one another in the streets to ask if it were possible.

In as short a time as may be conceived, astonishment resolved itself into satisfaction. Metternich to his wife wrote:

> All Vienna is interested in nothing but this marriage. It would be hard to form an idea of the public feeling about it, and of its extreme popularity.

The official announcement in the *Gazette*, February 24, 1810, ran in these terms:

> The formal betrothal of the Emperor of the French, King of Italy, and her Imperial and Royal Highness the Archduchess Marie Louise, the eldest daughter of his Imperial and Royal Majesty, our very gracious sovereign, was signed at Paris, on the 7th, by the Prince Schwarzenberg, Ambassador, and the Duke of Cadore, Minister of Foreign Affairs. The exchange of ratifications of this contract took place on the 21st of this month, at Vienna, between Count Metternich Winneburg, Minister of State and of Foreign Affairs, and the Imperial Ambassador of France, Count Otto de Mesloy. All the nations of Europe see in this event a gage of peace, and after so many wars look forward with delight to a happy future.

Stranger than anything else, perhaps, was the bedazzlement of Marie Louise's stepmother, the empress. This lady, erstwhile Napoleon's most implacable opponent at the Austrian court, was as emphatic as anyone in praise of the match. Count Otto de Mesloy wrote in a dispatch:

> The empress shows herself extremely favourable to the marriage.

Into this enterprise which was to provide him with an heir and carry on the State that he had founded, Napoleon, at forty-one, threw

Marie Louise

himself with a schoolboy's ardour. The brain that had bent itself to the uptilting of a world was now absorbed in chiffons, in planning the *meubles et immeubles* of the imperial bride's appanage, in heaping the *corbeille* with stately vesture and more intimate delicacy of lace and linen, meet alike for the daughter of an emperor and for the consort of a Napoleon.

Here let us see something of the outfit which the emperor planned for his girl-bride. The *corbeille* itself alone, of white velvet, cost 12,000 *francs*, the marriage robe another 12,000. Then among the court dresses we come upon one of silver tissue, another of pink tulle decorated with gems and spangles, a trained robe of *blonde*, silver and chenille. These ran into hundreds of pounds apiece.

Then there were the ball-dresses, one with violets (the Bonaparte flower) and silver in a design of architectural columns. Historic retrospect furnished a gown of pink and silver in the style of Francis I, patterned with fish-scales, and a girlish dress of white tulle would serve for the less imperial moments of the bride.

Then came a dozen evening gowns. Tulle with silver flowers and buds; white satin and pearls; a white dress, trimmed, somewhat unusually, with raspberries.

A velvet gown trimmed with double rows of fringe on the bodice and scarf. This had descended to the moderate price of 588 *francs*.

The simple dresses of crepe and tulle, with high neck and long sleeves, came to quite small prices of £14 apiece, and why one of imitation *cachemire* mounted to £40 is not explained.

Blonde again appears for a more sumptuous garment, and is worked in chenille with ivy leaves, and cost nearly £100; violet sprays adorned another of the simpler gowns.

Long coats were supplied in a variety of materials and of substance. The white satin with double capes, the pink satin, pink *frisé* velvet made in shawl fashion—this was a prevailing mode—and the more trivial blue *crêpe* appear among the number.

The simpler outdoor garments were furnished for £12 to £15 each.

Hunting outfits were designed with an eye to pageantry, such as one in white satin with golden tassels, and another in velvet with gold trimming, and, for this ornamental kind of sport, *blonde* veils were also included.

Fichus were the order of everyday attire, and these, both large and small, were there in quantity.

Sixteen dozen of gloves were not excessive for an empress, and the price at 40 *francs* a dozen (judged, even, upon relative values) may make modem mouths water by its moderation.

Fans, shawls of *cachemire* and wraps of velvet finish the more public adornment of the imperial consort.

Now we come to more hidden wonders. There were over one hundred pairs of white silk stockings—and a few cotton ones, which were perhaps for bedroom use, where we find included *fichus*, nightcaps and other unidentifiable items. Some of the nightcaps were of the mode "Caroline," others of "Napoleon," and one ran up to the price of 840 *francs*.

Dozens of underwear, embroidered and lace-trimmed, but confined to cotton and linen materials, are in the list. Some of the petticoats were of Scotch mull, though foreign goods were not loved by Napoleon.

There were nearly three hundred pocket-handkerchiefs of cambric, some lace-edged. Among the lace objects appeared a veil, a shawl of *point d'Alençon*, two dresses of *point d'Angleterre* and three shawls of the same, one of which was in a design of rose and laurel intertwined in garlands, with the monogram M.L. at each corner.

The court train of lace, at about 600 guineas, seems far removed from a fancy price. The whole of the lace cost no more than 3,000 guineas. It would be interesting to compare such items of expenditure with those in the *trousseau* of the recent Bonaparte bride of a prince of the royal house of Greece.

The jewels included a *parure* of emeralds and diamonds, in which a comb of specimen emeralds figured, and thus came to over £8,000, while the case which held it was charged at £4 by the court jewellers.

A fine specimen of goldsmith's work was the box of graven gold for toothpicks. It was further adorned by a miniaturist with portraits of the imperial pair.

Jewelled fans, one set with diamonds, one with emeralds, were added to the simple ones of the general outfit.

A cameo portrait of the emperor on *agate-onyx* was the work of Argenti, a famous Roman cutter. A large collection of war medals was also presented to the bride.

Victim though she was, Marie Louise, being still in her teens, must surely have felt some elation at the spectacle of such apparel for the sacrifice.

Berthier, Prince of Neufchâtel, made his State entry as marriage envoy into Vienna on March 5. On the 6th a gala banquet and masked ball at the palace—festivities often enough described. Next came the formal demand for the hand of the archduchess, preferred by the ambassador. On the 9th the bride-elect made her act of solemn renunciation of all her rights and claims as princess of the Imperial family of Austria. On the 11th, in the evening, in the Augustine Church, took place the marriage by procuration, the Archduke Charles standing as proxy for Napoleon.

Two days later, the 13th, Marie Louise set forth on her eventful journey to France. Some of the incidents of this journey were not too agreeable. On the Bavarian frontier, for instance, Marie Louise was met by Napoleon's sister, Caroline Murat, Queen of Naples, who informed her, "to her infinite distress, that her lady-in-waiting. Countess Lazanska, who had been with her since her childhood, would not be permitted to proceed farther on the journey. She was to part with all she had brought from Austria." Apparently, even the little favourite Spitz had to be sent back to Vienna: Napoleon wanted no more pet dogs with a bride.

Was it partly to atone for these slights that the emperor suddenly resolved to dispense with etiquette and ride out to meet his bride in the manner of a knight? At noon on March 27 (what a rate of progress !), as he was excitedly tramping up and down the park at Compiègne, a letter from Marie Louise was delivered to him. She was just leaving for Soissons, she said. There are two or three stories as to what followed. A familiar one is that Napoleon jumped into a carriage without suite or escort, and was driven at full speed to Soissons. This would be by no means bad for an emperor, but what knight-errant condescends to a carriage? Napoleon was up to a trick more romantic than this, and we choose rather to conceive him scouring on horseback the road to Soissons in the guise of a messenger or courier carrying a letter to the bride. Marie Louise had never yet set eyes on him. The surprise was charmingly imagined, and ought to have succeeded: it was spoiled by an outrider too well trained to appreciate an operatic situation. The girl-empress and Caroline Murat were driving from Soissons in a storm of rain. The outrider, recognizing the emperor as he reined up against the carriage, gave the cry of "*L'Emp'reur!*" and the secret was out. However, when the door was opened and the steps were let down, Marie Louise was kissed like any *bourgeoise*.

All halting-places were ignored. Compiègne was reached; the final presentment of splendid pageantry collapsed like a pasteboard scene. Alone with the bride, whose high colouring must have been dashed by the fatigue of the long hours (and by the absence of the dinner promised at Soissons, and missed by a healthy appetite such as hers), Napoleon supped. The chaperon of Naples alone made a third at the shorn feast.

As with everything else, the complementary ceremony of the nuptial benediction is waved aside. Napoleon in his wedding harks back to Henri le Grand—and the next morning boasts to his intimates that he has "anticipated his conjugal rights."

For it was not until the first day of April that the nuptials were solemnized. There were the public ceremonies of the civil marriage at St. Cloud, the State entry into Paris, the religious solemnities in the Chapel of the Louvre. Marie Louise at last was Empress of the French.

Napoleon stated at St. Helena that although the reign of his second consort was brief she ought to have enjoyed it, inasmuch as "the world was at her feet."

We note, however, that in exchanging one palace for another, the young empress had not altogether freed herself from the nursery. Napoleon—in no spirit of distrust—surrounded her with a multitude of precautions. There is the story of the secret drawer in her *bureau*, which the maker of that piece of furniture was showing Her Majesty how to open; while the lady-in-waiting, from motives of delicacy, had withdrawn herself from the presence. The lady did not wish to seem a prier into secrets, but the emperor was angry that the empress had been left alone for that short spell. Napoleon himself, on his nuptial visits to his wife's room, must pass through the antechamber, where a lady-in-waiting slept always as guardian to Marie Louise.

She resumed her music lessons and her practising; continued to use her pencil, and received her first riding lessons, rather nervously, under the supervision of the emperor—who may have taught her rather more than he knew, for he himself habitually bumped in the saddle. Until she had been well and truly married, by the way, no princess of Austria could learn to ride. It was a point of etiquette in the family.

Napoleon was probably not very long in learning that he had wedded a somewhat colourless young woman. Her dread of him passed almost immediately, and she told Metternich that His Majesty was really more afraid of her than she of him; yet in her feeling for Napoleon there seems to have been something; bordering in an almost tragic degree upon the commonplace. Neither fear, nor awe, nor worship, nor the glamorous obsession of passion could for one moment have visited the serene shallows of this Austrian girl-wife. "I never had romantic feeling of any kind for him," was her frank avowal in after years.

One of the most bewildering facts about these historic figures, whom the haze of our own imaginations has magnified to heroic form, is the absence of enchantment they seem to have possessed for those in next proximity. A thousand woman souls may have swelled with romantic ardour for the hero their eyes had never seen, dead long before their day; yet no single thrill has traversed the being of the woman set at the idol's right hand. Imagination is ever the Promethean life-giver; the creature also, like its Creator, makes all things out of nothing.

Curiously or not. Napoleon himself was more than satisfied with the situation, more than pleased with the bride. He chuckled to Metternich over the grand success of his bargain, and did not tire of telling his friends that there was no wife like an Austrian.

Sir H. Rumbold says:

> He came down, so to speak, from the pinnacle to which he had raised himself and where, till now, he had dwelt sternly alone with his soaring dreams and his boundless ambition, and found a delight he had never deemed to be possible in the sober joys of married life. In short, he fell desperately in love with his young wife.

It added immensely to his pleasure in Marie Louise that she had made conquests of the redoubtable Clan! Josephine they had fought to the end, but:

> Marie Louise from the first unconsciously took by storm her husband's family, from the austere Madame Mère to the; jealous, intriguing sisters; while from the royal sister-in-law, Catherine of Würtemberg (wife of Jérôme Bonaparte, King of Westphalia) she won the meed of praise that 'it was impossible to see her without loving her.'

Her fancy, to be sure, was gratified at every turn; but it is fair to add that she showed tact, grace, and good nature. The Chamberlain Rambuteau says (*Memoirs*) in his kindly way:

> Her very timidity added a certain grace to her; there was some-

thing so pathetically appealing about her. She inspired her surroundings with a mixture of respect and sympathy, and these sentiments, added to a general conviction of her real omnipotence, won all hearts for her. I was at every *fête*, and was often selected to open the balls during the time I was waiting for my special duties to begin, which they did after a journey to Trianon, whither the emperor took the empress to rest at the beginning of her pregnancy.

Of this great event the tidings filtered presently from the palace to the capital and the provinces. The emperor's *bonne Louise* was admirably fulfilling her mission! There is a pathetic little touch in a letter written at this date to her bosom friend:

> You know how little courage I have.

She was but nineteen, she had no mother, and the father who could pour strength into her for anything was far away. On the evening of March 19, during a *cercle* at the Tuileries, it was told the emperor that the first symptoms had set in, but the night passed, and no climax. Betwixt night and morning of March 19-20, 1811, the emperor with every mark of gentleness stood frequently for long spells at the bedside. At a critical moment the surgeon was flustered, and from his behaviour Marie Louise inferred the worst. "Must my life be sacrificed, only because I am an empress?" she wailed.

"Come, Dubois," said the emperor, asserting himself at the crisis, "don't lose your head! Think only of the empress."

There was a half-hour of combat before which Napoleon, who had witnessed, imperturbable, the spectacle of the battlefield, sickened and fled, pale and unnerved. The warrior at least can stretch his arm against the assailant, but with what cruel odds is the mother-victim fronted! The trial was soon ended, however.

At 9.20 on the morning of March 20, guns one hundred and one boomed the birth of l'Aiglon, Napoleon's son and heir, the King of Rome. All the night past the people of Paris had crowded the churches to pray for this arrival of arrivals, and through the windows of the empress's room Napoleon watched the joyous gestures of the crowd.

What an infinite melancholy fills this brief career! This is the prince, Napoleon's one lawful child, who on his deathbed, twenty-one years and four months later, said to his friend Count Prokesch-Osten:

> My birth and my death—those two words are my biography:

they tell my whole story.

It was almost absolutely true.

Posterity has known this child and youth by three resounding titles: King of Rome, Napoleon II, and Duke of Reichstadt. Chiefly, however, it has known him as one of the unhappiest and most luckless princes born to France. His birth was "an onerous complication," wrote Lord Acton; and in sooth it was, but this there was no foreseeing. We first see the beautiful baby (beautiful he was) in his gorgeous "cradle of mother-of-pearl and gold, surmounted by a winged Victory," in which he lay to be smiled at by all. Then he comes before us in his cloak of silver tissue lined with ermine, a lovely little postulant borne to his public baptism at Notre Dame. After this fine ceremony we may behold him faring through the glades of Saint-Cloud in his gilded baby-coach drawn by two milk-white sheep.

Gérard found the child a charming subject for his brush, painting him with cup and ball in his cradle. This portrait, on the eve of Moscow, Napoleon placed on a stand before his tent; and the veterans of the Guard, as they passed before it, "cried with joy." Alas! for the baby boy: Moscow, we may say, decides his fate.

> Within less than two years Cossacks were the escort of the King of Rome. When the Coalition made him a prisoner, he was forever torn from his father. Napoleon, March 20, 1815, on the return from Elba, re-entered the palace of the Tuileries triumphantly as if by miracle, but his joy was incomplete. March 20 was the birthday of his son, the day he was four years old, and the boy was not there."

His father never saw him again.

They remembered one another, though in differing degrees of intensity. Napoleon at St. Helena is much moved on receiving a lock of the boy's hair, and a letter from him which some hand traces over the little prince's hand. With the lad himself, the memory of his father expanded into a sort of ecstatic dream. What thoughts he had of his mother we know not, for from childhood onwards till his death they were almost strangers. The growing prince, his great title gone from him, lived with his grandfather. Emperor Frances; his mother queened it in her toy duchy of Parma. But thoughts of an abiding and harassing love for his father are his chief emotional sustenance. The love is harassing, because he is always contrasting his own nothingness and his own steady physical decline with the immensity of his father and his father's relentless grip on life.

As his malady of consumption deepens he is more and more impressed with the blind cruelty of his fate. He was handsome and proud and gentle, with at least a touch of Napoleon's personal ascendency. Glances followed him in the ballroom; and once when he rode to perfection a fiery horse at a review, the soldiers, "accustomed to maintain a profound silence in the ranks, broke suddenly into shouts of admiration." It is not permitted to say that in Napoleon II we lost another great creature, for the seeds of death were laid in him at birth; but he seems to have taken to the grave some sweet and noble qualities, and "as the earth left him, he turned to heaven."

We have glanced at Moscow, and return to Marie Louise. The days of fate drew on. The glitter of the Tuileries paled and went out almost as swiftly as in the few anarchic and dissolving months that had sent to their account Louis XVI and Marie Antoinette. Abdication, return, the utter *débâcle* followed one another in stifling sequence, till the tempest joined with the deluge. The emperor was needed in the field; he appointed the Empress Regent. The daughter of the Caesars held an office for a precedent for which the archivists sought back into the middle centuries. But her power, even of such formal kind, was short-lived. Under the advance of the Allies, she left Paris with her son and proclaimed herself in Blois, in May 1814, in empty grandiloquence upon the walls of the city. Alas! upon the very day of the *affiche* Napoleon was signing his abdication, in the desperate hope that his son would be recognized as the succeeding monarch.

The more trivial taint in the empress peers forth in an episode at Blois. It fell to the lot of General de St. Alaire to break the news of the abdication to the regent. He was received by her while she was still in bed, and her feet were half uncovered.

"Not wishing to stare into her face in so direful a moment, he cast down his eyes, respectful of her grief.

"'Ah!' said the empress, 'you are looking at my foot. I have always been told it is a pretty one.'"

The general's head drooped at the banal vanity.

From this hour, it must be confessed, the sympathies of French readers are terribly against Marie Louise. She has been judged, found wanting, condemned. France has continued to regard her as the "ungrateful wife" who forsook her husband in the day of his disorder. She, to be sure, did not abandon Napoleon more hastily than he had been abandoned by the French. If she quitted Paris when the Allies were in sight, she could have pleaded the definite commands of Napoleon that their son was to be saved from the enemy. If she took ultimate refuge in Vienna, it was when she had, not virtually but actually, ceased to be a sovereign, and had passed again under the all but absolute control of the imperial father in whose will she had always sunk her own. Pray also let it be remembered that the Marie Louise of these days that would have tried the nerve and staunchness of a Marie Thérèse was still a young person of three-and-twenty.

Meneval, as it seems to us, puts the case not unfairly. The ambition of Napoleon and the policy of the Austrian Cabinet had elevated Marie Louise for a moment to a rank she had not coveted and would gladly have declined. "Be a good wife, a good mother; do everything to please your husband," her father Francis had counselled her. To this, says Meneval, Austrian policy added beneath its breath: "So long as your husband's fortunes prosper, and he is useful to our House." These counsels Marie Louise had submissively and implicitly obeyed. True, she had not succeeded in identifying herself with the country of her adoption. But she had entered France a schoolgirl, and she quitted it a young and inexperienced woman. The time that she actually passed with Napoleon was two years and eight months.

We are not, of course, to forget her activities, when the crisis came, in sending envoys to her father, and in attempting as far as possible to gain support for the claims of her son. "All of us," says Bourrienne, "would have defended these *si defendi possent*." Alas! the collapse was complete. Then the domestic autocrat spoke, and once again the obedient daughter listened. The Emperor Francis told his daughter that she must adopt the safest course. Her son's life even was not secure in France, now in large part hostile and turning eagerly to welcome Louis XVIII. Her proper action would be to retire to the Duchy of Parma, one of the Austrian appanages. Up to that moment Marie Louise had hesitated, had moved from Paris to Blois, thence to Orleans, had reverted to Rambouillet. Then she took her final flight, and began those years of residence, placid and uneventful, so far as any great political crises were concerned, in her duchy.

As for Napoleon himself, we know how he preserved ever for his young consort sentiments of approbation, we might even say of gratitude, for the exactness with which she had performed her appointed part. In all that concerned Marie Louise, Napoleon took to the last a quasi-paternal interest. When in a riding accident she fell into the River Po, he heard of the event with every appearance of solicitude.

In his will, that wondrous "light before death," drawn up in the retreat of the South Atlantic to which he had transported so small a part of his valuable belongings, he stated—

I have every reason to be pleased with my dear wife, Marie Louise. I retain for her to my last moments the most tender feeling.

A chain of her fair hair was among the relics he bequeathed to his son. He directed, too, that his own hair should be made into a bracelet, clasped with gold, which should be sent to the ex-empress. Her deposed condition and her title as Grand Duchess of Parma he ignored. "To the Empress Marie Louise, my lace." And he appointed her as his executrix.

M. Masson, in his work *L'Impératrice Marie Louise*, takes the view of a quite dispassionate observer. Admitting that Marie Louise has been for a hundred years "*un objet de détestation*" in France, he remarks that his countrymen have judged her as if she had been French by birth and blood, or at least as if she were a naturalized Frenchwoman who had embraced "*nos ambitions, nos goûts, nos passions, nos rêves.*" But Marie Louise was born German, she was brought up in hatred of the country that had temporarily adopted her, and of this country she had acquired scarcely one definite notion. She had spent in all some four years in France—"*mais en quelle vie, en quelle captivité, sans rapport avec les êtres, sans tendresse pour le sol et le paysage.*"

She was always in some degree an exile who had been sacrificed to politics; she always felt herself in some degree a stranger. Come we where we may, continues M. Masson, we are still part and parcel of the race that we belong to; and to belong to a race implies that its temperament is ours, "*physique, mental et moral.*" Marie Louise being essentially of her race, her acts, if we would render them intelligible, must be viewed through the prism of her race. Farther, she came into the world an Archduchess, and to France she carried with her something of historic atavism and her imperial education. But the whole national prejudices of the French are against her.

One singular champion Napoleon (in his character of exiled and abandoned husband) found in Vienna. This was the grandmother of Marie Louise, Queen Marie Caroline of Naples. Her Majesty (also at this date a fugitive) was the last of the daughters of Marie Thérèse and a sister of Marie Antoinette. "No longer able," says Meneval, "to endure the authority which the English had arrogated to themselves over Sicily," she had come to Vienna—arriving there at about the same time as her granddaughter—to beg for the restitution of her kingdom. She had abhorred the French Revolution and everything that it could and could not be held responsible for, and Napoleon she regarded—not without reason—as her peculiar foe. Now, however, she beheld him destitute, and was touched. History has not informed us of what Queen Marie Caroline said directly to her granddaughter, but the Baron de Meneval has told us what she said to him.

De Meneval, a secretary of Napoleon's, was one of the few French persons who had accompanied the ex-empress to Vienna. The queen grandmother sent for him, and gave her opinion of the situation in good set terms. Time was, said Her Majesty, when she had had cause enough to cry out against Napoleon, but now that she saw him in his distress she could and did forget the past. It angered her to learn of the efforts the Viennese Court was making to detach her granddaughter from the bonds that had given her glory, and to deprive the emperor of the sweetest consolation he could receive in this hour of his wounded pride. If the court still held out against the reunion of husband and wife, it was Marie Louise's duty to tie her sheets to her window and make off in disguise ("*il fallait que Marie Louise attachât les draps de son lit à sa fenêtre et s'échappât sous un déguisement*").

What a figure would Dumas or our Stevenson have made of the archduchess and ex-empress sliding down her rope of knotted sheets! What a heroine would romantic drama have claimed in all countries! What a dainty page would have been secured to Napoleon's biographers! What a charming little corner would history have kept for Napoleon's Marie Louise!

She reserved herself for a fate less picturesque. In 1814, says Saint-Amand, Marie Louise "had met the man who was to make her forget her duty towards her illustrious husband." This was a middle-aged gallant, General the Count of Neipperg, "as he called himself," the one-eyed gentleman with the black patch—"one of the most persistent and one of the most skilful of Napoleon's enemies." To Neipperg, after the tragic death on the Rock, Marie Louise was morganatically married. She bore him two daughters and a son, and lived in his subjection till he died in 1829.

Yet another successor, and one not less obscure, did Marie Louise give to the Caesar of these times. Her third husband, whom she married in 1833, was De Bombelles, a Frenchman in the service of Austria. There seems to have been English blood in De Bombelles, but we have escaped hitherto the reproaches of the French on this score.

Marie Louise died in 1847 (just one year before the Revolution that brought Napoleon's nephew to the front) at the age of fifty-six. Time had not frosted her memories of France—it had done worse: it had changed them again into the hostile fancies of her childhood.

13

The 'Tragi-Comedy' of the Rock

Sir Hudson Lowe has hinted that there were gallantries even at St. Helena. Gossip of intrigues no doubt there was, but he makes too much of it. Had he flatly denied it, he would not improbably have been in the right. Napoleon at St. Helena is not, of course, in the dreadful situation of the Masked Man in the keeping of Saint-Mars at Pignerol; but he was held with some degree of closeness by Sir Hudson, the gaoler-in-chief, through whom alone access to the captive could be won. Sir Hudson could name names, he whispers us: well, without enormous indiscretion he might have named them. He does not do so, and the unromancing man seems here to be romancing a little. In circumstances easily imagined it would have been dangerous to leave Napoleon at St. Helena open to the wiles of certain women; but no woman could get to him save by express permission of Lowe himself, and Lowe was a very jealous guardian.

On the whole, and having regard to all the circumstances of the case, a drearier situation than that of the Rock is scarcely to be conceived. Stripped alike of empire and of title, Napoleon, outlawed of Europe, sits down at last to the problem of such a total failure in life as no other man in the world had ever been confronted with. It is a ruin almost as absolute as that of the "arch enemy" in Milton. Escape? Where, and to what? There is no notion more hopeless. Elba had been successfully evaded; but the return into France from Elba, the return to *power* in France, was far more difficult for Napoleon than we have generally believed—and return from St. Helena there was none. The attempt was never made.

It was in the last week of July 1815 that the British Government decided on St. Helena. On August 7 Napoleon was the prisoner of H.M.S. *Northumberland*. Ninety-five days later, towards eight in the evening of October 17, he was landed with his suite at Jamestown, the capital of the island. Among the twenty-five who followed him, General Bertrand had been comptroller of his household at Elba, Count Montholon and General Gourgaud had served as adjutants in the last campaign. Count de Las Cases was a converted *émigré*, and Dr. Barry O'Meara had held the post of chief surgeon on the *Bellerophon*. Countess Montholon and Mme. Bertrand were the two ladies of the party. After one night at Jamestown, Napoleon moved to "The Briars," the villa residence of the merchant Balcombe (sometimes called Balecombe), where, with Las Cases and a servant or two, he spent six or seven weeks. In December he moved to the house called "Longwood," a secluded dwelling high above the port, and here the "tragi-comedy of five years" was enacted.

"A little company of French gentlemen and ladies, accustomed to the stirring life of a brilliant capital, found itself pitched on a desolate island, far from friends and home and all the great movement of the world. The attendants of Napoleon were not cast in the stoical mould; and, even if considerations of policy had not been involved, temperament would have inclined them to exaggerate minor discomforts, to strain against the restrictions of the governor, to shudder at the rocks and ravines, to condemn the rain when it was rainy, the sun when it was sunny, and the wind when it was windy, to compare the sparse gum-trees of the Longwood plateau with the ample shades of Marly and St. Cloud, and the rough accommodation of the Longwood house with the comforts of a well-appointed Parisian hotel. To a man like Napoleon, whose whole soul was in politics, seclusion was a kind of torture. He had no administrative occupations to absorb his energies as had been the case in Elba; and time, to quote his own bitter phrase, was now his only superfluity."

We know precisely what were the instructions of the British Government to Sir Hudson Lowe. It is stated in the dispatch of September 12, 1815:

> You will observe that the desire of His Majesty's Government is to allow every indulgence to General Bonaparte, (this title was in itself no inconsiderable grievance), which may be compatible with the entire security of his person; that he should not by any means escape, or hold communication with any person whatever, excepting through your agency, must be your unremitted care; and these points being made sure, every resource

and amusement which may serve to reconcile Bonaparte to his confinement may be permitted.

That his prisoner should be held fast, and be corrupted by no unauthorized communications: these were undoubtedly regarded by Lowe as the cardinal points of his instructions. He has been censured, as we all know, for his manner of enforcing them; but it is probable that if, at an early date, some terms could have been agreed upon between Sir Hudson and the exiles, little would afterwards have been heard on this score. In fact, Napoleon had not more than five or six interviews in all with Sir Hudson Lowe; and at most of these he showed—as was by himself admitted—to very poor advantage. He could not work Lowe up to banging the door!

What we need to remember is, that the policy of the little band forbade them to come to terms or live peacefully with the Governor. Lowe's methods were not perfect, but the captives for their part did not choose to be accommodating: it did not suit their scheme. Mr. Seaton says truly that "the whole of their conduct was based on a system, and when that system necessarily came to an end on the death of Napoleon they acknowledged that they had nothing to say against the governor." Towards the end, Napoleon, realizing that he must inevitably die upon the Rock, melted somewhat, and on his deathbed "charged Bertrand and Montholon to seek a reconciliation with the governor." Both of them dined with Lowe immediately after Napoleon's death.

A few lines are worth taking from the interesting *Events of a Military Life*, by Walter Henry, assistant-surgeon of the 66th Regiment, who was at St. Helena from July 1817 until the end:—

> The governor appeared to me much occupied with the cares and duties of his important and responsible office, and looked very like a person who would not let his prisoner escape if he could help it. From first impressions I entertained an opinion of him far from favourable; if therefore, notwithstanding this prepossession, my testimony should incline to the other side, I can truly state that the change took place from the weight of evidence, and in consequence of what came under my own observation at St. Helena. Since that time he has encountered a storm of obloquy and reproach enough to bow any person to the earth; yet I firmly believe that the talent he exerted in unravelling the intricate plotting constantly going on at Long-

wood, and the firmness in tearing it to pieces, with the unceasing vigilance he displayed in the discharge of his arduous and invidious duties, made him more enemies than any hastiness of temper, or severity in his measures, of which the world was taught to believe him guilty.

Among the specific commands laid by the government upon Sir Hudson were that Napoleon was always to be styled General Bonaparte (a point that certainly "might have been conceded without loss of dignity" on our part); that no letters or packets were to be sent or received by the French unless they had first been seen by the governor; that Napoleon himself should be seen by the orderly officer twice in the twenty-four hours, and that sentinels should patrol Longwood after nightfall; finally, "that certain limits should be assigned within which Napoleon should be at liberty to walk or ride unattended." There were to be *some* limits, but they were to be "reasonable." Napoleon had, in fact, a circuit of some twelve miles within which he might walk or ride unattended.

In an existence thus straitly ordered for him there was little room for irregularities on his part, and if quest were made of amorous intrigue it would be quite fruitless. Had any light-behaved lady desired to dispel the gloom of the outlawed emperor, she would have had to be bold enough to ride up to Longwood under an escort provided by Lowe! Napoleon himself, however, seems to have sought no distractions of the kind. It was difficult to get him abroad from Longwood for any sort of social intercourse. An invitation to meet the Countess of Loudon at dinner was brusquely declined—and no wonder, for it was addressed to "General Bonaparte." As time went on there was little of the gallant in his appearance. He breakfasted once at the house of Sir William Dove, (on the other side of the island), who pronounced him "as fat and as round as a China pig."

The *amours* of the First Consul and Emperor were not indeed wholly forgotten by Napoleon on the Rock, but there is no craving for new ones. Passion flies St. Helena! The deserted man talked much of his wife, the unresponsive Marie Louise, from whom he could get not so much as a scrap of paper. He talked of and lauded his mother. He talked often and fondly of his son.

He was full of moods, as may be fancied.

To quicken all the leaden hours was a task too heavy even for his busy genius. He learnt a little English, he dictated memoirs, he played chess, he read books and newspapers, he set Gourgaud mathematical problems, and in the latter half of 1819 and the earlier half of 1820 he found some solace in gardening. In the first two years of his captivity his spirits were sometimes high and even exuberant; and in the exercise of his splendid intellect he must have found some genuine enjoyment. But at heart he was miserable, spiting himself like a cross child, and allowing petty insults to fester within him. Now he was calm, proud, and grand, now irritable and wayward.

He could not make the great peace with fate; the world of his enemies was not worth the strife he kept with it (did he not, even when fronting death, leave a legacy to Cantillon for attempting to assassinate Wellington?); and he, the captain of men, had no "captain Christ" to whom at last to yield his soul in resignation.

The most interesting account that has come down to us of the first period at St. Helena is Mrs. Abell's (*Recollections of the Emperor Napoleon at St. Helena*[1]), published about twenty-three years after Napoleon's death. Mrs. Abell was the little Betsy Balcombe whose father was Napoleon's first host on the island. The Briars, Balcombe's estate, a mile and a half out of Jamestown, was long celebrated, says O'Meara, "for the genuine old English hospitality of the proprietor." Napoleon had for his six or seven weeks' residence a small pavilion, twenty yards or so from the dwelling-house, "consisting of one good room on the ground-floor and two garrets." In the lower room, where his camp-bed was set up, he slept, ate, read, and began the dictation of his memoirs. Balcombe fitted up a kitchen for him. So exiguous was the accommodation in the pavilion that the man who had tenanted, the Tuileries "good-naturedly walked out after he had finished his dinner, in order to allow his domestics an opportunity of eating theirs in the room which he had just quitted."

Little Betsy Balcombe, who spoke French with fluency, was made a pet of by Napoleon. She was his "Meese Betsee," when he began to trust himself with a word or two of English, and he romped with her, playing blindman's-buff, and running from a cow that he pretended was charging him in a meadow. He chaffed the child and her father about the English habit of sitting over the wine at dinner; Frenchmen, he said, were never so ungallant. It is from Betsy that we hear

---

1. *Recollections of Napoleon at St. Helena - The Remarkable Story of a Fallen Emperor and a Teenage Girl* by Mrs. Abell (late Miss Elizabeth Balcombe) also published by Leonaur.

of Napoleon's wrestlings with English, over which he stumbled heavily till the end. Chaffing a lady of the suite, he would explain: "This is my lofe, this is my mistress," till the British matron in good Mrs. Balcombe rose in explanation of the objectionable meaning attached by the nineteenth century to this romantic appellation of the Shakespearean age.

From these sweet childish recollections, the *naïveté* of which seems to visualize the years of Betsy's teens with the crystalline perception of a baby soul, we learn something of the impression made on the sensitive plate of femininity by the chained demon of the island—as to many, by hearsay, and by imagination, he had presented himself. Scarce had the inhabitants of St. Helena heard of Waterloo, when, lo! the vanquished sovereign was in the offing. Vulgar eyes spied on his landing, thoughtless feet pressed on his pathway upwards from the town to the purveyor's cottage. Then did the clear eyes of childhood behold as a man (as one, moreover, who had a genial side, turning to childhood's playfulness) this ogreish vision of the nursery. Hear what little Betsy tells of her own conception.

To her, Napoleon had been a monster "with one flaming red eye in the middle of his forehead and long teeth protruding from his mouth, with which he tore to pieces naughty little girls, especially those who did not know their lessons." This dreadful dream resolved itself into a personality struggling with broken English, teasing Betsy, perhaps by hiding her first ball-dress almost to the hour of dressing, but who, in general, gave to the little companion a kindly patience which stands out against the intolerance of adult opposition. Betsy sings her little songs to the captive, prison linnet that she was. Betsy dares to invade the garden tent wherein Napoleon dictates the memoirs of those wondrous twenty years of lordship. She handles fearlessly that beautiful service of *Sèvres* china, given to the emperor by the City of Paris, painted with scenes from his campaigns. He, as we know, regarded these familiarities with the amusement he had often experienced at a masked ball. The child carried away with her, from the island, a lock of Napoleon's hair, a souvenir she had begged of her playmate. "Meese Betsee" had indeed memories for which the hero-worshipping would vainly have bartered gold. The girl stood by when that Frenchwoman, wife of an island official, knelt to kiss the garden turf at The Briars where an "N" had been marked by the faithful courtiers. These things the child, with her child's instinctive delicacy, kept in her little heart.

Some other children, too, come into the picture: little Bertrands, little Montholons, and a young Las Cases, captives like their parents. Some were born on the rock of exile; their advent welcomed by Napoleon as reconciling the caged mother to her doom for one more year. "*Faites lui un enfant*" was his adjuration to the Comte Bertrand, when the *comtesse* sickened in the tropic steam so far from France, or from the Irish land of her ancestry. When the pretty and vivacious Comtesse Bertrand was confined in the winter of 1817, she brought the newly-born into Napoleon's presence with the words:

> Sire, I have the honour to present to your Majesty *le premier Français* who, since your arrival, has entered Longwood without Lord Bathurst's permission.

This child, by the way, was rather curiously named after the Emperors of Austria and Russia and the Duke of Wellington.

Then, as the years dragged on, first one and then another of the little feminine band dropped away. Betsy to England with her parents, when Balcombe had fallen under suspicion of some injudicious, if not nefarious, dealing with the imperial captive, to whom he acted as purveyor; Madame de Montholon, later, to France with much misgiving on the part of the authorities lest she should have carried off the emperor's memoirs on her person, or packed among her clothing. None left at last, save Madame Bertrand, who had been the most unwilling of them all to make the journey into banishment.

There is, besides the engaging Betsy, one other English girl of whom we catch a moment's glimpse. The French *entourage*, who promptly christened her the Nymph, had observed the young lady one day in her rustic chasm, and reported on the incident to Napoleon. He, by and by, set out on horseback for a peep at the fair islander; but she, it seems, had somehow got wind of the design, and donned the outfit of the Philistine. The spell was thereby broken. The girl's relatives, too, felt uneasy at the notice accorded by the prisoner-of-war. The attentions of an ex-emperor of whom tales, not underspiced we may believe, had reached their isolation were open to suspicion. Napoleon himself perceived or heard of their timidities; he was in no way inclined to give occasion to the enemy (it was in any case a matter of small interest), and he sought the Nymph no more.

Report was put about that the youthful and pretty Miss Susanna Johnson, Lady Lowe's daughter by her first husband, had "ventured to come alone to Longwood," where, meeting the ex-emperor, she received a rose from his hand. A stepdaughter of the governor would scarcely have taken so risky a jaunt, and Miss Johnson's half-sister, Miss Lowe, declared the story "a pure invention; such a thing was impossible."

Between the rare forms of womanhood seen at St. Helena, so remote from the world that had shaped itself trembling beneath Napoleon's hand, and those women—whether of the Tuileries, of the *coulisses*, or of foreign courts—among whom the dictator had reigned, what contrasts may the fancy make! Napoleon himself, if the contrasts were ever made by him, was doubtless very little moved. Already the vulture gnawed: the malignant disorder of the body joined with the lessened vigour of the mind (for he had lived a thousand lives in one, and Nature strikes at last) conspired to draw on the apathy of age forestalled: already there had fallen a shadow of the silent shores of death. The immense cerebration was being reduced to the flywheel operation of trivialities, of the everlasting hysterics of the younger members of the suite. The exasperated nerves took outlet in petulance, the conqueror skulked behind the shutters of dismal Longwood, behind the curtains of the bed, shrinking like the stricken beast from the pertinacious efforts of officialism to set an eye upon him, to certify that he was still within the prison.

Anon, pleased as a child with a new toy, the conqueror sat at the chess-board, rendered careless in his play by admiration of the beautiful Chinese chessmen. They were sent by a member of the Elphinstone family who had touched at the island on his way home from the Celestial Empire to England: an offering in recollection of a cup of cold water, for Napoleon on the field of Waterloo had sent drink from his own canteen to another member of the family wounded in that "Valley of Decision." A sister of the family, Lady Malcolm, has recorded (*A Diary of St. Helena*), like little Betsy, her surprise at the real Napoleon of the captivity. The embodiment of all evil in one countenance, which she had awaited, ended in a face not expressive to her judgment of any immense capacity, but with the aspect of benevolence.

This feeling of surprise was common to many of the visitors to the island who were for the first time confronted with the bogey-man of rumour. Little Betsy's notion was perhaps more comically materialised; it was hardly more grotesque. We hear of the young Scotswoman, Mrs. Stewart, who visited St. Helena on her way home from India, and with whom Napoleon discussed his favourite Ossian. "How entirely different from what we fancied him to be!" was her exclamation. This man, who had made—as all the world was then saying—a shambles of Europe, what could he be but a ghoul! How indeed were any of them to understand that the Napoleon of their imagination should in a day of utter weariness find rest in laying down the mask and unbending to these small variants of the island solitude?

On the constant petty troubles within the walls of Longwood we need dwell but little longer. These bickerings, jealousies, and squabbles were not so much between the two women—Mme. de Montholon and Mme. Bertrand—who shared the emperor's fate, as among the younger menkind of the small establishment. Napoleon bore with surprising self-control many of the disagreeables entailed by the conditions of life in that narrow spot. Then upon occasion, goaded beyond endurance, he would rap out a reminder to the foolish children—what indeed were their misfortunes, what indeed the contrasts of their present to their past, as compared with his own?

The gentle Comtesse de Montholon, ever for making the best of an unhappy situation, set herself against all quarrelling; and she, though not remaining to the end of his expiation on the Rock, did more perhaps than Bertrand's wife to soothe the closing years and months of Napoleon's exile, of his physical torment, when the malignant gastric ulceration sent him in anguish to the floor. For five years she bore her part in the tragi-comedy, a gentle companion and guest at Napoleon's table; and to her, as to the Bertrands, children were born. She did not quite escape calumny. We hear that Madame Bertrand, her Celtic nature fired with jealousy, at some real or imagined preference of Napoleon for the French Comtesse, cast it in her teeth that she had shared the emperor's room.

M. Philippe Gounard has dealt with this painful subject, arguing its *invraisemblance*; there is a good deal of ungenerous and rather scurrilous writing on this subject, but not an ounce of proof against Mme. de Montholon. The de Montholons were favoured by Napoleon at St. Helena, and both of them were in his confidence; but, were there a suspicion of truth in the statements about Mme. de Montholon, the husband's reputation would suffer even worse things than the wife's, for he knew her every movement, and there is not a trace of the pander in his affection for and devotion to the emperor. Napoleon openly regretted to Montholon the departure of Mme. de Montholon from St. Helena, and Montholon wrote to her of this with pride.

The emperor very much regrets your departure. His tears

flowed for you, perhaps for the first time in his life.

So far is this case from being proved, that any argument would *dis*prove it.

When death struck off the shackles, Mme. Bertrand alone of the little feminine band looked upon the quiet face "before decay's effacing fingers" had swept from it the heroic lineaments. She looked down from her tall height, for she was nearly six feet, she the handsomest woman seen in St. Helena, says the chronicler Betsy, recalling her childish admiration for the new-comer. She, who had been the most reluctant of the little company of exiles, was to be the only woman fated to stand before the lifeless hero.

We see Mme. Bertrand, first of all, in her girlhood, as Miss Frances Dillon. Her father was an Irishman who had thrown in his cause with Royalist France, and whose head had fallen in the Terror. The Lady Jerningham of the day was her aunt. Fanny Dillon must have towered above Bonaparte as she danced the "*Boulangère*," a country-dance, with him in the camp at Boulogne.

Some betrothal had occurred in her early girlhood—then she married Bertrand the faithful *maréchal*. With him she shared Napoleon's stay at Elba.

The decision that Bertrand should be one of the ex-emperor's suite at St. Helena drove Madame Bertrand almost to despair. We are told that she attempted suicide while on the *Bellerophon*. Her attempt at drowning failed, and she spent the last five years and a half with Napoleon. Between Mme. Bertrand and Napoleon, as time went on, there was considerable friction. Even upon Bertrand himself the fret of the long imprisonment told before the end. He would have been glad to get away and attend to the education of his children. For Madame Bertrand, even if she did prove fretful and petulant, we can find a great deal of pity and excuse. She did not at any time share her husband's devotion to the captive, and, prisoned as she was in a tropical region, the complications of maternity tried the unhappy woman's health. The Duchesse d'Abrantès praises her as one of those "qui *ont adouci l'agonie de l'Empereur*" but there was little warmth in her attentions.

If, for any dealings with the Sex, Napoleon deserved chastisement at the hand of Fate, he perhaps received it in the absence from his dying hours of one single loving woman.

Napoleon, Lover and Husband

Contents

Youth	207
Thoughts of Marriage	215
Josephine de Beauharnais	222
Citizeness Bonaparte	229
Madame Fourès	238
Reconciliation	245
La Grassini	252
Footlight Beauties	260
Readers	268
Josephine's Coronation	276
Madame ★★★★,	283
Stéphanie de Beauharnais	290
Eléonore	298
Hortense	304
Madame Walewska	310
The Divorce	333
Marie-Louise	341
Marie-Louise: part 2	349
Elba	356

The Hundred Days.	365
Summary	372

CHAPTER 1
Youth

Paris, Thursday, 22nd, 1787,
Hotel de Cherbourg,
Rue du Four-Saint-Honoré.
After leaving the opera I wandered about in the garden of the Palais-Royal. Strongly impressed by the scenes which I had just witnessed, my mind in ebullition, exhilarated by the music, I was at first insensible of the cold; but, as the scenes which I had beheld faded, I became conscious of the wintry air and turned to seek shelter under the colonnade. I was upon the threshold of the iron gates when my glance fell upon a woman, and I stopped to look at her. The hour, her extreme youth, and general appearance left no doubt as to her social status, yet she looked modest, and when she stopped and confronted me it was not boldly but in a manner perfectly in accord with her appearance. Her diffidence encouraged me and I spoke to her; I, who have always been so impressed with the odiousness of such a calling as hers, have always shunned such women and considered myself contaminated by so much as a look from one of her class, now voluntarily addressed one; but this girl's pale face, delicate appearance, and sweet voice effaced all my old prejudices, and I said to myself: 'Here is a person whom it would be wise to study, as I desire to know something of this class of women.'

'You look cold,' I said to her. 'How can you wander about on such a chilly night?'

'The cold exhilarates me, and then—it is my life; I must seek acquaintances.'

The indifferent and business-like tone of her answer pleased me, and I walked on beside her. 'You look delicate,' I said. 'I don't understand how you can endure such a life as yours must be.'

'*Dame!* I must do something. I know no other way of earning a livelihood and I don't wish to starve!'

'But could you not find some other occupation—something less wearing physically?' I asked.

'Not now, it is too late.'

I was delighted with her frankness, never having elicited such replies in my previous experiences.

'You must come from the North,' I said, 'since you do not mind the cold.'

'Yes, I come from Nantes, in Brittany.'

'I know that part of the country well. *Mademoiselle*, I wish you would tell me the story of your downfall.'

'It was an officer, like yourself, who caused it.'

'Do you regret it?'

'I do indeed!' she answered, in a voice whose depth of feeling surprised me. 'I assure you I do; my sister is happily settled, and you cannot imagine how I wish that I too had a home.'

'How did you happen to come to Paris?'

'I was abandoned by the officer who seduced me and obliged to flee from my mother's anger; having made the acquaintance of another officer I accompanied him to Paris; then, he too left me, and a third, with whom I have lived for three years, succeeded him; although a Frenchman he was called by business to London and is still there, so I am obliged to shift for myself. Let us go to your rooms.'

'Why should we go there?'

'Don't be a silly! We will warm ourselves and then—perhaps you will be glad to have me there.'

I was far from scrupulous and had piqued her only that she should not run away from the sermon I was mentally preparing, and the modesty I intended to parade—before proving to her that it was a virtue I did not possess.

At the time when this was written Bonaparte was aged eighteen years and three months, having been born on the 15th of August, 1769. We have the right to suppose that this was the first woman with whom he had any connection, and reviewing rapidly the history of his youth we shall find sufficient reasons to confirm this opinion. Napoleon himself made a note, with dates, of such love-affairs as left an impression upon his memory; those which I have been able to investigate I have found to be absolutely correct.

He left Ajaccio for France on the 15th of December, 1778, when he was but nine and a half years of age. The feminine memories which he carried with him from his island were those of his nurse, Camilla Carbone, who was the widow Ilari, and of a little schoolmate, "*La Giacominetta*," of whom he often spoke in the sad days at Saint Helena. Later in life he showered benefits upon his nurse, her daughter, Mme. Tavera, and her granddaughter, Mme. Poli, whom he had himself christened Faustina; he was unable to do anything for his foster-brother, Ignatio Ilari, because when very young Ilari had espoused the cause of the English party and enlisted in the English Navy.

Of the nurses who had charge of Napoleon's infancy and childhood one, Minana Saveria, remained until her death with Mme. Bonaparte; the other, Mammuccia Caterina, died before the Empire was established, as did also little Giacominetta, for whose sake, when a lad, Bonaparte had borne much teasing.

At the college of Autun, where he was a pupil from the 1st of January to the 12th of May, 1779; at the college of Brienne, where he was from May, 1779, to October 14th, 1784, at the military school in Paris where he spent the year from October 22nd, 1784, to October 30th, 1785, no woman entered his life. Even admitting the statement advanced by Mme. D'Abranèes that, contrary to the strict rules of the *Ecole Militaire*, Bonaparte, under the pretext of a sprain, spent eight days in the apartment of M. Permon, No. 5 Place Conti, I see no reason to change my belief, for at that time he was but a stripling of sixteen.

Napoleon went to Valence on the 30th of October, 1785, and left that place to pass his vacation in Corsica on the 16th of September, 1786, after a sojourn of less than a year; he did not return from the island until the 12th of September, 1787, and it was then that he made his journey to the capital; therefore an adventure, prior to that of the 22nd of November, 1787, could hardly have taken place between his leaving the *Ecole Militaire* and his return to Paris.

He did not engage in any gallantries while in Corsica, nor yet in Valence; indeed, during his sojourn in the latter place he appeared to be timid, rather melancholy, absorbed in his studies and desirous only of standing well in his classes and being well received socially. He had carried to Valence a letter of introduction to Mgr. de Tardivon, Abbé de Saint-Ruff, from the Marbeufs, and to this ecclesiastical dignitary, who, crossed and mitred, gave tone to the town, he owed his *entrée* into the best houses of the city, to Mme, Grégoire du Colombier's, Mme. Lauberie de Saint Germain's and Mme. de Laurencin's.

These ladies, particularly the latter two, held the best positions in the province, belonged to the lesser nobility and lived handsomely. They were prejudiced against the lives of the officers whom they admitted to their houses, and never permitted any intimacy between their daughters and young men whose conduct they did not consider irreproachable.

Bonaparte may have entertained some vague ideas of marriage with Caroline du Colombier, who was permitted by her mother rather more liberty than other girls enjoyed. He was barely seventeen at that time, and she was considerably his senior; if he admired her, the attentions which he paid her were chaste, deferential and boyish: à la Rousseau. It was not long, however, before Mlle. du Colombier married an officer, M. Garempel de Bressieux, and left Valence and went to live in an old *château* in the country.

Nearly twenty years later, when Napoleon was in camp at Boulogne, he received a letter from her recommending her brother to his notice, and although he had not seen the object of his boyish admiration since her marriage, he answered by return of post, assuring her that he would seize the first occasion to be useful to M. du Colombier and saying:

> The memory of your mother and yourself has always been dear to me. I see by your letter that you live near Lyons, and I must reproach you for not calling while I was there, as it would have given me great pleasure to have seen you.

This advice was not lost, and when, on April 12th, 1806, Napoleon passed through Lyons on his way to the coronation at Milan, Mme. de Bressieux was among the first to request an interview. She was terribly changed, aged, and no longer the pretty Caroline of bygone days, nevertheless she obtained all she asked for: the erasure of certain names on the list of *émigrés*, a position for her husband, and a lieutenancy for her brother. On New Year's day of 1807 Mme, de Bressieux recalled herself to the emperor's memory by a letter asking for news of his health. Napoleon responded promptly, and in 1808 he made her lady-in-waiting upon *Madame Mère*, called her husband to preside over the electoral college of Isière, and in 1810 created him a baron of the Empire.

Such was the grateful memory Napoleon cherished for all who had been kind to him in his youth; there were none whose fortunes he did not assure, as there were none whom he forgot to mention during his captivity; women, if possible, received the greater share of his gratitude, and even when he had reason to feel some bitterness towards them it was enough that they should once have shown him kindness. Thus Mlle. de Lauberie de Saint-Germain, like Mlle. du Colombier, had preferred another to him and married her cousin, M. Bachasson de Montalivet; but Napoleon harboured no resentment, and it is well known that he made M. de Montalivet's fortune, creating him successively *préfet de la Manche* and of Seine-et-Oise, director general for bridges and public roads, minister of the Interior and count of the Empire with an endowment of eighty thousand *francs*. Mme. de Montalivet, of whom he once said, "Of old I loved both her virtues and her beauty," he named a lady of the empress's household in 1806.

Mme. de Montalivet, however, did not accept this honour unconditionally, saying to the emperor:

> Your Majesty knows my belief regarding a woman's duty in this world; the favour which you have had the goodness to accord me, and which many will envy, would seem to me a misfortune if it prevented me from attending my husband when he has the gout, or nursing my children when Providence gives me any.

The emperor at first frowned at Mme. de Montalivet's frankness, but after a moment said graciously:

> Ah, *madame*, you wish to dictate terms; I am unaccustomed to that, but on this occasion I submit. Accept the position, and all shall be so arranged that your duties as wife and mother shall not be interfered with.

Mme. de Montalivet's position remained a nominal one, but that did not prevent Napoleon from showing her particular attention; he was fond of the whole family and said of them:

> The family integrity is indubitable; it is composed of lovable people and I believe firmly in the disinterestedness of their affection.

Such were the recollections which Napoleon had of Valence. They were dear to his heart, and of a kind which those young girls might well be proud of inspiring. He had no other intimacies that we know of, and in his private journal no others are mentioned; like Hippolite, he appears to have been more in love with glory in those days, than with women; in confirmation of this witness this extract from a letter written at that time:

> If I had to compare the days of Sparta and Rome with our modern times I would say *here* reigns love, *there* reigned love of country. Judging by the opposite effects which these passions produce one seems authorized in believing them incomparable. One thing is certain: people who abandon themselves to gallantry lose the ability to even conceive of the existence of a patriot, and we have reached that point today.

It is almost with a sense of certitude that we conclude that the girl he met in the Palais-Royal was his first mistress. The adventure, vulgar though it was, does not the less reveal his character; there is his misogyny, his critical spirit, brusque speech, and the habit of interrogation which he never renounced; his good memory, also, is noticeable in his account of it, for he reproduced in striking fashion the girl's manner of speech, even to the exclamation, *Dame!* which proved her Breton origin.

It is doubtful if Napoleon ever saw this girl again, for although among his papers, dated during that sojourn in Paris, there is a dissertation on patriotism which is addressed to a young lady, it is hardly a topic upon which one would write to a woman of her class.

After this sojourn in Paris, which lasted from October to December of 1787, Bonaparte again returned to Corsica, where he arrived on the 1st of January, 1Y88. He spent six months on the island, rejoining his regiment at Auxonne on the 1st of June; no trace of any love-affair at that place remains to us.

In the early part of 1789 he was sent to Seurre with a detachment, and is accredited with holding relations there, first with a Mme. L———z, *née* N———s, the wife of the collector at the salt depot, later with a farmer's wife, Mme. G———t, to whose house he went to drink milk, and, lastly, with the daughter of the house wherein he lodged. This seems crowding a good deal into twenty-five days, during which time his books are silent witnesses to his assiduous study; nevertheless, when, fourteen years later, on the 6th of April, 1805, Napoleon passed through Seurre on his way to Milan, it is claimed that M. de Thiard, who was at that time his chamberlain, introduced into his presence the boarding-house young woman, and that he presented her with a scholarship in a government school for her son, a lad of twelve. The stated age of this child precludes the idea that Napoleon believed him to be his son; moreover, had the emperor entertained the least doubt upon the subject he would have done far more for the boy, and that without its being asked of him.

In Corsica, where he spent the entire year of 1790, at Auxonne, at Valence, again in Corsica, then, in the middle of 1792, at Paris, there were no love-affairs; we hear of none during the first campaign in the South against the Federalists, of none at Toulon.

We must deliberately skip over a period of four years, during which the young lieutenant became a general of brigade and was placed in command of the artillery in Italy, where, in 1794, the Convention sent one of its influential members, the Citizen Louis Turreau, on a mission to the army.

Representative Turreau was accompanied on his journey by his bride, who was the daughter of a surgeon at Versailles and a remarkably pretty woman; he arrived at Cairo, in Piedmont, where Bonaparte was stationed, on the 21st of September, and, finding the young officer congenial, cultivated his acquaintance; while Mme. Turreau and the artilleryman soon arrived at an understanding, Bonaparte's intimacy with Mme. Turreau never assumed the proportions of a *liaison*, for she was too fickle to remain long constant, and, evidently, it never aroused the husband's jealousy, for he retained a high opinion of the young officer's ability, and when the Convention was in danger it was he, as well as Barras, who urged confiding the command of the troops to Bonaparte and, with the Corsican deputies, became his surety.

Bonaparte did not forget this service, and when placed in command of the army in Italy he took Turreau, who had not been re-elected, with him as commissary-general. Mme. Turreau again accompanied her husband, and, in default of the general-in-chief, made the best of such lovers as courted her; her conduct gave rise to continual scenes of jealousy, and Turreau, so it is said, died of a broken heart. The widow returned to Versailles, and in the early days of the Empire was dragging out a dreary existence there, when, one day, the emperor chanced to mention her before Berthier, who was also a native of the town. The general had known Mme. Turreau from childhood, but for years had carefully shunned her; however, when he saw that the emperor took an interest in his old schoolfellow, he renewed the acquaintanceship and espoused her cause, while Napoleon, never forgetful of a kindness, made haste to extricate *madame* from her financial embarrassment, granted all her requests and assured for her the realization of her rosiest dreams.

With the exception of Mme. Turreau, who threw herself at his head, women paid but scant attention to the little, pale, thin officer who was always badly dressed and regardless of his appearance, and Napoleon's early loves resolved themselves into trivial flirtations or vulgar adventures. He himself thought but little about women, being absorbed by his ambitious projects, and there was another, and valid reason for his chastity, he was poor. Poverty, however, did for him what it has done for many another man—forced him to consider matrimony that he might be the sole recipient of a woman's caresses.

Chapter 2

Thoughts of Marriage

While at Marseilles Napoleon played at love with Mme. Joseph Bonaparte's sister, Désirée-Eugénie Clary, then a pretty girl of sixteen; she believed his attentions to be serious. Her girlishness vanished and she developed a woman's affection for him. Sixty-five years later the rough drafts of her letters to Napoleon were found among her effects; they were all signed "Eugénie," for after the fashion of the time the young girl, whom her family called Désirée, had wished to be called by her lover by a name not used by others; these letters, which are the spontaneous outpouring of a pure affection, breathe the spirit of the period following upon the Reign of Terror, when women made love a religion; indeed, it was the only religion which existed on the ruins of society.

Mlle. Clary wrote in one of her letters:

> Oh, my friend take care of yourself for my sake, for I could not live without you; guard as sacredly as I shall the promise which binds us, for were it broken I should die.

Napoleon's acquaintance with Mlle. Clary dated from January or February, 1795, and the engagement, if there was a formal one, must have taken place on the 21st of April, when Bonaparte passed through Marseilles on his way to Paris. There was no opposition to the marriage from the Clary family, for Joseph and his wife had long desired it, and Désirée's father, who is reported to have said "that one Bonaparte in the family was quite enough for him," had died on the 20th of January, 1794, and the remaining members of the family, Mme. Clary and her son, readily yielded to the young girl's wishes; her youth was no obstacle to the marriage, for at that time girls were usually wed in their eighteenth year, and the First Civil Code had just fixed the thirteenth year as the legal age for a female to marry. Désirée Clary afterwards claimed, and officially stated, that at this time she was between thirteen and fourteen years of age, but she must have been nearer seventeen, as she was born on the 9th of November, 1777.

Bonaparte arrived in Paris in May; he was out of favour, out of funds, and his only hope lay in this marriage, failing in which nothing remained for him but to take service in Turkey, or, like many others, to speculate in national securities. Even when, by degrees, his position improved, and he was employed by the Committee on Public Welfare on plans for the campaign, his position was precarious, and realising its instability, believing that his sole salvation lay in this marriage, he urged Joseph to have a date fixed for the wedding, and in every letter which he wrote his brother at that time messages for Désirée appeared.

For a while Mlle. Clary was a faithful correspondent, but while at Genoa with her sister and brother-in-law she neglected her lover, and in one of Napoleon's letters he said, "The road to Genoa leads through the waters of Lethe," called her the "silent one," and constantly reproached her for not writing. Finally, becoming impatient, he determined that a definite understanding should be arrived at, and wrote to Joseph that he *must* interview Désirée's brother and bring the matter to a head, and the following day, without giving his first letter time to reach Joseph, he wrote again saying:

> This affair must either be concluded or broken off. I await an answer with the greatest impatience.

Then a month passed, and save for friendly messages there was no correspondence between the pair.

The truth is, that Paris, the unknown, fascinating city which he had entered with a worn uniform, leaky boots, and a suite composed of a couple of hungry *aides-de-camps* had interposed itself and its captivating women between Napoleon and the little Marseillaise. What a contrast there must have been between the immature girl and the elegant and worldly women of the capital! Désirée could hardly have been beautiful, though there must have been a certain charm about her soft eyes with their pencilled brows, *retroussé* nose, laughing mouth and reserved yet tender manner; but between the young provincial and the elegant, graceful, well-dressed and beautiful, if artificial, Parisian women, there was the same difference as lies between hothouse fruit and that which ripens in the open air. The Parisians, created for a life of gaiety and excitement, highly refined in manner and adepts in the art of pleasing, were like hothouse fruit, which, carefully tended, reaches the highest state of perfection, and when exhibited to the best advantage by the fruiterer appears, with its fine colour and bloom, which the winds of heaven have never visited too roughly, much more appetizing than the fruit of the orchard which, kissed by the sun, whipped by the breeze, and not quite ripe, leaves in the mouth a fresh but somewhat tart taste.

Napoleon wrote:

> In Paris alone live women capable of holding the helm, A woman should live six months in Paris to learn what is her just due, and where her rightful domain.

A few days later he wrote:

> The women here, who are certainly the most beautiful in the world, play a great *rôle* in all the affairs in life.

The women who figured conspicuously in the society of that day certainly were beautiful and possessed of even a greater charm, a perfect knowledge of the amenities of life; better versed in the art of inspiring affection than able to give it, they completely fascinated the young officer, and, having nothing save his hand to offer, he proffered that freely, laying his heart and hand first at the feet of Mme. de Permon, then proposing to Mme. de la Bouchardie, later to Mme. de Lesparda and finally to Mme. de Beauharnais who took him at his word.

During all this time he never wrote to Désirée, and at last she lifted her voice in complaint, but so gently, so sweetly, that it sounds in one's ears like the sad strains of an Æolian harp. She wrote him:

> You have broken my heart, yet I am weak enough to forgive you everything. You are married and I have no longer the right to love and think of you; the only consolation which remains for me is to be assured of your belief in my constancy, then I long for death, for life is a burden, now that I may not consecrate it to you. I cannot accustom myself to the thought that you are married—it is too hard, too cruel! I will prove to you that I am more faithful to my engagement than you to yours, and, though you have broken the chain which united us, I shall hold it binding; I shall never marry. I wish you every happiness and all prosperity in your marriage, and I hope that the woman

you have chosen will make you as happy as I had meant to do, and as you deserve; but in the midst of your happiness remember poor Eugénie and pity her sad fate.

Forgetfulness was foreign to Bonaparte's nature, and the memory of this love which he had inspired was always a tender point with him; from a flirtation he had insensibly drifted into an entanglement which had ambition for its basis, and which had resulted in the breaking of a heart, and throughout his life he strove to undo the wrong and win forgiveness. While at Milan, in 1797, he planned a brilliant marriage for Désirée, who was in Rome with her sister and brother-in-law, Joseph being then ambassador at the court of Pius VI, and gave a warm letter of recommendation to General Duphot in which he spoke of him as "a fine man and distinguished officer;" and in a personal letter to Joseph he said, that an alliance with General Duphot would be a desirable one. Duphot made a favourable impression upon Mlle. Clary, and their marriage contract was about to be signed when the terrible scene of December 28th took place and Désirée's dress was stained with the blood of her betrothed.

After refusing several offers, Désirée finally consented, while Napoleon was in Egypt, to marry General Bernadotte. It was considered a fine match, but he was a most insupportable Jacobite, narrow-minded and opinionated; a Bearnais by birth, he yet had none of the Gascon's sprightliness or readiness of speech, but possessed all their shrewdness and hid under apparent frankness a scheming brain. He held Mme. de Staël to be the cleverest of her sex because she was the most pedantic, and he spent the honeymoon in laying down the law to his young wife.

The news of this marriage reached Bonaparte at Cairo, and although Bernadotte was his enemy, and the union displeased him, he wrote most kindly to Désirée, wishing her all happiness.

When Napoleon returned from Egypt the first person to solicit a favour was Mme. Bernadotte, who asked him to stand godfather to her infant son. Intuitively she knew that a son was the one thing lacking to complete Napoleon's happiness, and, as if to spite Josephine, whom she hated, and whom she always spoke of as the "old woman," Désirée boasted of her maternity. Bonaparte kindly consented to stand for the child, and with Ossian's martial ballads in mind named the baby Oscar. Years later Napoleon said:

Bernadotte's becoming a Marshal of France, Prince of Pontecorvo and King of Sweden was all owing to his marriage with my first sweetheart.

It was for her sake that Napoleon pardoned all Bernadotte's disloyalty during the Empire.

From the very first Bernadotte manifested his opposition to Bonaparte; nevertheless, he was called to a seat in the Council of State, then named general-in-chief of the army in the West, where he not only opposed, but openly conspired against the First Consul, aspiring to gain command of the army. For this he received no punishment. Bonaparte simply, in order to get rid of him, appointed him minister plenipotentiary to the United States, a post which Bernadotte expressed himself as perfectly willing to accept, playing his game so well, however, that the frigate which was to bear him to his destination was never ready to sail.

The following year saw the conspiracy in which Moreau was implicated, and Bernadotte again escaped unpunished, because Napoleon so willed it, Désirée's welfare being always in his mind; he did still more for her, for, redeeming Moreau's estate, his property at Grosbois, and his hotel in the rue d'Anjou, for which he paid four hundred thousand *francs*, he presented it to Bernadotte. The Empire established, Napoleon, for Eugénie's sake, created her husband a marshal of the empire, chief of the eighth corps of the Legion of Honor, president of the electoral college of Vaucluse and *Chevalier de l'Aigle Noir*; for Désirée's sake he gave the couple an income of three hundred thousand *francs*, a lump sum of two hundred thousand *francs* and the sovereignty of the principality of Pontecorvo.

For the love of her Napoleon forgave Bernadotte after Auerstaedt, Wagram, and Walcheren, condoned two military blunders, which were probably something more serious than blunders, coming as they did on top of a flagrant conspiracy in which Bernadotte, Fouché and Talleyrand, in complicity with the royalists, brought into play the same tactics by which, in 1814, the return of Louis le Désirée was effected.

Thus, over her husband's shoulders, Napoleon's one-time sweetheart received attentions and favours which would be surprising did we not know that he was ever actuated by the desire to atone for the sorrow and mortification he had once caused her. Two days after the Battle of Spandau, in which Bernadotte was wounded, Napoleon wrote to him, saying:

I am glad to learn that Mme. Bernadotte is with you; pray give her my affectionate regards and add that I have one little thing to reproach her with. She might have written me a line giving me the news of Paris, but I will have it out with her when we meet.

Although Mme. Bernadotte never appeared at court, for she detested Josephine and the entire Beauharnais family and was at no pains to conceal her dislike, Napoleon showered gifts upon her. He presented her with priceless *Sèvres* vases and Gobelin tapestries, it was for her that he reserved one of the three magnificent fur pelisses which the Emperor of Russia presented to him after Erfurt; yet, appearances to the contrary, his friendship was entirely disinterested. Was it not of Désirée's aggrandisement that he was thinking, when, after Walcheren, he meditated sending Bernadotte to Rome as governor-general to represent the court of France at the Quirinal, thus creating him a high imperial dignitary with an emolument of three million *francs*, and putting him upon an equality with Borghese who was at Turin, Elias at Florence, and almost with Eugène who was at Milan?

When the sovereignty of Sweden was offered to Eugène de Beauharnais he declined the honour, not wishing to become an apostate, and it was due to the good-natured neutrality of Napoleon that Bernadotte was elected hereditary prince of that country. If Napoleon's political moves at this period are incomprehensible to some historians, it is because they failed to take into account the part which his heart played in the affairs of state; he was seduced by the pleasure of seeing the woman in whom he took so warm an interest become a queen, his godson heir apparent to a throne. He regulated minutely the details of Désirée's presentation and leave-taking as princess of Sweden, and, unprecedented favour, he invited her to one of the family's Sunday dinners. He conferred upon the newly-elected Prince of Sweden a purse of a million *francs* from the public treasury, repurchased the property with which he had originally presented him, negotiated with him the return of Pontecorvo and gave a title and sum of money to Bernadotte's brother; certainly Napoleon was justified in writing to Désirée.

You must long since have been convinced of the interest I take in your family.

Four months after the receipt of all this kindness Bernadotte combined with Russia against Napoleon; less than a year afterwards everything indicated that a rupture between France and Sweden was imminent, and Désirée, who had most reluctantly consented to take a short journey to Stockholm, then made haste to return to her hotel in the rue d'Anjou.

Then, exercising the greatest caution, Napoleon wrote to the Minister of Foreign Affairs requesting that he speak to the Swedish ambassador regarding Désirée's presence in France, and state, as delicately as possible, that he was sorry to see that the princess royal had come into the country without permission, which was not customary, and that he regretted her leaving her husband under the existing circumstances. Désirée paid no attention to the ambassador's admonitions, but proceeded to install herself, and in November, when war was about to be declared, the emperor wrote a second time and sent Cambacérès to the Queen of Spain (Julie Clary) saying that he wished the princess to leave Paris and return to Sweden as it was not proper that she should be in France at that time.

His wishes availed nothing, and Désirée remained in Paris, continued to order her dresses from Leroy, to receive her friends and hold her receptions; she went to the baths with her sister and returned to Paris as though nothing unusual was taking place; she even considered it singular that the Frenchmen whom she received should blame the former marshal of the Empire who had then assumed command of the allied forces in the north of Germany. If one can believe those who claim to be well informed, Désirée was both ungrateful and a traitor, and while conveying to her husband Napoleon's adjurations, acted between Bernadotte, Fouché and Talleyrand as an intermediary.

If demonstrated that Désirée profited by the emperor's weakness for her to become a link in an intrigue between conspirators who knew each other of old, one must think badly of her character, and it is pleasanter to believe that she remained in Paris because of her love for the city, that she might not leave her sister, nieces and friends, or be obliged to alter the habits of a lifetime.

She was in Paris in 1814, and took part, with other people of rank, in the visit of Alexander of Russia; she was still there in 1815, during the hundred days, and on the 17th of June, the eve of Waterloo, she ordered a nankin riding-habit and a percale dressing-gown trimmed with valenciennes from Leroy; her lack of interest in Napoleon's success in the stupendous game he was playing, with all Europe for his adversaries, clearly proves that hers was the forgetful spirit.

CHAPTER 3

Josephine de Beauharnais

Towards the end of October, 1795, hazard brought together the Vicomtesse de Beauharnais and General Bonaparte. The latter had sprung suddenly from obscurity to publicity, and his name, but recently so little known that Barras had written it "*Buona-Parta,*" had been spoken in thunderous tones to the whole of France by the cannon which crushed the rebel sections of the Convention.

Second in command of the army of the Interior, soon to be commander-in-chief, Bonaparte had ordered the disarmament of the Parisians. A youth came to his quarters begging permission to keep his father's sword; Napoleon saw the boy and, being attracted by him, granted his request, and the mother then called to express her thanks. She was a great lady, a *ci-devant vicomtesse*, the widow of a president of the constituency, of a courtier, of the commander-in-chief of the Army of the Rhine, and she was a revelation to Bonaparte; her title, birth and education, the easy, graceful manner in which she expressed her thanks, all charmed him.

For the first time in his twenty-six years of life the young provincial, to whom no woman of quality had ever paid the slightest attention, found himself in the presence of one of those elegant, accomplished and desirable creatures whom he had seen and admired from afar. He was in a position which gratified his pride, that of a protector, and this role which he played for the first time suited him marvellously; while Mme. Beauharnais, who was reduced to all sorts of expediencies, discerned at once what manner of man she had to deal with.

A Creole, native of the island of Martinique, she had been married at the age of sixteen to the Vicomte de Beauharnais; a marriage arranged by her aunt, who lived openly with the Marquis de Beauharnais, the bridegroom's father. From the time she first came to Paris, in 1779, Josephine Tascher de la Pagerie, Mme. de Beauharnais, led a wretched existence; deceived and abandoned by her husband, and finally separated from him, through no fault of hers, she had no social distractions; she was never presented at court, for she lived with her aunt whose position was equivocal, but it is claimed that after her separation from her husband she made use of her liberty. Returning to Martinique she remained there until her safety was threatened by the insurrection, when she escaped to France, and becoming reconciled with M. de Beauharnais, who was then deputy of the *Etats-Généraux*, president of the constituency and general-in-chief of the Army of the Rhine, she enjoyed a brief period of happiness; her *salon* was then frequented by men of note and letters, and for the first time she tasted the sweets of social position. Then came the Reign of Terror; Beauharnais was imprisoned and guillotined and she escaped only by a miracle.

When released from prison Josephine de Beauharnais was thirty years of age, the mother of two children and penniless. Aided by some feminine connections which she had formed in prison, for she . had none elsewhere, she launched herself into society. With the money which she received from Martinique, loans which she made wherever possible, debts which she contracted in every direction, she managed to keep up an appearance. She left her apartment in the rue de l'Université and rented from Louise-Julie Carreau, the wife of Talma, for the sum of four thousand pounds a year in cash, or ten thousand in notes, a small hotel. No. 6, rue Chantereine, where she installed herself in October, 1794.

A year passed, debts accumulated, and nothing came in; probably with Creole *insouciance* Josephine failed to give proper consideration to her financial affairs, or hoped that some miracle might extricate her from her difficulties, and, while showing herself everywhere where the society of that day amused itself, she picked up acquaintances who were instrumental in the restoration of some of her husband's property, but she ran through it as fast as it came into her possession. She possessed nothing, neither capital nor fixed income. At her marriage she had received a dot of one hundred thousand *francs* from which she was to receive a yearly interest at the rate of five *per cent.*; but her father was dead, her mother very poor, and the island blockaded by the English.

Her aunt, Mme. Renaudin, had given her some unimproved real estate, but it had long since been disposed of; moreover, no one can squeeze an income out of unimproved property, and of credit she had none. Mme. Renaudin helped her a little by loans, and there were one or two obliging bankers who accepted drafts on Martinique, who even advised her going to Hamburg where she could receive her remittances with less trouble; but she was in a desperate position, credit exhausted and age creeping on; it was at this critical moment that General Bonaparte rang the bell of the house in the rue Chantereine and returned the visit of Mme. la Vicomtesse de Beauharnais.

Napoleon did not know that the house, which was rather imposing in appearance, was the property of Citizeness Talma, who, when she was Mlle. Julie, had received it as a price of her favours to a lover; nor did he know that this property, in an out-of-the-way corner of Paris, within a stone's-throw of the rue Saint-Lazare, on which its garden, in almost its original extent, touches to this day, was worth only fifty thousand *francs*. A man-servant responded to the bell and ushered the general through a long open passage, on one side of which, in a sort of pavilion, the stable was situated, its open door revealing two black horses and a red cow; the carriage-house, which contained a shabby carriage, was carefully closed.

The passage gave into a garden in the centre of which stood the house, a modest structure of one story and basement surmounted by a mansard; four high windows pierced its *façade* and a low porch, with a simple balustrade in the style of a terrace, ran across it. Bonaparte mounted the steps, entered an antechamber, scantily furnished by a brass fountain, the lower half of an oak wardrobe and a pine settee, from whence the servant introduced him into the dining-room, where he was free to choose between a seat on one of the four black haircloth-covered chairs which surrounded the mahogany table, or to wander about and look at the engravings which, framed in black and gold, decorated the walls. The room was not luxurious, but here and there serving tables, of mahogany or of the yellow wood of Guadaloupe with marble tops and gilded trimmings, bore witness to former opulence; while behind the glass doors of two cabinets a collection of table accessories, and a tea-service of English plate made a fine showing; of silver, in the proper sense of the word, there was none.

Josephine, all tricked out by her maid, the Citizeness Louise Compoint, hastened to the dining-room to greet her guest; she could not receive him elsewhere as the first floor of the house comprised only that apartment, her bed-chamber and a small apartment which served as a dressing-room.

Josephine's bedroom, though simple, was tasteful and pretty, the furniture was of mahogany and the yellow wood of Guadaloupe; there was a gay toilet set of blue nankin with decorations of red and yellow coxcombs, the low double bed was daintily draped, and the room was ornamented by a harp of Renaud's make and a little marble bust of Socrates; the dressing-room, with the exception of a Renaud piano, was chiefly furnished with looking glasses; there was one on the toilet-table, another on the chest of drawers, one on the night stand, and over the chimney hung a double pier-glass.

Such were the surroundings of this high-bred woman. Except on festive occasions, when she brought out a small service of blue and white porcelain, she ate off earthen-ware; the table linen was composed of eight tablecloths, of which four were of bird's-eye, and all so worn, that when the inventory was taken the entire supply of household linen was estimated at a value of four pounds. Bonaparte was ignorant of all this; he did not know that the elegant and charming woman who stood before him, whose tasteful toilet pleased his eye, whose infinite grace troubled his senses, possessed scarcely enough underwear to clothe her decently; he saw only a charming and elegant woman, a woman to arouse desire.

Josephine's hair was brown, of a fine quality but not over luxurious; however, in those days, blonde wigs and a suspicion of powder were in vogue; her complexion was rather dark and already somewhat faded, but art concealed the ravages of time; her teeth were poor, but were never displayed, and she had a dear little mouth which was always curved in a slight smile, the sweetness of which accorded with the exceeding softness of her eyes, with her gentle expression and the touching quality of her voice, to catch a sound of which the servants, in later years, loitered in the corridors of the Tuileries. Her nose was small, with sensitive, quivering nostrils, and slightly inclined to be *retroussé*.

Her head, however, was not to be compared with her tall, supple body, which terminated in slender, arched feet, whose beauty may yet be divined by a glance at the shoes she once wore. Her form was unfettered, she did not even wear a girdle to support the bosom, which was, however, very small. General effect is everything, and this woman possessed a charm and grace peculiarly her own; long practice had rendered her every movement graceful and refined; she never lost an advantage, was constantly on her guard, leaving nothing to chance, and she had that indefinable nonchalance of the Creole which is so attractive, while about her floated like a perfume that sensuality which makes the Creole woman essentially feminine and is so intoxicating to man. Napoleon, younger and more inexperienced than the majority of men, was peculiarly susceptible to it; it was that about the woman which had appealed to him at their first meeting, even while she dazzled him by her imposing manner, which he spoke of as being "that calm and dignified demeanour which belongs to the old *régime*."

Mme. de Beauharnais saw that the young officer was completely captivated, and when he called the following day, and the day after, and so on day after day, she understood that her empire over him was absolute. Seeing Mme. de Beauharnais surrounded by men of the old court who were his superiors by rank and birth, Ségur, Montesquiou, Caulaincourt, all of whom treated him with a certain degree of familiarity, Napoleon failed to perceive that these men, who, in his estimation, had lost nothing of their former prestige, came to her house as bachelors, to divine that their wives would not visit there. Coming from the Jacobin circle in which he had always lived, and which at Vaucluse, Toulon, Nice, and Paris had advanced his interest, he took infinite delight in the company in which he found himself. The luxuries of the lady, like her nobility and social position, were all delusions, but his senses aiding, were accepted by Napoleon as realities.

A fortnight after his first visit they were lovers. Judging from writings they were still only friends, but a witness of the times tells us that transitions were rapid, that fine distinctions were not made, and the world moved fast.

They loved passionately. Such love was natural enough on his part; on hers—well, possibly it was equally so, for Bonaparte was a new toy, a savage to be tamed, and the lion of the day.

To a woman like Josephine, no longer in her first youth, such ardour, such intense passion, burning kisses and constant craving for her presence, was the most flattering of tributes, for it proved that she was still beautiful and able to please. All this made Napoleon attractive as a lover, but hardly recommended him for a husband; however, when he offered himself, he was accepted, for she was in a desperate situation and had nothing to lose by the marriage, while it offered a chance of betterment. Bonaparte was young and ambitious, was general-in-chief of the army of the Interior, the Directory had not forgotten that it was he who arranged the plans for the last Italian campaign, and Carnot proposed creating him commander-in-chief in the approaching campaign; such a marriage, therefore, might be her salvation and committed her to nothing, for divorces were easily obtained in those days when there was no longer any question of priests and religious ceremonies, and it was simply a contract which endured as long as both parties desired to observe it, but which meant nothing either to the woman's conscience or to society.

Bonaparte was a man capable of great things, and Josephine argued that if she played her part well she would share any honours accruing to him, while if he was killed she was sure of a pension as his widow. Nevertheless, she took some precautions; in the first place she dissimulated about her age, for she did not wish either her young lover, or any one, to know that she had passed her thirty-second year. Accompanied by Calmelet, her confidential adviser and one of the guardians of her children, and by a person of the name of Lesourd, she went to a notary's where those two certified:

> That Marie Josephine Tascher, widow of Citizen Beauharnais, was well known to them, that she was a native of the island of Martinique, and that as the island was at that moment occupied by the English it was impossible for her to secure a certificate of her birth.

Armed with this legal document Josephine was able to declare to the civil officer that she was born on the 23rd of June, 1767, whereas she was born on June 23rd, 1763.

Josephine also deceived Napoleon regarding her fortune, which one would suppose was a difficult thing to accomplish, but Napoleon accepted all her statements, and there was drawn up privately, with only the general's *aide-de-camp*, Lemarrois, as witness, the strangest marriage contract which had ever come under the notary's observation. There was no property in common of any sort, complete authority was given by the prospective bridegroom to the prospective bride, the guardianship of her children by her first marriage remained entirely with her, and a dowry of fifteen hundred pounds of rent was bequeathed her in the event of his death, and in that event all property belonging to her previous to this marriage was to be restored.

Personal property there was none; all that the future wife possessed belonged to the estate of herself and the late M. de Beauharnais, and no inventory of it existed; it was therefore impossible for her to decide whether she would keep it for her personal use or share it with Bonaparte. Such an inventory was taken two years later and Josephine refused all claim to the property. In those two years she had bettered herself. Napoleon frankly avowed his lack of fortune, declaring himself possessed of no real estate and no worldly possessions other than his wardrobe and military equipments which were valued by him at a nominal sum suggested by the notary. He was really, as the notary said to Mme. de Beauharnais, "as poor as a church mouse." Bonaparte himself thought the declaration of his worldly possessions ridiculous, and simply erased that paragraph from the marriage contract.

The contract was dated March 8th, 1796, and the following day the marriage was celebrated by a civil officer, who was gracious enough to register the groom's age as twenty-eight, and the bride's as twenty-nine instead of thirty-three; Barras, Lemarrois (who was not then of age), Tallien and the inevitable Calmelet were the witnesses. There is no mention of the parents of either party having sanctioned the marriage, and probably they were not consulted.

Two days afterwards General Bonaparte left to join the army in Italy, while Mme. Bonaparte remained at her home in the rue Chantereine.

Chapter 4

Citizeness Bonaparte

Napoleon was ten days on the road between Paris and Nice, and from every posthouse where he stopped for relays, he dispatched a letter to the "Citizeness Bonaparte, in care of Citizeness Beauharnais."

In these letters there is naught save love; ambition finds no place; there is no reference to his plans, no incertitude expressed regarding the future; he was so sure of himself, that he felt no need of a confidant, or of discussing his intentions and the likelihood of his success. He was like a prince of bygone days sallying forth to an assured victory. and his letters to his bride breathed only passionate love.

From the moment that he arrived at Nice, even while speaking a few brief words to the demoralised troops which constituted his army, words which encouraged their hopes and roused their enthusiasm, even while enforcing obedience from the revolting generals, while organizing, equipping and providing for the nourishment of the disorganized forces which he was to lead across the Alps, he found time to write letter after letter to Josephine.[1] He wrote:

> When tempted to curse my fate, I lay my hand over my heart, and, feeling your picture there, love renders me supremely happy, and all of life seems bright, save the time which I must spend away from you.

Napoleon never parted from the miniature to which he referred, showed it to everyone and prayed to it at night, and when by accident the glass was broken, he was terribly distressed, fancying it presaged death.

Bonaparte's love for Josephine was like the adoration of the faithful, the exaltation of the believer; if the soldiers knew of his infatua-

1. *Napoleon's Letters to Josephine* by Henry Foljambe Hall also published by Leonaur.

tion they did not make sport of it, for the majority were of his age and race, and extravagant dreams filled their brains as well as his.

In spite of his youth. Napoleon was just the man to lead such a strangely assorted army; his thin, pale, immobile face, framed by long locks, which he wore slightly powdered, impressed the soldiers by its inscrutability, his piercing eyes seemed to read their very souls, his glance cowed them. Below him in command, were such men as Augereau, a deserter from half the armies of Europe, a familiar old fellow and a bully, and Massena, one-time smuggler and pirate, as fond of women as he was of money, and indifferent to the means of securing both. These men would gladly have overthrown the young upstart who was in command of them, but he looked them straight in the eye, and, like wild beasts before the tamer, they growled, but grovelled. The mass of officers and soldiers, for there were not many such ruffians as Landrieux, did not need to be cowed, for their hearts were Napoleon's from the first; the greater part of the men had been in the Egyptian Army and had served an apprenticeship of abnegation; each had in his soul something of the spirit of La Tour D'Auvergne, and was animated by patriotism and love of glory.

In this war, officers refused advancement as an insult, corporals turned the tide of battle, common soldiers improvised themselves into generals and devised strategic movements; an electric current of genius circulated in the ranks; men disdained death and were gay in the face of it with joyous stoicism. In all these respects Napoleon was a worthy commander; to vanquish, to conquer the enemies of France, were the means by which he would be enabled to see his beloved and have her at his side, and with this desire urging him on, he won, in April, 1796, six battles, took twenty-one flags and forced Piedmont to capitulate. " My brave boys," he said to his troops, "I appreciate and am grateful for your gallant conduct!" and doubtless he was thoroughly sincere, for, thanks to their gallantry, Josephine could join him.

Napoleon despatched Junot to Paris with the hard-won trophies and with orders to bring Mme. Bonaparte back with him, and to his wife he had written:

Hasten, for I warn you that if you linger you will find me ill; fatigue and your absence combined are more than I can bear.

It was no lie to draw her to his side, for he was consumed by a continual fever and exhausted by a persistent cough; the itch, from which he had suffered at Toulon, had reappeared and affected his stomach, making him almost consumptive, while his incessant craving for Josephine also wore upon his health. He wrote to her:

> You are coming, are you not, my darling? You will soon be here at my side and I can hold you in my arms, close to my heart which beats only for you. Oh, take wings, beloved, and fly to me!

No other woman had the least attraction for him. At Cairo, a prisoner of war, the mistress of a Piedmontese officer was brought to his tent; she was young and beautiful and at sight of her his eye gleamed for a moment, then he greeted the captive with calm and gentle dignity, and keeping his officers with him, arranged for her transportation to the outposts and return to her lover.

In this case he may possibly have been actuated by motives of policy, but at Milan, when Grassini made every effort to seduce him, singing for him so exquisitely that the whole army were enthralled, he paid the singer but repulsed the woman. There was only one woman in the world for him then, and the voluptuous happiness he found in her arms satisfied all his desires, he longed only for her caresses and was impatient for her arrival.

Following the fortunes of war was not to Josephine's taste; she found it far more agreeable to remain in Paris and enjoy the fruits of her husband's success, which had made her one of the most courted women of the capital, than to share his fortunes in camp. No one refused credit to the wife of the general-in-chief of the French forces in Italy; moreover, Bonaparte had sent her power of attorney, so that she was able to indulge her extravagant tastes; she was at every *fête* and ball, at all the receptions at the Luxembourg, which under Barras had recovered their princely splendour, and where, next to Mme. Tallien, who was the social leader, Josephine was the most important of the ladies.

She was the cynosure of all eyes when, after Junot had presented the Directory with the trophies of her husband's battles, she left the hall leaning on his arm, and she gloried in the adulation which her husband's victories had brought her. When she entered her box at the theatre the parquet rose as one man and cheered; at official *fêtes*, at the celebration of the victories, it almost seemed to Josephine that the honour was hers, so great was the attention paid her. Paris, too, enchained her; the city had taken such a hold on her that the idea of living elsewhere was intolerable, and ever afterwards that feeling predominated; she strove to the end of her days to remain in Paris.

Napoleon awaited her arrival in a state bordering on frenzy; he was both anxious and tormented by jealousy, and wrote letter after letter, sent courier after courier to hasten her coming.

What are you doing? Why do you not come? If it is a lover that detains you, beware of Othello's dagger!

Josephine found it necessary to invent excuses for her delay, as Joseph Bonaparte had been sent to hasten her departure, and Junot, in spite of the pleasure he took in exhibiting himself in his hussar uniform, was about to rejoin the army, so, unless she could hit upon a really good excuse for remaining in Paris, she knew she must accompany him. After Chérasco had followed Lodi, and the army was at that moment at Milan, therefore it was no longer a bivouac but a palace which awaited her.

Poor health was an old story, but an illness occasioned by the beginning of pregnancy she thought would be an excellent excuse, and, indeed, when that news reached Bonaparte he was delighted. In one of his letters he says to her:

> I have wronged you greatly, and I do not know how I shall ever expiate my fault; I reproached you for remaining in Paris when you were suffering. Forgive me, darling, for the love with which you have inspired me has deprived me of my common sense; I shall never regain it; I am incurable. I am filled with gloomy fore- bodings; I fear for your safety; could I but hold you in my arms I should be happy; but the distance which separates us fills me with misgivings. A child, as adorable as yourself, will soon lie in your arms! . . . It seems to me that could I but see you once, hold you for an instant in my arms, I should be content, but, unfortunate man that I am, I cannot go to you even for a moment.

On that same day he wrote to Joseph:

> My friend, I am in despair, for my wife, the only creature in the world whom I love, is ill, and I am oppressed with the most gloomy forebodings because of her condition. I beseech you to tell me exactly how she is, and by the tie of blood and the tender friendship which unites us, beg that you will give her the tender care which it would be my greatest joy to give her. You cannot love her as I do, but you are the only person on

earth who can, even in a measure, take my place; you are the only man on earth for whom I have always entertained a warm and constant affection, you and my Josephine are the only beings in whom I feel any interest. Reassure me; tell me the truth. You know my ardent nature, that I have never loved before, that Josephine is the first woman I have ever truly cared for, and you can understand that her illness drives me distracted. I am alone, given over to fears and ill health, nobody writes to me and I feel deserted by all, even by you. If my wife is able to stand the journey I desire that she should come to me, for I need her. I love her to distraction and I can no longer endure this separation. If she has ceased to love me my mission on earth is finished. I leave myself in your hands, my best of friends, and I beseech you to so arrange matters that my courier will not be obliged to remain in Paris more than six hours, to hasten his return with the news which will give me new life.

Napoleon had become really desperate and threatened, if his wife did not join him, to send in his resignation, abandon everything and return to Paris. Josephine realized that further excuses were futile; she could not deceive Joseph by pretending illness, for he saw that she was able to go to every entertainment and bore the fatigues of pleasure remarkably well; while as for her last and best excuse, that which had touched her husband so deeply, it was too evidently a fiction for her to insist longer upon it. So at last she was obliged to prepare for the hated journey, and after a farewell supper at the Luxembourg, in the lowest of spirits, blinded by tears, she stepped into a travelling carriage and, in company with Joseph Bonaparte, Junot, Citizen Hippolyte Charles, the assistant of Adjutant-General Leclerc, her maid Louise Compoint and her dog Fortune, she started for Milan.

Louise Compoint, nicknamed the officious, ate at the same table with her mistress, was almost as well dressed, and had little of the menial about her. Her room in the rue Chantereine in nowise resembled a servant's, but with its curtains and *portières* of Siamese stuff, alabaster and gilt candelabrum, Sèvres statuettes and *jardinieres* and handsome brass-trimmed furniture was really better appointed than Mme. Bonaparte's. Louise Compoint's relations to Josephine were doubtless those of a confidante whom it was desirable to conciliate, for, although they afterwards disagreed, she paid the girl a pension up to 1805. During the journey, which was slow and seems to have been designedly prolonged, Junot managed to ingratiate himself into Mlle. Louise's good graces, and although Josephine subsequently showed herself far from indifferent to the admiration of M. Charles, she was for the moment furious because Junot preferred her maid to herself.

Although the travellers left Paris at the end of June they had not reached Milan on the 8th of July, and Bonaparte, who was obliged to leave there and go to face Wurmser's army, sent a courier begging his wife to join him at Verona.

> I need you, for I feel that I am on the eve of a severe illness.

Josephine, however, preferred to await his return to Milan, whither he rushed the moment he could leave the field, and they spent two days together, then he was obliged to face the crisis at Castiglione.

Never was there a graver situation, danger more imminent, it was not simply a question of avoiding defeat, but of annihilation; yet during the terrible mental strain which followed, when he was massing his divisions and manoeuvring to prevent disaster, at the moment when his destiny was at stake and his star seemed to waver, when, for the first time, he was assailed with doubts of himself, Napoleon still found time for a daily love-letter.

> Show me some of your faults, be less beautiful, less gracious, tender and good, above all never be jealous and never weep, for your tears drive me crazy, they fire my blood.... Rejoin me as soon as you possibly can, that ere death can part us we may have more happy days together.

Throughout their entire separation the same wild passion was daily expressed; in order that Josephine should rejoin him, so that he might sometimes spend a day or an hour in her society, he entreated, implored, and finally was forced to command; and she, grown a little more submissive in the face of conquered Italy and that fantastic army, feeling vaguely that her husband belonged to the race of chiefs whom one must obey, made the effort to join him.

It was a strange journey which Josephine made across a country torn by war; sometimes she was forced to flee before the Austrian forces, sometimes she made a triumphal passage through the towns of new Italy, where she was welcomed like a sovereign; it was made through armies sometimes victorious, sometimes disbanded; she travelled in carriages, which were continually being upset, and on horseback; and in the brief intervals of her perilous journey Bonaparte made ardent love within the sound of drums beating a charge, under fire, and by the light of bombarded cities.

When Josephine was with him Bonaparte spent the entire time at her side in an attitude of devotion; when absent, he sent courier after courier bearing messages of affection; from every one of those unknown towns, whose names he rendered immortal, he dispatched letters in which passionate declarations of tenderness, of confidence and even of gratitude are mingled with jealous imprecations. It was a constant cry from a hungry heart, from a man who had lived chastely, towards the mistress older, more worldly, more sophisticated than himself, who satisfied his heart and senses.

Unintentionally, Bonaparte borrowed his epistolary style from Rousseau, not that he was insincere or that his love was a pretext for literary efforts, but because he was imbued with that style; he did not know, and never learned how to speak of love in any other fashion; he was a disciple of Jean-Jacques to the end of his days. Josephine was neither of the same nationality, education or temperament, and his perpetual elation and continuous demands upon her affection wearied and bored her. It was pleasant to hold the first place in the heart of so extraordinary a man, and his youthful fervour interested her at first, but there was a brutality in the expression of his love which shocked, rather than appealed to her jaded senses, and often rendered her husband's caresses repugnant.

She was recompensed in a measure for the unpleasant experiences of her sojourn in Italy by the offerings from cities, princes, generals and merchants which poured in upon her; but although she received and spent a great deal of money, she was not a mercenary woman. As prodigal as short-sighted, easily tempted and yielding, Josephine accepted willingly and gave capriciously, seeing no wrong in either course, and simply obeying her instincts; nevertheless she managed that Bonaparte remained in ignorance of her doings, knowing that he entertained scruples which were incomprehensible to her. Among the first presents offered her in Italy was a box of rare medals, *à propos* of which Bonaparte had so strongly expressed his disapproval that she had felt obliged to return them; after that experience she took good care to keep him in ignorance, and whenever he questioned her as to how jewels, valuable pictures and priceless antiquities came into her possession she accounted for them by clever inventions, in which proceeding she was ably seconded by her accomplices.

There were many things of which Bonaparte was ignorant, among them the existence of General Leclerc's assistant, M. Charles, who had remained in Milan, and paraded the streets, foppishly arrayed in a cavalry uniform, invariably appearing at the Palace Serbelloni during its master's absence. M. Charles was a well-built, active young man, gay, witty and possessed of the most imperturbable assurance. Josephine claimed that their friendship was purely platonic, that the young man was merely a pleasant companion who helped her to while away the time, but it is certain that he was also the go-between between the Creole, who was always in need of something, and the shopkeepers who fancied that the general's wife could be useful to them, and he was a lavish contractor, levying gaily upon whatever was needed with the jolly inconsequence of a soldier foraging.

Bonaparte finally became suspicious of M. Charles, as he had of Murat, and upon some pretext the young man was arrested; upon his release he left the army and returned to Paris, where Josephine secured him a position with the Compagnie Bodin, and he made a large fortune in the provision business.

M. Charles had been a companion to Josephine's taste, someone from her beloved Paris, gay, noisy, amusing Paris which she missed so much, and she needed some one of his calibre to help her bear the intolerable *ennui* to which she was a victim. "I am bored to death," she wrote her aunt, and indeed she was; she was bored by the demonstrative affection of her young husband, bored at Milan and Genoa where she was received like a queen, bored at Florence where the grand duke welcomed her as "My Cousin," at Montebello where she held her court, at Passeriano and Venice, bored everywhere outside of Paris, yet, when Bonaparte finally turned his face homeward, she did not accompany him; she had taken a fancy, so she said, to see Rome, and she did not reach the rue Chantereine until her husband had been a week settled in the house whereon, at her orders, one hundred and twenty-five thousand *francs* had been expended in furniture and decorations.

Thus, for a caprice, Josephine renounced the triumphant journey across Switzerland and Italy, during which Bonaparte was everywhere greeted with shouts of acclamation, the victorious return to France by the side of the man with whose praises the whole country was ringing, the man whose glorified name she bore.

Although at that time Napoleon's ardour had somewhat abated, his wife was still the only woman whom he loved, and he made a public confession of his affection, saying to Mme. de Staël, "I adore my wife," he never left her, and was not displeased by the report that he was extremely jealous. Josephine was no longer pretty, she was nearing forty, and showed her age, but in Bonaparte's sight she had not changed, and, his first passion passed, there remained so sweet and tender a memory of his first love that throughout his life she exercised over his heart and senses an immutable influence.

Note.

A chronicler, whom I only cite because in such matters it is wisest to take note of all that is said, affirms that on the morning when Bonaparte received the oaths of the civic guard, he had in his apartment an actress, who was a mistress of a Piedmontese general, and whom he had ordered brought there for his amusement, and that, the ceremony terminated, he went on foot to the *Passage des Figini*, where he purchased from Manini the jeweller, feminine ornaments valued at a hundred and twenty-eight pounds. Another account, that previous to the taking of Milan he had for a mistress the Marquise de Bianchi, a woman of remarkable beauty, who had called upon him to reclaim twenty-five horses belonging to her husband which the French had stolen. After the *marquise* he is accredited with having entertained an opera singer named Ricardi, to whom he presented a carriage and six horses; after that, a youthful dancer of seventeen, Mademoiselle Thérèse Campini, and, lastly, the daughter of a furrier. That makes five, and none of the adventures, and I have carefully investigated the subject, appear to be authentic.

CHAPTER 56

Madame Fourès

Bonaparte stood on the deck of the transport *l'Ocean* as she sailed out of the harbour of Toulon on the 29th of April, 1798, and watched Josephine until distance hid her from his sight. He still loved her fondly, if not with the burning ardour of the first days of their married life, and admired her as the incarnation of grace and elegance, of all that was sweet and feminine, and as the first woman who had been completely his own and rendered him supremely happy.

It had been settled between them that as soon as Egypt was conquered (and he did not doubt that he should conquer) he should send a frigate for her and she should join him, in the meanwhile she was to go to the baths; but if Josephine was sincere when she promised to go to Egypt, the idea of making such a journey, of going into an unknown land, soon became a bugbear to her, the old Parisian life reconquered her, society and the world resumed their sway, the attachment she had formed at Milan was hard to break, and she lingered in France.

Reports of her indiscretions reaching Napoleon on the passage between Malta and Alexandria, his old suspicions were awakened, and he felt he must know the truth; so he called aside those whom he judged to be his sincerest friends and least likely to deceive him, and, determined to learn what had been said of his wife in Italy, pressed them with questions. Men were blunt in those days and he was soon fully informed.

Josephine's life before he married her did not interest him and he asked no questions about it. When he had written her from Milan:

> Everything pleases me, even your errors and the trying scene which preceded our marriage by about a fortnight.

He gave the keynote to his character and explained his comprehension of love. In his opinion the right a man has over his wife dated from the day they are wed, and from the day when Josephine de Beauharnais had bound herself to him by an oath, accepted his love and professed to share it, she belonged wholly to him; if she had deceived him he was done with her.

The idea of divorce germinated in the hour when his eyes were unsealed and the illusion under which he had lived was dispelled. Had Bonaparte remained in ignorance of Josephine's infidelities he would doubtless have been as faithful in Egypt as he was in Italy, but under the circumstances he felt under no obligation to restrain himself, and saw no reason why he should not lighten the tedium of the hours by the distractions, which, a few months previous, would have seemed to him like treachery to his wife, but which under the existing conditions appeared but natural to a man of his years.

He had a fancy to taste of the far-famed charms of Oriental women, as so many other Europeans had done, and a number were introduced to him, but their obesity was repugnant, for no one was ever more easily disgusted, more sensible to odours, or more impressionable than Bonaparte.

He was more fortunate at the Egyptian Tivoli, a garden constructed on the model of the Tivoli at Paris and managed by a member of the old bodyguard, once a schoolmate of Bonaparte's at Brienne, who had obtained *permission* to follow the army. Like its prototype, the Egyptian Tivoli had a club with all kinds of games, swings, jugglers, snake-charmers and dancers, and its *habitués* could take an ice while listening to the strains of a military band. The place would have been pleasant if frequented by the feminine *habitués* of similar European resorts, but of European women there were few, the only ones who frequented the Tivoli having come with the army to Egypt; for, in spite of the order that officer's wives were to remain behind, a few, disguised in male attire, managed to evade the scrutiny of the sentinels and make the passage in the holds of the transports; they were mostly hold, audacious creatures, old campaigners accustomed to a life of adventure, and, like the wife of General Verdier, able to handle a gun as well as their husband.

The prettiest among these women was a little blonde with dazzling complexion and white teeth, by name, Marguerite-Pauline Bellisle. She would have been attractive anywhere; in Egypt she was simply adorable. Apprenticed to a milliner at Carcassonne, she had succeeded in marrying her employer's nephew. Lieutenant Fourès, a good-looking young fellow in the 22nd Chasseurs. In the midst of their honeymoon came the order to embark for Egypt; the bride arrayed herself in cavalry uniform and sneaked aboard the same vessel which carried the groom; arrived at Cairo she resumed her feminine *habiliments* and devoted herself so exclusively to her husband that the union was cited as a model one.

During a *fête*, given at Esbekieh after a review of the troops, Bonaparte's young *aides-de-camps*, Merlin and Eugène de Beauharnais, caught sight of Mme. Fourès and admired her so vehemently that his attention was directed to her, and he inquired who she was; that evening he saw her again at the Tivoli, was introduced and paid her marked attention. Afterwards, intermediaries, who are to be found everywhere, undertook to smooth the way for him.

Whether from calculation or virtue, it was some time before the little woman yielded; it required protestations, letters and rich gifts to overcome her scruples, but at last she succumbed. On the 17th of December Lieutenant Fourès received an order to embark, alone this time, on the *Chasseur* commanded by Captain Laurens, with orders to make the coast of Italy and carry dispatches to the Directory; at Paris he was to see Lucien and Joseph Bonaparte, and, after receiving such letters as they desired to send, to return to Damiette. He returned sooner than was expected.

The day after the lieutenant's departure Bonaparte gave a dinner at which Mme. Fourès occupied the seat of honour. The host was most attentive, but towards the end of the repast, with apparent awkwardness he upset a carafe of ice-water over her, and rising, with many apologies, led the way into another room, under pretext of assisting her to rearrange her disordered toilet. A chronicler of the times tells us that:

> They paid some regard to appearances, but unfortunately their absence was so prolonged that the guests who remained at table entertained grave doubts as to the genuineness of the accident.

They had still more cause for doubt when a house adjoining the palace Elfi-Bey, the general's residence, was hastily furnished, and the fair Marguerite stalled therein.

Madame Fourès was scarcely settled in her new abode when her husband returned. The *Chasseur* sailed from France on the 18th of December, and the following day fell a prisoner to the English man-of-war *Lion*; the English, who were pretty accurately informed regarding what was going on in the French Army, were malicious enough to send Fourès back to Cairo on his parole not to serve against them during the war. The lieutenant, who Marmont vainly essayed to detain at Alexandria, arrived in a furious temper, and cruelly did his wife expiate her faithlessness; to escape his rage she petitioned for a divorce, which was pronounced by a military justice, and on the return of the Syrian expedition Lieutenant Fourès was again ordered to return to France, and an express order to expedite his journey was addressed to the naval commander.

After her divorce, Mme. Fourès, who had resumed her maiden name of Bellisle, paraded herself as Bonaparte's favourite. Richly apparelled, living in most luxurious fashion, entertaining generals and doing the honours of the palace to some army women, she was to be seen everywhere; sometimes driving with Bonaparte, while the *aide-de-camp* on duty trotted by the side of the carriage—Eugène de Beauharnais like the rest,—sometimes galloping about in a general's uniform, a cocked hat perched on her head, and mounted on an Arab horse which had been especially broken for her use. "Here comes our general!" said the soldiers, while those addicted to flowery language nicknamed her, "Cleopatra."

About her neck she habitually wore a long chain to which hung her lover's miniature; it was a public *liaison* at which no one manifested any astonishment.

From the year 1792 young women in masculine apparel were to be found at all the headquarters of the Army of the Republic, sometimes acting as *aides-de*-camp, as did the *demoiselles* de Fernig, but more frequently in another capacity, like Illyrine de Morency, Ida Saint-Elme and many others. At that epoch a man's costume was to be found in the wardrobe of every woman of easy morals, the generals' custom of taking their mistresses, and even their wives, on military expeditions was so deep-rooted that during the campaigns in Spain, and up to the fall of the Empire, hardly one failed to follow it; for example, witness Massena in 1810 and 1811. Nevertheless Eugène de Beauharnais rebelled against his duties as escort to his stepfather's mistress, and was excused from that service, though he was still retained as *aide-de-camp*.

So deeply enamoured was Bonaparte of Marguerite Bellisle, that he did not conceal from her his intention of repudiating Josephine; and even meditated marrying her should she bear him a child, but as he laughingly remarked: "The little idiot does not know enough to have a baby," which being repeated to her drew forth the retort: "Who knows if I am the idiot?"

During the Syrian expedition Marguerite remained at Cairo, and Bonaparte wrote her the tenderest letters, and when, after Aboukir, the general embarked on the *Murion* to return to France, he left orders that the *ci-devant* Mme. Fourès was to rejoin him as soon as possible, and that she should sail by the first armed vessel.

General Kléber, however, did not take that view of the situation. He had succeeded Bonaparte in command, and doubtless he regarded La Bellilote as one of the perquisites of the position; at all events he threw obstacle after obstacle in the way of her departure, and it was owing to Desgenettes that she finally embarked on a neutral vessel, the America, in company with Junot and some of the savants of the Egyptian expedition, Rigel, Lallemand and Corancez, Jr. Unfortunately the America fell into the hands of the English, and Mme. Fourès was not released from captivity and able to return to France until too late.

When she reached her native land the reconciliation between Bonaparte and Josephine was an accomplished fact, and her lover metamorphosed into the First Consul of the Republic, a position which rendered it incumbent upon him to set the country an example of a dignified and upright life. It is claimed that Bonaparte forbade Mme. Fourès coming to Paris; if so, his injunctions were disregarded, for she came and showed herself in company with her friends at *"Les Français"* and other theatres; the consul, however, firmly refused to see her, but gave her as much money as she demanded. On the 11th of March, 1811, he presented her with sixty thousand *francs* out of the appropriation for theatres, he bought a *château* for her in the suburbs of Paris, and arranged a marriage between her and M. Henri de Ranchoup, an *émigré*, an ex-infantry officer, and the scion of a good Auvergne family; the marriage took place at Bellevile in 1800, and the husband received as a wedding-present the vice-consulship of Santander, from which he was promoted, in 1810, to the consulate of Gothenburg.

In spite of her husband's duties, Mme. de Ranchoup appears to have been seldom absent from Paris; she was there in 1811, and still there in 1813. In 1814 she was well known in society and visited the Baroness Girard, the Countess de Lucy, and the Baroness Brayer; she went in for literary work, and had published by Delaunay a two-volumed novel entitled *Lord Wentworth*. The romance of her life, however, is far more interesting. She painted also, and was not without talent if one can judge by the charming portrait she made of herself, wherein she appears pulling the leaves from a daisy; it was a singular idea to thus represent herself essaying to read her fate by the aid of a flower. Alas, for her! while searching for "passionately" she found "not at all." The portrait represents a charming woman with a vivacious face under a mass of short, babyish curls, slight, graceful figure and really beautiful arms, and it atones in gracefulness for what it lacks in technique.

Towards 1816 Mme. de Ranchoup came to an open rupture with her husband, sold her furniture, which was valuable, and departed for Brazil in company with an ex-officer of the Guard, Jean-Auguste Bellard. It was rumoured in Paris that, having realized on her property, she proposed to renew her relations with Napoleon and aid him to escape from St. Helena. She was not thinking of such a thing, having grown to detest the emperor, and to affect royalistic opinions. When Mme. d'Abrantès published her memoirs she mentioned this rumour, praising Mme. de Ranchoup highly for her loyalty and devotion; but the latter protested, as such a statement rendered her a suspicious character in the eye of the police, who, knowing her to be an old friend of Bonaparte's, were inclined to keep an eye upon her and who watched her narrowly when she returned from Brazil with Bellard in 1825.

In reality her journeys between Brazil and France were taken simply to secure to herself a competency; she took out merchandise, which she exchanged for rosewood and mahogany, these she brought back and sold in France, returning again to South America with furniture; oscillating in this fashion between the Old World and the New until 1837, when she settled in Paris. She continued writing, and published another novel, *Une Châtelaine du XII. Siècle*, and installed in a modest little apartment in the rue de la Ville-l'Evêque, surrounded by monkeys and birds, she led a cheerful, contented existence until the 18th of March, 1869, when she died at the age of 92 years. She retained all her faculties unimpaired to the last; she wrote, played on the harp, and painted; she bought pictures, kept up her friendships with the women she had known in other days and even made new friends, among others, Mlle. Rosa Bonheur.

Mme. de Ranchoup's taste in art is discerned by the numerous pictures with which she endowed the museum at Blois (to which city she was attracted by her friend the Baroness de Wimpffen). Many of these pictures which claim to be Raphael's, Titian's, Léonard's, and Boucher's, are really only copies; some canvases are attributed to Prud'hon, others to Reynolds, Terburg, Jean Meel, Carlo Maratti, Jeaurat, and there are also two modern pictures, one a Rosa Bonheur, the other a Compte-Calix; infant Jesus', Bohemians, Venuses, Cupids, Psyches and Hermits, abound; but not one recalls the days in Egypt, the palace of Elfi-Bey, and the man who played the most important *rôle* in her life. Before she died, Mme. de Ranchoup, or the Countess de Ranchoup, as she preferred to be called, burnt every letter which had been written her by Bonaparte. It appears as though she wished to annihilate every memory of the love to which she owes her place in history; that youthful, sensual love which had, nevertheless, an ingenuous side, and in which, above all, we see how imperious was Napoleon's desire for a child; a child of his own, to whom he could transmit his name and his glory.

Chapter 6

Reconciliation

Josephine was dining at the Luxemburg, a guest of Gohier, president of the Directory, when the news that Bonaparte had landed at Fréjus was announced: it was totally unexpected and almost overwhelmed her, for she had well-nigh forgotten that he existed, had seemingly overlooked the possibility of his return, and arranged her life to please herself, her conduct closely resembling that of a widow no longer inconsolable.

While in Egypt the husband meditated a divorce, in France the wife was making her repudiation imperative; having broken off her relations with Barras, whose influence was declining and whose power was weakening, she did everything to ingratiate herself with the Gohiers, husband and wife, from the moment he held an important government position.

Gohier was a native of Rennes, belonged to the middle-class, and had been the minister of Justice during the Reign of Terror; he it was who drew up the legal formulas which Fouquier-Tinville enforced; he was the *casuiste* of the guillotine. Nothing gives an air of austerity like the hunt after judicial expediencies, it is the indispensable mask which hides the law's prevarications, and Gohier affected a Spartan-like integrity and sternness.

Because of his austerity he was elected a member of the Directory, and because of it also he made a recruit of Josephine, who confided to him her passion for M. Charles, and was counselled by him to apply for a divorce in order to espouse her lover.

Josephine, though tempted, hesitated; but in the meantime, because of M. Charles, she quarrelled with her brothers-in-law, Joseph and Lucien, who were the most violent adversaries of the Gohier party, and inspired their life-long enmity.

On the Bonaparte side were all Napoleon's friends, those who waited, hoped and counted upon his return to re-organize France, while the Gohier party comprised his bitterest enemies, Bernadotte, Championnet, Jourdin, Moulin, all the political generals. The Jacobins had pushed forward Gohier, who was a republican and a civilian, solely that they might encompass the downfall of the conqueror. The more hostile Gohier was to Bonaparte, the better it suited Josephine, and, in order to secure to herself the protection and support of the Gohier family, she schemed to marry her daughter Hortense to their son; planning to sacrifice the poor child (whose happiness was always a secondary consideration) if it proved to her interest to do so.

This scheme was progressing finely, and they were dining *en famille*, when the startling news that Bonaparte had disembarked and was on the way to Paris came upon them like a thunderbolt.

It was clear that he would not have come in so secret and unheralded a fashion save for grave reasons; Gohier realized that a crisis was at hand, and Josephine that she had not a moment to lose if she would save herself, for, seeing a struggle for supremacy, she meant to be on the winning side. Gohier might yet be a useful friend, but the most important thing was to regain her empire over Bonaparte. With this end in view, she instantly determined to go to meet him, and announced that determination to Gohier. "Do not fear. President," she said, as she took leave of him, "that Bonaparte comes with designs fatal to liberty, but it is wiser to prevent traitors from gaining his ear."

She hurriedly ordered post-horses and set out; this time without Louise Compoint, or Fortune; and, unincumbered by baggage, flew to meet her husband. Her plan was to throw herself into his arms, rekindle his burnt-out passion, and win him back, and by thus avoiding all explanations return with him to Paris, and be at his side to receive the chagrined Bonapartes who would again hesitate to speak, or, if they dared, would find they spoke to deaf ears.

While Josephine was urging on her postilions, and eagerly scanning the horizon for the travelling-carriage she so wished to meet, Bonaparte arrived in Paris by the Bourbonnais route; learning this she hastily retraced her steps, but she had lost three days, during which Bonaparte had interrogated his brothers, sisters and mother, who confirmed the gossip he had heard in Egypt, and cemented his determination to obtain a divorce. There was no longer any doubt as to what Josephine's conduct had been in Milan, or of the life she had led during the past seventeen months. It seems that the Bonapartes, either out of regard for her or their brother, did not tell all they knew, possibly they did not know everything; however, what they said sufficed; Napoleon's decision was taken, and the whole family approved it.

In vain did the friends, to whom he recounted his troubles, remonstrate and point out to him that the acclamations with which the people had greeted his return proved that they looked to him for their salvation, that they did not expect a scandal, that he must wait until he had done his duty to his country before he dismissed his wife, that to advertise his domestic troubles was to lay himself open to ridicule, and that in France ridicule kills; to all Bonaparte turned a deaf ear.

"She must go," he said, "no matter what people say; they will gossip for a day or two, then all will be forgotten." No consideration could soften or touch him, no interests were great enough to overthrow his just indignation. To avoid a meeting wherein he feared he might be moved to pity for he realized the hold Josephine had over his senses, and would not trust himself to meet her—he deposited with the concierge her jewels and effects; he then made an appointment with his brothers for the following morning, intending to settle the last formalities, and alone in his room on the first floor of the house, awaited their arrival.

Josephine, half frantic, at last reached the rue Chantereine; it was a desperate game she was about to play, and her chance of success was poor, for her cause was already half lost.

During her journey, for perhaps the first time in her life, Josephine had reflected upon her position and the horror of it had burst upon her, forcing her to see that if she did not succeed in seeing, and reconquering her husband, she had nowhere to go. Men like M. Charles were well enough for a pastime, but how could she have been so stupid as to permit her relations with him to have become a scandal and for his sake to jeopardize her best interests? That, the affair with Barras and others, the Bonapartes antagonized, debts everywhere—what *was* to become of her? Her head was in a whirl. Not realising the value of money, she had bought continually on credit, fancying that all her bills were settled when she had only paid something on account, and she dragged after her then, as she did during the Empire and up to her last hour, a train of creditors who always gave her fresh occasion for expense and whose bills she increased without a thought of the day of reckoning.

When payment became due she wept and sobbed, lost her head, resorted to every possible expedient, called on God and the devil to help her, and, when she succeeded in gaining a little time, thought herself saved. This was how she stood at that moment; to her tradespeople alone, it is said, she owed twelve hundred thousand *francs*, and it is not unlikely, for that was the usual sum of her indebtedness. She had purchased in the canton of Glabbaix, in the department of Dyle, national bonds to the amount of one million, one hundred and ninety-five thousand *francs*, and still owed two-thirds on it; the other third was to have been furnished by her aunt, Mme. Renaudin, then become Mme. de Beauharnais, but she had not a penny and could not fulfil her promise. She had bought of Citizen Lecoulteux the lands and *demesne* of Malmaison for two hundred and twenty-five thousand *francs*; thirty-seven thousand, five hundred and sixteen *francs* for furniture, utensils and provisions, and nine thousand, one hundred and ten *francs* for rights and privileges; on this she had paid for the furniture with "the price of diamonds and jewels belonging to her:" but the rest was demandable, and who was to pay it?

Josephine knew she might claim that the general, who had visited Malmaison before his departure for Egypt, had offered two hundred and fifty thousand *francs* for the property, and that that was about the sum which she had agreed to pay for it; but after having seen Malmaison Bonaparte had seen Ris, and had favourably considered its purchase, and finally his choice had fallen upon a place in Bourgogne; moreover, he had not given her power of attorney. His brother Joseph was his business manager; it was through him that Josephine received her annual allowance of forty thousand *francs*, and to Joseph alone had Napoleon communicated his projects. The latter had advanced fifteen thousand *francs* on account to Lecoulteux; the receipt, however, which bore the date of 17th *Messidor*, year *VII.*, was in the general's name, and Josephine therefore still owed fifteen thousand *francs*, because she had stipulated at marriage for the separation of property.

Nothing belonged to her; not even the hotel in the rue de la Victoire, for it had been bought and paid for by Bonaparte; all that she owned were the spoils of her Italian campaign, which she was pleased to display, and which one of her contemporaries tells us was worthy to have figured in *A Thousand and One Nights*. She still possessed pictures, statues and antiques, but what were they against what she owed; and what did they amount to in comparison to what she was losing?

Thus Josephine was again in desperate straits and no longer at an age when she could hope to repair her fortunes by a lucky marriage. The years had left their traces, her figure remained supple and graceful, but her face had faded; a Creole, married at sixteen, matured at twelve (for Tercier claims to have courted her in 1776) she was much older than a northern woman at the same period of life, and, looking the situation in the face, she clung to the hope that her husband would see her and be touched.

She went to the rue Chantereine, forced her way into the house and to the door of the room in which Bonaparte had intrenched himself; but she knocked and implored vainly; finally she threw herself upon her knees, and the sounds of her sobs and lamentations rang through the house. She remained there for hours endeavouring to make him open the door; at last, utterly discouraged and exhausted, she was about to depart when her maid, Agathe Rible, thought of an expedient and begging her mistress to stop where she was, rushed for Eugène and Hortense, and returning with them had them kneel beside their mother and join their supplications with hers; at last the door opened, Bonaparte appeared, and without uttering a word held out his arms to his wife; his eyes were suffused with tears, and his face bore evidence of the terrible strain he had undergone.

It was no half pardon which was extended to Josephine, but forgiveness, utter and complete. Bonaparte had the wonderful faculty of forgetfulness, and once he had forgiven a fault and renewed his confidence, was able to erase from the tablets of his mind the faults or crimes which it had pleased him to condone, so that it was as though they had never been committed; not only did he forgive his wife, but, more wonderful, he ignored her accomplices; he never deprived one of them of life or liberty, did nothing to impede their success; nevertheless, when, by chance, he encountered certain of them he became suddenly extremely pale. He argued that those men were not to blame, but that the fault was his, for he had not taken good care of his wife, that she had not been properly guarded, but left too long alone and unprotected, and so another had been able to penetrate into his *harem.*

It was natural, the necessity of sex ordered that man should be insistent, that woman should succumb; it was the law of nature. Bonaparte reasoned that if the erring wife was no longer beloved, she should be repudiated; if she was still dear, the only thing to do was to take her back; reproaches were senseless. Before an accomplished fact Bonaparte yielded, he accepted things as they were and people as he found them, and he did not exact of women a virginity which they did not possess.

This is less French than Oriental in his nature, but so it was. Knowing, or fancying that he did, what to believe regarding the morality and virtue of women, convinced that marital security could be ensured only by watchfulness, he determined to take his precautions and to make it a rule that no man, under whatever pretext, was to remain alone with his wife, and to keep her constantly under surveillance. If this rule was not strictly adhered to with Josephine it was because he no longer hoped for offspring, and we shall see later how he managed with his second wife.

Josephine, triumphed over the Bonapartes, who having deplored the marriage, had desired, schemed for, and almost achieved a rupture. She made Napoleon contribute to her triumph, for on the following morning, when Lucien, the most ardent advocate of the divorce, called at an early hour in obedience to his brother's summons, he was ushered into Josephine's bedchamber, where Napoleon was still in bed. The family realized that, having pardoned so much, Bonaparte would not wrangle over a question of money, and that it was useless to talk of his wife's debts, so for a time they subsided.

On the 21st of November he paid the one million, one hundred and ninety-five thousand *francs* due on the national bonds of the department of Dyle, later they served as a dowry for Marie-Adélaide, commonly called Adele, the natural daughter of M. de Beauharnais, for whom Josephine arranged a marriage with François-Michel-Auguste Lecomte, captain of infantry, and appointed collector at Sarlat immediately after the marriage. Napoleon also paid what was still owing on Malmaison, a bagatelle of two hundred and twenty-five thousand *francs*, and settled the tradespeople's accounts, amounting to one million, two hundred thousand *francs*; these he took the trouble to investigate, and it repaid him, for by deducting charges for goods which had never been delivered and righting over-charges he reduced the sum exactly one-half.

Josephine had cause for reflection; a husband who would thus pay debts to the amount of two million *francs* was a protector such as is not often found, and certainly one for whom a woman could well afford to make some sacrifices; she did so, and her apparent conduct up to the moment of her divorce gave her enemies no cause for gossip; she herself said that she was too afraid of losing her position to be indiscreet. She proved her gratitude to the Gohiers, for on the evening of the 17th of November she sent them an invitation to breakfast with the First Consul and herself on the following day, and, Gohier declining, she urged his wife to press upon him the acceptance of an important position under the new government.

Gohier, always austere, indignantly refused; but when, after pouting for two years, he solicited the First Consul's favour, it was Josephine who obtained for him the position of commissary-general at Amsterdam, where he was so well contented that he remained for ten years, and would doubtless have passed the rest of his life if, in 1810, the post had not been abolished; it is said that then he refused to go to New York, but he later accepted a pension which was paid him during the restoration; nevertheless, he was a good republican to the end of his days and stipulated for a civil interment.

CHAPTER 7

La Grassini

Bonaparte had been able to forgive and forget, but he could not, in 1799, rekindle the passion he had felt for Josephine in his early manhood when, inexperienced in love or life, he had been intoxicated by the possession of a woman of rank. With Mme. Fourès he had tasted the charm and freshness of budding womanhood, and the comparison forced itself upon his memory; he had enjoyed the change, and had no longer either the desire, or the will to remain a faithful husband.

The relations which he wished Josephine to bear him in the future were rather those of a friend and confidante than a wife; he wished for a wise friend to whom, when in an expansive mood, he could tell some of the thoughts which agitated him, from whom he could seek advice regarding a society which he had had no time to study, and for a tender nurse who, should illness befall him, would give him almost maternal care, who would listen to, condole with, and coddle him; upon whose bosom he could lay his aching head and be comforted as if he were a child.

He wished her to be mistress as well as friend, a mistress with whom he need be under no restraint, who without apparent *ennui* would accept all his moods, cheer his melancholy or share his pleasures; one who would always be ready for a journey, who would wait for but never keep him waiting, who, while not sharing his feverish activity would sympathize with all his undertakings; who would drive with him behind the four horses he delighted to handle, follow his hunting expeditions, accompany him to the theatre, have a smile always on her lips and a gentle answer at her tongue's end.

For Josephine he reserved a special place in his political plans; France, which he planned to reorganise, lacked, according to him, two of its primary elements, the nobility and the clergy; he believed that he could rally the latter, and counted upon his wife to draw the former. Not taking into account the mysterious hierarchy to which the old society of France had submitted, the invisible lines which had divided it into diverse coteries, and the impassable gulf which separated them, he viewed it as a whole. Josephine, he thought, had been of it, and could draw it back to him; she would be one with the *émigrés*, with the people of the old court and the nobility, with all those who belonged to the old *régime*, a natural intermediary between himself and them. Josephine could dispense benefits, distribute favours, repair injustices; little by little she could draw from the camp of the enemy those whom he wished to see re-enter the country; later she would serve as a link between what remained of the old regime and the new one he was building up.

Certainly, it was a fine and cleverly conceived role, and Josephine was apparently well qualified to play it; she had the necessary ease, elegance and grace of manner, possessed the happy faculty of speaking the right word in the right place, was exceptionally graceful and tactful in proffering a gift, and had a charming fashion of receiving people; she was possessed also of wonderful tact in address, which enabled her to approach people of all ranks and appear at ease in all company; what she lacked were those relations with the nobility upon which Bonaparte counted; those she had formed since the revolution would not serve his purpose, but would indeed have been injurious to the new government had not the First Consul from the first signified his intention of sundering them.

In the beginning Josephine found herself isolated, but, in proportion as Bonaparte rose, obstacles fell away, social distinctions melted before him, and ambitions woke. In foreign lands and in France alike people set their wits about to discover, if by any lucky chance, they were even distantly connected with either the Beauharnais or Tascher families; they inquired into remote alliances and distant kinships until then unacknowledged, had recourse to inferiors and old family servants for information, and ere long a current set in which swept all the old titled, office-seeking, soliciting sycophants either towards the yellow *salon* of the Tuileries or the *stucco* drawing-room at Malmaison.

It must not be supposed that this state of affairs was due to Josephine, that it manifested itself because she was born a Tascher and married a Beauharnais; it existed solely because she was Mme. Bonaparte; people flocked around her because she was close to the master, the satellite of the planet from which they hoped for light, and they would have swarmed to toady her just the same no matter what her name, origin or past had been. Nevertheless, Josephine, perhaps sincerely, believed herself an important factor in the movement, and strove to impress Bonaparte with the invaluable service she rendered him, and, strange to relate, she succeeded in convincing him; as he firmly believed that *he* had conquered the clergy, he could easily believe that his wife had won the nobility.

What woman would not be proud to be raised to such a position, who would not have been satisfied with missions so diverse and so great? Had not the consul the right to think that Josephine, with the memory of her infidelities and of all that had been forgiven her before her eyes, realizing the disparity in their ages and remembering the weaknesses to which she herself had yielded, would let pass *amours* which could neither detract from her position nor from her husband's affection, and that from fear lest Bonaparte be involved in a scandal and realizing what was due their position, she would always be extremely complaisant?

Josephine, unfortunately, failed to see matters in this light; not because she had become enamoured of her husband's physical charms, nor because gratitude and admiration of his character had roused in her a love so profound that it rendered her jealous, but because she thought of her own interests, of *her* position. She reasoned that if Bonaparte detached himself from her physically he would end by divorcing her, and she lived in a state of perpetual apprehension; she watched him, and debased herself to set hired spies upon his track; she bored him with scenes, tears and hysterics, made a confidant of everyone who would listen to her, and, in default of realities, imagined events which she recounted as facts, related incidents she would assert she had seen, and to the truth of which she would swear if needful.

The consul's first gallantries, however, were not very serious. A day or two after his triumphal entry into Milan, the 14th or 15th *Prairial*, a concert was improvised, where, for his benefit, Italy's greatest artists, Marchesi and Grassini, sang. The latter was twenty-seven years of age (for she was born at Varese in 1773), and she was no longer in appearance what she had been two years previous when, enthusiastically infatuated by Bonaparte, she had essayed to attract his attention and win him from Josephine. She was still handsome, but it was a style of beauty commonly seen in the streets of Italy; her figure was already over-developed, her face with its large features and black eyebrows, framed in thick black hair, looked a trifle heavy; her dark flashing eyes and swarthy skin gave her the appearance of a woman of amorous temperament, which, it appears, was deceptive. She had no end of lovers, not from sordid motives, for she was not mercenary, but resulting from mutual contempt and weariness; there was not one of them whom she had not proclaimed an angel at the beginning of the intimacy, but her honeymoons waned ere they had passed the first quarter.

Although Grassini's physical beauty was already on the decline, her artistic career was at its height; she was not a great musician, nor deeply versed in the principles of her art, but she was art itself; her contralto voice, always the most sympathetic of voices, was pure and smooth throughout its entire register. Hearing her, one listened not only to a great singer but a muse; no one phrased as she did, no one interpreted so understandingly grand opera (in opera *bouffe* she was wretched), no one deployed such amplitude of voice, such depth of expression in tragic roles, or could so sway an audience.

Music was the only one of all the arts—above all, vocal music—for which Bonaparte had a particular taste; the rest he protected, from policy, because he considered it incumbent upon his position and wished his name handed down to posterity as a patron of the arts; music alone he thoroughly appreciated, enjoyed and loved for itself and the pleasurable sensations it evoked; music calmed his nerves, charmed away melancholy, warmed his heart and set him a-dreaming. It matters little that he sung false, did not know a note and could not carry an air, he was so moved by music that he was carried out of himself, and that proves a higher appreciation of it than is felt by many claiming to be musicians. He valued fine singing so highly that he decorated the soprano Crescentini with the order of the Iron Crown.

In Grassini, it was less the woman than the songstress that captivated him. For two years Bonaparte had dwelt in her thoughts and her resistance was naturally not protracted. The day after the concert she breakfasted at the consul's apartment, Berthier making a third, and it was settled that she should precede Bonaparte to Paris, where she should fill an engagement at the "*Théâtre de la République et des Arts*," and this arrangement was recounted in the fourth bulletin of the army in Italy; doubtless with the view of disarming Josephine's umbrage at the *prima-donna's* arrival.

The article read as follows:

The First Consul and the commander-in-chief (Berthier) attended a concert on the 15th *Prairial*, which, though improvised, proved very agreeable: Italian music has ever new charms. The celebrated Billington, Grassini and Marchesi are expected in Milan, and we are informed that they are shortly going to Paris to give concerts there.

This notice was printed for Josephine's benefit. Bonaparte dissimulated his infidelity behind a change of dates, and masked behind the name of Billington, the only person in whom he took any interest.

At Milan, during the days which preceded Marengo, he spent every hour which he could spare in listening to Grassini. He was possessed by her marvellous voice, and held it to be the finest trophy of the campaign, and he wished that she should celebrate his triumphant return to France and sing his victories. He desired Grassini to be in Paris by the 14th of July for the *fête* of "*La Concorde*" and that she and the tenor Bianchi should sing an Italian duet. With this object in view he despatched an order to the minister of the Interior, desiring the composition of a song celebrating "The deliverance of the Cisalpine and the glory of our arms, a fine poem in Italian," insisted the consul, "set to good music."

Twenty-three days later, in the church of Les Invalides, the Temple of Mars, which was magnificently decorated, official France assembled in solemn state to celebrate the nation's victories, and when the First Consul had taken his seat upon the platform, Grassini and Bianchi sang their duets, for there were two Italian numbers sung in succession. "Who could better," inquired the *Moniteur*, "celebrate the victory of Marengo than those to whom it assured peace and prosperity?"

It was audacious of Bonaparte to have his mistress sing at an official fete, and had the world suspected their relations there would certainly have been a clamour raised, but it seems their connection was then unknown, even Josephine being unsuspicious, for she placed reliance in the article in the army bulletin; moreover, the caprice, the physical caprice at least, was not of long duration. Before leaving Milan, Grassini, intoxicated by a success long and vainly desired, imagined that she was going to play a great *rôle*, not only in the theatre but in politics; she fancied that she had a great influence over her lover, and, being naturally good-natured, she left Italy laden with petitions from her compatriots.

Bonaparte was not a man who permitted anyone to talk business when he desired to talk love, and Grassini bored him; moreover, he exacted that she should not show herself anywhere, but should live like a recluse in a little house in the rue Chantereine; this did not suit the lady at all, for she had dreamed of quite a different existence, of a *liaison à l'italienne*, which would have advertised at once her name, her person and her talent, and as fidelity was not her forte she was bored to death; there was not even a theatre open to her, for her terrible jargon closed the door of the opera, and at that time there was no Italian Opera in Paris, so she took to herself a lover in the person of Rode, the violinist.

Bonaparte learned of her infidelity and severed his relations with her, but whatever fear Rode may have felt for his subsequent artistic career, neither he nor Grassini were made to suffer; twice even the consul accorded them the *Théâtre de la République* for their concerts, the second of which was particularly brilliant, the box-receipts amounting to thirteen thousand eight hundred and sixty-eight *francs* and seventy-five *centimes*, and the account given of it by Suard in the *Moniteur* being almost lyric.

Later Giuseppina Grassini returned to the wandering life of a star, and came and went between Berlin, London, Milan, Genoa and Paris; she was *fêted* and flattered everywhere, and made engagements for three thousand pounds sterling for five months; nevertheless, when she passed through Paris and knocked at the door of the private apartment of the Tuileries it was always opened to her. The interviews led to nothing, but they distressed Josephine greatly. She wrote to one of her *confidantes*:

> I have learned that Grassini has been ten days in Paris, and it seems that it is *she* who causes my present sufferings. I assure you, my dear, that if I were in the least to blame I would frankly admit it; you would do well to send Julie (her friend's maid) to watch and see if Grassini calls, try also to find out where the woman lives.

The whole nature of Josephine is revealed in this letter. What could Grassini matter to her? Did she not understand that there was no serious tie between the Italian and Bonaparte; that it was only one of those meetings wherein memory plays a greater part than desire? No, she had to pry and spy and address her complaints and her lamentations to a woman whom the consul disliked and whom he had almost turned out of the Tuileries: such was Josephine.

She seems, however, to have calmed down in 1807, for when they were organising the "chamber music," Napoleon recalled Grassini to

Paris and offered the *prima-donna*, uniquely to the *prima donna,* a fixed salary of thirty-six thousand *francs*, fifteen thousand *francs* of annual gratuities, without counting gifts, and fifteen thousand *francs* pension on her retirement; besides which she was to have the use of the opera or *Les Italiens* once each winter in which to give herself a benefit; and was to use her vacations, if she chose, in travelling from city to city, advertising herself with her sonorous title as "*Prima-donna* to His Majesty the Emperor."

This title, however, did not serve to defend Grassini from the bandits who swarmed on the roads, and on the nineteenth of October, 1807, near Rouvrai on the confines of Yonne and the Cote d'Or, her travelling carriage was attacked by four deserters from a Swiss regiment and the poor creature was outraged, stripped and maltreated; but two days afterwards justice befell the aggressors and the emperor admitted to the Legion of Honor M. Durandeau, commander of the national guard at Viteaux, who had slain two of the bandits and arrested a third.

It is said that Grassini implored the bandits, who had taken a miniature of Bonaparte set in diamonds, to keep the jewels, but to return the miniature. It is recounted that, in a drawing-room where great indignation was expressed over Crescentini being decorated with the Iron Crown, Grassini exclaimed: "Ah, but you forget her wound!" (referring to the former's chagrin at her own appointment as first *prima-donna* to His Majesty.) A man of the world of that time tells us that La Grassini was clever and witty, spoke slangy French with a strong Italian accent, and that her habitual outspokenness gave her a reputation for sincerity and honesty.

Such was the situation from 1807 to 1814. Grassini received from the emperor alone seventy thousand *francs* a year, which was more than she received from the public, for the latter became less enthusiastic with time, as was plainly shown at *Les Italiens* in November of 1813 when, with great ado, *Horace et les Curiaces* of Cimarosa was produced; but she always achieved a success at the "*Théâtre de la Cour,*" and received the same consideration from the emperor,

Gratitude was not one of La Grassini's virtues, nor were memory and affection characteristics of hers, for, after Napoleon's banishment to Saint Helena, she attached herself to his conqueror the Duke of Wellington and deployed her charms of voice and person for his benefit.

The "Iron Duke" had a fancy for that which Napoleon had praised, and it is related that he asked David to paint his portrait, to which request the artist replied "that he only painted historical subjects."

CHAPTER 8

Footlight Beauties

Bonaparte's infatuation for Grassini was transitory, and Josephine's jealousy of brief duration; and although other actresses visited the consul's private apartments in the Tuileries, their visits need not have caused her any great anxiety, for they were persons of mediocre virtue to whom Bonaparte could not become seriously attached, and of whom he simply required that they be pretty and complaisant during the few hours he passed in their company; but it sufficed that such callers came to the Tuileries, and the wife prowled about the staircases and corridors, candle in hand, with the hope of surprising them and enacting some scene which would put her husband plainly in the wrong.

Had it not been for Josephine, these passing fancies of the great conqueror would never have come to light; it was she who discovered and told of them; but, commonplace as these brief romances were, there is sufficient reason for reviewing them as they reveal certain phases of his character which might be vainly searched for elsewhere.

Aside from Grassini, and perhaps Mme. Branchu, who was so homely that to accuse him of a weakness for her would seem absurd were it not possible that the *dilettante* in him might have rendered her attractive because of the wonderful talent she displayed in tragic opera; he never affected the queens of the lyric stage.

No dancers visited the Tuileries, although it was the moment when dancers were in vogue; when Clotide was supported by Prince Pignatelli, who allowed her one hundred thousand *francs* a *month*, and was outbid by Admiral Mazaredo, who offered her four hundred thousand; when Bigottini was showered with favours from all sides, and thereby accumulated a fortune for her numerous progeny, for whom in later years she arranged advantageous marriages. No *comédiennes*, neither

Mlle. Mars, who was not at all pretty when she made her debut, nor Mlle. Devienne, the incomparable *soubrette* whose bright face betrayed her cleverness and wit, but who was unable to utter a word in answer to the flattering speech the emperor once made her when *en route* for a hunt, nor Mlle. *Mézeray*, who was greatly interested in Lucien Bonaparte, nor yet Mlle. Gros, who made Joseph happy, ever went in at the famous "little door" of the Tuileries.

In 1808, Bonaparte may have been interested in Mme. Leverd, for after a single performance at Saint-Cloud she was admitted to the *Société Française*, and it would scarcely have been at the instigation of M, Rémusat the manager, for later, *despite* the emperor's wishes and orders, he positively persecuted her. Mme. Leverd was an exceptionally graceful and charming woman, so sprightly, *coquettish* and bewitching that her lack of real talent was generally condoned; but if Napoleon had a fancy for her—which is not certain—she was the sole *comédienne* who appealed to him, for by nature, temperament and choice he was drawn to tragedians.

That was the most glorious period in the history of tragedy and the *Théâtre Français*, the time, when, before a highly-cultivated audience who would not permit the slightest inaccuracy to pass unnoticed; before soldiers who were in accord with noble and generous sentiments, a marvellous company kept alive the traditions of epic literature. While Bonaparte favoured the actors with his protection, and was not sparing with money, he was severely critical; he held that the lines which they spoke were precepts for the nation and were of less importance for its literary education than for the formation of its morals. He once said to Goethe: "Tragedy should be the school of kings and people, it is the highest point a poet can attain." One evening on retiring he said: "Tragedy warms the heart and elevates the mind; it does, and should, create heroes," and it was then that he added: "If Corneille was alive I would make him a king."

Bonaparte did not care for melodrama, which he claimed had no proper place in dramatic literature, and had little taste for comedy, considering, like Molière and Beaumarchais, that it was unreal, agreeing with Le Sage that it was repulsive, and with Fabre d'Eglantine that it was pitifully unnatural; farce was utterly incomprehensible, and failed to distract him. Jokes, witticisms and cleverly turned phrases, even when they touched upon the main subject, but which were not, as he said, "the spirit of the thing," pretty phrases and graceful couplets all escaped him; he despised and disdained, or, rather, he ignored them. Tragedy seemed to him strong, serious, noble; his equals spoke in the kings, heroes and gods of tragedy, in their words he imagined he heard his own voice, for it was in such fashion that he wished to be represented to posterity, when, with the lapse of time, his life should be depicted on the stage.

Having this passion for tragedy Napoleon was naturally drawn in his hours of leisure to seek those who interpreted it; the pretty faces of the *soubrettes*, the affected innocence of the *ingnéues*, and the airs of the great *coquettes* could all be met at his court, the whole company of the social comedy were at his beck and call; but the women who impersonated Phedra, Andromache, Iphigenia and Hermione, were no longer courtesans but beings idealized by the characters they assumed, and viewing them at the play it was not the actress he desired, but the heroine she represented, and the artist's actual presence did not detract from this impression, the satisfaction of a purely sensual desire being hid from his eyes behind the shadow of poetry.

Recalled to reality by the press of business, having but a moment to give to the creatures of his fancy, unfamiliar with courteous phrases and unable to dissimulate the scorn he felt for those who, at a message from a valet, would rush to pamper his senses, Napoleon manifested, in both speech and action, a brutality which in another would have been pure cynicism: actually no one was less a cynic than he. "To everything pertaining to sensuality," says one of his intimate servitors, "he gave a poetic colour and name;" even his brusqueness of speech dissimulated a certain embarrassment which he always felt in the presence of women. He professed a viciousness which he did not possess; thus, in conversation at Saint Helena, he wished to appear more familiar with sensations than sentiments, while in reality no one was more sentimental than he.

Desire in him did not have its rise in sensuality, but from an overexcited imagination, and it happened not infrequently, that by the time the fair one was at hand the current of his thoughts had changed, that he was occupied with affairs of state and anything which distracted him was a bore. A tap at the door was the signal that the expected guest had arrived: "Bid her wait," the consul would exclaim. Upon a second, and impatient tap: "Bid her disrobe," the harassed consul would command. At the third tap he lost all patience and would cry: "Send her away!" and then would return to his work.

Such was the experience, so we are informed, of Mlle. Duchesnois, but she was accustomed to such adventures. At the beginning of the consulate a young elegant, who had just inherited a fortune, invited some of his friends to celebrate his good luck at a country house in the environs of Saint Denis; they breakfasted, sang and played cards, then they began to feel bored, and the host sent to a well-known house in the Chaussée d'Antin for some of the gentler sex to enliven his guests.

One of the young women remained without a gallant, being too plain to be attractive, although possessed of fine eyes, a svelte figure, an air of amiability and an expression of sadness which rendered her interesting; the party played at hide-and-seek in the park, and this girl, who was Mlle. Duchesnois, ran like a fawn, all her movements being graceful and supple, while her musical voice and clever conversation made her appear more intellectual and cultivated than her companions. Among the company was a young man who took pity upon her, conversed with her, and, finding her clever, cultivated her society and finally spoke of her to Legouvé who was curious to meet her, and who, on hearing her read some verses, was astonished at her talent.

Legouvé gave Mlle. Duchesnois advice and introduced her at Mme. de Montesson's where she met General Valence; he in turn became interested in her and promised to interest Mme. Bonaparte in her behalf and arranged for her *début*. She made her first appearance in Phedra, and it was not until a year or two later that her adventure at the Tuileries took place. Women have certain memories which nothing can obliterate, and Mlle. Duchesnois guarded throughout her life the apprehension that the words so often heard in her early youth and in the days of servitude, "she is *too* ugly," would again ring in her ears.

Thérèse Bourgoin was also dismissed in the same unceremonious manner, but she who so insolently answered: "Neither seen nor heard of," in response to a letter of inquiry from a duchess of the Empire and wife of a marshal of France regarding a lost parrot, was not likely to accept such treatment in a spirit of humility, particularly when the affront to her vanity was augmented by a personal loss—that of a rich lover, the minister of the Interior, Chaptal. After Thérèse Bourgoin's second appearance, in which she had been greatly harassed, Chaptal secured an engagement for her at the *Théâtre Français*, and to confirm this favour he wrote a public and official letter to Mlle. Dumesnil, announcing the bestowal of a ministerial gratuity and thanking her for having profitably used the leisure of her retirement in the formation of such a pupil.

Mlle. Dumesnil, at his request, gave the debutante some worldly advice, and Chaptal and the young actress were to be seen everywhere together; he placed the newspapers at her orders, and gave Paris food for scandal. Mlle. Bourgoin was just suited to a man of fifty; she had an ingenuous air and roguish smile, clear, infantile eyes, which gave her an appearance of innocence, a ringing voice and spiciness of speech, which, combined, gained for her the appellation of "the goddess of joy and pleasure."

Chaptal's great mistake lay in disregarding appearances and so compromising himself; blinded by Mlle. Bourgoin's specious manner, he believed implicitly in her fidelity; a belief of which Napoleon was malicious enough to disabuse him. One evening, when he had a business engagement with the minister, he also made an appointment with Mlle. Bourgoin, and the actress was announced within Chaptal's hearing; Napoleon sent word that she must wait, and a little later excused himself entirely, but Chaptal, on hearing his mistress announced, had gathered up his papers and departed, and he sent in his resignation that same night. The young woman on her side openly declared war, and at St. Petersburg, where she went after the peace of Tilsit, she regaled her adorers with all the epigrams and lampoons regarding the emperor which were amusing Paris.

At Erfurt the emperor took *his* revenge and entertained the *Czar* with epigrams on Mlle. Bourgoin, warning him against her over-generosity in affairs of the heart, which naturally militated against her success. At the restoration she espoused the royalist cause, all the more intensely because she had been presented to the king by the Duke de Berry and had good reasons for clinging to the Bourbons. During the hundred days she did not hesitate to array herself in their colours, for which no one interfered with her, but as the Duke de Berry failed to renew their relations on his return, her enthusiasm died a natural death.

Although Napoleon's relations with Mesdames Duchesnois and Bourgoin were unimportant, it was not the same with Mlle. George. Napoleon was installed at Saint-Cloud when Mlle. George visited him for the first time; she was received in the small apartment opening into the orangery, and it is claimed that it was on this occasion that he stung her pride by saying: " You must have hideous feet for you keep your stockings on. " Her animal beauty was so perfect in every other respect that this defect struck Napoleon's eye and so impressed him that the remark escaped involuntarily.

No one was more keenly alive to the beauty of well-modelled feet and hands than Bonaparte; it was one of the first things that he looked at in a woman, and when they were ill-formed he used to say: "Her extremities are common." Such was the case with Mlle. George, who, at seventeen, was superbly handsome, whose head, shoulders, arms and body were fit for a painter's model, but whose extremities, particularly the feet, were very ugly; doubtless the coarse, ill-made shoes which she had worn when sweeping her father's doorsteps at Amiens had helped to deform them. The father was manager of a theatre and led its orchestra.

Napoleon passed nearly the whole of that winter at Saint-Cloud, and Mlle. George was frequently his guest; aside from admiring her beauty, he was entertained by her cleverness and aptness at repartee; she recounted to him all the stories, and imitated for him the actions of the *habitués* of the *Théâtre Français*, and in those days there were lots of good stories going about. Her visits were continued after he returned to Paris, where he received her in an apartment of the *entresol* at the Tuileries; he never went to her house, and so never encountered Coster de Saint-Victor, or any other of her lovers. Mlle. George claimed that her intimacy with Napoleon endured for two years, and that during all that time she was absolutely faithful: it was more than was expected of her.

Josephine soon learned of this affair, was unusually disquieted by it, and treated her husband to innumerable scenes. Bonaparte wrote:

> She worries a great deal more than is called for she is always fearful that I may fall seriously in love; can she not understand that love is not for me? Love is a passion which makes one willing to abandon everything for the sake of the beloved person; certainly I am not of a nature to give myself up so completely, and what can it then matter to Josephine that I amuse myself with women for whom I feel no such sentiment?

No one could reason better, but reason went for nothing with Josephine. She was obliged to acknowledge, however, that Napoleon was very discreet; there was no scandal, no favours shown Mlle. George as an actress, for when she failed to keep her engagement she was rudely enough menaced with imprisonment and knew that the threat was not an idle one; when she played at court she received the same fee as her comrades, and it is said that when she made bold enough to ask Napoleon for his portrait he handed her a double *napoleon*, saying: "Here it is, and said to be a good likeness."

Probably he gave her money, for on the books of the privy purse the item, "handed to His Majesty the Emperor," is frequently repeated, designating sums of from ten to twenty thousand *francs*, although nothing indicates the uses for which they were destined; on one occasion only, the 16th of August, 1807, does Mlle. George's name appear on these books, against a gift of ten thousand *francs*, but three years had then elapsed since the cessation of her visits to the Tuileries, and this present was doubtless simply a memento presented on her saint's day. Less than a year later, on the 11th of May, 1808, Mlle. George left Paris surreptitiously in company with Duport, an opera dancer, who, fearing to be arrested at the barriers, had disguised himself as a woman. Ignoring alike her engagement at the *Théâtre Français* and her creditors, she fled to Russia to rejoin a lover, who, they say, had promised to marry her; this lover was Benckendorff, brother of the Countess d'Liéven, who came to Paris in the suite of the ambassador Tolstoi; he had just been recalled and purposed to show off his mistress in St. Petersburg, and above all before the *Czar*.

Underlying all this there was quite an intrigue, the object of which was to win the *Czar* from Mme. Narishkine, by a brief *liaison* with the French actress, from which, it was thought, he could be easily lead back to the empress. Mlle. George most assuredly suspected nothing of these fine schemes, and in letters to her mother she expatiated upon the charms of her "good Benckendorff," and signed herself, in August of 1808, "George Benckendorff."

She was presented to the Emperor Alexander who gave her a handsome diamond ornament and had her called to Peterhoff, but she was never asked the second time; she claimed that the grand duke, who, after a performance of Phedra, said: "Your Mlle. George is not worth as much in her way as my charger in his," visited her daily and "loved her as a sister."

According to her, the Russian nobility and gentry alike were her adorers, but this was not the end the conspirators had in view when they encouraged her going to St. Petersburg, nor was it what Napoleon had permitted them to plan when the plot had been revealed to him; nevertheless, when, in 1812, Mlle. George desired to return to France and rushed to rejoin the principal actors of the *Société Française* who had been summoned to Dresden during the armistice, the emperor not only had her reinstated in the society, but ordered that she should receive a salary for the six years of absence; her comrades never forgave that.

During the hundred days Mlle. George sent word to Napoleon that she could give him papers which would compromise the Duke d'Otrante, and Napoleon sent a trusted messenger to her; on his return he asked: "Did not *mademoiselle* tell you that her affairs were very much embarrassed?"

"No, sire," replied the messenger, "she only spoke of her desire to hand those papers personally to your Majesty."

"I already know what they refer to, Caulaincourt has mentioned them," returned the emperor, "and he told me also that Mlle. George was in straitened circumstances; you are to give her twenty thousand *francs* from my private purse."

Mlle. George at least was grateful, and undoubtedly the sentiments which she frankly avowed militated against her, and caused her brutal expulsion from the *Théâtre Français*. Even in her old age, when nothing remained either in face or figure of the onetime triumphant beauty, her voice trembled when she spoke of Napoleon, and she manifested such unfeigned emotion that she deeply impressed the young men who listened to her, and it was not the lover whom she lauded, but the emperor. This woman, not from the prudery of old age, for she spoke freely enough of other lovers, but from a sort of awe, seemed to forget that Napoleon had ever found her beautiful and sought her love, and she spoke not of the man he had been for her, but of the man he had been for France. Mlle. George reminds one of one of those nymphs whom the gods honoured by a brief caress, and who, blinded by the heavenly effulgence, failed to see the face of the deity.

CHAPTER 9

Readers

Tragedians alone climbed the dark staircase, and under the guidance of Constant or Roustam traversed a gloomy corridor, lighted night and day by *argand* lamps, and finally reached a room in the *entresol* from which a secret staircase led to Bonaparte's private apartments. Every morning Mme. Bernard, the imperial florist, placed a bouquet in this room, there was an appropriation of six hundred *francs* a year for that express purpose, but the flowers, which were renewed daily, died less quickly than the sentiment which inspired the visitors.

As Bonaparte rose in power these visitors—the solicitous, the ambitious, the *intriguants*—became so numerous that it would be impossible to keep count of them all. Every man who fills a position of power finds himself solicited by like callers, who await only a sign to give themselves to him, and, keeping themselves constantly in view, beg for a glance, seeking a profitable dishonour. Napoleon was thirty in 1800, thus, up to 1810, he was in the prime of life, and in vigorous health; he neither sought nor shunned amours, but, aside from Josephine, only two women ever inspired him with deep affection; he thought but moderately well of the sex, none of them ever interfered with his work, distracted his thoughts, retarded his progress or caused a modification of his plans; and these little episodes were not unlike the supper which was nightly set out for him upon one end of his writing-table: he would not have taken a step to procure food, but, finding it at hand, very naturally partook of it, and at once returned to his work. The important fact is not that a few veiled women stole by night into the emperor's secret apartment, but that no woman, wife or mistress, habitually frequented the study and the ministerial cabinet.

If Napoleon were not the person in question, if certain of his *liaisons* had not been recounted with details invented at pleasure, and if some of his favourites had not become authors, either for the pecuniary profit accruable from their memoirs, or for the pleasure of appearing before the public in a role they had never played, it would hardly be worthwhile to take note of these transitory love-affairs, but the calumnies have been too widely spread to render the *truth* unimportant.

One of the women who have become best known as a writer, and who received innumerable favours from both consul and emperor, must still escape censure; for circumstantial evidence, no matter how convincing, should not replace positive proof, and the study of characters analogous to hers will place her in the rank she should occupy.

Another, much less celebrated, but who up to the present time has done good service to pamphleteers, is a certain Mme. de Vaudey, who, when the Empire was proclaimed, was named lady-in-waiting on the strong recommendation of M. Lecoulteux de Canteleu. She was well-born, being the daughter of that remarkable soldier, Michaud d'Arçon, who invented the floating batteries used at the siege of Gibraltar, furnished the plans for the campaign in Holland in 1793, took Bréda without striking a blow, and was one of the most prominent senators of the council; she was well connected, also, for her husband, M. de Barberot de Vellexon, Lord of Vaudey and captain in the royal Bourgundians, was descended from an old Alsatian family, residents of Gray since the fifteenth century; moreover, she was an extremely pretty person, sparkling with wit and unusually clever, sang exquisitely, and wrote even better.

Mme. de Vaudey was appointed lady-in-waiting in 1814, and as the empress was about starting to take the waters at Aix-la-Chapelle, she accompanied her; and when Napoleon, early in September, rejoined Josephine at Aix, for the triumphal journey on the Rhine, Mme. de Vaudey accompanied them everywhere, and employed her time in amusing His Majesty. On her return to Paris she thought herself in a position to brave the empress, whose jealousy was aroused, and to set up housekeeping on the footing of a favourite in a pretty little *château* near Auteuil where she entertained largely, gave *fêtes*, lived like a princess, and, following her imperial mistress' example, ran deeply into debt. Once, after a prolonged audience, she laid the state of her finances before the emperor, and her debts were paid; a second disclosure of her pecuniary embarrassment met with the same success; but when she petitioned for a third audience.

Napoleon refused downright to see her. "I have not," he said to Duroc, "either sufficient money nor good-nature to pay such a price for what I can get so cheaply; thank Madame de Vaudey for the kindness she has shown me, and never mention her to me again."

On the receipt of this message Mme. de Vaudey wrote a pathetic letter, declaring that she would poison herself if her debts—debts of honour!—were not paid in twenty-four hours. The *aide-de-camp* on duty was hastily dispatched to Auteuil, and found the lady disposed for anything—except suicide;—it was immediately requested that she send in her resignation as lady-in-waiting, and that is why her name does not appear on the imperial almanac.

Some years later, after her mind had become unbalanced, Mme. de Vaudey called upon M. de Polignac and offered to assassinate Napoleon; later still, reduced to destitution, almost blind and with a paralyzed arm she peddled her *Souvenirs du Directoire et de l'Empire* as a pretext for asking assistance, and it was she who furnished Ladvocat, the librarian, with the greater part of his *Memoires d'une dame du Palais*; but she was in want and mentally unbalanced, others had not the same excuse. It was Josephine who, on the solicitation of Lecoulteux, had introduced Mme. de Vaudey at court, and she had numberless *protégés* of the same, and of an inferior order, none of whom merited her patronage and who appear to have had no other reason for being at court than their willingness to cater to Napoleon's fancies.

This state of affairs was not premeditated by Josephine, but her Creole nature had need of companionship and distraction; she liked to surround herself with agreeable and compliant people who were neither her equals nor yet servants, whose pretty faces pleased her eye, whose conversation amused, and whose accomplishments helped to distract her, who, in short, peopled pleasantly the palace wherein she claimed she lived in sad and solitary state; she engaged them without making many inquiries, sometimes touched by a sad story, sometimes attracted by a pretty face or an unexpectedly bright response. These young women, from some of whom the bloom of innocence had already been rubbed by friction with the world, were all hoping for conquests; poor and not educated to entertain conscientious scruples, they were thrown suddenly into the midst of a court which was one of the most splendid in history, and in the long idle days which they spent in the empress' private apartments they had nothing to do but accept the attentions of the officers with whom they constantly came in contact and to angle for husbands.

Naturally they aspired to find husbands among the officers who thronged the palace, as so many women no better than themselves had done; women who were then wives of marshals of the Empire; they saw constantly and familiarly him from whom emanated all favours, who at a sign could make or destroy one's fortune, and put themselves in his way, ambitious for that sign, ready to risk anything in order to obtain it; they were complaisant, presented themselves only when desired, and exerted themselves to please, and as the subalterns kept a sharp lookout to see if the emperor admired any of them, arrangements were speedily concluded and affairs followed their natural course without the slightest attempt at seduction on one side, or the least love on the other.

But, no matter how carefully concealed the intrigue, Josephine always discovered it; then there was a scene, and the young person was discharged; however, she had usually received a good dot and was apt to crown her career by marriage with some gentleman who was not over-scrupulous, and thus become the progenitor of people of some importance.

A typical case was that of Félicité Longory, daughter of a petty officer of the cabinet, whom Josephine had called to fill the position of lady usher. As such she was stationed in the *salon* into which the private apartments opened, and her duties consisted simply of throwing open the double doors for the passage of the emperor or empress; for this service she received three thousand, six hundred *francs* a year, which sum Josephine supplemented by six hundred *francs* in 1806. Félicité was a personage of no importance, almost a servant, yet she succeeded in attracting the attention of the emperor, and, the inevitable scene with the empress ensuing, was naturally discharged, and later married well.

Mlle. Lacoste stood a little higher on the social plane. She was a slight and pretty blonde, an orphan without fortune, who had been brought up by an aunt who was said to be a schemer, and who managed her niece's presentation to Josephine. The empress, touched by the girl's forlorn state, gave her an ambiguous position, vaguely entitled a reader. Mlle. Lacoste certainly did not find her duties fatiguing, for hardly had she assumed the position when the court departed for Milan where the coronation was to take place, and she followed the court, without being of it, for she had no clearly defined position. As reader, Mlle. Lacoste was denied access to the drawing-room of the ladies-in-waiting; and, too well-bred to associate with the ladies' maids, near to whom, however, she was lodged, she felt isolated and forlorn in her new surroundings.

At Stupinitz the emperor caught sight of her and remarked her pretty face; at Milan he spoke to her and an understanding was arrived at. Josephine, however, soon became aware of it and there was a terrible scene; the reader was ordered to leave and her aunt summoned from Paris to escort her home; but before her departure the emperor insisted that she should appear once at least among the empress' retinue. This created a great scandal, for a reader was not supposed to appear outside the private apartments. On returning to Paris Napoleon undertook to find a husband for Mlle. Lacoste, and married her to a rich financier; she made an honest wife and devoted mother, and never reappeared at the Tuileries.

During this same journey to Italy, in the midst of the fetes given at Genoa in celebration of the union of France and the Ligurian Republic, a lady by name of Gazzani or Gazzana (her name has been written both ways), crossed Napoleon's path; she was the daughter of a Mme. Bertani, a dancer, or, according to some historians, a singer connected with the Grand-Theatre.

Out of compliment to Josephine a number of Italian ladies had gone to Milan, and it had been arranged that La Gazzani should accompany them; it was a strangely assorted party, comprising ladies of the Negrone, Brignole, Doria and Remedi families, and women like Mme. Gazzani and Bianchina La Fléche, who was destined to such a brilliant career in Westphalia.

Carlotta Gazzani was tall, rather too slight perhaps, but with a most graceful and elegant carriage; her hands and feet were not remarkable for their beauty, indeed she invariably wore gloves, but her features were of the purest type of Italian beauty and her eyes large, dark and very brilliant. Even women praised La Gazzani's beauty, which is positive proof that it was great, but also, that she lacked that peculiar and indescribable charm which renders some women so captivating and the envy of all their sex. Mme. Rémusat admitted that it was her husband, then first chamberlain, who charged himself with the Italian beauty's introduction at court, and who persuaded the emperor to nominate her reader to Josephine; evidently it was not Talleyrand alone who, as Napoleon once said, "always had his pocket full of mistresses."

Mme. Gazzani, then called Mme. Gazzani Brentano, and who long afterwards assumed the title of Baroness de Brentano, replaced Mlle. Lacoste, at a salary of five hundred *francs* a month; from 1805 to 1807 little was heard of her, for during that period which comprised the

Battle of Austerlitz and the campaign in Prussia and Poland the emperor was little in France, but on his return to Paris and later at Fontainebleau she saw her opportunity and seized it. She was so lodged that she could easily reach the emperor at all hours, and when summoned by him immediately hastened to obey. She never attempted to pose as a favourite, but accepted with modesty her role of occasional mistress, and the empress, at first inclined to be jealous, was quickly reassured by Napoleon's making her his *confidante*.

The Italian retained a respectful and submissive attitude towards the empress, and remained unpretentiously in her place. She was accorded the *entrée* of the drawing-room reserved for the ladies-in-waiting, but, that favour bestowed. Napoleon did not publicly interest himself in her and permitted the ladies of the palace to treat her as they pleased and shun her if they chose; their hostility, however, was of a short duration, and soon several of them, and not the least haughty, relented sufficiently to admit her into their circle. Mme. Gazzani obtained something more substantial, however, from her relations with the emperor than the flatteries of the court, as she secured the general receivership at Évreau for her husband.

After the imperial divorce Mme. Gazzani rejoined her lord, and being close to Navarre, where Josephine was residing, she became an intimate of the household to which she was strongly attracted by a *liaison* with M. de Pourtalès, a groom of the empress' household. Her intimacy with the emperor terminated at Fontainebleau, after that he only saw her by chance. He never loved her and appears never to have talked of her, but she was consoled for his forgetfulness by the success in life of her daughter, Charlotte Joséphine-Eugénie-Claire, self-styled Baroness de Brentano, who made a brilliant match and married M. Alfred Mosselman, by whom she had a daughter who married M. Eugène Le Hon.

Although oblivious of Mme. Gazzani, Napoleon often spoke of a certain Mlle. Guillebeau, the daughter of a bankrupt banker, who was, in 1808, appointed to assist Mme. Gazzani as reader. Mlle. Guillebeau's mother was Irish by birth, and had three daughters, two of whom were grown and contributed to the family income by dancing and playing the tambourine in the drawing-rooms of the nobility. The eldest compassed an introduction to the Princess Elisa, who assisted her to make a good marriage, and the younger, who the gossips affirmed had not been cruel either to Murat or Junot, was clever enough to secure the protection of Queen Hortense, who was taken with her pretty face and clever dancing.

At a masquerade ball, given by Caroline at the Elysée, Hortense, who was to lead a costumed *quadrille*, took a fancy to dress Mlle. Guillebeau as Folly, and to have her, tambourine in hand, lead the procession of her maidens into the ballroom. Caroline had double reasons for jealousy, and as soon as she perceived Mlle. Guillebeau she rushed to Hortense's side and a lively scene ensued, which resulted in Folly's dismissal from the ballroom. This was an episode in the continual warfare which raged between the Bonapartes and the Beauharnais, and to avenge both herself and her favourite, Hortense presented Mlle. Guillebeau to her mother, who, to annoy Caroline, attached the girl to herself in the position of reader.

This incident occurred just previous to the journey to Bayonne, and when the imperial household was installed at Marrac, Mlle. Guillebeau found herself in an isolated position; court etiquette closed the door of the drawing-room against her during the day, and she only entered it occasionally of an evening in order to entertain the company with her music and dancing, and was therefore reduced to passing most of the time in her bedroom, which was in reality nothing better than a garret, for the *château* of Marrac was small, and had not been constructed with a view to lodging an imperial household. Being a great *coquette*, the girl was fearfully bored, and was well content when a servant—a Mamaluke—tapped at her door and announced an imperial visit.

Matters were progressing quite to her taste when Lavallette, who, by right of his position of postmaster-general, watched the correspondence of the household, sent Napoleon a letter written to Mlle. Guillebeau by her mother, in which she had clearly traced the role her daughter had to play, and recommended her to lose no occasion to make herself agreeable to His Majesty, and to strengthen his fancy for her to the utmost; pointing out to the girl how greatly to her interest it was to follow this course, and how she could profit by the imperial weakness. Napoleon was so disgusted with the lowness of the intrigue, in which he afterwards discovered that Prince de Bénévant was implicated, that he immediately commanded a post-chaise for *mademoiselle*, and she was packed off to Paris escorted only by a valet.

Mlle. Guillebeau met and married a M. Sourdeau who, thanks to the emperor, was given a receivership, but he appropriated the funds and prison stared him in the face when the restoration occurred and proved his salvation. Mme. Sourdeau was clever enough to secure an introduction to the Duke de Berry, who found her "charming and possessed of the most beautiful eyes in the world," and as a recompense for favours' received appointed her husband consul at Tangier.

In the life of Napoleon, these passing fancies count for little; they barely appealed to his senses, never touched his heart; they give us no insight to the active side of his nature, but demonstrate his hatred of intrigue, his generosity and certain of his habits. It would be easy to relate many adventures of the same kind, but none more interesting; tales of garrison adventures for which, as emperor, he paid two hundred *napoleons* where one of his captains would have paid twenty *francs*; he was not constituted differently than his marshals and his soldiers; he was a man, but he was not a man whose senses were so imperious that he was always forced to yield to them.

At Vienna he observed a young girl, who, on her side, was apparently infatuated with him; he had her followed, and invited her to visit him in the evening at Schoenbrunn; she accepted, and as she spoke only Italian and German they conversed in the former language. Napoleon discovered almost immediately that the girl belonged to a most respectable family and did not comprehend in the least what the invitation to meet him implied, and that while she felt a passionate admiration for him it was ingenuous and innocent; he ordered that she should be immediately reconducted to her home, and provided for her future, giving her a dot of twenty thousand florins.

This act was far from being unique in Napoleon's history, it was repeated three times at least in his life; on the last occasion at Saint Helena.

CHAPTER 10

Josephine's Coronation

In the idleness and disquietude of her daily life, which resembled closely that of an aged *sultana*, Josephine had ample leisure for reflection, and the outgrowth of her continual agitation, anxiety and jealousy was the knowledge that by one thing only could her position be secured—the birth of a child. Without understanding Napoleon's ambitious projects, she yet knew that he had a consuming desire for male issue, and, as his fortunes rose, gradually comprehended why he so desired an heir, and realized that for her maternity should no longer be a pretext for obtaining favours in the shape of journeys which gave her relaxation from the monotonous life at the Tuileries—but an aim; that the throne of which her husband was slowly climbing the steps *should* have an assured heir.

To Bonaparte, chief of a republic, Bonaparte re-establishing the Bourbons and content with a life-long place of honour under the restored monarchy, a son was not indispensable, but, unfortunately for Josephine, the contingent glory of a *rôle à la Monk* did not tempt him, nor the disinterestedness of a life like Washington's satisfy him. A great flood of opinion, one of those popular currents which nothing stems, swept all obstacles from his path and raised him first to a consulate which was republican, later to one which was autocratic and differed from a monarchy only in name, and above all in the insolvable question of heredity.

Around this question of heredity surged the ambitions of some and the projects of others. Josephine saw that Bonaparte's brothers already aspired to the succession; that the sisters debated whether their husbands, too, might not have a chance, and that the nation itself desired, after so much turbulence, a government that would endure more than a lifetime; but if a monarchal form of government was established, who was to succeed Napoleon? There were the consul's brothers, but by what right could they be called to the throne? An hereditary monarchy in its Christian form is a derivative of the Hebrew form of government, and is supposedly a divine institution, but it applies exclusively to the chief of a dynasty and his descendants, however far removed, provided that they are male and descended in direct line from him. In order that Napoleon's brothers should succeed him it would have been necessary to have recourse to an expedient, common enough with the ancients, and proclaim that the late Charles de Buonaparte had been emperor of France, but it was unlikely that the country would accept such a fiction.

Another expedient was to abandon the Hebraic law of succession and institute the Roman law of adoption; under that regime the consul would be free to choose as his successor whomsoever he judged best fitted to fill his place; but it was a question whether the nation would overcome its prejudice in favour of the old monarchal system and accept such a solution of the problem. The simplest, most natural solution, which would both annihilate the ambitions and please the populace, was the birth of a son to Napoleon.

In her anxiety to give to her husband the heir so ardently desired Josephine visited innumerable mineral springs whose waters were supposed to cure sterility, consulted various physicians and submitted heroically to any treatment recommended, made pilgrimages, and even had recourse to sorcerers; whenever she had the least ground for believing herself with child she immediately made Bonaparte a sharer in her joyous hopes, and he in turn confided his happiness to his intimates; as each hope died Napoleon became more and more morose, and indulged in hard and bitter speeches which attested his disappointment. Once at Malmaison, he decided to get up a hunt in the park, when Mme. Bonaparte came to him weeping and said: "How can you think of hunting in the park when all our animals are with young?" at which he retorted in a loud voice: "Well, then, I suppose it must be abandoned; everything here seems to be prolific except the mistress?"

Publicly he threw all the blame for their childlessness upon his wife; but recalling Mme. Fourès and many others, none of whom had borne him children, he entertained secret doubts of the justice of the aspersion he cast upon her; doubts which Josephine stimulated by talking incessantly of *her* children, and by forcing Eugène and Hortense constantly upon his notice; she harped so much upon the subject that Mme. Bacciochi lost all patience, and one day silenced her by remarking:

> There may be something in what you say, but remember, sister, when those children saw the light you were much younger than you are now!

The majority of the family, however, were prevailed upon to accept her view of the situation, and Napoleon himself did not combat it vigorously. On several occasions he said to his brother Joseph:

> I am childless, you all think me impotent, and Josephine, despite her anxiety, is not likely to bear children now; so after me the deluge!

When, on his return from Spain, Lucien preached divorce, and suggested the advisability of a marriage with an *infanta*, Napoleon rejected the proposition; undoubtedly he had diverse motives for so doing, but possibly the strongest of all was of a personal and private nature; he may have reasoned that while a union with a Bourbon princess would unquestionably further his ambitious schemes, it was foolish to struggle for a throne if unable to transmit his name and glory to a son.

The Spanish union was nevertheless urged by Lucien, for whom Josephine had but scant affection, remembering that he had been the first advocate of a divorce, and from that time she made no further effort to conciliate her husband's brothers, but did not hesitate to report any story which might injure them, however false, nor to embellish the truth; and she was not sorry when a rupture finally occurred. Napoleon often said of Josephine that "she bears no more malice than a pigeon," but this was true only when her personal interests were not at stake.

Although the doubt which she had inspired in Napoleon served to avert a divorce in 1801, Josephine knew herself to be at the mercy of chance; it was neither the actresses whose company he frequented, nor the ladies of the court whom she feared, for if one of them happened to bear a child she reasoned that Napoleon could not be assured of his fatherhood unless a striking physical resemblance proved it; what she dreaded was a *liaison* similar to the one with Mme. Fourès, for a child born under such conditions meant the shipwreck of all her hopes and ambitions, as Bonaparte had reached a point where he felt himself upon a level with the old dynasties, and knew that a union with him would not be disdained by the purest blood of France, while there was no lack of men like Talleyrand, "the accursed limper," ready to tempt him, suggest advantageous marriages and act as intermediary.

In default of a child, which alone, as Napoleon himself said, "could insure Josephine's peace of mind and put a stop to her unceasing jealousy," how could she attach herself to her husband so firmly that he would not dream of breaking the chain? For years associated with him in his public life, received everywhere as a sovereign, holding her *salon* at the Tuileries or at Saint-Cloud, obliged by Napoleon himself to take precedence over all other women, even above his mother at family and informal gatherings, presented to the country and to Europe as the first lady in France, she could not be repudiated without a scandal, and such a proceeding would certainly be badly received by the public. She had been the medium for the distribution of too many favours, had exercised her influence to obtain too many pardons, not to have warm and faithful adherents; but, as Napoleon's popularity grew and his power increased, the worldly prestige of his wife diminished, and she realized more and more that no tie could bind him to her save a living token of their union.

Josephine finally conceived a most ingenious plan, namely, to constitute a heredity by persuading Napoleon to adopt his nephew and her grandson, the child of Louis Bonaparte and Hortense de Beauharnais; such a procedure would conciliate all factions, satisfy the Bonapartes, because the heir-presumptive would be one of their name, and assure her own future, and the question of succession would then be settled. She convinced Napoleon of the wisdom of this law and he spoke of it to Louis; but Louis indignantly refused invoking the rights of his brother Joseph and himself, and before these imaginary and baseless claims, which were without precedent in history and totally at variance with the monarchal doctrine.

Napoleon gave way and renounced the sole expedient which would have enabled him to establish an heredity without having recourse to divorce. Failing to achieve the adoption of her grandson, Josephine saw no other means of consolidating the tie which linked her to Napoleon and his fortunes, and while suffering the greatest disquietude she was obliged to accept the situation with such fortitude as she could summon to her aid.

The First Consul being proclaimed emperor, she naturally became empress, received the homage of the ministers of state and was addressed as "Your Majesty," and after the triumphal journey from Aix la-Chapelle to Mayence, after the cannons of the Invalides had announced her return to the Parisians and the authorities had defiled before her throne, her position seemed assured, and a divorce highly improbable; but her own jealousy nearly occasioned the dreaded calamity.

At Saint-Cloud she observed that a lady who had called to pay her respects, left the apartment sooner than was strictly in accordance with court etiquette, and having long suspected an undue intimacy between this lady and the emperor, she herself left the drawing-room and mounted the secret stairway leading to the private apartment in the *entresol* where he was in the habit of receiving fair visitors, and, recognizing the lady's voice, she insisted upon being admitted and made a scene which provoked Napoleon to violent anger. As a result he declared himself weary of such espionage and determined to end it, and saying that he should follow the counsels of his friends and secure a divorce, he sent for Eugène to arrange the details.

Eugène arrived, but both for his mother and himself he declined all favours or any pecuniary assistance; thus several days passed, Eugène remained unapproachable, while Josephine did not recriminate, but wept unceasingly, and Napoleon's resolution weakened before her tears; moreover, he knew himself to be in the wrong, and that it was not thus so grave an act should be accomplished, and a final conversation took place between them. "I have not the courage," said he at its close, "to carry my threat into execution, and if you will only be affectionate and obedient I shall never *oblige* you to leave me, but I will admit that I wish that you yourself would relieve me from the embarrassment of our present relations."

Josephine, however, had no taste for self-sacrifice, and did not propose to decide her fate. Napoleon must be the arbiter; she was ready to obey, but she intended to await his order to descend the steps of the throne to which he had raised her. Influenced by his habits, political uncertainty, the hope of a possible paternity, affection for his stepchildren, the necessity of ruining the life which he had linked with his, of renouncing forever the woman whom he still loved, touched by the resignation of the Beauharnais family, and provoked at the joy manifested by Josephine's enemies, Napoleon once more abandoned the idea of divorce, and, as though to prevent its return, commanded his wife to give serious attention to the preparations for his coronation, in which she should be associated.

Certainly Josephine should have been content; her most ambitious dreams could never have reached this height; she, the Creole, who had been brought to France owing to the caprice of a courtesan, was to realize the ambitious dreams of past queens of France, be crowned by the Pope, and participate in the triumphs of the new Charlemagne.

She was, however, desirous of forging still another link in the chain which bound Napoleon to her. For eight years she had been perfectly content with the civil ceremony which alone cemented their union, but it now occurred to her that the benison of the Church would lend additional strength to her position. She did not ignore the fact that she would have great obstacles to surmount before overcoming Napoleon's objections to such a step; she knew he would argue that, as the ceremony had not already taken place, it was useless to call public attention to its omission, that the greater number of the men who surrounded him were in the same position as himself, and that by setting them such an example he would cause numerous acts of rehabilitation, which would appear to be in opposition to extant civil laws, and would seemingly indicate that the head of the government did not acknowledge the validity of the only mode of marriage which the state recognized, that he would find no lack of reasons to advance for his refusal, any of which might mask a furtive one.

Napoleon knew that the Church is accommodating, when she has to deal with the powerful ones of earth, and that when it is advisable she will cut a knot which she had tied, but he felt that if later he was constrained to sunder his marriage relations he would prefer being free to act for himself and not be under obligations to the Holy See.

Josephine divined all this, and was fully alive to the fact that she had nothing to gain by appealing to Napoleon, and had no valid reasons to advance for the religious solemnization of their union; she knew, too, that to assign conscientious scruples as her motive would give not only Napoleon, but the whole court, cause for mirth: but the Pope would not laugh at her.

For several years she had been in correspondence with Pius VII. and quietly paving the way for a religious marriage, so when the Pope called on her at Fontainebleau, she confessed that her union with Bonaparte had not received the sanction of the Church, and the Holy Father, after felicitating her upon her commendable desire to obey the laws of the Church, promised to insist upon the Sacrament. Thus Napoleon's hand was forced, for the Pope was quite capable of postponing the coronation if he postponed the marriage; to refuse to anoint the emperor, if Napoleon refused to obey the canons of the

Church. The ceremony had already been thrice adjourned, and each postponement entailed immense expenditures, gave rise to discontent among the people, and provoked distrust. Paris was filled to overflowing with civil and military deputations, it would have created an awful scandal if the Pope, who had come to Paris solely to anoint and crown the Emperor, returned to Rome without having performed the ceremony; it was absolutely necessary to yield, and on the morning of the 9th December, Cardinal Fesch pronounced the nuptial benediction.

If ever a marriage was forced that one was, and later Napoleon could truthfully affirm that undue influence had been brought to bear upon him, that his consent having been unfairly obtained the marriage was, according to the canons of the Church, null and void; but this Josephine could not foresee, and married by a cardinal, anointed by a Pope and crowned by the emperor, she fondly believed her position unassailable.

Chapter 11
Madame ★★★★,

Napoleon would not have been the man he was had he never felt the need of a love not purely animal, of a friendship which should satisfy the sentimental and intellectual side of his nature as well as the physical, and as he advanced in years and his position isolated him more and more from ordinary mortals, the longing for sympathetic companionship grew upon him.

During the early days of the consulate this longing was but faintly felt, but as the fires of youth burned down his intellectual nature assumed the ascendency, and we find ourselves in the presence of a new Napoleon, a man prone to periods of melancholy, possessed by a feverish desire to be understood, and as apt to indulge in dreams of an ideal affection as in ambitious ones, a man delicately tender, who found for the expression of his sentiments language suitable for a hero of romance. As Napoleon has not previously been presented to the world in this light one feels some hesitancy in so doing, but the proofs that his character did thus change, though covering a somewhat later period of his life, are still sufficiently authentic to warrant the assertion.

The women to whom Napoleon addressed himself at this time were no longer actresses and adventuresses, who made capital out of their relations with him, but women of the world who had husbands to deceive and reputations to consider, who were cautious in their indiscretions, destroyed all proof of their relations with the emperor, and whose descendants carefully guarded the secret, while those who were indiscreet enough to gossip about these ladies took good care to disguise their names; even at this late day he who lifts the light veil which conceals their identity would be most discourteous; moreover, one cannot be *positive* that the veil screens but *one* woman.

Naturally one can identify certain traits of person and character, particularly when retaining from childhood a strong and clear impression of a certain face, but such proofs are not documentary, and even at the risk of being obscure and leaving some points unexplained, one must proceed with the greatest caution. There was at the consular court a young woman of twenty, wedded to a man thirty years her senior. The husband was a most respectable person, a great worker, and left the best of reputations behind him; he was one of those faithful servants of the state of whom the old *régime* made head clerks, and the new, general directors; he possessed wonderful ability as a financier, and it was he who organized and directed a financial institution which is conducted today upon the same lines that he laid down.

The wife was charming, graceful and amiable; her features were irregular, but her face was rendered remarkable by an extremely winning smile and the thoughtful expression of her dark blue eyes—eyes which, it must be admitted, were somewhat deceptive, as they expressed whatever their mistress willed; her hands and feet were marvellously small and beautiful, she danced like a fairy, sang like an artist, played the harp like a *virtuoso*, was an excellent listener, and did not display unduly her most remarkable intelligence. This lady lacked neither a strong will, worldly wisdom, ambition nor unscrupulousness, but she concealed her real hardness by a suave manner which enhanced her beauty, and, though of *bourgeoise* origin, she understood the art of politeness better than many a high-born dame, and instinctively comprehended the requirements of good society (a knowledge which must be innate and cannot be acquired); and she carried herself with as haughty and disdainful an air as if she had been born in the purple rather than of middle-class provincials.

According to certain authorities it was in November, 1803, that Napoleon fell in love with Mme. ****; but the affair with the woman whom Josephine surprised in the orangery at Saint-Cloud seems to destroy this hypothesis, and it is more likely that Napoleon paid his first addresses to Mme. ****; about nine months later, in August, 1804. The child which was born to Mme. **** during that year resembled Bonaparte neither in mind nor feature, a fact which, though it inspired Napoleon with some doubt as to its parentage, was a safeguard to the wife and confirmed her husband's faith in her. It is not uncommon, however, for features as characteristic as those of the Bonapartes to skip one generation and appear, strongly developed, in a second, and it was such a manifestation, occurring a generation later in this family, which revealed a connection which up to that moment had been kept fairly secret.

Was the lady at Saint-Cloud the person who, towards the end of the consulate, frequented a little house in the Allée des Veuves where Napoleon also went secretly? Was she the same woman whom Napoleon, disguised and alone, visited by night at her own house in Paris? It is impossible to say. The adventure at Saint-Cloud seems to have been one of those transitory amours which endure but a day; nocturnal and secret excursions on the part of a man who was ordinarily such a stay-at-home as Napoleon, demonstrate however, an irresistible attraction of which there are few instances in his career. There is some uncertainty regarding the identity of several of the women who played a part in Napoleon's life about that time which, for the moment, it is not advisable to clear up, and about which, memorialists and their editors have been careful not to enlighten us, out of consideration for the woman about whose memory they surge, and above all, for her descendants; nevertheless, there are certain facts regarding which all witnesses agree, and which, though not positive proof, are the strongest sort of circumstantial evidence and permit us to fathom the mystery with which these ladies surround themselves and to divine their names.

A few days before the arrival of the Pope for the coronation. Napoleon, with his whole court, proceeded to Fontainebleau, and his retinue were not slow to perceive that he appeared unusually serene and approachable. One evening, after the Pope had retired to his apartments, the emperor remained with the empress, chatting with her ladies-in-waiting; this proceeding did not strike Josephine as natural; her jealousy was awakened, and she began to search for proof of a new intrigue; not knowing exactly whom to suspect, she pounced upon Mme. Ney, who denied emphatically to Hortense, her old schoolfellow at Mme. Campan's, that the emperor was in any way interested in her, but asserted that he was simply curious about one of the ladies of the court whom Eugène de Beauharnais found quite to his taste. Eugène was but a screen; the lady accepted his attentions and appeared to take pleasure in his society solely to avert suspicion; she was intimate with Caroline Murat, who lent her assistance to the intrigue in order to spite Josephine, as she did in many other instances.

No definite understanding had been arrived at when the court returned to Paris, but Napoleon was captivated by the lady's charms; he was loath to leave the empress' apartments when she was on duty, and was always ready to join Josephine at the theatre if that lady accompanied her; and, though ordinarily he objected to his wife's going to the play except in state, he was then ready to organize little theatre parties, provided always that Madame **** was of the company. Josephine grew more and more uneasy and attempted to remonstrate, but her remonstrances were so ill received that she dared not insist, and although publicly Napoleon seemed more affable and frank than ever before, in reality, unless a certain lady was present, his temper was irritable and uncertain. "Bonaparte makes me a daily and reasonless scene," Josephine wrote a friend about that time; "he is unbearable."

About that time Napoleon was seized with a violent fancy for playing cards in the evening, and invariably called his sister Caroline and two ladies of the palace, one of whom was the object of his affection, to be his partners. He played badly, giving but scant attention to the game, which indeed served only as an excuse for remaining in the society of the woman he so admired, and procured him an opportunity to gaze upon her and to ponder over the charms of an ideal and platonic love; without mentioning names he frequently indulged upon these occasions in long and vehement tirades against jealousy and jealous women; and poor Josephine, drearily playing whist with court dignitaries, was forced to listen to the invectives which, uttered in his sonorous voice, rang out in the respectful silence of the room and were plainly audible to all.

At a *fête* given by the minister of war, in honour of the coronation, the women, in accordance with the usage of the day, were alone seated at supper, the empress with several of her ladies and the wives of state dignitaries occupying the table of honour. Napoleon refused to seat himself but walked about, chatting with various ladies in an unusually gracious and affable manner; he was assiduous in his attentions to Josephine, and taking a plate from the hands of a page served her himself. When he fancied that he had manoeuvred enough and had been sufficiently polite to the company in general, he approached Madame **** and engaged in conversation with her neighbour, gradually including his charmer, and, perceiving that she wished some olives which were set upon the table at a little distance, he fetched them to her, saying: "You do wrong to eat olives at night, they will make you ill," then, turning to the other lady, he added, "and you, *madame*, do well not to eat them, above all you are wise not to imitate Madame **** for in all things she is inimitable."

The emperor's stratagem did not impose upon Josephine, whom

nothing escaped, and who, in the middle of the winter, had been obliged to yield to a sudden fancy of his and go to Malmaison, a journey which had upset all her plans and made every one excessively uncomfortable, for the visit had been so suddenly undertaken that there had been no time to light the fires, and the first night was spent in a veritable icehouse; the cold, however, had mattered very little to Napoleon who made a nocturnal visit which he flattered himself had been unobserved, little suspecting that Josephine, after a long station behind a glass door, had learned his secret.

After the ministerial fete, the court returned to Malmaison, and the following morning the empress summoned to her presence the lady who had not partaken of olives, and after an aimless conversation, abruptly asked what the emperor had said to her on the previous evening, then, what he had said to Madame ****. The lady answered that His Majesty advised Madame **** not to eat olives; "Ah," exclaimed the empress, " while he was giving her such good advice he might have told her that it is ridiculous for a woman with such a long nose to essay the *rôle* of Roxelane; "then, taking a book from the chimney-piece, she added: "Here is the book which is turning the heads of all the blonde and thin young women." The volume in question was Mme. de Genlis' novel, *La Duchesse de La Vallière*, and the empress' sarcasm was not idle, for the romance was to be found in the room of every lady-in-waiting; the book had the enormous sale of ten editions, and doubtless the fact that many aspired to a position similar to La Vallière's had not been detrimental to its success.

The emperor had no intention of installing a favourite. He said upon one occasion:

> I do not wish women to govern in my court, their influence was harmful to Henri IV and Louis XIV, my mission is more important than theirs was, and the French have become too serious to pardon scandalous *liaisons* of their sovereigns.

His real mistress, as he often said, was power, and he had worked too hard to attain it, to permit of its being stolen or even coveted. Madame **** who was both very astute and very intelligently advised, asked nothing for herself, indeed, she was not able to accept many favours, as they might have roused the suspicions of her husband, who was far from being indifferent to his wife's good name and conduct; the most that she was able to secure individually was a position as lady-in-waiting, an appointment which was warranted neither by her position, birth or anything in the past which had endeared her to Bonaparte, and which caused some gossip and many malicious smiles; but little as her relations advantaged her personally, she profited by them to advance the interests of others and her one time protectors became her *protégés*.

Murat, already Marshal of the Empire, was promoted to the dignity of a prince and made admiral in-chief, which classed him, after Cambacérès and Lebrun, among the serene highnesses; but at the same time and of his own accord the emperor named Eugène de Beauharnais prince and arch-chancellor of state, thus placing him upon the same level as Murat, and establishing the balance between the Bonapartes and the Beauharnais, inclining it even in favour of the Beauharnais. There was a marked difference in the terms which he employed in announcing both decisions to the Senate, and he made the positions which his brother-in-law and his stepson held in his affections most evident; on the one hand it was clear that he yielded to outside pressure and the solicitations of the family, on the other, that he gave freely, actuated by the dictates of his own heart:

"In the midst of the anxieties and the bitterness inseparable from the high rank where we are placed, our heart has felt the need of affection and sincere friendship, and its wants have been gratified by this child of our adoption our paternal benediction will accompany this young prince throughout his career and, seconded by Providence, he will one day be deserving the approbation of posterity."

Such was the speech which announced Eugène de Beauharnais' aggrandizement to the senate; and he had asked for nothing, expressed no dissatisfaction with the position of grand officer of the Empire and colonel of *chasseurs* which had previously been conferred upon him, as he was on the way to Milan at the head of the mounted guards. It was in truth a fine command, and it was a strange error on the part of Mme. de Rémusat, to represent in the light of a disgrace the greatest favour which the emperor could bestow upon a general of twenty three years.

At all events this disgrace, which, according to her, was occasioned by an access of jealousy against Eugène, was of singularly short duration, for he left Paris on the 16th of January in obedience to an order dated on the 14th and which was prompted by the necessity for the appearance of the guards at the coronation at Milan, and it was but fifteen days later that he received a personal letter from the emperor with a copy of the message to the senate and his nomination as prince and arch-chancellor of state.

Nothing could prove more clearly that Napoleon was drawn closer to Josephine, that he did not propose to be led by anyone, and that the affection inspired by Madame **** was already on the wane: satiety comes soon when there is no restraint. It was at Malmaison in the heart of winter that the intrigue culminated, and at Malmaison, ere spring-flowers had blossomed, that the chains were broken.

It was while the court was enjoying a fortnight's sojourn at Malmaison, during which Napoleon enjoyed perfect freedom, and could walk, talk and enjoy the society of Madame **** to his heart's content, while Josephine mourned and pined in the seclusion of her chamber, that the final rupture occurred. One morning the emperor went to his wife's apartments and returning to his old confidential manner, admitted that he had been very much in love but was disillusioned, and finished by asking Josephine to aid him to sunder his relations with Madame ****. The empress took the matter in hand and summoned the lady, who, perfectly mistress of herself, did not manifest the slightest emotion and opposed to the empress' remarks a mute disdain and a face as impassive as marble.

Although the emperor never renewed his allegiance, Madame **** always remained tenderly attached to him, while he invariably manifested for her the greatest consideration, according her every favour compatible with her husband's position, and designating her among the first for court honours and favours. During his hours of trial she was one of his most faithful adherents, she enhanced the *fêtes* of the hundred days with her beauty, and when, after Waterloo, the vanquished hero was about to leave his country forever, Madame **** was one of the last to visit Malmaison and offer to the dethroned emperor the tribute of her respectful attachment and unalterable devotion.

CHAPTER 12

Stéphanie de Beauharnais

Prior even to Austerlitz, Napoleon resolved to establish family relations between his house and the sovereign houses of Europe which would serve to consolidate political alliances; he was of the opinion that his government would never be firmly established in Europe until the blood of the Napoleons mingled with that of older reigning families, and not believing himself marriageable, he mobilized around him all who were, boys and girls, with the view of strengthening the only bond to which he attached any value, because he did not think it subject to political hazards. From his point of view nothing was more binding, even to princes, than ties of blood.

His first step, on returning from the campaign, was to arrange a marriage between Eugène de Beauharnais and the Princess Augusta of Bavaria; she was betrothed to the Prince of Baden, but that was of no importance. Napoleon finding another wife for the discarded lover in the person of Stéphanie-Louise-Adrienne de Beauharnais, the daughter of Claude de Beauharnais, Count of Roches-Baritaud, and of Adrienne de Lezay-Marnésia his first wife, and cousin, sixteen degrees removed, to Hortense and Eugène.

Stéphanie de Beauharnais was born at Paris on the 26th of August, 1789, and, losing her mother at the age of four years, spent some time in the convent of Panthémont; a certain Lady de Bath, an old friend of her mother's, then took the young girl under her protection and, when the convents were closed, confided her ward to two of the sisters, Mmes. de Trélissac and de Sabatier, who took Stéphanie with them, first to Castelsarrasin, then to Périgueux and later to Montauban. Her paternal grandmother, Fanny de Beauharnais, occupied herself at Cubières with poetry and flirtations, her father was an *émigré*, and her grandfather, Marquis de Marnésia, was travelling in America, so that, save for the kindness of Lady de Bath, the child would have been left to public charity.

One day, in the beginning of the consulate, Josephine happened to speak of her little cousin before her husband, and Bonaparte, who thought so much of ties of blood, was indignant at his wife for leaving one of her name to the care of a stranger and an Englishwoman. He immediately sent for the child, but the nuns refused to deliver her to the messenger, whereupon he sent a courier armed with legal authority to take Stéphanie de Beauharnais, and the sisters were forced to obey, though not without tears and grave misgivings. Upon her arrival in Paris the child was placed with Mme. Campan, and thenceforth she was one of the little group of young girls who came to Malmaison each *décadi* (the republican day of rest), and whose white-robed forms and cheery laughter enlivened the park as they flitted about under the shade of the great chestnut trees.

Both Josephine and Hortense were extremely kind to Stéphanie, but she did not appear on gala days, had no rank, was of no importance, and seemed destined to such a marriage as had been arranged for her cousin Emilie de Beauharnais, Mme. Lavallette; the little lady, however, did not take that view of the situation, but assumed the airs of a princess and treated those of her relations who were not honoured with a lodging in the imperial palace very haughtily.

Such was the situation when Eugène married and it became necessary to provide a wife for the Prince of Baden; Napoleon first thought of another ward of Josephine's, her niece, Stéphanie Tascher, but afterwards decided upon Stéphanie de Beauharnais, and the arrangements for the marriage were definitely concluded by him while on his way to Carlsruhe, on the 20th of January, 1806, and were confirmed by an agreement signed at Paris on the 17th of February.

Stéphanie was at that time seventeen years of age, was clever, bright and gay, with a certain childishness of manner which was very taking; she had rather a pretty face, a fine complexion, sparkling blue eyes and beautiful blonde hair. Upon the emperor's return to Paris she was taken from her boarding-school to the Tuileries and installed in an apartment near that of the empress and became at once the life of the palace; gay, piquant and agreeable, she enlivened the dreary salons, and not being in the least embarrassed by the emperor she indulged her mischievousness as freely in his presence as elsewhere, which greatly pleased and amused him; she was not long in perceiving this and increased her efforts to divert him, and they were soon engaged in a lively flirtation.

Possibly Napoleon hoped for something more, but Mlle. de Beauharnais was not so inclined; she only wished for distraction and to make the most of Napoleon's friendship and admiration without compromising herself; she was well aware that it was not because she was Mlle. de Beauharnais that she was to espouse the Prince of Baden, but because she was a Napoleonite, that the manner of her reception by the prince's family depended entirely upon the emperor, and that it was therefore prudent to find out how much he would do for her.

Stéphanie's struggle was not with the empress, but with the sisters of Napoleon, who had no intention of yielding her precedence, and who, Caroline Murat particularly, snubbed her mercilessly, but little Stéphanie made light of their rudeness and laughed gayly at everything until Caroline, exasperated, became insolent. One evening, while they were waiting for the emperor, Stéphanie seated herself on a folding chair, upon which the Princess Caroline ordered her to rise, saying, that it was not customary for young persons to remain seated in the presence of the emperor's sisters; Stéphanie rose immediately, but she no longer laughed, on the contrary, she wept bitterly; the emperor, entering at that moment, perceived her tears, and inquired their source. "Is that all!" he exclaimed when Stéphanie told her grievance, "well, come and sit on my knee, and you won't incommode anybody!"

This anecdote is lent an appearance of authenticity by a note which is found upon the register of the master of ceremonies:

> Our will is, that the Princess Stéphanie-Napoleon, our daughter, shall in all circles enjoy all the privileges due her rank, and that at *fêtes* and at table she shall be seated at our side, and in case we are not present that she shall be placed at the empress' right hand.

This gave Stéphanie precedence over the emperor's sisters, sisters-in-law, Hortense, and even over the Princess Augusta of Bavaria.

On the following day a message announced to the senate the adoption of Stéphanie de Beauharnais and her approaching marriage with the Prince of Baden, and ordered the State to send a deputation to pay her respects, in which ceremony M. Claude de Beauharnais, the princess's own father, figured conspicuously.

M. de Beauharnais, on his return from exile, had entered the senate, and was then a member of some years' standing, with a salary of twenty-five thousand *francs* a year, and he was about to enjoy the benefits accruing from the parentage of a charming daughter. Napoleon appointed him to the senatorship of Amiens, which brought him an income of twenty-five thousand *francs*; in 1807 endowed him with twenty-five thousand eight hundred and eighty-two *francs*, and in 1810 made him *chevalier d' honneur* to Marie-Louise, a position which commanded a salary of thirty thousand *francs*, and on the 22nd of September, 1807, made him a personal present of two hundred thousand *francs*; but all this was a mere bagatelle in comparison with what the emperor did for Stéphanie.

He took a personal interest in her *trousseau*, ordering for her a tulle dress covered with an embroidery of gold thread and interwoven with precious stones, the cost of which was twenty-four thousand *francs*; from Lenormand he commanded twelve dresses, at prices ranging from nineteen hundred to twelve hundred *francs*; from Leroy he commanded forty-five thousand, one hundred and seventy-eight *francs* and ninety-six *centimes*' worth of millinery and trinkets, and from Roux-Montagnat, two thousand, five hundred and seventy-four *francs*' worth of artificial flowers; in addition to all this he gave her a dot of fifteen hundred thousand *francs*, a superb *parure* of diamonds, and presented her with a thousand *louts* from his private purse.

Both the civil and religious marriages were celebrated with the utmost pomp and magnificence; Napoleon could not have done more for his own child, and the festivities were not confined to the palace, but overflowed into the city, which was illuminated by fireworks set off on the Place de la Concorde. When the last spark had died, the last note of the band had sounded, and the guests had departed, the emperor and empress, according to usage, conducted the bride and groom to the bridal chamber, but it was found impossible to induce Stéphanie to occupy it; she wept and sobbed, and insisted that her school-fellow, Mlle. Nelly Bourjolly, should sleep with her.

The court went to Malmaison on the following day, but Stéphanie, in spite of all the arguments brought to bear upon her, still remained obdurate. Someone told the prince that his wife's repugnance arose from the manner in which he dressed his hair, as she detested a cue, thereupon he had his hair cut short; but as soon as Stéphanie perceived him she burst out laughing and declared that he was uglier than before. Night after night the prince went to her door, supplicating and praying for admittance, and at last exhausted threw himself upon a couch in the ante chamber and fell asleep; in the morning he went and complained to the empress, while Napoleon smilingly watched the couple who naturally were the talk of the *château*.

That this state of affairs gave the emperor a certain amount of satisfaction, that he bore Stéphanie no ill-will was proved by the superb *fête* which he gave at the Tuileries in honour of her marriage: the first great ball to which not only the court but the gentry of the city were bidden. Nothing equalling the two *quadrilles*—one in the gallery of Diana conducted by the Princess Louise, the other in the *Salle des Maréchaux*, conducted by the Princess Caroline— had ever been seen, while the lavishness of the refreshments set all the world talking: there were sixty *entrées*, sixty roasts and two hundred desserts; one thousand bottles of Beaune, one hundred of Champagne, one hundred of Bordeaux and one hundred of sweet wines were consumed; but the festivities did not soften Stéphanie's heart.

Political reasons intervening, Napoleon saw himself obliged to interfere. Mlle. de Beauharnais' *coqueteries* had amused him and supplied a pretext for teasing his wife, but he had permitted himself rather too much latitude in according to the young girl a rank disproportionate to her birth and fortune and in celebrating her marriage in princely style; he now saw that the patience of the ruler of Baden was nearly exhausted, and, as a war with Prussia was imminent, felt it expedient to conciliate all the German princes who might become auxiliaries, or at least give valuable information.

Having respected Stéphanie previous to her marriage, he did not afterwards meditate making her his mistress, and the flirtation which was suitable neither to his dignity, his age nor his temperament, grew wearisome, and it was becoming embarrassing to have her longer at Paris, while she might be of service at Carlsruhe, if only in counterbalancing the hostile influence of Markgraf Louis and the little German court.

Napoleon hardly took time to investigate the little stories contained in certain intercepted letters, which proved only too plainly what an inhospitable reception awaited his adopted daughter, but hastened her departure. Stéphanie left France despairing; she took with her three of her schoolfriends: Mlles, de Mackau, Bourjolly and Gruau, and as soon as she arrived in her father-in-law's principality, she wrote to the emperor:

> Sire, each day when I am at liberty I think of you and the empress, of all who are dearest to me; in imagination, I am in France and near you, and I find a certain pleasure in my sadness.

Napoleon responded rather severely, without making use of any paternal or tender expressions.

Carlsruhe is a charming place of residence. Make yourself agreeable to the Elector, who is now your father, and love your husband, who merits your affection by the tenderness he lavishes upon you.

When she had answered in a manner which pleased him, saying that she was contented at Carlsruhe, Napoleon wrote more kindly, calling her *daughter*, but recommending the same line of conduct; and he did not become thoroughly amiable until the hereditary grand duke asked him to make the campaign with him, and in the same letter announced that Stéphanie was about to become a mother; then he wrote, saying:

I only hear good news of you and hope you will continue to be kind and gentle to all who surround you.

He then authorized her to rejoin the empress and Hortense at Mayence, and to remain with them while her husband was with the army, and thereafter, to all his letters to Josephine he added a kindly message for Stéphanie. In 1807, Stéphanie and her husband were invited to Paris on the occasion of the marriage of Jérôme Bonaparte with Catherine of Wurtemberg, and she hastened to accept; but if she retained any illusion concerning the emperor's affection and the exceptional rank which only a year previous he had bestowed upon her, she must have been cruelly disappointed, for the place assigned her was the very last among the princesses, and it was only by courtesy that she took a place in the Imperial family; by favour that she was given a folding-chair when the family were seated. She had become a princess of the German confederation, and had there been any of the reigning German princesses present, they would have taken precedence over her.

At first Stéphanie did not seem to perceive her downfall, and took pleasure in flirting with Jérôme, the new King of Westphalia, but her aunt remarking upon her conduct, the situation became clear, and realizing that she could only hold her position through her husband, she managed to inspire him with so much affection that he became unsupportably jealous.

Did the prince stand by Stéphanie in 1814, when, after the emperor's downfall, he was urged to repudiate her and turn out of the palace of Zaehringen this unwelcome witness to broken oaths, whose presence constantly recalled favours whose authors the reigning house of Baden desired to forget? Was it because of his fidelity that at the age of thirty-two, this man, previously in the most vigorous health, fell suddenly ill, and after dragging for a year died of a strange malady in 1818? Stéphanie, although the mother of numerous children, was unable to preserve one son; when she lost the second, or believed him dead, she wrote broken-heartedly to the emperor:

> I was so happy to tell your Majesty that I had a son and to beseech your protection for him. A son made me forget my griefs and was necessary to my position which is often a difficult one—now I have lost my only hope!

She grieved unceasingly over the fatality which followed her sons and took from her race, stricken because of her with political sterility, the heredity of the throne of Baden.

Ten years after the death of the grand duke, between four and five o'clock on the morning of the 26th of May, 1828, a *bourgeois* met a young man of seventeen, who muttered only one or two phrases in low German in the Tallow Market of Nuremberg; the youth had never walked, his eyes had never seen the sun's light, his stomach was unable to support animal food, but he would never have been thus deformed had he not since babyhood been sequestered in solitude and obscurity.

Stéphanie was the first to ponder, calculate, and be convinced that the mysterious and unknown youth at Nuremberg, who was called Kaspar Hauser, was her own son—her child, in whose place a dead baby had been substituted, and who, a victim to the hatred of Markgraf Louis, and the ambition of Countess Hochberg, had for nearly sixteen years expiated in darkness and solitude the sin of having a Napoleonite for his mother. Poor Stéphanie was unable to do anything, for her enemies were triumphant and powerful; one reigned upon the throne of Baden, and she could tremble for Kaspar Hauser, and weep over his sad fate, when, after escaping three ambuscades, he was finally assassinated.

Was hers one of those illusions with which a mother loves to comfort her heart, or one of those revelations, which, better than all the investigations of justice, sometimes throw light upon a great crime? However this may be, Stéphanie firmly believed to her last hour (she died on the 29th of January, 1860), that Kaspar Hauser was her lost son, and to the few friends whom she received in the tumble-down palace of Mannheim, she asserted that her son did not die in 1812, but that he had been stolen from her, designating the authors and accomplices in the crime. Some German authors have attempted to demonstrate that the poor mother deceived herself; for the credit of the reigning house of Baden, it is to be hoped she did.

CHAPTER 13

Eléonore

Towards the close of the revolution, Mme. Campan, once a confidential member of Marie Antoinette's household, established a school for young ladies at Saint-Germain-en-Laye; Josephine became the patroness of the institution, and there her daughter and nieces were educated. This group of young girls, so closely allied to the imperial family, drew around them the daughters of those who had, or sought for, some appointment under the Consulate, and Mme. Campan's nieces making excellent marriages, thanks to their intimacy with Hortense, the school was still further augmented by the daughters of intriguing parents who hoped their children might also profit by the acquaintance of their royal schoolfellows.

Mme. Campan was supposedly an influential person, having obtained positions for numerous people, pardons for exiles and the restitution of confiscated property; her school was the fashionable one of the day, and on the list of pupils can be seen, side by side with names of people who had recently attained eminence, the old historical ones of Noailles, Talon, Lally-Tollendal, and Rochemond,

After the Consulate, the reputation of the school diminished somewhat, and among the scholars there was a young girl of whose origin Mme. Campan was somewhat in ignorance, and who could probably never have been a pupil had the principal then been as strict regarding the parentage of those whom she admitted as she was in the days of the school's great popularity. This young lady was Mlle. Louise-Catherine-Eléonore Dénuelle de La Plaigne. The father claimed to be a man of wealth, but his business ventures were not always successful; the mother, who was still very pretty, was rather gay, and the family lived in a sumptuous apartment on the Boulevard des Italiens, received a great deal of rather mixed company, and managed as best they could from day to day, awaiting the time when their daughter should make a rich marriage.

Time passed, Mme. Dénuelle aged, the father ran into debt, the quarterly tuition was hard to pay, and, moreover, since the departure of the Beauharnais from Mme. Campan's, the chances of meeting a desirable *partie* in that establishment, had greatly diminished; so, as Mme. Dénuelle had not access to salons where her daughter might have made such acquaintances, she determined to show her at the theatres. One evening at the Gaîté, a good-looking officer entered the box where Mme Dénuelle and her daughter occupied seats, and took the vacant place; the ladies were not haughty, the officer was gallant, and an acquaintance grew apace.

Mme. Dénuelle invited the young man to visit them and he did not fail to do so; he soon became so enamoured of Eléonore as to ask her hand in marriage, and the wedding took place on the fifteenth of January, 1805, at Saint-Germain.

This officer, Jean-Honoré-François Revel, who claimed to be a captain of the 15th regiment of Dragoons and the *aide-de-camp* of General d'Avrange d'Haugeranville, was a knave. He had resigned from the regiment of which he was once quartermaster, and claimed that he expected to get a contract for supplying the army with provisions; in the meanwhile he lived on credit. He appears to have counted more upon the beauty of his young wife to extricate him from his embarrassment than upon any efforts of his own, and two months after the wedding he was arrested and imprisoned for attempting to pass a forged check.

Eléonore then bethought herself that the Princess Caroline Murat had been her schoolfellow, and, warmly recommended by Mme. Campan, solicited her highness' protection. The princess first placed her in a sort of asylum at Chantilly, where unfortunate women like herself were received; later, in despite of Mme. Campan's advice, she yielded to Eléonore's solicitations and installed her in her own household.

Mme. Revel was an extremely handsome brunette, tall and graceful, with large, dark eyes and a lively, *coquettish* manner; she had not been educated to entertain scruples, and she certainly had not acquired any in the two months she spent with Bevel. At first her duty was to announce the princess' guests, later she was promoted to the dignity of reader, and when, after the emperor's return from Austerlitz towards the end of January, 1806, he came to visit his sister, Mme. Eléonore deftly managed to make herself noticeable and as soon as propositions were made to her accepted with enthusiasm, and allowed herself to be conducted to the Tuileries; from thenceforth she went there habitually, spending two or three hours in the emperor's society.

Revel had been condemned by the criminal court to two years' imprisonment, and on the 13th of April his wife asked for a divorce, which was granted on the 29th of April, 1806; it was high time, for on the 13th of December, 1806, at No. 29 rue de la Victoire, she was delivered of a male child who was registered as "Léon, son of Mlle. Dénuelle, property-holder, aged twenty, and of an absent father."

There was no doubt as to the child's parentage; Eléonore who in her prayer for divorce had stated that she was "attached to the person of Mme. la Princess Caroline," had, from the time she returned from Chantilly, lived in a small house in the rue de Provence, which she never left save for her visits to the Tuileries—visits of which Caroline knew the secret—moreover, the child's resemblance to Napoleon was so striking as to confute doubt. Thus the event which Josephine so dreaded came to pass; the charm was broken, for henceforth the emperor entertained no doubts regarding his ability to provide an heir to the throne.

The emperor was at Pulstuck, when, on the 31st of December, the news of Eléonore's *accouchement* reached him, and doubtless the birth of this illegitimate son was strongly instrumental in the formation of plans which two years later he carried into execution.

The child Léon was at first confided to the care of Mme. Loir, foster-mother of Achille Murat; later, in 1812, M. Mathieu de Mauvières, mayor of the commune of Saint-Forget, baron of the Empire and father-in-law of Méneval, the emperor's private secretary, was appointed guardian to the boy, and an independent fortune was settled upon him by his imperial father. Not content with this, in January, 1814, when about to leave Paris to join the army, Napoleon authorized the Duke de Bassano to add twelve thousand pounds income, and to this, on the 21st of June, 1815, was added canal stock valued at one hundred thousand *francs*, and finally, actuated by conscience, the emperor added a codicil to his will in which he bequeathed to Léon three hundred and twenty thousand *francs* for the purchase of a country seat, and as long as he lived interested himself in his son's welfare. The thirty-seventh paragraph of his testamentary instructions to his executors, proves that the lad was never forgotten. Napoleon wrote:

If his taste runs in that direction I should be pleased to have little Léon enter the magistracy.

To avoid a rupture with Josephine, to whom he was still sincerely attached, and at the same time to comply with the law of heredity in a manner which seemed to him both satisfactory and natural, Napoleon conceived the idea of adopting his natural son, spoke of it to the empress, sounded many of his confidants on the subject, and invoked precedents to justify his inclination. That he did not carry these plans into execution is probably due to the fact that he realized that the days of Louis XIV. were past, and that the country would not permit him to follow the example given by that monarch, who had designated the Duke de Maine and the Comte de Toulouse as his heirs to the throne.

Napoleon became very much attached to this child, and frequently had him brought either to the Elysée or to his sister Caroline's, sometimes received him even at the Tuileries while dressing or at breakfast; he played with him, gave him dainties to eat and was amused by Leon's childish chatter. As time passed Napoleon was necessarily unable to bestow the same personal attention upon Léon, but in 1815 he recommended the boy to the care of his mother and Cardinal Fesch. Mme. Bonaparte was already interested in the boy and seemed disposed to do a great deal for him, but unfortunately Leon's was not a character to inspire warm affection.

In 1832—he was then twenty-five—Dénuelle was already nearly ruined, owing to his passion for gambling, and applied for assistance to Cardinal Fesch, swearing that he would never again lose forty-five thousand *francs* at a sitting. It was a gambler's oath, for a year later he was as badly off as ever, attempting to brazen out his affairs, mixing with visionary politicians and engaging right and left in duels, for he was brave and somewhat of a bully.

In 1834, by trading on the name of the grand man to whom he owed his existence, he was elected chief of the communal battalion of the national guards of Saint-Denis; he was soon suspended for disobedience to orders, but afterwards reinstated, and attempted to justify himself by the publication of a number of pamphlets, which are, however, so hazy that they could hardly have served to clear his character before the public.

In 1840 he was one of the official *cortége* on the return from Cendres, and, being absolutely ruined, began a series of lawsuits against his mother with the intention of wringing money from her, she having preserved her fortune intact.

The emperor had never renewed his relations with Leon's mother, had, indeed, refused to receive her when, in 1807, she presented herself at Fontainebleau, but he acquitted his debt to her by giving her a house in the rue de la Victoire, and a dot of twenty-two thousand pounds, which was not transferable. She married, in 1808, a lieutenant of infantry, M. Pierre-Philippe Augier, who took her to Spain with him, and who died in captivity after the Russian campaign. Eléonore was not inconsolable, for at Seckenheim, on the 25th of May, 1814, she was married for the third time to M. Charles-Auguste-Emile, Count de Luxbourg, and a major in the service of the King of Bavaria.

Returning to Paris with her third husband she was obliged to combat the first, for Revel, profiting by the fall of Napoleon, posed as a victim and essayed to blackmail his ex-wife; Mme. de Luxbourg resisted, and Revel, to avenge himself and to make a few pennies, published innumerable pamphlets whose titles were startling, and admirably combined to attract attention and create a scandal, but he was defeated in everything he attempted against his former wife. Léon was somewhat more fortunate in his suits against his mother, for, although he lost a suit wherein he charged her with swindling and attempted to force her to render an account of her income, he succeeded in having himself acknowledged as her natural son, and on the second of July, 1846, he obtained a lump sum of four thousand *francs* instead of the yearly allowance which he had sued for.

In 1848 he seems to have been somewhat better off financially, for he meditated presenting himself as a candidate for the presidency of the Republic in competition with the Prince Louis Napoleon, with whom, eight years previous, in March, 1840, he had been ambitious to fight a duel. Leon's conduct in this respect was so singular that it can only be explained by the supposition that he was mentally deranged. In 1848 he put forth his claims in a manifesto beginning:

> Citizen Léon, ex-count Léon, son of the Emperor Napoleon, director of the Pacific Society, to the French people.

The empire reinstalled, Dénuelle obtained from Napoleon III, a pension of six thousand *francs*, and the payment of Napoleon's first legacy to him of two hundred and twenty-five thousand, three hundred and nineteen *francs*, but that did not content him, and in 1853 he reclaimed five hundred and seventy-two thousand, six hundred and seventy *francs* in virtue of some visionary decree, and in 1857 sued the minister of Public Works for the sum of five hundred thousand *francs*, which he claimed was due him for draughts made by him for the *chemin de fer du Nord*. Not a year passed that he did not bring forward some claim or petition, and the civil list paid his debts five or six times; but he was irrepressible and his brain was in a state of perpetual evolution up to the time of his death, which occurred at Pontoise on the 15th of April, 1881.

CHAPTER 14

Hortense

The year 1807 was a decisive one in the life of Napoleon; the month of January being marked by the birth of Léon, which gave to him the certitude that he could have a direct heir, and May by the death of Napoleon-Charles, eldest son of Louis and Hortense. With him died Napoleon's dream of creating an heredity by adoption, and the child's death was also a sad blow to his affections. Napoleon-Charles had been doubly dear to the Emperor, being the son of the girl, who, from the moment he met her, had taken such a hold upon his heart that he had accorded to her tears the pardon refused her mother, and to whom he had been both father and guardian. Napoleon-Charles was the child also of his best-loved brother, "the little brother" who had been to him almost as a son, whom he had lodged, fed and educated when he had but a lieutenant's scanty pay; whom he had made his *aide-de-camp* and the witness of his victories, whom he had ennobled as he himself rose in rank, until he stood close to the throne.

In his nephew Napoleon saw all the characteristics of the Bonapartes, undisfigured by Louis' blobber-lip and ugly nose, and unbeautified by the slender grace of his mother's family, but a Bonaparte through and through, idealized only by an aureole of golden hair. To this child, the first male of his generation. Napoleon had given his father's name, and he had shown such a lively affection for the boy that gossips had begun by insinuating, and had finally asserted, that he was the child's real father, that his stepdaughter had been his mistress before becoming Louis' wife.

Hortense's marriage-contract was signed on the 3rd of January, 1802, the marriage celebrated on the 4th, and her son was born on the 10th of October, 1802, therefore she was certainly not *enceinte* when she married, since there were two hundred and eighty days between the time she was wed and the birth of her child.

Louis Bonaparte was the most jealous and suspicious of husbands; he tyrannized over his wife from the hour of their marriage; he never left her, had her constantly under surveillance, and forbade her to pass even one night at Saint-Cloud. Suffering from an illness due to youthful indiscretions, he at first essayed to effect a cure by taking tripe baths, the stench of which infected the old orangery which stood at the end of the Terrasse des Feuillant; later, to draw out the humour, he slept in the nightgown and sheets which had previously served a hospital patient afflicted with the itch, and he obliged his wife to sleep on a little bed in the same room with him. Every maid who showed the slightest affection for Hortense was pitilessly discharged; his mother-in-law was a target for the gravest accusations, yet Louis had never the slightest doubt of his wife's virtue.

In his *Documents Historiques sur la Hollande*, he affirms that he was the father of the three children whom his wife and he "loved with equal tenderness;" this affirmation he repeated both in prose and in verse, for he thought himself a poet; and when, on the emperor's proposal to adopt Napoleon-Charles, Louis alluded to the current reports regarding the boy's paternity, it was not because he attached the slightest importance to them, but because they served as a pretext for not yielding to his brother's wishes. Louis-Napoleon had an unfortunately melancholy and peculiar disposition, but he loved his son as much as he could love anyone, and the child's death was a severe trial; after this loss he was for a time reconciled to Hortense, with whom he previously lived so unhappily that his imperial brother had more than once seen fit to remonstrate with him, and he wrote kind and affectionate letters to Josephine, whom ordinarily he detested.

Shortly after the death of her son, Hortense, who was in poor health, went to Cauterets accompanied by her husband, and it was there, under circumstances the details of which are well-known, that she became *enceinte* with her third son, Charles-Louis-Napoleon, afterwards known as Napoleon III.; thus Louis Bonaparte never believed for an instant that Hortense had been his brother's mistress, and not only did he bear witness to his faith in her virtue, but his conduct was an affirmation of his convictions; as for Hortense, until 1809, she remained ignorant that such gossip was afloat.

Josephine's marriage with General Bonaparte had wounded her daughter to the quick, for she felt it to be almost a crime for her mother to wed one who was a soldier under the Republic, a man whose political principles were similar to those entertained by the men who had caused her father's execution. Previous to her mother's marriage, Hortense lived at Saint-Germain-en-Laye, near her grandfather, the Marquis de Beauharnais and her aunt, Mme. Renaudin, whom he had recently married. At the beginning of the Consulate she was entered at Mme. Campan's, and she did not go to live at the Tuileries until about the time when the consul left France for Marengo; thus it was not until Bonaparte returned from Italy that Hortense saw him continually and familiarly.

Napoleon always entertained a tender and paternal affection for his wife's daughter, which she returned only with timid respect; she trembled when addressing him, dared ask nothing of him, and when obliged to make a request employed intermediaries. "The little goose," Napoleon frequently said, "why don't she speak to me; why is the child so afraid of me?" He did not interfere when Josephine arranged the marriage between her daughter and Louis Bonaparte, because he hoped that this marriage might unite his own family and that of his wife, and foresaw that it might be politically judicious, and he also felt a delicacy in interfering with any of Josephine's plans for her children; but whenever he thought it necessary he did not hesitate to counsel Louis as to his conduct towards Hortense, and with the most admirable tact and delicacy strove to calm his jealous fears and point out to him wherein his conduct was faulty. He pitied his stepdaughter, venerated her, and guarded his speech in her presence; on more than one occasion he said: "Hortense obliges me to believe in virtue."

Napoleon was not ignorant of the rumours which were afloat regarding his relations with his stepdaughter, rumours which some of those who were very near to him were assiduous in spreading and which were amplified by the English papers. In order to put a stop to the calumnies he bethought himself of a plan which does greater credit to his knightly intentions than to his discrimination; he commanded a ball to be given at Malmaison, and that Hortense, although then in her seventh month, should assist at it; he invited her to dance, but Hortense declined, alleging that she was weary, although in reality her refusal arose from her knowledge of her stepfather's dislike of seeing women who were *enceinte* upon the floor of a ballroom, above all, when, as was the fashion of the time, they were clothed in such clinging garments that the outlines of the figure were plainly discernible.

The emperor, however, insisted, asking simply for a contredance, and, after persisting for some time in her refusal, she finally yielded.

The following morning a newspaper published some gallant verses upon the subject, and Hortense, furious, complained to the emperor, but received no satisfaction; the truth being that the ball had been given solely to furnish occasion for the verses, and so force the public to acknowledge that she was not so far advanced in pregnancy as was currently reported; it was with this view also that the *Moniteur*, which up to that time had never spoken of the consul's family, inserted In its edition of October 12th, 1802, the following announcement:

> On the 10th inst., at 9 o'clock in the evening, a son was born to Monsieur and Madame Louis Bonaparte.

Napoleon did all in his power to crush the calumny, but his efforts proved unavailing; so he gradually accustomed himself to look upon the report from a political standpoint and cogitated how he might turn it to account. He felt an almost paternal affection for Napoleon-Charles, and some of the happiest hours of his life were spent in play with him; it delighted him to hear the child cry: "Long live Nanon the soldier!" when he saw a grenadier pass, and he frequently had the little fellow sit by his side while he dined, being highly amused by the child's desire to touch everything and by the agility with which he seized and upset everything within reach of his baby hands.

The emperor frequently took Napoleon-Charles to the garden to feed tobacco to the gazelles, and, seating him astride one of them, would roar with laughter at the baby's antics; he often sent for the child when in his dressing-room, and, after caressing him and making the most extraordinary grimaces for his amusement, would end by sitting down upon the floor, the better to play with him. Napoleon loved the little nephew, whom the people claimed was his own son, as though he were verily bone of his bone and flesh of his flesh, and therefore the idea of adopting him as his heir was not repugnant, even if by so doing the people were convinced of the truth of their suppositions. In this lad he believed they would find impersonated the characteristics of his race and his own genius, and that they could not claim that the line which he had founded was built upon a fiction.

It must be admitted that this plan was contrary to all established ideas, but Napoleon had no prejudices and believed that his exceptional destiny placed him above humanity at large, that the nation would not judge him according to accepted moral formulas, and that the people's desire to assure the stability of his government would cause them to overlook the unconventionality of the proceeding, the more easily as they could not confirm the existing suspicion.

It must not be supposed that it is upon simple supposition only that we accredit the emperor with these ideas and projects; we base our statements upon a conversation which he had with Hortense, two years after the death of her son, and which is related at length in her unpublished *mémoires*. He then spoke freely to his stepdaughter regarding the consequences attendant upon the death of Napoleon-Charles, who, as he said, was thought to be his son as well as hers. "You know," Napoleon said, " how absurd such a supposition is, but you could not convince all Europe that the child was not mine," he stopped a moment, arrested by a movement of surprise from Hortense, then continued:

> Your reputation does not suffer on this account, as you are generally esteemed; nevertheless, the idea receives credence everywhere; it was perhaps best that it was so, and for that reason I regard his death as a great misfortune.

Hortense wrote:

> I was so surprised, that I was unable to utter a word, I no longer heard what he said. That reflection, '*it was perhaps best that it was believed*,' tore a veil from before my eyes and pierced me to the heart; was it possible that he who had been so kind and generous, in whom I seemed to find my own lost father, had been actuated throughout by political motives and not by affection!

Hortense was mistaken, for if Napoleon had been actuated by policy he also was moved by affection, but her indignation was quite natural, considering that she looked upon the situation from a woman's point of view, and was unable to conceive of the profound subtlety of Napoleon's reasoning. If he had showered kindnesses and attentions upon Hortense it had not been in order to confirm the story that Napoleon-Charles was his son, on the contrary he had made every effort to refute it; but the gossip persisting and a conviction of its truth being firmly established in the public mind he had sought to utilize it for his own interests and the consolidation of his dynasty; it was a battlefield inspiration which he had had, for one of his most remarkable faculties was the ability to look situations clearly in the face, to discern at a glance precisely where he stood, make the best of affairs, and act promptly upon his intuitions.

It was owing to his belief in a philosophical acceptance of all situations, that, while he felt keenly the loss of Napoleon-Charles, he accepted the inevitable with calmness. The remark, "I have not time to indulge in sentimental regrets like other men," has been accredited him; it might better be admitted that the death of his poor little nephew was a grief to him, for he wrote to all his correspondents, at least twenty times to Josephine, six or seven to Hortense, and severally to Joseph, Jérôme, Fouché and Monge, expressing his sorrow, but adding, "that it was destiny." It was not in Napoleon's nature, nor in accordance with the philosophical formula which the continual spectacle of war and death in all its most terrible forms had imposed upon his spirit, to yield to idle tears when a destiny was accomplished,

Napoleon-Charles was one of the ties which attached Bonaparte to Josephine, and this tie broken there only remained between them those bonds of tenderness which were woven by ten years of wedded life; years broken by long absences, marred by frequent quarrels and strange misunderstandings. Could these bonds resist such a strain as they were subjected to in 1805 by his *liaison* with Madame ★★★★?

.

CHAPTER 15

Madame Walewska

On the 1st of January, 1807, the emperor, on his way from Pulstuck to Warsaw, stopped to change post-horses at the little town of Bronie; a noisy and enthusiastic crowd awaited the liberator of Poland, and rushed to surround the imperial carriage as soon as it came in sight. As the carriage stopped before the post-house. General Duroc descended and cleared an entrance; he was about to pass the door when he heard a cry of entreaty, saw hands lifted in supplication, and a voice addressing him in French, said: "Oh, sir, pray get us out of this crowd, and arrange so that I may obtain even a glimpse of His Majesty!"

Duroc paused and looking about saw that the demand came from two ladies, who seemed sadly out of place in the multitude of peasants and workmen; the one who spoke to him seemed almost a child, she was very fair and fragile, with great, blue, innocent-looking eyes which at that moment glowed with patriotic enthusiasm; her skin, of the texture and freshness of a tea-rose, was flushed with embarrassment, and her slender yet supple and graceful form trembled with excitement; she was dressed very simply, and wore a dark hat wound about with a black veil.

Duroc took in the situation at a glance, and extricating the two ladies from the crowd gave his hand to the blonde and led her to the carriage door. "Sire," he said to Napoleon, "deign to greet these ladies, who braved the dangers of the crowd to see you."

The emperor lifted his hat and leaning towards the lady began to talk to her, but she, as she afterwards recounted, was so excited by the emotions which agitated her that she did not permit him to finish his sentence. "Welcome, Sire," she exclaimed, "a thousand times welcome to Poland! Nothing which we can do can sufficiently demonstrate the affection we bear you, nor the pleasure we Poles feel in having you step upon this land which looks to you for deliverance,"

While the lady spoke, Napoleon watched her closely, and when she ceased, took a bouquet from the carriage, presented it to her and said: "Keep this as a guarantee of my good intentions, we shall meet at Warsaw, I hope, and I shall reclaim a reward from your fair lips."

Duroc then took his seat beside the emperor, and the carriage drove rapidly off, while Napoleon waved a parting salute to the young woman.

The person who had made such an effort to see the emperor, and welcome him to Polish soil, was Marie Walewska, *née* Laczinska, She was the offspring of a very old but poor and numerous family. M. Laczinski died when Marie was a baby, leaving six children, and the widow, who was absorbed in making the best of the small domain which constituted their fortune, sent her daughters to boarding-school, where they learned to dance, acquired a smattering of French and German, and a slight knowledge of music. Between fifteen and sixteen years of age Marie returned home, with but a mediocre education, but with a pure heart, which knew but two passions—religion and country—her love for her God was balanced by her love for Poland; those were the pivots upon which her nature turned, and to arouse her from her usually gentle sweetness it sufficed to say that she would marry a Russian or a Prussian, her country's enemies, a Protestant or schismatic.

She had hardly returned to her home, when, by a singular chance, she had two excellent opportunities for marriage, and Mme. Laczinski permitted her daughter to choose between the aspirants for her hand. One was a charming young man who seemed to have everything in his favour, and who had pleased her from the first; he was very rich, well-born and remarkably handsome—but he was a Russian, and a son of one of those generals who had cruelly oppressed Poland. Marie could not consent to become *his* wife, so her choice fell upon the other suitor, old Anastase Colonna de Walewice-Walewska, who was seventy years of age, a widower for the second time, and whose oldest grandchild was nine years her senior, but he was very rich, the *Seigneur* of the province which the Laczinskas inhabited, owned most of the land, laid down the laws, inhabited *the château* of the neighbourhood, and was the only person who invited his poor neighbours to dinner.

He had been the late king's chamberlain, and on important occasions decorated his coat with the order of the White Eagle; he was the head of one of the most illustrious families of Poland, who were authentically connected with the Colonnas of Rome and bore the same coat-of-arms, and he was of more ancient lineage than any other family in the kingdom. It was not strange that Mme. Laczinska was enchanted at the prospect of having so illustrious a son-in-law, and Marie made little resistance, for her first appeal to her mother was met with an unanswerable argument; she fell ill, however, of an inflammatory fever, and for four months hovered between life and death. When barely convalescent she was led to the altar, and the miserable young woman spent three years in the dreary *château* of Walewice, finding her only consolation in her religion.

At last she gave birth to a son and a desire for life re-awoke in her. She determined to live for her child, who had a right to the happiness which she had missed, but she did not wish that he should live upon annexed land which was no longer a country, that he should be, like her, in servitude, or that, like his father, he should beg of the conqueror his property and title; she wished her son to be a free man and a Pole, and to attain that end it was necessary that his country should rise and free herself.

Napoleon had already vanquished Austria, measured his strength against Russia at Austerlitz, and was about to strike at Prussia and her allies; he was a providential adversary of her country's enemies and seemed destined to save Poland.

When the campaign of 1806 opened and Napoleon's forces marched with incredible rapidity across France and Germany to Berlin, the Prussians melting like phantoms before them, Mme. Walewska reached such a state of feverish enthusiasm that she could no longer remain at Walewice, to which remote spot news penetrated but slowly, and her husband being as great a patriot as herself, they went to Warsaw, where they established themselves as became their rank.

Mme. Walewska, conscious of her lack of education and worldly knowledge, fearing to blunder when she spoke French, unsupported by family or friends, dreaded to go into society, and above all to appear at La Blacha, the palace of Prince Joseph Poniatowski, and the rallying-place of Warsaw's best society, and though in obedience to her husband's command, she made a few formal and obligatory visits, she held aloof from the gaieties of the capital, thus remaining, despite her loveliness, almost unknown.

The whole city was in a tumult of excitement over the approaching arrival of the emperor, all being desirous that his reception at Warsaw should outdo the welcome given him at Posen; the city was turned topsy-turvy by the citizens in their determination to give Napoleon a royal welcome, for they felt that the fate of Poland lay in his hands. Mme. Walewska longed to be the first to greet him, and, without weighing the importance of the step she was taking, persuaded one of her cousins to accompany her and rushed to Bronie.

After the meeting which we described in the beginning of the chapter she stood gazing after the imperial carriage until it was lost to view; then, carefully enveloping the bouquet which the emperor had given her, she stepped into her carriage and returned to Warsaw.

Her intention was to keep her journey a secret, to shun all the *fêtes* and thus avoid a presentation to Napoleon; but her companion, though sworn to secrecy, was far too elated over the adventure to keep the story to herself, and one morning Prince Joseph Poniatowski sent to inquire at what hour Mme. Walewska could receive him, and, calling in the afternoon, invited her to a ball he was about to give in honour of the emperor, saying that Napoleon wished particularly to meet her a second time. As she blushingly refused to understand his reference to her first meeting with His Majesty, the prince, laughing heartily over the matter, explained his knowledge of the affair.

It appeared that at one of the dinners given in the emperor's honour, he had been observed to look attentively at the Princess Lubomirska, and she was immediately presented, but after meeting her. Napoleon paid but scant attention to the lady; this indifference surprised Prince Joseph, but was explained by Duroc, who related the episode of Bronie, and explained that his royal master had fancied that in the princess he had discovered the charming unknown. Duroc gave all the details of the meeting at Bronie, describing minutely the face, figure and toilet of the mysterious lady, but Poniatowski was unable to divine who it could have been, and was about to give up his search in despair, when the indiscreet chatter of Mme. Walewska's companion enlightened him, and, knowing the emperor's desire to cultivate the acquaintance, he determined that she should come to the ball.

Mme. Walewska refused absolutely to go, and remained unmoved even by his argument that under Heaven she might perhaps be an instrument towards the rehabilitation of her country. Hardly had the prince departed when the principal representatives of Poland were announced; they were statesmen, whose authority was based upon public esteem and consideration and the deference due to their irreproachable conduct and wisdom; all of these men foresaw what benefit might accrue to Poland from Napoleon's admiration for one of its daughters and they joined in urging her acceptance of the prince's invitation; their arguments, however, failed to move her and she was still firm in her determination to remain at home, when her husband arrived and came to their rescue.

M. Walewska was ignorant of the adventure at Bronie, and saw in the insistence of these gentlemen nothing save the consideration due his rank and the services he had rendered his country, and promptly accepted for his wife. Marie pleaded, almost with tears, to remain at home, but her husband insisted, ridiculed her fears, and finally commanded that she should go. She made one condition, however, which was, that, as almost all the other ladies had already been presented, care should be taken that her presentation should not be conspicuous.

The great day came, and her husband hurried her toilet, fearing that they would be late and reach the ballroom after the emperor had departed. M. Walewski would have liked to see his wife magnificently apparelled, and he found great fault with the severely simple dress of white satin which she had selected to wear and with the garland of leaves which was her only ornament; others, however, were not of his opinion, for a murmur of admiration greeted her entrance into the ballroom. She was installed between two ladies, with whom she was, unacquainted and was feeling strange and uncomfortable, when Prince Poniatowski stationed himself behind her. "Your arrival has been impatiently awaited, *madame*," he murmured, "and your entrance to the ballroom greeted with pleasure; your name has been repeated until it must be known by heart, and after scrutinizing your husband someone said, shrugging his shoulders: 'Poor little victim;' and I am commanded to invite you to dance."

"I do not dance," she answered, "and have no inclination towards that form of amusement."

The prince explained that his invitation, being at the instigation of the emperor, was paramount to an order, that His Majesty was watching them and that if she refused he should be considered at fault, and also that the success of the ball largely depended upon her; but persuasion and explanation were alike wasted. Mme. Walewska positively refused to dance, and the prince had but one resource: to find Duroc, who received his confidences and repeated them to Napoleon.

Mme. Walewska was soon the centre of a brilliant circle of staff-officers who were charmed by her beauty and unaffected manners, for her presence, which was an open secret to the Poles, was not understood by the French. Napoleon, however, was not long in effecting the removal of his unconscious rivals; Louis de Périgord seemed the most devoted of her admirers, so the emperor made a sign to Berthier and ordered him to send the *aide-de-camp* at once to the sixth corps on the Passarge, and the next in order was Bertrand, who, on a second sign, was ordered to report to Prince Jérôme before Breslau.

The emperor wandered about the ballroom with the intention of making himself generally agreeable, but his preoccupation led him to make singularly *mal à propos* speeches; he asked a young girl how many children she had, a homely old maid, if her husband was jealous of her beauty, and inquired of a lady who was enormously stout if she was very fond of dancing. When he arrived before Mme. Walewska her neighbours nudged her as a sign that she should rise, and standing, her eyes fixed on the ground, strangely pale, she awaited the emperor's pleasure. "White upon white is not becoming, *madame*," he said aloud, then added in a low tone, "This is scarcely the reception I expected—" He paused and looked at her attentively, but as she made no response he passed on, and a few moments afterwards left the ballroom.

His departure was the signal for greater liberty of action, each recounting to her neighbour what the emperor had said to her, and all anxious to learn what he said to Mme. Walewska, and to what he referred when saying that he had expected a different greeting, for those nearest had caught his remarks, and the wildest curiosity prevailed regarding it, some daring spirits even going so far as to question Marie herself. As soon as possible she made her escape, but on the way home her husband also catechised her, and, receiving unsatisfactory replies, announced that he had accepted an invitation for a dinner at which the emperor was to be present, and requested her to order a more elegant costume for that occasion. Marie was on the point of telling him of her imprudent trip to Bronie, of its consequences up to date and her disquietude; but he left her brusquely at the door of her room, which she had hardly entered, before her maid handed her a note which she had some difficulty in deciphering :

> I have seen, admired and desired but you this evening. A kind and prompt answer alone can calm the impatient ardour of
>
> N.

Mme. Walewska crushed the note in her hand, disgusted and revolted by its language. "There is no answer?" she said to her maid, who departed to convey her mistress's reply to the bearer of the note; but the messenger who waited in the street was no other than Prince Poniatowski, who did not propose to be so easily beaten, and, despite the servant's remonstrances, entered the house and followed her to her mistress's room with such promptitude, that Mme. Walewska had barely time to lock the door. From behind the closed door she informed the prince that her decision was immutable; and at the risk of a scandal the prince alternately implored and menaced, but was at last obliged to depart, discomfited and angry. She was scarcely awake on the following morning, when her maid handed her a second note, which she did not open, but sealing it up in an envelope with the first ordered that both should be handed to the messenger.

Before noon her drawing-room was crowded, all the personages of the nation, influential members of the government, Prince Joseph and Grand Marshal Duroc, being assembled there, but Marie, pretexting a sick headache, remained in her own room stretched out upon a lounge. Her husband was furious, and to prove that he was not jealous, as was artfully insinuated, he conducted the prince and his countrymen into his wife's apartment, and in their presence insisted that she should allow herself to be presented and should attend the dinner, to which she was bidden. To this the Poles agreed in chorus, and one of their number, an old man, who was highly respected, and whose advice was deferentially listened to by the chiefs of the government, fixed his eyes sharply upon her, and said in an impressive manner: "I hope that between this and the date set for the dinner your indisposition will have disappeared, for you cannot refuse the invitation without laying yourself open to the accusation of lack of love for your country."

How could this inexperienced girl of eighteen, alone, without a friend to counsel her, defend herself against so many?—she did her best, but the pressure was too great. She was obliged to rise, and, obeying her husband's mandate, called upon Mme. de Vauban, who was Prince Joseph's mistress, solicited her advice as to the toilet she should wear, and asked her to be initiated into the mysteries of court etiquette; thus she was delivered into the hands of the enemy, for Mme. Vauban was deep in the intrigue.

Née Pugot-Barbentane, Mme. de Vauban had lived at Versailles and was familiar with the life of the old court; at the outbreak of the revolution she fled to Warsaw, and there lived publicly with the prince, who had previously been her lover. She thought that to give a mistress to a sovereign, whether he be Louis XV. or Napoleon, was the most important mission which a courtesan could fill, and as for scruples, purity, duty, or conjugal fidelity—it never occurred to her that a woman of the world would balance such virtues against certain advantages. Mme. de Vauban was clever enough to perceive that the woman with whom she had now to deal could not be tempted by worldly considerations, that she must manoeuvre skilfully and make use of weapons with which she was not familiar, before she could overcome Mme. Walewska's scruples, and, feeling unequal to the task, she contented herself with paying her visitor numerous compliments, advising as to her dress and conduct, and protesting friendship; then she turned Marie over to a young woman who lived with her somewhat as a companion.

This lady, Mme. Abramowicz, was a divorcee without fortune, young, gay, and clever, and, being nearer Mme. Walewska's age, possessed every requisite to attract her confidence, even the most exalted sentiments of patriotism—real or feigned. She insinuated herself into Mme. Walewska's confidence and won the affections of the lonely girl, who had never had an intimate friend, and whose heart longed for a confidante. Mme. Abramowicz ingratiated herself with the husband, and was inseparable from the wife, and when she thought that the time was ripe, she read to Mme. Walewska a letter, signed by the most prominent men of the nation, and members of the provisional government:

> Madame:
> Slight causes sometimes produce great results, and women from time immemorial have exercised great influence over the world's politics; ancient history, as well as modern, bears testimony to this fact, and so long as men are dominated by passion women can sway them.
> Had you been a man, you would gladly have given your life to your country; as a woman you cannot serve as her defender, but there are other sacrifices which you can make for Poland, and which you should gladly impose upon yourself, however painful they may be.
> Do you imagine that it was for love that Esther gave herself to Ahasverus? Does not the fact that he inspired her with such fear, that she swooned when he looked upon her, prove that affection had no part in that union? She sacrificed herself for her country, and, to her everlasting honour, she saved it. May history record as much for your glory and our happiness!
> Are you not daughter, sister, wife and mother to zealous Poles who, with us, form the national sheaf, the strength of which

can be augmented only by the number and union of those who compose it. Remember, *madame*, the words of a celebrated man, a saint and pious ecclesiastic, Fénelon, who wrote: '*Men, in whom all public authority is vested, can achieve no effective result from their deliberations, if women do not aid in the execution of their designs.*' Heed his voice, which unites with ours, that you may promote the happiness of your countrymen, of twenty million souls.

Thus every spring was brought into play to precipitate the downfall of this young woman, who, inexperienced and guileless, had neither a husband in whom she could confide, nor parents to defend her, nor friends anxious to save her; the family, country and religion were invoked to force her compliance, all conspired against her, and to complete the work, she was made to read the note from Napoleon, which she had once refused to open.

I fear, *madame*, that I have displeased you; yet I had a right to hope the contrary—was I so mistaken? Your enthusiasm has waned while mine has augmented. You have banished sleep from my pillow! Ah, deign to give a little joy to a poor heart which is ready to adore you. Do you then find it so difficult to write to me? You owe me two letters.

N.

Her husband, proud of the success of his wife, for which he took all the credit, without understanding the situation nor having the slightest suspicion of what was expected of her—for he was an honest gentleman—insisted upon her going to the much discussed dinner. The poor girl herself understood that the step was a decisive one and committed her; but all the world wished it, and she yielded. Her drawing-room was constantly filled with visitors, who mutely felicitated her, and in order that she should not change her mind during the time preceding the dinner, Mme. Abramowicz kept her company.

On her way to the dinner, Mme. Walewska comforted herself with the idea that as she did not love Napoleon, she had nothing to fear, and on her arrival the marked attentions of some of the guests, who already had in view the solicitation of her protection, completely disgusted her with her supposed conquest and she was firmly resolved to remain unapproachable when the emperor appeared. Napoleon was more self-possessed that evening than at the ball, and better prepared to be generally courteous; when Marie was presented he said simply:

"I thought *madame* was indisposed, has she quite recovered?" and this purposely simple speech overthrew her suspicions and even struck her as being extremely delicate.

At table she was placed next the grand marshal and almost opposite the emperor, who, when all were seated, began in his curt fashion to question his neighbours upon the history of Poland; he appeared to listen attentively and to take a deep interest in the subject, but whether speaking or listening his eyes never left Mme. Walewska save to exchange a glance with Duroc, with whom he seemed to have established a sort of optical telegraph. It seemed as though the remarks which Duroc addressed to his neighbour were dictated by a glance or gesture of the emperor, who kept up all the time a grave discussion upon European politics; once he lifted his hand to the left side of his coat, Duroc hesitated for a moment, looked attentively at his master, and at last, divining what was required of him, heaved an "Ah!" of satisfaction. It was the bouquet of Bronie which was in question and Duroc hastened to ask Mme. Walewska what had become of it.

Marie responded that she religiously preserved the flowers which the emperor had given her for her son. "Ah! *madame*," said the grand marshal, "you must permit us to offer you something more worthy of you."

Imagining that his speech had a double meaning she retorted loudly, flushed with anger. "I care only for flowers!"

Duroc was dumfounded, but after a moment recovered his presence of mind sufficiently to say: "Very well, *madame*, we will pluck laurels from your native soil for you;" and observing that that touched her, knew that his second speech had been a lucky one.

When the company rose from the table and returned to the drawing-room, the emperor took advantage of the confusion to approach her and fixing upon her his strangely piercing eyes, the power of which no human being had ever resisted, he took her hand and pressing it, said in a low tone:

"With eyes so sweet and tender, with such an expression of goodness, it cannot possibly be a pleasure to torture a man, or else appearances are deceitful and you are the most *coquettish* of women, the most cruel of your sex."

On the emperor's departure the party broke up and Mme. Walewska was persuaded to go to Mme. de Vauban's where a number of the dinner guests and those who were initiated into the intrigue, awaited her coming; upon entering the room she was immediately surrounded by those who flattered her and assured her that the emperor had had eyes only for her, that she alone could plead the nation's cause, touch his heart and determine him to rehabilitate Poland. Little by little, as if in obedience to some secret understanding, the guests departed, leaving Marie and Mme. Abramowicz alone; almost immediately Duroc was announced and when the doors were closed, he seated himself at Mme, Walewska's side and laid a letter on her knee, then taking her hand, said in the gentlest possible manner: "Can you refuse the request of one who has never brooked refusal? His position, though glorious, is lonely and sad, and it lies in your power to give him some hours, at least, of happiness."

Duroc spoke at great length but she made no answer and hiding her face in her hands wept and sobbed like a child; the other woman, however, answered for her and guaranteed that she would go to the rendezvous. When Marie indignantly remonstrated, she shamed her with her lack of patriotism, telling her, that she was a renegade daughter of Poland, that they should all willingly sacrifice anything for him who would be their country's deliverer, and finally bowed the grand marshal out, assuring him that Mme. Walewska would finally comply with his master's wishes; then opening the note which he had brought, Mme. Abramowicz read it aloud :

> There are moments when the weight of my rank seems more than I can bear, and I am now living through such a period. How can I satisfy the desires and needs of a hungry heart which longs to throw itself at your feet and is arrested only by weighty considerations which paralyse its most ardent desires and deprive me of freedom of action? Oh, if you would but come to me! You alone can surmount the obstacles which separate us; my friend Duroc will arrange everything.
> Come to me, and all your desires shall be fulfilled, and your country will be dearer to me when you have taught me to love it.
>
> N.

Thus the fate of Poland lay in her little hands; it was not her countrymen alone who said so, but the great conqueror himself, who affirmed it; it depended upon her, that her country should be reborn, the shameful divisions abolished, the torn parts reunited, and the White Eagle fly proudly over all. It was no wonder that such a glorious dream almost intoxicated her; yet she still struggled, claiming that she was not equal to playing such a role, to which they answered, that she should not lack for advisers, and had only to follow their counsel. Her modesty revolting, she was told that the sentiments she entertained were provincial, ridiculous and out of date, that many another woman, quite as virtuous as she, would willingly exchange places with her and lend Poland the aid of their beauty were the chance given them,—why, they asked, should she doubt her ability to do good?

Though an emperor, Napoleon was but a man—and a man in love; she would be able to wind him around her finger and achieve the realization of the patriot's brightest dreams. Thus at last they wrung from her a reluctant consent. She refused, however, to answer Napoleon's letter, feeling physically incapable of writing, and they left her alone to advise together, taking the precaution, however, to lock her in, lest she might change her mind and run away; but she was not thinking of such a thing, she reflected, or rather, exhausted by the prolonged struggle, she dreamed.

She wondered if she could not without losing her self-esteem have an interview with Napoleon, inspire him with friendship and respect and persuade him to listen to the prayer of her people; surely he would not force his caresses upon her, knowing that she had no love to give him, for she would tell him that he inspired her only with sentiments of enthusiasm, admiration and gratitude. There was nothing depraved in the imagination of this girl of eighteen, whose only knowledge of love was derived from the almost platonic affection of her septuagenarian husband, and drifting into the world of dreams, where the virtue of woman has nothing to fear from the passions of man, where the senses are abolished and souls speak and understand each other, she dreamed of an ideal friendship, which should both comfort Napoleon in his loneliness and benefit Poland.

The conspirators, having settled everything, returned and Mme. Walewska agreed to comply with all their wishes, only stipulating that she should remain where she was until those who were to conduct her to Napoleon, should call; she remained all the next day, which dragged by slowly, alternately watching the hands of the clock and the closed door by which her executioner must enter.

At half-past ten in the evening someone knocked, and Mme. Abramowicz, hastily arraying Marie in a hat with a thick veil and a long cloak, which completely disguised her figure, led her like one in a dream to a carriage which waited at the street corner, and assisted her to enter it; a man with a long coat and a slouched hat, who had held the door open, drew up the step and took a seat beside her. Not a word was exchanged on the way, and when the carriage drew up before a private entrance to the grand palace, her silent companion assisted her to leave the carriage and almost carried her to a door which was opened impatiently from within, and, quietly departing, left her alone with Napoleon.

Blinded by tears Mme. Walewska could not discern the features of the emperor who knelt by her side, took her hand, and began speaking to her in a caressing manner; nor was she clearly conscious of what he said until the words: "Your old husband" escaped him, when the full realisation of the ignominy burst upon her and with a cry of horror she sprang to her feet and looked about for means to escape.

Napoleon was momentarily paralysed with surprise, not knowing what to make of this woman, who after so many entreaties had yielded to his solicitations and granted him a nocturnal rendezvous, yet who now manifested such unmistakable and unaffected horror at her situation. Not holding the key to her presence there, he questioned an instant if she was not acting a part with the intent to increase his desire, but her grief and dismay were too genuine, and determined to solve the riddle of her conduct, he drew her gently away from the door against which she was leaning, seated her in an armchair and began to question her kindly regarding her history; resolved not to alarm her, he sought to put his questions in a manner which would least wound and shock her sensibilities, but in spite of his kind intentions, his habitual masterfulness pierced the veil of gentleness and he could only obtain brief and fragmentary answers from the trembling woman, but even those he turned to weapons against herself.

"Had she voluntarily given herself to the man whose name she bore, was it for rank and wealth that she had sacrificed her youth? No;—then who forced her to unite her young life with an old and decrepid man? Her mother;—then why had she any remorse, since the marriage was not of her chosing?"

Marie stammered between her sobs that it was her duty to be faithful, that that which God had joined together, man should not seek to sunder. Napoleon could not control his mirth, and at the sound of his laughter Mme. Walewska's tears fell all the faster.

More and more mystified and correspondingly interested by this woman, the like of whom he had never before encountered, he was the more determined to discover the solution to her presence in his apartments. Here was a woman who wished to be a faithful wife, to hold fast to the principles of her religion, a woman who was unquestionably pure and virtuous, and yet, she was there in his apartments at the dead of night, in compliance with his wishes. Never had his curiosity been so aroused, and he pressed his questions, asking about the education she had received, the life she had led in the country and the society she frequented, of her mother and family,—he wished to know everything, even to the name she had received at baptism: the sweet name of Marie, by which he ever afterwards called her.

At two in the morning someone rapped at the door. "What!" exclaimed Napoleon, "so soon? Well, my gentle dove, dry your tears and go home to rest; you need never again fear the Eagle, for he will exert no other influence over you than that of passionate love. You will end by loving him, for he will be everything to you—everything." He assisted her to fasten her mantle, put on her veil, and conducted her to the door, but before he let her out he exacted a promise that she would return the following night. She was reconducted to her home and retired almost reassured, it seemed as if her dream might be realized, for as Napoleon had been kind and tender and spared her that time, she fancied it would be the same in the future.

At nine o'clock the following morning the confidential friend was at her bedside, holding in her hands a large package, which, after prudently locking the door, she carefully unwrapped, and drew forth several jewel-cases in red morocco, a quantity of hothouse flowers intermingled with branches of laurel and a sealed letter; but scarcely had she exposed to view a magnificent brooch and spray of diamonds than Mme. Walewska snatched them from her hands and flung them to the end of the room, furious that they should have been sent her. She ordered that they should be immediately returned; she wished the emperor to comprehend that she was not for sale, and that if she gave herself to him it would not be from a desire for jewels; then, unsealing the letter, she read :

> Marie, my sweet Marie, my first thought is for you, my greatest desire to see you again; you will keep your promise and return, will you not? Otherwise the Eagle will fly to you! Our friend tells me we shall meet at dinner, deign, therefore, to accept this bouquet which shall establish between us a bond by which we may communicate in the midst of the crowd which will surround us, and even under the gaze of others. When I lay my hand over my heart you will know that it is filled with

thoughts of you and you can respond by touching your bouquet. Love me, my precious Marie, and never take your hand off your flowers.

N.

The letter was all very fine, but it could not make her accept his diamonds, nor even the flowers and laurels. She had an excuse ready: One did not wear flowers on one's dress save at balls, and it was to a dinner she was going. She vainly essayed to excuse herself from this dinner, but she was forced to fulfil her engagement by those whose ambitions were roused and who firmly believed that, through her, they would see their dearest wish fulfilled. Her husband remained perfectly blind, he never suspected for a moment the intrigue which was being carried on about him, and urgently desired her to accept all invitations.

On her arrival at the house where the dinner was given, she was immediately surrounded by her acquaintances and by those who were anxious to be presented, and it seemed to the poor woman as if all these strangers were cognizant of her adventure of the night previous. The emperor had already arrived and appeared dissatisfied, he frowned and regarded her with an angry expression, his eyes seeming to read her very soul; as he advanced towards her she trembled, fearing that he was going to make a public scene, when suddenly recalling the words of his letter, she laid her hand on the place where his flowers should have been, and had the satisfaction of seeing his contracted features relax into a smile and his hand respond by a similar sign.

Before going to table he called Duroc aside and spoke with him for an instant; she had barely taken her place at the table, where, as at the preceding dinner, she was seated next the grand marshal, when he attacked her about the bouquet; she responded haughtily that she was insulted by the diamonds, and wished it distinctly understood that she would accept no presents of that kind, that the only thing which could repay her devotion was hope for the future of her country.

"Has the emperor not already given you the right to hope?" retorted Duroc; then he recalled to her a number of acts which proved his master's good faith, and throughout the dinner he continued to talk of the emperor's affection for her, the loneliness of his high state, and the need he had of a heart which would love and understand him, and of the glory of the mission which was hers, reminding her, too, of her promise to return to the palace that night.

She was conducted to the palace with the same precautions as on the previous evening, and found Napoleon gloomy and thoughtful.

"You have come at last," he said, "I had abandoned all hope of seeing you!" He assisted her to lay aside her cloak and hat, and when she was seated, stationed himself before her, and commanded her to explain her conduct. Why did she go to Bronie? Why had she sought to inspire him with a sentiment which she did not share? Why had she refused his flowers and even the laurels? Why had she ever made a rendezvous with him? What were her intentions when she came to the palace? As she did not answer he gave way to a paroxysm of anger and exclaimed: "You led me to hope for everything and you give nothing; you are a true Pole, and your actions confirm the opinion I have always held of your nation."

Moved and troubled by her reception, and anxious to know what he thought of her people, she said: "Ah, Sire, forgive me, and tell me what you think of us Poles."

He informed her that he considered the Polish race passionate and unstable, emotional and lacking in system; that their enthusiasm was impetuous and genuine, but short-lived, and that this portrait of her race was her likeness. Had she not flown, like one crazed with enthusiasm, to gain a glimpse of him? Had she not led him to believe by her earnest and passionate expressions of esteem that she was most kindly disposed towards him? He had allowed himself to be duped, but she must know that, when anything was withheld from him, it became the object he most coveted, and that nothing could daunt him in the pursuit of it. Whether real or feigned, the violence of his excitement grew apace and Mme. Walewska shrank before him. "I want you to understand," he thundered, "that I will force you to love me! I have already lifted the name of your country from the dust, thanks to me that it has not been wiped from the face of the earth! I will do more—but, remember, that even as I crush this watch in my hand, so shall your country and all your hopes be crushed if you push me to extremes, repulse my love and refuse me yours."

Overcome by this violence, Mme. Walewska fainted—when she recovered consciousness she no longer belonged to herself.

Henceforth it was a *liaison*, if one can so designate the habit she acquired of going nightly to the palace and passively submitting to caresses which she hoped would someday bring her a great reward. Napoleon established a provisional government, the embryo of an army and several companies of light cavalry were attached to his guard; but it was not for so little that Mme. Walewska had sacrificed her virtue, the only thing which could content her and condone her conduct in her own eyes, was the re-establishment of Poland as a nation and a state. Incapable of feigning a sentiment which she did not entertain, or a passion which she did not feel, she had none of the requisites for the domination of a lover, and was not even cunning enough to conceal the motive which actuated her. Nightly she referred to the one topic which interested her and was consoled by promises and buoyed by hopes; but the promises were always for the future, in the present there was only misery which seemed interminable.

She met with no censure in her own country; aside from her husband, whom she had been obliged to leave, all hastened to do her honour, not as a favourite but as a victim, for none were in ignorance of her sacrifice, and by all she was esteemed, respected and pitied. Her husband's own sisters. Princess Jablonowska and Countess Birginska, constituted themselves her chaperones; had she so desired, she could have taken the first place in Warsaw's society and maintained almost regal state; but Mme. Walewska shunned society, lived unpretentiously, and gave no cause for enmity; therefore, though less flattered, she received greater sympathy.

To a society which concealed oriental habits under a veneer of French elegance and customs, which still retained the moral code of Catherine the Great, there was nothing shocking in Mme. Walewska's position. There was no fine Polish gentleman of the time who had not an authenticated mistress, of whose existence his wife was well aware and to whom she exhibited no animosity; scarcely a noble did not support, at some one of his country seats, one or more Georgian favourites; consequently, as he did not travel with a *harem* in his train. Napoleon appeared to the Poles as a singularly chaste sovereign; when he established himself in Warsaw they felt that he should have a female companion to divert him, and but natural and right to secure for him the society of the only woman in whom he manifested the least interest.

Fortuitously, the emperor admired a woman of exceptional character and one who could be made politically useful; virtuous, unaffected, disinterested, animated solely by love of country, incarnating in her person the best traits of her nation, Marie Walewska was capable of inspiring in the heart of her royal lover a deep and lasting affection, and the Poles reasoned that she would become like a second wife to Napoleon, that, without sharing his imperial state and splendour, she would fill a special place in his life and be an ever-present ambassadress for Poland.

Napoleon was alive to the fact that Mme. Walewska did not love him for himself, that her country held the first place in her heart, indeed, she never essayed to make him think otherwise, but frankly avowed that she had become his mistress in the hope of softening his heart and awakening his sympathies towards her unhappy land, and he, who usually mistrusted anyone whom he suspected of a desire to make use of him, placed implicit confidence in this simple, sincere and earnest girl; he knew her to be so far above the ordinary ambitions of women that he longed to content her, and keenly regretted his inability to bestow the one boon she coveted.

He frequently said to her:

Rest assured that my promises to you shall be fulfilled. I have already forced Russia to relinquish what she had usurped; time will do the rest, but you must be patient; politics is a cord which snaps if subjected to too great a strain, and the time is not yet ripe for the realization of your hopes. In the meanwhile, your politicians must work, the country must be organised; you are rich in patriots and can command plenty of brave arms—honour and courage start from every pore of you Poles—but that will not suffice, there must be great unanimity.

It was strange how this man, who never discussed politics with a woman, continually recurred to the subject of Poland's future, and discussed with her the best means for the amelioration of her countrymen, how to benefit all classes and insure a united movement even if at the expense of the aristocracy.

You well know that I love your nation, that my wishes and my political views lead me to desire its entire rehabilitation; I am most willing to second its efforts and uphold its rights, and all that I can do without endangering the interests of France, I will do; but remember that the distance that separates us is tremendous, that what I establish here today may be annihilated tomorrow. My first duty is to France, I cannot shed French blood for a cause which is not theirs, nor arm my people and rush to your succour each time that it may be necessary.

From these grave matters he would turn to social gossip, current anecdotes and the tittle-tattle of the drawing-room with a rapidity which amazed his listener. He wanted her to inform him regarding the private life of every personage whom he encountered, his curiosity was insatiable and went into the minutest details; it was his way of forming an opinion upon the leading class wherever he found himself, and here, where such great interests were at stake, he made use of every means to inform himself. From the accumulated tales, which engraved themselves upon his memory, bits of information regarding this one and that one, he drew astute conclusions which astonished the woman who listened and showed her that she had furnished him with arms against herself; she would protest indignantly against the deductions he drew and the judgments he pronounced; the quarrel usually ending with his giving her a slight tap on the cheek and exclaiming: "Good little Marie, you are worthy to be a Spartan and to have a country!"

Napoleon would not have loved Mme. Walewska as he did, had he not taken an interest in her toilet, in which matter he considered himself an excellent judge, having once written to Savary:

You know that I am an authority upon woman's dress.

From the time of the Consulate he had selected the presents sent to any queen, and the dress of the court ladies did not escape his criticism; even Josephine, whose taste in dress was exquisite, was not exempt. Above all he disliked sombre costumes, and Mme. Walewska insisted upon dressing in the most simple fashion and always in black, white or gray, which displeased him extremely, and regarding which he remonstrated with her, and she retorted, that "a Polish woman should wear mourning for her country; when you resuscitate it I will wear nothing but rose-colour."

Thus in every way she brought him back to the same subject, but without annoying him, so great was his love for her. It did not suffice him to see his mistress by appointment, he desired that she should attend all the dinners and *fêtes* at which he was obliged to be present, and as he wished to be constantly in communication with her he initiated her into the mysterious system by which he communicated with Duroc, and she became more expert at it than the grand marshal himself, and at the very instant when Napoleon seemed engrossed in some serious subject he would tell her in his sign language that his heart was filled with thoughts of her. When she expressed her astonishment that so great a general, so shrewd a politician, should condescend to such boyish means of communication, he said:

Reflect that I am obliged to fill with dignity the post assigned to me, I have the honour to command nations. I was an acorn, I have become an oak and I am watched on every side; this situation obliges me to play a role which is not always easy, but which I am obliged to keep up in order to preserve the character with which I am invested, and while I must play the monarch for all the world, I love to be your subject, and how can I manage to tell you that I love you at a state dinner (which I want to do every time I look at you), unless I employ the sign language?

When he removed his headquarters to Finckenstein Marie was obliged to follow him, and the melancholy existence she led there resembled closely that which she had once led at Walewice with her old husband. The long, quiet days were broken only by the meals which she ate *tête-à-tête* with the emperor, and which were served by a single valet, the rest of the time was spent in reading and embroidering, and her only distraction was watching the parade from behind closed blinds. It was the life of a recluse subject to the will of a master, without society, pleasure or distraction, and yet it satisfied her better than the brilliant society which she had left at Warsaw.

Thus Mme. Walewska realized the type of woman which he had hoped to find in Josephine: sweet, complaisant, timid, attentive, unambitious and seemingly without will, who lived only for him and who, though she asked a favour of him, asked so colossal a one that it became impersonal and impossible of conception save by a soul singularly pure and disinterested, and to hope to receive it from the hands of a mortal, was to think of him almost as a god; all this appealed strongly to Napoleon and augmented his Polish love's hold on him.

When the emperor was about to leave Poland, without having realised the dream for whose sake Mme. Walewska had given herself to him when, despairing and disillusioned, Marie refused to follow him to Paris and announced her intention to retire into the heart of the country, there to await in sadness and solitude the fulfilment of his vows, it became his turn to supplicate:

I know that you can live without me, that your heart is not mine; but you are good, kind and generous, can you find it in your heart to deprive me of my only happiness—of the few moments that I spend each day with you? You are my sole joy, the one being who brightens my life, and yet I am supposed to be the most highly blessed of mortals.

His tone was so bitter, his smile so sad, that, overwhelmed by a new sentiment of pity for this master of the world, she promised to follow him to Paris.

Mme. Walewska reached Paris in the beginning of the year 1808, and thenceforth this mysterious *liaison*, to which Napoleon was sometimes unfaithful, but which was nevertheless the grand passion of his life, was established on so strange a footing that, if one could not find its confirmation in isolated details and dates which are authenticated by divers witnesses, it would be difficult to follow the chain of events and one would not dare to affirm the continuity of facts which the best informed contemporaries ignored.

It is known that during the campaign of 1809 Mme. Walewska went to Vienna, where an elegant establishment awaited her near the Palace of Schoenbrunn, that she became *enceinte*, and after peace was declared went to Walewice for her confinement, and that there, on the 4th of May, 1810, Alexandre-Florian-Joseph Colonna-Walewska, was born. Knowing so much, have we not a right to question whether Napoleon's hesitation when treating with Austria, his indecision regarding the fate of Poland was not due to the presence of her to whom he had solemnly promised the rehabilitation of her country?

What contemporaries do not tell us is that towards the close of 1810, Mme. Walewska, accompanied by her sister-in-law the Princess Jablonowska, and her infant son, returned to Paris, where she lived first in a pretty house on the Chaussée d'Antin, afterwards at No. 2 rue du Houssaie and then at No. 48 rue de la Victoire. Every morning the emperor sent to ask her orders; boxes in all the theatres were placed at her disposal; the doors of the museums opened to her; Corvisart was charged to look after her health and Duroc to see that her every desire was satisfied and her life made as agreeable and easy as possible. The following anecdote gives an example of her power:

At Spa, a young Englishman indulged in a joke of doubtful taste at the expense of the Princess Jablonowska. On her return to Paris the princess invited him to accompany Mme. Walewska and herself to the museum of artillery; in the gallery where armour was displayed the party stopped before the armour worn by Jeanne d'Arc, and while the young man was looking at it the Maid of France opened her arms and, seizing him, pressed him violently to her heart; suffocating, he struggled to escape, but it was only upon the order of Mme. Walewska that

Jeanne d'Arc[1] released him. Knowing the jealousy with which Napoleon guarded his museums, is this not a positive proof of her power?

Whenever he could escape from the cares of state the emperor went to her, or had her come to the *château* with her son, upon whom he had conferred the title of Count of the Empire. None in the company, with the exception of the Poles, suspected their relations, and Mme. Walewska went little into society and received only a few compatriots; her household was mounted upon a modest footing and her conduct extremely circumspect. When she went to take the waters at Spa her sister-in-law ac- companied her, and it was at her sister-in-law's home, a house at Mons-sur-Orge, called the Château de Brétigny, which was rented from the Duchesse de Richelieu, that she passed the summer. They essayed vainly to draw her into society, but her greatest preoccupation was to hide from the world the relations of which the majority of women would have been proud.

Her country home was situated in a secluded spot and conducted in an extremely simple style, but it was her universe, and she left it as seldom as possible; nevertheless, she was obliged to accept Josephine's repeated invitations to go to Malmaison with her son, whom the empress loaded with presents and playthings, but it does not appear that she mingled in court society before the year 1813, and it is only at that epoch that in her personal accounts two court-dresses are mentioned; one was a dress of black velvet with gold-spangled tulle, the other of white tulle; however *recherché* her costumes may have appeared she was certainly not an extravagant woman, for her annual bills at Leroy's never exceeded six thousand *francs*.

It was needless for her to appear at court in order to recall herself to Napoleon's memory, proof of which lies in a letter written by him from Nogent, the 8th of February, 1814; in the midst of the terrible strain incident to the French campaign, on the day following the Battle of Brienne, and on the eve of that of Champaubert, he thought of Mme. Walewska and endeavoured to secure her future. He had charged the treasurer-general, M. de La Bouillerie to settle fifty thousand pounds upon the young Count Walewska in such fashion that, in the event of his death, his mother should be his heir, and the idea that all the formalities had not been fulfilled caused him to write this letter :

---

1. *Personal Recollections of Joan of Arc - A classic novel of the 'Maid of Orleans'* by Mark Twain also published by Leonaur.

I have received your letter relative to young Walewska, I give you *carte blanche* to do whatever is proper; but act at once. That which preoccupies me most at present is first that boy and then his mother.

N.

Mme. Walewska knew nothing of all this, and there never was a more disinterested heart than hers. During the last days at Fontainebleau when the emperor, abandoned by all, had sought to find in death a refuge which destiny refused him, she hastened to his side and spent an entire night in an antechamber awaiting his commands. Napoleon, absorbed in his gloomy reflections, exhausted by the physical crisis through which he had passed, never thought of asking for her until she had already been gone an hour. "Poor woman," he said, "she will believe herself forgotten."

He little understood her, for a few months later, at the end of August, 1814, she landed at Elba, accompanied by her son, her sister and her brother. Colonel Laczinski, and spent a day with the emperor at the hermitage of Marciana. From the moment she learned of Napoleon's return to Paris in 1815 she was among the most devoted and assiduous of the women who visited the Elysée and at Malmaison, faithful to the emperor through his fall and misfortunes.

But after he had gone to St. Helena she thought herself free, and M. Walewska having died in 1814, she married at Liege in 1816, General Count d'Ornano, who had been obliged to take refuge there after the second return of the Bourbons. General d'Ornano had been one of the bravest officers of the Grand Army, and Mme. Walewska's union with him was brief but happy, for she died within the year, expiring in her home in the rue de la Victoire on the 15th of December, 1817.

One of the emperor's companions at St. Helena tells us, that the news of Mme. Walewska's marriage affected His Majesty keenly, as he had preserved a warm affection for her and could not reconcile himself to the thought that one whom he had loved should care for another. In his will the emperor had expressed his desire that Alexandre Walewska should enter the French Army; his career was a brilliant one, and as soldier, writer, diplomat and statesman his life is too intimately associated with the history of his time to render it necessary for us to dwell upon it here.

CHAPTER 16

The Divorce

The death of Napoleon-Charles destroyed Napoleon's dream of creating an heredity by adoption; the birth of Léon disabused his mind of all doubts of his inability to create a direct line, and love for Mme. Walewska completed the work by weakening Josephine's influence. It is impossible that at Tilsit the emperor directly negotiated an alliance with a Russian grand-duchess, but certain that from the moment of his return to France he began paving the way for divorce; his ordinary method of procedure was to carry a project into operation as soon as it was conceived, but he took two years for the execution of this one.

Mentally Napoleon was fully alive to the advantages which would accrue to him from a divorce and second marriage, but, though his brain was willing, his heart's dictates were in opposition to his political sagacity, and it was this war within himself which kept him in a state of uncertainty from 1807 to 1809, an uncertainty which causes his actions to appear inexplicable to the historian, cannot be accounted for by political reasons, and was due solely to conscientious scruples.

Before Napoleon could acquire the energy necessary for the rupture of his marital relations with the woman whom he had once passionately loved, and raised to share the throne with him, who was bound to him by ten years of close companionship, and whom, with her children, he had preferred above his own flesh and blood, it was essential that the ties which bound him should break one by one, and a divorce became a necessity.

Feeling that he was about to do her a great wrong, Napoleon attributed to Josephine even more amiable qualities than she possessed, and repeatedly said to his advisers: "She will not be able to bear it, it will kill her!" and possibly he was superstitious enough to believe that his fortunes depended upon her and her star; yet neither vain superstition, fear of the criticism of his companions in arms nor of public opinion, caused his hesitation, he simply paused for a time, listening to the dictates of his heart.

Weary of the emperor's vacillations some of those who were ardent advocates of the divorce, such as Fouché, essayed to hasten the rupture by adroit insinuations to Josephine, with the view of determining her to take the initiative and voluntarily sacrifice herself. Napoleon understood that this excess of zeal rose from the projects he had formed and allowed to be divined, but the more he realized his weakness the more it irritated him, and, indignant that one of his ministers should fancy he could coerce him, that this police spy should have dared to probe into his domestic life and show his ugly face in the conjugal chamber, he treated Fouché as he had never treated any man before, and Josephine, astutely advised by Talleyrand, who for some reason or another wished to throw an obstacle in Fouchés path, profited by her husband's momentary indignation and boldly accused him of intending to repudiate her. Napoleon shrinking from the scene which was bound to follow an admission of his intention, hesitated and was reconquered.

This renewal of affection for his wife did not render him more faithful, for in the sentiment which he entertained for Josephine, fidelity had no part; it was a kindly feeling, combined from memory, pity and gratitude, but permitting of no illusions regarding the youth and beauty of his wife, and when he found himself in the society of younger and prettier women he saw no reason why he should not enjoy it without detriment to his marital relations.

During the sojourn at Paris and Fontainebleau, between August and October of 1807, Mme, Gazzani exercised her influence over Napoleon, and it is said that at Fontainebleau he also fell a victim to the charms of Mme. de B. ★★★★, who was a companion to the Princess Pauline. This Mme. de B. ★★★★ whose husband was distantly related to the Beauharnais and owed his place at court to his kinship with them, was one of the prettiest of women; she was very tall, and some claim that her head and features were too small for her figure, but she was generally considered a remarkably handsome woman; she was extremely clever, poor, and morally unprejudiced. The emperor saw her at first at a hunting-breakfast and signified his admiration for her, going so far, it is said, as to write to her.

Her apartment was on the first floor of the *château*, and gave into the garden of Diana, so it was conveniently situated for nocturnal visitors, and His Majesty was always welcome. Mme. de B. **** was well content with her position, and the husband, who was aged and little troubled by scruples, rubbed his hands over it. "My wife," he said one day, in a drawing-room, "is a woman of wonderful resources; we are not rich, yet, thanks to her cleverness, we appear to be; she is a perfect treasure." She worked so well that she made him a chamberlain to one of the emperor's imperial brothers and a baron of the Empire.

This *liaison*, however, was conducted with such secrecy that some have doubted if it really existed, and as it was not continued after the emperor left Fontainebleau, the complaisant husband's pleasure abated and he had some unpleasant experiences, for Mme. de B. **** quarrelling with the princess because of a brilliant young officer, was dismissed from the imperial household and obliged to retire to her country-seat, while the officer was sent to Spain, where he was grievously wounded; on his return, Mme, de B, **** secured a divorce and they were married.

Although Bonaparte had allowed Josephine to reassume her sway over him he was still haunted by the thought of divorce, the wisdom of which his counsellors never permitted him to forget, and it was with this step in view that he went to Italy in 1807. One of Josephine's greatest disquietudes in connection with the divorce was the effect it would have upon her son, for although Napoleon had established Eugène in Italy as viceroy in 1805, and had married him, in 1806, to the Princess Augusta, giving him the title of "Son of France," his promises had not been sanctioned by legislative act; he wished, therefore, to reassure both his wife and the House of Bavaria, and also to inform himself regarding a union which had been proposed to him, namely, a marriage with the Princess Charlotte of Bavaria, and it was doubtless with this alliance in view that he arranged a meeting at Milan with the Bavarian king, queen and princess. The young girl, however, proved less prepossessing than he had anticipated, and discarding the idea of that alliance he left the princess to her strange destiny, and considered the advisability of a family alliance.

Although Lucien Bonaparte's first wife, Catherine Boyer, was a woman of most humble origin, the uneducated daughter of an innkeeper at Saint-Maximin de Vâr, Napoleon had loved her like a sister, and her young daughter, Lolotte, having reached a marriageable age he seriously considered the advisability of making her his wife. There was an estrangement between his brother Lucien and himself, and the emperor, who considered family unity essential, was desirous of effecting a reconciliation, and argued that this step might cement Lucien's affection for him; he reasoned that if the dissimilarity between Lolotte's age and his proved too great and the young girl showed any repugnance at the idea of becoming his wife, or if, on close acquaintance with her, he should alter his intentions, it would be easy to find her a suitable husband from some of the royal houses of Europe.

He thought that, should the marriage take place, the succession which he would establish in France would be more purely Bonaparte, and hoped that the girl who had been very fond of him as a little child would find it easy to renew the affection of her youth, Lolotte was brought to Paris and placed under the protection of her grandmother, Madame Mère, but she did not remain long. She amused her father with her letters about the doings of the French court, seemingly unsuspicious that her correspondence was watched, and it was soon clear to Napoleon that a union with his niece was not feasible, whereupon he sent her back to Italy. Lolotte Bonaparte never wore a crown, but in 1815, she married the Prince Gabrielli, and lived until 1865.

The Italian journey, then, was unproductive as far as Napoleon's matrimonial projects were concerned, but Fouché continued to agitate and disseminate the idea of divorce, thus exposing himself to wrathful letters from the emperor, which did not, however, cause him to cease intriguing; his ordinarily clear perception seemed obscured, his usual sagacity at fault, for he failed to see that this was not the moment to urge his plans. The perils of Eylau, and the conspiracy which was hatched during his absence had not made sufficient impression upon the emperor for him to deem it essential to leave a living representative in Paris when war called him away, and in order to decide him to repudiate Josephine and wed another an extraordinarily desirable alliance must be proposed: such a one was not at hand, the idea of a Russian alliance having long been abandoned, and Austria having no marriageable daughter to offer.

Almost immediately following Napoleon's return from Italy, Mme. Walewska arrived in Paris and Napoleon's heart was completely filled with her, while his mind was occupied with affairs of state; the Spanish question perplexed him greatly, and claiming that that must be settled before he could reopen with Alexander the conference begun at Tilsit, he gave little thought to the question of divorce. Talleyrand, however, began to urge the step, and to insist that the emperor should at least come to some decision upon the subject. Under the pressure brought to bear upon him Napoleon became so excited and nervous that a serious illness seemed inevitable; he had frequent attacks of excruciating stomach trouble, and when ill would draw his wife down beside him on the bed and weeping sob out that he *could* not leave her.

It seemed as if Josephine possessed some talisman by which she held her husband's affection, and although he sometimes said that she was old and ugly, during their sojourn at Marrac his conduct towards her was like that of a youthful lover. In those days he apparently forgot that a divorce had ever been talked of; they amused themselves like a couple of children let loose from school; frequently, in the presence of the guard of light cavalry that escorted them, he chased Josephine across the beach and pushed her into the water, laughing like a boy, and when the empress, in her haste, lost her shoes, he threw them out to sea and forced her to drive home in her stockings, that he might the better see and feel her feet, which he greatly admired.

At this period he was more alive to Josephine's worth than ever before, indeed she never appeared to better advantage than upon this journey to Bayonne; she showed herself intelligent, adroit and full of tact in the strange interview they were obliged to hold with the Spanish sovereigns, and later during the triumphal march across the south and west provinces, when the temperature was so high that in order to be at all comfortable they were obliged to travel by night, when at each halting place they were feted and entertained in exactly the same dull manner, when Napoleon was bored in the extreme by the ovations, Josephine, in spite of fatigue and illness, was always punctual and ready with a gracious smile and fitting word for all.

It was wonderful how she managed to appear interested in everything, in household affairs and children, in all which could best please the women; how she managed to temper Napoleon's dominant power by her gracious smile and caressing manner and to win love where he won admiration. She had wonderful tact in giving a present, and a way of taking a jewel from her own person and offering it to a matron or maid which was simply captivating, and understood how to make the presentation to an official of an obligatory present appear like a token of personal esteem.

Although for four months constantly under the charm of Josephine's presence, the desire for divorce again took hold of Napoleon; doubtless it was the incentive for the journey of Erfurt, to which place he was accompanied by Talleyrand, whose mission it was to insinuate to the Emperor Alexander that Napoleon was ready to share his throne with one of the grand duchesses; but Talleyrand, instead of serving his royal master, unscrupulously betrayed him; it was he who furnished the Russian emperor with a plan for eluding Napoleon's proposal, suggested the basis for a new coalition against France, and paved the way for the war of 1809.

From Erfurt, Napoleon was obliged to return at once to Paris and the Spanish frontier. He relied upon Alexander's good faith, and fancied that when he had quelled the Spanish mutiny, nothing would be easier to arrange than the proposed Russian alliance. However, it was not a mutiny which he had to subdue in Spain but an insurrection, and, instead of taking two months to put it down, as he had anticipated, he was detained three months, and finally achieved but a barren victory. Then came news from Paris of plots in his own family, who were figuring upon his death, that Austria was again in arms, that the archdukes were instigating revolt in Germany, and the sacred war kept alive by secret societies.

Leaving Benavente, he spurred to Paris with incredible rapidity, and in three months he unmasked traitors, put his affairs in order, organized an army, and pushed on to the Danube, Austria having attacked and Archduke Charles invaded the territory of the confederation; but when at Schoenbrunn, after seventeen months of indefatigable action, he had time for reflection, the urgent necessity for divorce was made apparent; he not only realized clearly the obligation of assuring an heredity, but the necessity of having a representative in Paris during his absence, one around whom his friends would rally in the case of an English invasion or an uprising of the royalists. Josephine was no longer at hand to confuse and trouble him by appeals to his conscience, and the memory of the years they had passed together, to startle him by suggesting that, with the sundering of their lives, the star of his destiny would begin to wane; another woman, as agreeable, younger, and more beautiful, next whose heart lay a child of his, was at his side, and so the question, which for two long years had vexed his spirit and wrung his heart, was finally settled.

So long as Napoleon doubted if he could have children he had schemed, planned and invented every imaginable combination for the foundation of an heredity, but now that he *knew* that he could found a line of kings, that his descendants might sit upon the throne of France, it was plain to him that a second marriage was the only practical step, that a direct heir alone could ensure the stability of the Empire.

In order to spare both Josephine and himself, and avoid further painful scenes, he wrote from Vienna ordering that the communicating doors between his apartments and the empress's at Fontainebleau be walled up, and when Josephine joined him at the *château*, he refused to grant her a private interview and remained closeted with his ministers; from that time, he so arranged that they were never alone together, and thus avoided any explanations or private conversation regarding his intentions. Napoleon essayed to make Hortense announce his decision to her mother, and, when she refused, summoned Eugène from Italy for the purpose; but when he knew his stepson to be on the way, he mustered up his courage and provoked the supreme conversation wherein he must declare to his wife his irrevocable determination to divorce her.

So at last fell the blow which Josephine had been dreading for years, for the avoidance of which she had deployed all her charms, the fear of which had poisoned her life; she knew that further effort was futile, and although she wept and fainted when the emperor finally announced his decision, it was rather with the view of making the best of the situation for herself and children than from excess of feeling; she wished her son's position firmly established, her own debts paid, and an ample income settled upon her; she desired to preserve the rank and prerogatives of an empress, and above all that she should not be forced to leave Paris.

Napoleon granted all that she asked, the Elysée was given her as a town residence, the domain of Malmaison for a country seat, and the *château* of Navarre as a hunting-lodge; and a yearly income of three millions, the title, the escort, and the customary retinue of a reigning empress were assured her; thus he prepared for his divorced wife a place in the state which was unparalleled in history, unless a like example could be found among the annals of Rome and Byzantium..

But Napoleon gave his divorced wife more than money, palaces and titles, he gave her his sympathy and his tears. He sent almost hourly for news of her, desiring to know how she passed her time away from him, and like the most faithful and tender of lovers, wrote her letter after letter, and insisted that all who surrounded her should visit him that he might glean from them every item of interest regarding the daily life of the woman he had repudiated; there was no attention, kindness, or favour that he did not lavish upon her, so conscious was he of the wrong he had done; what he wished was that she should accept the inevitable with fortitude, and, making the best of her new situation, relieve him of the pain of knowing her unhappy through his will.

Nevertheless, when he went to Malmaison to see and console Josephine he never embraced her or entered her private apartments, but so arranged that his visits should have an air of formality, for he wished that both she and the world should know that all was ended. This conduct bears witness to his respect for Josephine, showing that he would not permit anyone to think that the wife of yesterday had become the mistress of today; perhaps, too, he doubted of his ability to maintain his distant demeanour save when supported by witnesses, and his conduct shows how strong, powerful and tender was his affection for this woman; an affection which had outlived youth and beauty, and, in spite of all strains, remained to the last the great love of his life.

Chapter 17

Marie-Louise

Up to this period all the women with whom Napoleon had been intimately connected had been considered by him as his inferiors, for, surrounded by women of the noblest blood of France, Montmorencies, Mortemarts and Lavals, he had learned to estimate the social worth of the Beauharnais family correctly, and the influence which Josephine had exercised over him through her supposed prestige had long since vanished. None of his mistresses had been sufficiently highborn to flatter his vanity by her rank and worldly position; indeed, he does not seem to have attempted conquests of that kind, or, if he did, must have been early discouraged; moreover, in order to satisfy his egotism and ambition something more than a marriage with a noble family of France was necessary.

Such an alliance was made possible by the Emperor of Austria's proffer of the hand of his eldest daughter Marie-Louise; this alliance Napoleon believed would assist him to climb the last step towards equality with his predecessors upon the French throne, and the Napoleonic system which he had endeavoured to establish and to strengthen by intermarriages between the Bonapartes and the various reigning families of Europe, would, by his marriage, become amalgamated with the house of Austria, even as the Bourbons had been before him, his dynasty would lose its improvised air, and on assuming the quartering of the house of Austria gain the relationships which seemed to him to constitute the only strong and durable political tie.

In this alliance Napoleon's ambition found satisfaction, but how could his dominant spirit accommodate itself to a wife who had from birth the consciousness of her rank and worth, and the belief in her own infallibility common to those born in the purple. By a strange hazard the young girl who was offered to him had been so educated as to have no will save that of her father, to realise that her interests were subordinate to those of her nation, that she was destined to play a role in some political combination, and that she must accept without a murmur the marriage which the political interests of her country imposed upon her; it was with this object in view that Marie-Louise's character had been moulded from earliest infancy. She had been taught all languages, German, English, French, Italian, Spanish, Turkish, Bohemian and even Latin, for it was impossible to foresee where her destiny would lead her; moreover, it was argued, that the more extended her vocabulary, the greater the number of words at her command for the expression of an idea, the less ideas she was likely to have.

Her talents for music and drawing had been encouraged and cultivated as those accomplishments provided an innocent means of distraction for a princess wherever she might find herself; the teachings of the Church had been given her literally, and minute attention to all its forms inculcated, but all questions of dogma were avoided, for it was possible that fate would give the Austrian princess a heretic for a husband. Her education included a system of morals which only the *casuists* of Spain could have advised; the archduchess was kept in ignorance regarding the difference in sex, the barnyard was peopled only by hens, she had no little dogs, only bitches, her riding horse was a mare, her books were pitilessly expurged, pages, lines, even words being cut out, without its occurring to the censor that the gulfs thus created would give the archduchess food for thought.

The princess was continually under the surveillance of a court lady, who directed the management of her apartments, was present at her lessons, invented her games, and watched the servants and teachers; this lady never left her pupil, either by night or day, and, as politics played an important part in the princess's destiny, the incumbent of this position changed with each new ministry, and Marie-Louise had five governesses in eighteen years; her education, however, was regulated by such rigid laws that, despite all changes in her suite, she remained the same.

Marie-Louise's amusements were such as are common to a conventual life; she had flowers to cultivate, birds to take care of, and sometimes lunched under the trees with her governess's daughter; her holidays were spent in the intimacy of the family in pleasant but *bourgeois* fashion; she never participated in the gaieties of the court, and had made but one or two short journeys in order that she might have change of air. The event which had made the greatest impression upon her, and which had given her the most distraction, were her flights before the French invasions, when discipline had been relaxed and tasks laid aside; thus it was not a woman who was offered to Napoleon but a child, accustomed to live under such strict rules that any life would seem sweet by comparison, and for whom the simplest pleasures would possess a charm.

Marie-Louise's education was identical with that given to the daughters of Marie-Thérèse and the result of this method, as exemplified by Marie-Antoinette at Versailles, Marie-Caroline at Naples and Marie-Amélie at Parma, was not desirable—and it was to be dreaded lest the nature of the young Austrian princess which had been so repressed would expand in the same way as her aunt's; Napoleon, however, reasoned that husbands are responsible for their wives' conduct, and laid his plans accordingly. The schoolgirl who was to pass into his keeping should simply leave the convents of Schoenbrunn and Laxenburg for that of the Tuileries and Saint-Cloud, she should live under the same inflexible rules, the same rigorous surveillance, she should have no freedom in the choice of friendships and read no book which had not been previously scanned; no masculine visitors should be permitted, and her governess should be replaced by a lady of honour and four ladies-in-waiting who should be perpetually on guard; the only difference in her life should be the presence of a husband.

Thus since the husband was obliged to teach his wife all that her parents had taken pains to conceal from her, he resolved to supplement the enlightenment by great precautions, and determined that no man, however high or low his position upon the social ladder, should remain for one instant alone with the empress. He re-established the etiquette of Louis XIV.'s time, the rigidity of which had been relaxed through the indifference of Louis XV., and the feebleness of Louis XVI.; but where royalty veiled its distrust under the disguise of traditional honours, employing the highest ladies in the land to watch the queen under the pretext of keeping her company, Napoleon brought into play undisguised military discipline; he was not actuated by jealousy, but simply by motives of prudence and precaution; he had once said at a state's council: "Adultery is the affair of a moment," and he was convinced, perhaps by experience, that a *tête-à-tête* between a man and a woman easily became criminal.

With such a distrust of woman Napoleon would doubtless have found the Oriental system quite to his taste, but as it was not customary among Europeans to seclude their wives in a *harem* he was obliged to replace eunuchs by ladies-in-waiting, and iron bars by etiquette, but, save for the name, the prison was the same. The imprisonment accepted, he intended to give to his wife every material pleasure which she could desire; but the pleasures which he offered her were almost identical with those which a *sultan* gives to his favourite *odalisque*.

While at Vienna Marie-Louise ignored the pleasure of elegant dresses, exquisite laces, rare shawls and dainty linen; in Paris, provided that no merchant approached her and she made her selections through the medium of a lady of the wardrobe, she should have every beautiful thing which French industry could produce, and Napoleon gave her a foretaste of the luxuries which were to be hers in the *corbeille* which he sent her, of which he inspected each article and had it packed under his supervision. The *corbeille* included twelve dozen chemise of the finest batiste, trimmed with embroidery and valenciennes, twenty-four dozen handkerchiefs, twenty-four nightdresses, thirty-six skirts, and twenty-four nightcaps, at a cost of fifty-one thousand, one hundred and fifty-six *francs*.

In addition the *corbeille* contained eighty-one thousand, one hundred and ninety-nine *francs*' worth of laces, exclusive of a point-d'Alençon shawl, which was valued at three thousand two hundred *francs*; sixty-four dresses from Leroy costing one hundred and twenty-six thousand, nine hundred and seventy-six *francs*; seventeen cashmere shawls valued at thirty-nine thousand, eight hundred and sixty *francs*; twelve dozen stockings, ranging in price from eighteen to seventy-two *francs* a pair, and sixty pairs of shoes and slippers of all colours and fabrics, which had been made according to measures sent from Vienna, and were so small that Napoleon, as he examined them, remarked that it was a good sign. Everything that Paris could produce that was beautiful and rare was presented to her, and yearly she might have almost as much. As for her toilet alone, she was to have an allowance of thirty thousand *francs* a month.

As a girl, Marie-Louise had owned but one or two jewels, whose value was so insignificant that the wife of a Paris shopkeeper would have disdained them; a couple of hair bracelets, a necklace of seed pearls and another of green beads had comprised her ornaments; as empress she was to have diamonds of enormous value; the thirteen stones which surrounded the portrait which the emperor sent her alone cost six hundred thousand *francs*, a diamond necklace costing nine hundred thousand *francs*, and a pair of ear-rings costing four hundred thousand *francs*, and a still finer *parure* composed of a diadem, comb, ear-rings, necklace and belt contained two thousand, two hundred and fifty-seven large stones and three hundred and six rose diamonds. She was to have a *parure* of emeralds and diamonds valued at two hundred and eighty-nine thousand, eight hundred and sixty-five *francs*; one of opal and diamonds costing two hundred and seventy-five thousand, nine hundred and fifty-three *francs*; one of ruby and diamonds and another of turquoise and diamonds, all of immense value, without counting the diamond ornaments furnished by the crown and appraised at three million, three hundred and twenty-five thousand, seven hundred and twenty-four *francs*.

The apartments which she had inhabited in Austria had been furnished in the simplest manner, in France magnificent rooms which had been redecorated and furnished under the emperor's personal supervision awaited her coming, and in order to spare her any feeling of strangeness the emperor ordered that all toilet articles and small pieces of furniture likely to be in daily use should be duplicated; thus, in whatever palace she went to reside, the articles to which she was accustomed should be at hand.

When the work of the furnishing of the apartments was complete the emperor was so proud of his success as a decorator that he invited all his guests to view them, and at the Tuileries he himself conducted the king and queen of Bavaria to inspect the rooms, taking them by the way of a dark and narrow staircase which led from his own dressing-room to the empress's bedchamber; the staircase was so narrow that the king, who was extremely corpulent, was obliged to descend sideways, and when they arrived at the foot, the door leading into the apartment destined for the empress was found to be locked and they were obliged to turn about in the dark and narrow space and remount the staircase—a movement which was executed with great difficulty because of his Bavarian Majesty's great size. At Compiègne it was the emperor also who did the honours of the empress's bathroom to the Queen of Westphalia, displaying to her the marble bath and furniture and hangings of India stuffs which had cost four hundred thousand *francs*.

For the good of her stomach Marie-Louise's governesses had forbidden all rich food, but the emperor, foreseeing that, like most Viennese, she would have a taste for goodies, took upon himself the ordering of her table, multiplying the deserts with cakes and ices and *bonbons*,

Marie-Louise had a generous nature, but up to the time of her marriage had had nothing to give save such samples of her own handicraft as she had been taught to make; as empress she was enabled to shower presents upon her family. Napoleon setting her an example by sending handsome presents to her people even before she arrived in France. It was not possible to assert that she had a taste for the theatre, as she had never seen a play, but Napoleon believed that she would not be of her country and her time if she had not, and planned for her amusement in that way, both when she accompanied him to the theatre or preferred to have the actors play in the palace; in short it was his intention that she should have everything which would distract and amuse her so long as it was in accordance with the secluded life he had planned. It was not his intention that she should leave her apartments save for great civil and religious ceremonies, state balls, the theatre, the hunt, and such journeys as might be necessary, and upon these occasions she was to be surrounded by her ladies of honour and officers, and, arrayed in court costume, laden with jewels, she was to remain in haughty isolation, to be worshipped by all classes from afar like an idol.

Thus he essayed to gild the bars of the prison which he had prepared for the Austrian princess, dreaming to keep her a child, and imagining that she would pass, without feeling the transition, from captive archduchess to captive empress; thus he sought to assure himself of her fidelity and so to arrange her life that she should be, like Caesar's wife, above suspicion. The woman whom he thus planned to seclude had in his eyes a mission to fulfil, to be the mother of his children; she was the mould destined to receive and develop the dynastic germ, and it was in order to assure the legitimacy of his descendants that he took so many precautions: he acted not unwisely, for the doctrine of monarchical succession hinges upon the unquestionable legitimacy of offspring.

Napoleon did not doubt that Marie-Louise would become a mother, having informed himself minutely regarding her health and physical being, and knowing her family to be prolific, her mother having had thirteen children, her grandmother seventeen, and her great grandmother twenty-six, and he was impatient for her arrival that he might insure the future of his race.

Napoleon had received Marie-Louise's portrait, which represented a young woman with long, blonde hair parted in heavy masses and brushed back on each side from a high forehead, eyes of china blue, a nose slightly indented at the base, thick lips, heavy chin, white but rather prominent teeth and a complexion marred by the ravages of smallpox; the shoulders were large and white, the bust remarkably full, and the arms, which were long and thin, terminated in small and pretty hands, while her foot was charming. He had been told that she was tall for a woman, and neither graceful nor supple, but an easy carriage Napoleon thought could be acquired, and what he most desired was that her appearance should show the characteristics of her race.

When Lejeune,[1] General Berthier's *aide-de-camp*, arrived at Compiègne, preceding Marie-Louise by several days, Napoleon had the portrait which he had received from Vienna brought into the room and proceeded to question the young officer as to the likeness; happily Lejeune was an artist as well as a soldier, and was able to show the emperor a sketch in profile which he had himself made of the archduchess. "Ah," exclaimed Napoleon, "she has the real Austrian lip!" and going to the table upon which lay a number of medals with the heads of various Austrian sovereigns thereon, he compared the various profiles and recognized with pleasure that his future empress was a true Habsburg.

From the moment the negotiations were concluded, that he knew his dream about to be fulfilled. Napoleon burned with impatience for possession; in vain he essayed to distract his thoughts by hunting, but the idea haunted him; he spoke of it to everyone and he wished the preparations for the reception finished before they had begun. On its being represented to him that it would be difficult to turn the grand *salon* of the Louvre into a chapel because of the immense pictures which it was difficult to dispose of, he responded: "Well, then, burn them!"

He was preoccupied with the impression which he would make and he ordered from Léger, who was Murat's tailor, a court costume literally covered with embroidery, but on trying it on found it so uncomfortable that he was unable to wear it. He ordered boots from a new shoemaker, in order to have finer shoes than those he had hitherto worn and took dancing-lessons, wishing to learn to waltz, but he only succeeded in bringing on an attack of heart trouble, which forced him to abandon the lessons. As Catherine of Westphalia wrote to her father:

> Neither you nor I would ever have imagined Napoleon capable of such things.

---

1. *Lejeune Volume 1* and *Lejeune Volume 2* by Louis-François Lejeune also published by Leonaur.

In measure as the cortege from Vienna advanced his impatience increased. At last he could wait no longer. Marie-Louise slept at Vitry on the 26th of March, on the 27th she was due at Soisson, and it was not until the 28th that the emperor was to join her. The programme of the ceremonial was printed, the pavilion where the meeting was to take place was built and decorated, the troops were commanded and the repast prepared, nevertheless, on the morning of the 27th, in a pouring rain. Napoleon left Compiègne in company with Murat, and without an escort or suite, rode to Courcelles where he awaited Marie-Louise's coming under the shelter of a church porch.

At last the coach with its eight horses appeared and stopped for relays. Napoleon advanced to the side of the carriage, the groom of the chambers announced him, his sister Caroline, who was conducting the bride, presented him to Marie-Louise, and dripping with rain he entered the carriage, which drove rapidly off. They rushed past villages where the mayors, address in hand, waited to receive them, through cities *en fête* and at last, at nine o'clock in the evening, without having broken the day's fast, they arrived at Compiègne. The emperor cut short the addresses of welcome, presentations and compliments, and, taking Marie-Louise by the hand, conducted her to his private apartment; there the young girl had reason to remember the lesson which her father had instilled—obedience to her husband in all things.

The following noon the emperor had his breakfast served at the empress's bedside by one of her maids, and during the day he said to one of his generals: "My friend, marry a German, they are the best women in the world, good, amiable, innocent, and fresh as a rose." Napoleon appears to have disregarded or disdained the criticisms which would naturally follow upon his action in assuming that the marriage by proxy was all that was necessary, and his consummation of it before the subsequent ceremonials had taken place, and justified his conduct by saying: "Henry IV. did the same."

CHAPTER 18

Marie-Louise: part 2

Three months after her marriage Marie-Louise said to Metternich: "I am not afraid of Napoleon, but I begin to think he is of me." Thus three months had sufficed to banish the terrible fear which from Vienna to Compiègne had caused her such mortal terror that it had affected her physical well-being. But how was it possible that Napoleon should have become timid in the presence of this girl of eighteen? In taking this Austrian princess to wife he realized the dream of years, and from a purely physical desire for the possession of the high-born girl had grown a desire to be the object of her affection, as well as the husband assigned her by the political interests of her country; he wished to know that he possessed her heart, and desired that she should proclaim her happiness.

One morning when they were at the Tuileries the emperor sent for Metternich and closeted him with the empress; at the end of an hour he rejoined them and said to the ambassador: "Well, have you had a good talk, has the empress laughed or cried, had she many complaints to make?" Then, seeing that the ambassador was embarrassed, he added: "Oh, I do not expect you to give me a detailed account of your conversation; it is private matter between you and the empress;" nevertheless, on the following day, he questioned Metternich minutely, and as the latter was not inclined to enlighten him, he exclaimed: "The empress has no complaints to make, and I hope you will say so to your sovereign, as he will rely implicitly upon what you say."

In reality it was rather himself than the Austrian emperor whom he sought to reassure; he wished to believe that his wife was devoted to him, that she was contented with the life he forced her to lead, and hid from him no lingering sentiment of distrust and dislike. Aspiring to domestic peace and happiness, he longed for the assurance of Marie-

Louise's affection and the realisation of his desires.

From childhood the Austrian princess had shared the universal hatred of Bonaparte. When only six years old her mother had told her that Monseigneur Bonaparte, the Corsican, had fled from Egypt, deserting his army, and had become a Turk; she believed firmly that he had been in the habit of beating his ministers, and had slain two of his generals with his own hand, and the year preceding her marriage—the year which had seen Vienna bombarded, and witnessed the Battles of Eckmühl, Essling and Wagram—she had considered him one of the most despicable of beings. After Znaïm Marie-Louise wrote to a friend:

> I am consumed with fury against Napoleon, yet I am obliged to sit at table with one of his marshals.

When his divorce was announced, and the question of a second marriage began to be discussed she never admitted for a moment that the French conqueror's choice might fall upon her. "My father," she said, "is too kind to coerce me in a matter of such importance." She pitied Napoleon's possible choice, being sure that it would not be she who would be the victim of political expediency; and when the project of her marriage was discussed, she wrote to a friend of her childhood:

> Pray for me, for, while I am ready to sacrifice my personal happiness for the welfare of my country, I am most unhappy.

Though in reality the Austrian princesses had no voice in the disposal of their hands and no opinion save that of their father, for form's sake, Marie-Louise's consent to the marriage was asked, and she resigned herself to the inevitable, while mentally regarding her future husband as an ogre. When one considers the situation her feeling was not unnatural; four times the French conqueror had devastated her country, twice he had entered Vienna as a victor; he had forced her royal father to go to his camp, suing for peace; every sentiment of patriotism and filial affection, the most sacred of human emotions, the most sensitive chord in noble pride had been outraged by him; yet, strange as it may appear, Marie-Louise once wed her repugnance was not apparent.

Whether this was due to the education which she had received, or whether her natural temperament was awakened and she enjoyed the good things which Napoleon provided for her—luxuries to which she was unaccustomed,—and found his personality not displeasing, or whether her contentment was feigned, it is impossible to affirm; but it is probable that the first supposition is correct, and Napoleon did all in his power to prove to her that he was, and would remain, a good husband. At the beginning of the Consulate he had ceased to share his chamber with Josephine, pretending that his work and duties rendered it necessary, but in reality to insure his own freedom; he was prepared, however, if Marie-Louise exacted it, to reassume the chain, for he said: "It is a woman's rightful appanage;" but their temperaments were too dissimilar; while he, always chilly, wished a fire kept up all the year round, she, accustomed to a cold climate and a Spartan-like existence in the immense and glacial palaces of the environs of Vienna, could not stand heated rooms.

Frequently, with the uxoriousness of a young husband, he urged Marie-Louise to spend the night with him, but she always responded that he kept his rooms too warm; while on going to her apartments he would find the temperature too low for him and order a fire lighted, but he invariably deferred to Marie-Louise's contrary opinion with the remark that "Her Majesty's will was law," and, after shivering for a short period, would go away.

This difference in their temperaments and indifference on her part paved the way for infidelities, but Napoleon does not appear to have thought of such a thing, or, if he did, he hid his *amours* carefully and they were but passing. In 1811 he appears to have paid some attention to the Princess Aldobrandini-Borghèse, *née* Mlle. de Rochefaucauld, to whom he had given a dowry of eight hundred thousand *francs* and married to the brother-in-law of Pauline Bonaparte, and whom he had, just named lady-in-waiting; but it is probable that he simply admired the manner and elegance of the young woman, who is said to have been charming. There was also some talk, and some gossip in private correspondence, regarding the Duchess of Montebello, who was one of the empress's ladies of honour, but there is no proof of a *liaison*; such adventures as he did permit himself were obscure and carefully dissimulated, creating no gossip, simply because no one knew anything about them.

The first *amour* which caused any gossip had its birth at Caen where the emperor met Mme. Pellapra of the Testa-Cubières suit. Napoleon again met Mme. Pellapra at Lyons on his return from Elba in 1815, and then pamphleteers attacked "Mme. Ventreplat" to their hearts' content. At Saint-Cloud there was a little love-affair with a certain Lise B **** but it never reached serious proportions; beyond this his marital behaviour towards Marie-Louise was exemplary.

Bonaparte imagined that the young empress felt aggrieved at his visits to Josephine at Malmaison and to Mme. Walewska in the rue de la Victoire, although the former had become yearly less frequent in proportion as Josephine's conduct became more and more displeasing, and were made with great privacy, while the latter were so secret that few were cognizant of them. On the officers who composed his suite when he visited Malmaison and on those who were aware of his friendship with Mme. Walewska he imposed caution and secrecy, saying on each occasion: "Knowledge of this visit would cause my wife unnecessary pain."

After his second marriage his entire manner of life changed; there remained to him from his poor, solitary and melancholy youth, which was devoid of the amusements natural to his age, a taste for noisy and active sports and in that respect he, with his forty-one years and Marie-Louise with her eighteen, were well matched; if possible he was the bigger child of the two, and he entered with zest into amusements suitable for a collegian. The young empress had proposed but one amendment to the cloister-like existence mapped out for her, she desired to ride horseback, which was an exercise habitual with the princesses of Lorraine as soon as they escaped the maternal rule; Marie-Antoinette had done the same, and there is a record of Marie-Thérèse's objurgations.

Napoleon himself acted as riding-master to his young wife, and during the first lessons ran at her horse's side, bridle in hand, until she had acquired sufficient confidence to ride alone, then daily the horses were ordered immediately after breakfast, and, without taking time to put on his boots, the emperor would throw himself into the saddle, and in his stocking-feet gallop up and down the Grande Allée after his wife, exciting the horses to run and greatly amused by her cries and laughter; about every ten feet a groom was stationed in order to avoid any accident to the empress, but it often happened that the emperor had the most falls.

In the evening, in the intimacy of the household, he organized all kinds of games, such as blind-man's-buff, puss-in-the-corner, cushion-and-keys and games of forfeits in which he took an active part. Up to this time Marie-Louise's only social accomplishment was the ability to move her ear without moving a muscle of her face, but she now learned to play billiards, for which game she developed such a passion and so much talent, that the emperor was obliged to take lessons of one of his chamberlains before he could meet her on equal terms; she also had a fancy for sketching his profile and he was always ready to pose for her, although he refused to sit for any painter; he listened attentively, when, seated at the piano, she played German *sonatas*, although he had but little taste for that style of music, and manifested a proper degree of interest when she showed him the suspenders or sash she was embroidering for him.

He was always at her side, devoted and attentive, endeavouring to amuse and distract his "good Marie-Louise," and his *bourgeois* habit of addressing her in the second person amazed the court, which had returned to the rigid etiquette of Louis XIV.'s time. Such an existence and such manners did not shock Marie-Louise, she soon accustomed herself to the new manner of life and addressed her husband with the familiar "thou," gave friendly nicknames to her sisters-in-law and called Madame Mère "mamma;" but all this affability rested upon a condition, that her husband should never leave her, but should always be at her disposition, and he who, up to that moment, had regulated his days according to his occupations and the demands of state, was now constrained to conciliate his occupations—sometimes to sacrifice them—to the tastes and caprices of his wife.

It had previously been the emperor's habit to breakfast alone and hurriedly, upon the corner of his writing-table (when business permitted him to breakfast at all), but he resigned himself to breakfasting with his wife at a fixed hour, taking from affairs of state the time for an elaborate repast which was most distasteful to him. Between the years of 1810 and 1812 the royal pair took five long journeys, visiting Normandy, Belgium, Holland, the Rhine and Dresden, and it was not she who waited for the emperor as Josephine had done, it was the husband's turn to cultivate his patience, for Marie-Louise was never on time for any social function; he made all his personal tastes subservient to hers and was not only a faithful but a loving and attentive husband, never missing an occasion to give his wife a pleasure.

The magnificent present which he made his wife of a *parure* of Brazilian rubies, costing four hundred thousand *francs*, when she had only wished for one valued at forty-six thousand, and the superb necklace, consisting of eight strings of pearls, which cost five hundred thousand *francs*, which he presented to her after her confinement and which was stolen from Blois, were simply imperial. The fact which shows the lover in the husband were the manifold little presents which he gave her, such as bracelets, bearing the date of some occasion which had been particularly joyous, loving words or names spelt out in precious stones, and was it not a proclamation of her affection when she had her own portrait framed in precious stones whose initial letters formed the words "*Louise, je t'aime*," and placed it upon her husband's writing desk.

If Napoleon had not loved his young wife he would not have taken umbrage at the slightest reference to his affection in the newspaper or to a verse wherein he was represented as a love-sick shepherd; as it was, the moment he saw the slightest reference to his affection in print he felt as though its sanctity had been violated, and immediately wrote a furious letter to the minister of police, wherein he did not deny his love, but insisted that the newspapers should not be permitted to comment upon it. Thinking to strengthen his wife's affection, he showered valuable presents of every description upon each member of her family, and favours upon all the Austrians at his court.

Despite time, the love which Marie-Louise manifested, and the precautions for his marital security which he had taken, and which were still carefully observed, he continued to be suspicious, and when the war with Russia called him from home he arranged that a detailed account of his wife's daily life and actions should be sent him by each courier; these letters were written by an illiterate person upon the commonest of paper, and upon these wretched scrawls he, who was usually so scrupulous and critical, wrote questions and notes; and yet in spite of this continual surveillance he dared not openly take his wife to task when anything displeased him, but strove to find an intermediary to express his disapproval.

Upon one occasion the empress, while walking in the park at Saint-Cloud with Mme. de Montebello, allowed the duchess to present one of her relations and spoke with him for some moments; the following morning after the levee the emperor detained the Austrian ambassador and recounted the affair, and upon Metternich's feigning not to comprehend what was wanted of him. Napoleon frankly explained that he wished the ambassador to speak to the empress, and the Austrian refusing he insisted, saying:

> The empress is young and might misunderstand my motives, attributing them to jealousy, while what you would say to her would make quite a different impression.

Napoleon's best beloved mistress, she who had most occupied his thoughts, was power, and this power which he had refused to give to Josephine, of which he had been so jealous that neither his two oldest counsellors, his brothers, nor any living being had he ever even given a shadow of authority, he gave, in 1813, in that time which was most perilous for his empire, to Marie-Louise; making her regent of the Empire.

Doubtless there was more shadow than substance in this abandonment, and that no grave decision could be taken without his consent; it is probable that a premonition of disaster assailed him even in Russia, and that by this act he intended to assure the transmission of his crown, but in any case it entailed a stripping of some of his dearly loved authority, and he had not hesitated. Decrees were signed in his name by the empress, by her pardons were accorded, nominations made and proclamations issued; the bulletins by which, since 1800, the master announced his victories, distributed his glory and gave the accounts of his conquests, were things of the past, and it was: "Her Imperial Majesty, Queen and Regent, who had received from the army information," and the conscripts for the unfortunate army were called "Marie-Louise men" by the people.

From head to foot of the governmental ladder weaknesses manifested themselves and treachery succeeded. Napoleon was no longer there, even his name had disappeared, while that of Marie-Louise was feared by none and meant nothing to the people; still, Napoleon would not alter his decree, applauded the step he had taken, and believed that his wife knew more than Cambacérès or than all the Bonapartes put together, and the nearer the catastrophe, the more imminent the peril, the more tenaciously he clung to the idea that she, she alone, would be his salvation.

By chance—for she was not responsible for his departure from Paris, the capitulation and all the rest—Marie-Louise caused his final downfall. Napoleon wrote her a letter, not in cipher, wherein he indicated the movements which he intended to attempt against the allied armies; this letter fell into the hands of Bleucher's courier, and General Bleucher made haste to lay it, *with the seal broken*, at the feet of the august daughter of his Imperial Majesty the Emperor of Austria.

Chapter 19

Elba

It is doubtful if Napoleon was actuated solely by love in the pursuance of the course described in the preceding chapter, and highly probable that his actions were entirely due to motives of policy. He probably argued that when the Austrian emperor found himself face to face with his daughter and grandson as the representatives of France, he would hesitate to strike the blow which would ruin them, and that the sovereigns of Europe, not finding himself, but one of their own rank seated upon the French throne, would hesitate to overthrow it, and, believing themselves interested in the tranquillity of France, would accept and confirm the substitution, that though he himself might be forced to abdicate, the dynasty which he had established would be assured.

In order to admit the truth of this hypothesis one must admit that, from the year 1813, before Lützen, before the first campaign, wherein he constantly manifested his confidence in his continued success, Napoleon was at heart despairing; that he had latent doubts about Austria, and considered Marie-Louise as a pledge of coalition, trusted in the bond of paternity, and relied upon the good faith of Francis II., the father.

To divine such a conspiracy as the aristocrats of Europe had woven against him, to foresee that the young girl who had been given him as wife was the lure prepared by the allied oligarchies to entrap him, would have required an insight into the depths of royal unscrupulousness which even a Talleyrand and a Fouché might be incapable of.

In order to conceive and carry out such a design, to coalesce around a nuptial bed the hate of all the old dynasties, the profound corruption which is met with solely in the highest circles was alone capable; in these circles education and tradition have rendered men unscrupulous, they become accustomed to disregard all laws, human or divine, which militate against their interests and to carry their designs into execution regardless of the means employed, seeing therein no dishonour. In this instance it was not a mistress but a wife which had to be furnished to encompass their object, and what mattered it if the wheels of their triumphant chariot, while crushing the impious being who had outraged the sacred monarchical system, also rolled over the shuddering form and blonde locks of an archduchess. Should she survive the ordeal, means should be found to console her, should she die—well, it could not be helped, for the attainment of such an end some things must be risked and Marie-Louise was only a woman.

Napoleon never suspected such a despicable conspiracy, never admitted that his wife was the accomplice of his enemies; nor was she, for care had been taken to conceal from her the role she was destined to play, and she enacted it the better because of her innocence. It was not until much later, at Saint Helena, that Napoleon traced the continuity between his second marriage and the disasters which followed it; even then he did not sound the plot to its very depth, either because it displeased him to elucidate the principal reason of his downfall, or because it pained him to smirch the memory of his wife by connecting her with so vile a scheme.

He frequently remarked: "My marriage was a flower-covered pit which they dug for me;" and instead of harbouring resentment against this woman who had been the cause of his downfall, he showed her more affection and greater confidence, as if to console her for the pain and disillusion caused by the aggressiveness of her native land and the menacing attitude of her father, which he believed she could not fail to regard as treacherous towards her and hers.

When the campaign of 1812 opened Napoleon apparently entertained no doubts of his ultimate success, it was his nature to hope even against hope, and it was not until much later that he was forced to admit the possibility of the enemies entering Paris and carrying away the empress and the King of Rome. He believed that theirs would be but a brief triumph, for the momentary occupation of Paris did not alter his strategic plans, but he could not suffer the thought that his wife and son should be, even momentarily, hostages in the hands of his adversaries, and it was to spare them such an insult that he ordered Joseph to abandon Paris, thus taking from it its statesmen and resisting elements and compromising the entire edifice of his plans, for Talleyrand knew how to avoid the injunction to follow the court.

His plans had long been laid, he had ingratiated himself into the confidence of King Joseph, the empress, the prefecture of the Seine and the police; he had accomplices everywhere over whom he exercised a strong and inexplicable influence and who seemed bound to him by an infernal pact; and with them he accomplished, in 1814, the treason which he began to plot at Tilsit in 1807. But the overthrowal of Napoleon's government was but half the task the Prince of Benevent had set himself, the whole would be accomplished only when he had succeeded in breaking the bonds which he himself had helped to forge between Napoleon and Marie-Louise.

The emperor believed that whatever misfortunes fate might have in store for him he should always have the supreme consolation afforded by the pleasures of home and the company of his wife and son, and that he had not secured a formal promise from the empress to rejoin him at Fontainebleau was because he still imagined that her tears might move the Emperor Francis and her future condition be ameliorated. He argued that a certain sovereignty would always be hers by right of birth, that she would be affectionate to him, who would resign himself to the existence of a petty prince, and, believing that she had loved in him rather the man than the sovereign, thought that there might yet be happiness in store for them and for the child whose mental and physical development they would watch over.

Marie-Louise was fond of her husband, disposed to sympathize with his hopes and plans, and willing to rejoin him when the occasion offered, but she was surrounded by people whose influence was all in a contrary direction, and accustomed from childhood to have others think for her, to be guided and ruled, it is not strange that she should have found it hard to follow the dictates of her heart and conscience. The love which she entertained for Napoleon was strong enough to impel her to faithfulness, and it was Talleyrand who took upon himself the task of blighting it.

With this object in view he had placed near Marie-Louise a woman who was heart and soul in his schemes, who was naturally an *intriguant*, and who, whenever she had been able to introduce herself into a diplomatic project, had been quite in her element; utterly unscrupulous, ignoring the virtue of gratitude, she was precisely the tool whom he required. As lady-in-waiting this woman had ready access to Marie-Louise's ear, and when the other ladies abandoned their posts and returned to their homes Mme. de Brignole remained with the empress, and, left almost alone with her, seized the occasion to obey

Talleyrand's instructions and to instil the poison of doubt into Marie-Louise's mind.

Instigated by her master, Mme. de Brignole first insinuated, then affirmed, that Napoleon had never loved his wife, but had constantly deceived her, and when the empress refused to believe she sent for two valets, who had just abandoned their sovereign and benefactor at Fontainebleau, and had them confirm all her lying tales.

There was no one at hand to inspire with courage and confidence the irresolute young girl who was more wounded by the accounts of her husband's infidelities than prostrated by the fall of her throne; and as she had once allowed herself to be sacrificed, like a modern Iphigenia, so now she acquiesced and stood inertly by, while political expedience sundered the domestic ties, which it had soldered. This compliance was not won in a day, for Marie-Louise struggled nearly a year against overwhelming obstacles, every sentiment was brought into play to alienate her affection from her husband: pride, jealousy, envy, vanity, all were employed, and Bonaparte's enemies triumphed only when they had succeeded in replacing his image in her heart by that of another, when the chaste Emperor of Austria had forced his daughter into a position which publicly compromised her: then monarchal Europe applauded, and the adulteress was recompensed by the sovereignty of Parma and Placentia.

Napoleon never dreamt of such abjection; from each of the stopping-places where he rested upon his sad journey he wrote a letter to his wife, as formerly he had written when she was making her triumphal journey towards Paris, greeted by the chiming of bells, the cannon's thunder, and the military salute of imperial marshals. The defeated emperor, wending his way across Europe under the watchful eyes of the military escort assigned by the allies, with the populace's cries of hatred ringing in his ears, never forgot his wife; but of all the letters which he wrote but two have been published; they are addressed to "My good, my dear Louise."

Forgetful of his own sufferings he wrote to her of the pain she must experience, made tender inquiries regarding her health and urged her to be courageous and brave. Care had been taken to inform Napoleon that Marie Louise's health rendered it imperative that she should take a course of the waters at Aix; it was a means of retarding their reunion and, consciously or not, Corvisart had lent his aid to the emperor's enemies; but of this, as of all the rest. Napoleon was unsuspicious, and, rejoicing in Corvisart's devotion, he addressed him a letter from Frejus which, if it was merited, is the physician's greatest glory, and far from opposing the journey to Aix the emperor encouraged it. He thought that though Marie-Louise might not be able to come immediately to Elba, she would surely hasten to install herself at Parma, and, in order that she should miss none of the accessories of rank to which she was accustomed, he dispatched a detachment of Polish light horse to that city to await her arrival and sent a large supply of carriage horses for her use.

Hardly had Napoleon reached Porto-Ferrajo than he began to arrange the empress's apartments in the palaces destined for his residence, hastening the work with the idea that she might arrive at any hour. He intended to celebrate her coming with fireworks and a grand ball, awaited her arrival to make various excursions to points of interest about the island, and, although foreign to his nature to give public expression to his sentiments, he ordered the painter who was decorating the drawing-room ceiling to depict there "two pigeons fastened together by a slip-knot which tightened as they separated."

It was on Marie-Louise's account that Napoleon kept the visit of Mme. Walewska shrouded in mystery. She had been to Naples to reclaim from Murat the endowment which the emperor had accorded her from the property which he had reserved, and which Murat had confiscated, and profiting from the relaxed surveillance at Porto-Ferrajo she had solicited an interview with the emperor.

Bonaparte was then installed at the hermitage of the Madonna de Marciana which was situated in the heart of a forest of aged chestnuts, in whose shade the intense heat of the Corsican summer was more endurable. The emperor occupied a small house close to the chapel, and the hermits, whom he had not wished to dispossess, were installed in the cellar, while for the accommodation of his suite which consisted of a captain of mounted police, named Paoli-Bernotti, an officer of ordinance, several Mamalukes and two *valets de chambre*, Marchand and Saint Denis, a large tent had been erected under the chestnut trees and close to a little spring which lost itself in a carpet of fresh moss besprinkled with wild lilies of the valley and violets. Dinner was never served at the hermitage, the emperor descending every evening to Marciana and dining with his mother, who was installed there.

On the receipt of Mme. Walewska's letter the emperor at once prepared for her visit, but the orders regarding the arrangements for her reception were so given that the name of the expected guest was kept a profound secret. She disembarked at Porto-Ferrajo during the night of September 1st, and found awaiting her on the quay a carriage and four, and three saddled horses in charge of Bernotti. Accompanied by her sister and little son she entered the carriage, while her brother, Colonel Laczinski, mounted one of the horses, and in the bright moonlight they set off for Marciana.

The emperor, accompanied by Paoli and two Mamalukes awaited their coming at Procchio, and there Mme. Walewska was also obliged to mount one of the horses as it was impossible for the carriage to go further; Bernotti took charge of the little boy and the party finally arrived at the summit of the mountain. Dismounting before the hermitage the emperor assisted Mme. Walewska from her saddle, and, hat in hand pointed to the house saying: "*Madame*, there is my palace to which you are heartily welcome;" and abandoning the house to the ladies he himself went to sleep in the tent which sheltered his suite and servants.

The close of the night was stormy, and in the early morning the emperor, who had been unable to sleep, called Marchand and questioned him as to whether any gossip had been caused by the arrival of his visitors; he was informed by the valet that it was rumoured in Porto-Ferrajo that the mysterious lady was none other than the empress, and the child the little King of Rome, and that, moved by this rumour, Doctor Foureau had hastened to the hermitage to offer his services and was at that moment awaiting the emperor's command.

Napoleon dressed and left the tent. The morning was bright and beautiful with no trace of the furious storm of the previous night, and on the mountain side in the bright sunshine, the mysterious child was playing happily. The emperor called the boy and seating himself in a chair which Marchand brought, took him upon his knee; he then sent the valet in search of Dr. Foureau and when the latter appeared said, pointing to the child: "Well, Foureau, what do you think of him?"

"Sire," responded the doctor, "the king has grown tremendously," at which answer Napoleon laughed heartily, for young Walewski was a year older than the King of Rome, but his beautiful features and the blond curls which fell in profusion over his shoulders caused him to resemble his half-brother closely, or rather, to resemble Isabey's popular portrait of the King of Rome.

Napoleon chatted for some moments with the physician, then, thanking him for the friendship manifested by the prompt offer of his services, dismissed him and turned to greet Mme. Walewska whom he espied about leaving the hermitage. Breakfast, which had been ordered from Marciana, was served under the chestnut trees; the meal passed off gaily, and the rest of the day was spent by the emperor and Mme. Walewska in walking and talking together.

At dinner the emperor desired that the boy, of whom he had seen but little during the day, should sit at his side, and when Mme. Walewska objected on the score of the child's boisterous ways he insisted, saying that he did not mind the child's roguishness, his own childhood having been a turbulent one. When they were seated at table the emperor recounted anecdotes of his boyhood telling how he used to beat his brother Joseph and force him to do his bidding, and how his mother had punished him by giving him only dry bread to eat—bread which he had given to the shepherd boys in exchange for their chestnut bread, or else thrown away and gone to his foster-mother's where he was fed on the best the house afforded and caressed to his heart's content. Young Walewska, who had at first been overawed by the presence of so many grown people at table and had behaved in most exemplary manner, was emboldened by the emperor's stories to give vent to his naturally high spirits, whereupon Napoleon said:

"I see, my lad, that you don't fear the whip.... well I advise you to! I never got a beating but once, but I've never forgotten it." He then went on to relate how Pauline and himself had once made sport of their mother and been soundly whipped by her in consequence. The boy listened attentively, and when the emperor had finished speaking exclaimed with an air of conviction: "I shall never be whipped for *that*, I would not make fun of *my* mother," whereupon the emperor embraced him tenderly saying, "That was well said."

At eight o'clock that evening the visitors returned to Ponte-Ferrajo, and re-embarked for Naples; in indemnification for the confiscations of Murat, Mme. Walewska carried with her a draft on the emperor's treasurer for sixty-one thousand *francs*. It is said that her stay at Naples was so prolonged, that March of 1815 still found her there.

In spite of all the precautions taken to keep Mme. Walewska's visit to Elba a secret, it became known, for there were too many people interested in the emperor's movements, too many spies about him, to keep such a visit from being talked of. The islanders insisted that the mysterious lady was Marie-Louise, but the English and Bourbon spies were better informed, and their employers believed that this visit heralded the renewal of the emperor's relations with the Polish woman. In reality, Mme. Walewska's journey to Elba was actuated rather by friendship and sympathy than by love, and the presence of her sister, Mlle. Laczinska, at the Hermitage, proves that the visit was a conventional one.

If Napoleon had any love-affair while at Elba, it certainly was not with the so-called Countess de Rohan, who was but a vulgar adventuress, and went to the island to reclaim no one knows what, from the emperor, and to offer him her company in his exile, but rather with a woman who has been much less discussed; the same whom he had received several times in his apartments in the orangery, at Saint-Cloud, and who, unsolicited, repaired to Ponte-Ferrajo. Whether this lady was married to Colonel B **** when she went to Elba, or married him there is not known, but, wed or not, her devotion to the fallen emperor was great, and it is unfortunate that so little is known regarding the details of her life. What we do know is, that, not content with having followed Napoleon to Elba, she went to Rambouillet in 1815 and besought his permission to follow him to St. Helena, that she was heartbroken at his refusal, and that with three thousand *francs* which were given her, she went to the United States, where she hoped to find him.

Little attention seems to have been attracted by Napoleon's intimacy with this woman, while certain letters, written by a miserable priest in the pay of the Duke de Blacas, have been republished periodically; these letters were written with the view of accrediting calumnious reports which were then afloat, and it is needless to dwell upon them here.

While at Elba, Napoleon passed through a moral and political crisis which rendered the greatest reserve obligatory; he knew that the slightest indiscretion would be related to Marie-Louise, and enlarged upon by his enemies who surrounded her, and that she would be deeply wounded thereby. He had sent Captain Hurault de Sorbée, the husband of one of her ladies, to Aix-les-Bains, with instructions to essay to speak with the empress, and deliver his messages in person, and had received news which led him to hope that a regular correspondence would soon be established between them; thus it was scarcely the moment to become entangled in a scandalous intrigue.

Time passed, the month of September dragged its weary length along without bringing the emperor a word from his wife or son, and at length, worn out by anxiety and unfulfilled hope, he determined to write to the Duke of Tuscany, upon whose friendship he still relied and whom he had designated to his wife as their natural intermediary. The letter he sent the duke was not supplicatory, from the manner in which he addressed, as "My dear brother and uncle;" it is evident that

Napoleon remembered the favours his highness had received at his hands, and believed that the one-time parasite of Compiègne must also bear them in mind.

> Having received no news of my wife since August 10th, nor of my son in six months, I beg your royal highness to inform me if you will permit me to send weekly letters to my wife in your care, whether you will undertake to keep me informed regarding her health, etc., and to forward letters from my son's governess, Mme. de Montesquiou. I flatter myself that, in spite of the events which have changed so many persons, your highness still entertains some friendship for me; if you assure me of this by granting my request, it will be a great consolation and comfort, and, in that case, I beg your highness to show yourself favourably disposed towards this little canton which shares the loyal sentiments of Tuscany for your person. I trust your highness does not doubt the sincerity of the sentiments I have always expressed, nor my esteem and regard; and I beg to be kindly remembered to your highness's children.

It was simply a question of a friendly service to be rendered one who confessed himself unhappy and admitted himself defeated, and who, to soften the prince's heart, almost avowed himself his subject, yet it was not a supplication, and the old equality, nay, superiority of rank, pierces through the carefully-worded lines. There was no answer to this letter, for the drama was ended, the Imperial house of Austria had succeeded in dishonouring its daughter, and the Empress of France had fallen so low as to become the mistress of her own chamberlain.

After such a letter, written to such a man. Napoleon would not take any further action; his wife and child had been stolen from him, the Bourbons no longer paid the annual sum stipulated for at Fontainebleau, and he saw that he should be forced to disband his guard, and, unable to offer even a semblance of resistance, be killed with his faithful followers, should the allied sovereigns order his transportation to some remote island, the Azores for example, as Talleyrand had suggested on the 13th of October, because, as he then said: "They were five hundred miles from any land."

The emperor foresaw that he must either submit to being transported by the sovereigns, or assassinated by the bandits in Brulart's pay; and preferring to make a supreme effort and risk all for France, determined upon his return.

CHAPTER 20

The Hundred Days.

On New Year's day, 1815, Napoleon had received a letter from the empress, giving him news of their son, telling what a handsome and charming child he was, and that he would soon be able to write himself to his father. It is impossible to say why this letter was written, possibly it was prompted by remorse, but whatever actuated Marie-Louise it served to strengthen the tie between herself and Napoleon, and confirmed his conviction that she had never abandoned the intention of rejoining him, that her silence was compulsory, and that, were she free to do so, she would hasten to his side.

He was convinced that, had he a throne to offer, Marie-Louise's jailors would set her at liberty, and as soon as he felt assured of the success of his enterprise he hastened to inform her, writing from Lyons on the 12th of March. Marie-Louise, however, did with this letter, as she had done with all those she had received from Elba, handed it over to her father who communicated its contents to the allied plenipotentiaries, and Napoleon received no answer.

Immediately upon re-entering Paris the emperor ordered that the empress's apartments should be put in order and re-established her household upon its old footing. Ten days later, upon the 1st of April, he wrote an official letter to the Austrian emperor wherein he reclaimed the "objects of my tenderest affection, my wife and son."

> As the long separation necessitated by circumstances has caused me the greatest sorrow I have ever experienced, I desire that my wife and child be speedily restored to me, and am assured that our reunion is as earnestly desired by the virtuous princess, whose destiny Your Majesty united with mine, as by myself.

And he terminated the letter by saying:

I know too well Your Majesty's principles and the value Your Highness places upon family-ties not to feel assured that, despite the disposition of your cabinet, or questions of political expediency. Your Majesty will accelerate the reunion of a wife with her husband, a son with his father.

Like the others this letter remained unanswered, and the obstinate silence, opposed alike to official and family letters, confirmed Napoleon's belief that it was the political attitude of the house of Austria and the pressure brought to bear upon her which paralysed the natural desire of his wife and prevented her rejoining him, he therefore determined to employ secret means for communicating with her. With this object he sent to Vienna carefully chosen messengers, Flahaut and Montrond, men who could be trusted and who possessed facilities for approaching Marie-Louise. Montrond alone pierced the lines, but when he was about to give to the empress the letter of which he was the bearer, Meneval interposed. The *ci-devant* secretary of Napoleon, who had become, in 1813, the empress's secretary and had followed her to Austria, understood only too well the relations existing between his royal mistress and Count Neipperg, and he felt that in burning the emperor's tender letter which he had written to his wife, he was rendering him a service.

Nevertheless, Meneval dared not write directly to Napoleon informing him of the real state of affairs, for he realised what a terrible blow it would be to his master, and he therefore determined to inform one in whose unwavering fidelity he had implicit confidence of the *liaison*, and wrote an anonymous letter to Lavallette; Count de Lavallette, however, saw in this anonymous communication only a political machination, and it is not strange that Napoleon shared his views. They were soon to be enlightened, however, for Ballouhey, secretary of expenses for the two empresses and a man whose fidelity and honesty were unquestionable, was en route from Vienna by way of Munich, where he was to receive some instructions from Prince Eugène. The emperor was so impatient to see Ballouhey that he ordered his arrival at Belfort to be telegraphed him, and stationed an orderly at his house in Paris with instructions to conduct the secretary to the Elysée the instant he appeared.

Ballouhey reached Paris on the 28th of April and was closeted for two hours with the emperor, but, though Napoleon received a clear and concise statement of Prince Eugène's ideas of the political situation, he failed to obtain definite information upon the subject nearest his heart. Ballouhey was a scrupulously exact accountant; he had been deeply attached both to Josephine and Marie-Louise; but he was a timorous man and dared not affirm the truth of the scandalous *liaison* which was an open secret in Vienna.

Meneval, expelled from Vienna, arrived a fortnight later, and from him the whole truth was learned. On taking leave of the empress she had charged him to say to his imperial master "that, while she would take no step towards securing a divorce, she believed he would offer no objection to an amicable separation." "Such a separation," she said, "was indispensable, but it would not impair the sentiments of esteem and gratitude which she entertained for him," and she added that "her decision to remain apart from Napoleon was irrevocable, and not even her father had the right to oblige her to return to France."

It was Marie-Louise who, putting herself under the protection of the allied plenipotentiaries in an official letter dated March 12th, provoked the furious declaration which was signed by them on the 13th, and in recompense for her act Count Neipperg was created court chamberlain; and it was with her consent that, on the 18th of March, the little King of Rome was separated from his governess, Mme. de Montesquieu, and deprived of all his French servants.

Undoubtedly, Meneval added other, and more private details, for it was no longer right to conceal the monstrous truth; possibly Marie-Louise was then in the early stages of one of those pregnancies which were to people the avenues of Burg with adulterous bastards, entitled princes and highnesses to the everlasting shame of the royal house of Austria.

When, after the birth of the King of Rome, Dubois, the *accoucheur*, affirmed that a second child would imperil Marie-Louise's life, Napoleon, despite his desire for numerous offspring and a second son to sit on the throne of Italy, had bowed to the physician's decision: M. de Neipperg had no such scruples and proved repeatedly that Baron Dubois had been mistaken. Although the emperor could no longer doubt the unfaithfulness of Marie-Louise, it was necessary to keep the truth from the nation and essential that the people should conserve their illusions regarding their empress; twelve months previous he considered that nothing would appeal more to the people than the thought of that woman and child confided to France; today the captivity in which they were held, the separation which violated all laws, human and divine, the attempted violation of conjugal faith and paternal love committed by the sovereigns in arms for the re-establishment in France of a government like their own, seemed to him of a nature to appeal to every generous and honest instinct in the heart of men and patriots.

The grief which the empress felt when she was torn from the post which it was her duty to fill, the thirty sleepless nights which she had passed in 1814, the real imprisonment to which she had been subjected, the treaty of Fontainebleau, violated by the kings who had torn from him his wife and son, the indignant cry of the old Queen Marie-Caroline to her granddaughter: "Since you are prohibited from going out by the door, escape by the window and fly to rejoin your husband," the King of Rome—then called the Prince Imperial—separated from his mother, Mme. de Montesquiou driven away and trembling for her pupil's life, the emperor wished Meneval to recount it all and ordered a report to be prepared in case the Chamber made a motion for the King of Rome. The Chamber!

Not once during the hundred days, not once during the six years of agony at Saint Helena, did a word of censure or bitterness against Marie-Louise escape him; he invariably spoke of her with affection and kindly pity; he thought of her only as she was when she first came to France, young, fresh, loyal and unsullied; there is not one of his companions in captivity who has not reported his conversations regarding her almost in the same terms. If a European ship dropped anchor in Jamestown Bay Napoleon was sure that he was about to receive a letter from the empress, and nervous, anxious and unable to work, would pass the whole day in expectancy; when one of his servants was taken from him his first thought was to send a letter by that sure hand to Marie-Louise, as for example the one he confided to his surgeon in which he said:

> Should the bearer of this see you, my good Louise, I beg of you to permit him to kiss your hands.

In his will, which was dated the 5th of April, 1821, he wrote this phrase:

> I never have had any fault to find with my dear wife, the Empress Marie-Louise; to my last moment I shall retain for her the most tender sentiments, and I beg her to watch over my son and guard against the dangers which still surround his childhood.

And, as if this was not enough, he bequeathed to her from the modest wardrobe which now constituted his sole fortune, all his laces, and on the 28th of April, a week before his death, he instructed Antommarchi to take his heart from his body and send it to her.

Preserve my heart in alcohol and take it yourself to Parma to my dear Marie-Louise; tell her that I love her tenderly and have never ceased to love her, recount to her all that you have seen, all that touches my situation and my death.

Truly Hudson Lowe did well in obliging Antommarchi to place the silver vase which contained Napoleon's heart in his coffin: What would Count Neipperg have done with it?

In default of the perfidious Austrian, many other women, from France, Ireland and Poland surrounded the emperor during the last glorious days of his short reign of three months, encouraging his spirit by their enthusiasm and devotion, pleasing his eye by their beauty; while even those who were least fitted for political intrigues became his spies and informants, and by instinct rather than reason, frequently gave counsel which might well have been followed; for example, George regarding Fouché; Mme. Pellapra who hastened to return to Paris from Lyons and warned him of the Duke d'Otrante's intentions, and Mme. Walewska, who, hastily returning from Naples, was immediately received with her son at the Elysée, brought messages from Murat.

Mme. **** was among the first to present herself to the emperor, and assuming her title and rank as lady of the palace, was among the faithful ones of the 20th of March, and among those who, in the brilliantly illuminated *salon* of the Tuileries, impatiently awaited the arrival of the exile of Elba. There were many others, Mme. Dulauloy, Mme. Lavallette, Mme. Ney, Mme. Regnauld de Saint-Jean-d'Angely, Mme. de Beauvau and Mme. de Turenne, all of whom vied with each other in the endeavour to encourage and please him. At that time there breathed upon these women of France that divine afflatus which creates heroines and martyrs, inspires acts of supreme devotion and courage, and strengthens souls to face courageously the severest trials.

During that sinister period, which is justly called, "the White Terror," a period of atrocities which today we vainly seek to palliate, the women of the Empire manifested, amidst the universal cowardliness of mankind, a courage, energy and presence of mind which immortalizes them; at the Tuileries during the hundred days, at Malmaison and after

Waterloo, they proved how well they knew how to show their loyalty and honour misfortune.

It was not alone the well known and the celebrated, but the humble and the obscure who showed their devotion; as, for example, a woman, who, at the review of the confederation, approached the emperor and handed him a petition, a roll of paper carefully fastened, from which, when it was opened, there fell twenty-five banknotes of a thousand *francs* each; and another who, on the 23rd of June, the eve of the day upon which Napoleon was to leave the Elysée for Malmaison, wrote to his *valet de chambre*, requesting him to meet her at the church of Saint-Philippe du Roule to receive an important communication.

Marchand went to the rendezvous, and found at the place indicated a woman engaged in prayer; she was veiled, but not heavily enough to hide her features, which were exceptionally beautiful; Marchand approached and asked in what way he could serve her. The mysterious lady hesitated for a moment, then, with extreme embarrassment, replied that the misfortunes of the emperor had touched her deeply, that she wished to see, to console and love him. Napoleon, on hearing of her desire, smiled and said: "Hers is an admiration which might lead to an intrigue; it must not be encouraged," but the *naïve* offer of this heart, coming on such a day and at such an hour, touched him profoundly, and later, upon several occasions, he spoke of the mysterious lady of Saint-Philippe du Roule.

Did he find in captivity some woman who gave to him the consolation which only a tender woman can give to a man? We know about his childish romps with Miss Elizabeth Balcombe,[1] during her sojourn at Briars; and we divine a familiarity with a woman whose conduct during the Empire would seemingly have forbidden her to approach him, and who, twice divorced, dismissed from court, had, by the simple fact of his marriage, brought disgrace upon her third husband. But if the testamentary liberality which the emperor showed this person gives some weight to the reports of the foreign commissioners, if her presence really occasioned discord among the emperor's companions, and her departure was one of the painful experiences which he was obliged to live through, one yet knows too little regarding this portion of the drama of Saint Helena to expatiate upon it; the woman plied her role upon the island; that is all that one can say.

---

1. *Recollections of Napoleon at St. Helena - The Remarkable Story of a Fallen Emperor and a Teenage Girl* by Mrs. Abell (late Miss Elizabeth Balcombe) also published by Leonaur.

Side by side with this retired courtesan, whom interest had taken to Rochefort, and whom interest retained at Saint Helena, we find another woman, who is really worthy of admiration. By birth and by her relationship with the Fitz-James family, Countess Bertrand was entitled to one of the best positions at court, and, had she remained in Paris, would doubtless have been one of the leaders of society, but she voluntarily shared her husband's devotion to his chief and followed him into exile; she lived in a cabin infested with rats, within reach of the emperor, but unable to succour or amuse him. She remained until the end, compassionate, sensible and dignified, guarding her honour like a Roman matron, and like a statue of grief she followed the procession which conducted the captive conqueror to his grave in the valley of Geranium, and she, an Englishwoman by birth, was the only woman who wept over the remains of him whom her countrymen had murdered.

CHAPTER 20

Summary

The sum of the preceding chapters only signified that Napoleon was subject to the same desires, passions and weaknesses as other men, and had taken no vows of continence; that the amorous side of his nature was twofold, on one side the physical alone reigned, on the other physical and moral united ... the moral being in the ascendant.

We have hidden none of the adventures wherein the animal part of his nature alone predominated; not because one can glean from them a special insight into his character, but because to hide them would give rise to the suspicion that they were wholly unfavourable to his general character. Because he was Napoleon all that he did was known, and no matter how carefully he hid his amorous intrigues they were sure to be discovered; ladies-in-waiting and ladies'-maids, *aides-de-cam*p and valets were ceaselessly on the watch, and no matter how insignificant the events which transpired they were all carefully noted. Everybody at the Tuileries lived in the governmental zone, whether they were soliciting favours or hunting for news, and all took a lively interest in the doings of the emperor, and each made a note of any incident which came under his observation.

As everything, Napoleon did, has an historical interest, as his lightest words, slightest actions, even the trifling ailments which from time to time afflicted him, have been of interest to the public for a hundred years, and as many erroneous tales have been accredited, the sole course for the author of this book to pursue is to establish facts, and relate such adventures as are authenticated by the according narrations of various reliable persons; if any have been omitted, or simply referred to, it is because they have been related by but one chronicler and it has been impossible to discover documentary proof of their authenticity, or sometimes because they were of so commonplace a nature as to render it useless to dwell upon them.

There were women always ready to gratify his desires, whether expressed by himself or made known by his messengers; he accepted their willingly-given caresses, sometimes from physical necessity, sometimes from voluptuousness; but he never experienced mental exhaustion or fatigue from his adventures, nor did any woman distract him from his work; of all these women none was seduced by him, for if there was a virgin among their number she was one who trafficked on her virtue.

In order to judge the men of the Empire, above all, Napoleon, by the narrow and hypocritical standard of contemporaneous times one must place them in similar environments; their lives were not the humdrum, monotonous lives of the modern business man, they were always in the saddle, death on the crupper, galloping from one end of Europe to the other amidst a rain of bullets, and if some of them, unknown to the emperor, trailed their mistresses after them, the majority gave little thought to the senses and remained chaste during the campaigns.

If, on their return from a long war, or when a city was conquered and there was a lull in the strife, brute passion gained the mastery, does it signify that they were the most debauched of mankind? To have followed the calling which they selected from preference and clung to from ambition must they not have been, by origin and nature, stronger, more brutal, more like the primitive man, than the men of this generation? Did not their profession develop, accentuate and foster all that was savage, combative and animal in their natures? Had they not the same tastes, desires and appetites as other men? Was it to be expected that they would remain scrupulously faithful to wives whom they rarely saw?

Some few, indeed, were faithful, and there are admirable examples of fidelity, tenderness and delicacy given by those men of war, but for the majority the distractions of the camp and garrison intrigues were the rule, and they placed no importance upon them.

Side by side with these animal appetites they entertained ingenuously sentimental ideas of conjugal tenderness, and nothing was too good or too precious for the wife who had almost invariably been married for love and from the most disinterested motives; to satisfy her tastes they pillaged Europe, throwing their spoils at her feet; to content her caprices and ambitions they deployed an amount of patience and diplomacy which would make one smile were it not so touching.

In generosity, in the care for his wife, in letters, presents, and in the wealth showered upon her. Napoleon was not outdone by any of his warriors, but his sentimentalism was of another origin and essence than theirs.

The soldiers of the Empire, who had neither by nature nor by education any scruples, fabricated a code of honour for themselves, and although they fondly believed the sword had made them the equals of the men of gentle birth whose places they had usurped, and whom they hated, their "soldier's code" differed in many respects from that attributed by Montesquieu to gentlemen; but in their days they could hardly search for the rules regulating that code of honour, and they did not care to take a Lauzun or a Tilly for their model; they still detested those whom they had replaced, and if they laid claim to the title of "gentlemen" it was because they considered themselves the equals of men of noble ancestry.

From 1806 everything in France was modelled on the troubadour style, novels, historical works, pictures, dress and drama, but it was less a question of the troubadour himself, than of him of whom he sang; the knight who professed the adoration of his lady, who for his exploits in the Holy Land received a scarf embroidered by her fair hands and considered his deeds of valour well rewarded by a glance from her dear eyes. The warriors of the Empire made every effort to model themselves after these ideal *chevaliers*, and though they did not gird themselves with the fair one's colours, many a man wore a sword-knot embroidered by her, or wore the beloved one's portrait over his heart, and decorated himself with some bauble of her giving upon state occasions.

Napoleon yielded less to this current than his followers, than Prince Eugène and certain of his marshals, but the ambient atmosphere finally affected him also, as certain incidents in his relations with Marie-Louise prove conclusively; but it was not, however, until the close of the Empire that a sentiment, until then unexperienced, awoke in him and effaced all others.

Up to that time Napoleon's sentimentalism was in no degree influenced by the literature of the time, but greatly by that of a previous era. Rousseau had influenced him, as his letters to Josephine, Mme. **** and Mme. Walewska show; in all of them may be found the same tone, the identical expressions and words which were used by the young Lieutenant Bonaparte when from Valence he complained of his loneliness and poverty.

A pupil of Jean-Jacques, Napoleon was so thoroughly impregnated with the ideas of his master, that he, who had striven for and obtained, even the impossible, in the order of events, encountered only impotence, negation and disgust in the range of sentiments. In Napoleon's continual search for a woman who would love him for himself, whose only thought would be for him, who would live but for him, and with whom he could dwell in a constant interchange of tenderness, he certainly acted in good faith; but who can tell up to what point he was influenced by his literary souvenirs, or how much he forced himself in the effort to experience sensations which he believed to be rare and strange.

That which gives us reason to think that he forced his nature is that he soon wearied; he received less pleasure than he anticipated in the society of the woman he wooed, and the real woman seemed invariably inferior to the ideal creature of his imagination; the sentimentalism which was cultivated found itself in opposition to the positivism which was natural, and he ruptured the much-sought-for relations; but only to run in search of a new sensation, a fresh experience, as soon as the occasion offered.

In such a man his fidelity, not of the senses, but of the heart, is surprising; he had mistresses whom he loved sincerely, and he divorced Josephine, yet she held a place apart in his heart and he ever felt a deep and tender affection for her, an affection so strong that he pardoned all her faults and the wrongs she had done him; nay, more, he forgot them.

Josephine's life, of which he did not fail to keep himself informed, must have revolted him, but he shut his eyes to it, and remembered only that the woman whom he had raised to be the first lady in France, who was associated with his destiny, was grace itself and elegance personified; he endowed her with all the virtues and graces which a passionate lover showers upon his mistress, and, although he reproached her for her prodigality, he proved his affection by giving her the means to gratify all her desires.

To the end of his days Napoleon ignored the true Josephine, and threw over the love of his youth a halo of imaginary charms and virtues which has immortalized her; if he thus deceived posterity it was because he was himself deceived, and to the very end he persisted in the illusions, holding before his eyes, in his heart and senses, at Saint Helena, the Josephine whom he had seen for the first time in the rue Chantereine, the woman in whose arms he first tasted the sweets of love.

Napoleon's love for Josephine was such as a man gives to his mistress, a love without respect, which puts no restraint upon itself, exacts instant satisfaction and does not fear disagreements; which voluntarily confesses its infidelities and relates *risquée* anecdotes; that such was Napoleon's affection for Josephine is proved by the fact that at each evolution of his destiny he realised more forcibly that his interests demanded he should break with her and rupture the union which was not a marriage in his eyes because it had not for eight years been sanctioned by the Church, and because, when it did receive the Church's blessing, he had appeared before the priest by force. Had Josephine given him a child he would have considered the contract valid, but, being childless, he considered himself free, and when he separated himself from her he treated her like a mistress, consoling her by large sums of money and arranging for her existence in an opulent style.

One may question whether, in spite of the weakness Napoleon had for Josephine, despite his showering favours and presents upon her, adopting her children and elevating her relatives to posts of honour, Napoleon ever regarded her as of his family; so great was the difference between the sentiments he entertained for her and those inspired by Marie-Louise, particularly after Marie-Louise had borne him a child. Then the conjugal spirit took possession of and dominated him; undoubtedly he never gave her the passionate love he had bestowed upon his first wife, but he entertained for Marie-Louise a respect which he never gave to Josephine.

While he had invariably refused all participation in affairs of state to his first wife he voluntarily accorded it to the second, discovering in her greater intelligence than he accorded to his oldest councillors or even to his brothers. With Josephine the sentimental side of his nature as developed by Rousseau was dominant, while with Marie-Louise his Corsican atavism and the traditions of his native mountains resumed their supremacy: Marie-Louise was sanctified in his view by her motherhood.

Napoleon would never admit that his wife had abandoned him and deceived him; she was his wife, the mother of his son, and that placed her above the temptations and weakness common to her sex. So dominant was the conjugal spirit in him that, to the hour of his death, he ignored her treachery, and that he, who was so jealous of the woman he had once possessed that he complained bitterly of Mme. Walewska's marriage, never uttered a complaint against his wife. Was his silence occasioned by the desire of securing for her the respect which a monarchal lord requires paid to crowned heads, did it make him happier to ignore her faults, did he find excuses for them in the extraordinary circumstances surrounding her, or did he hope that the secret he refused to reveal would be better guarded by history? Possibly he was actuated by all these motives, but his predominant thought was, that she was his wife, and therefore could not fall.

Thus, separating the purely sensual *liaisons*, which were brief, from the deep attachments of his life, we find in Napoleon as great a faculty for love as for thought and action, and are obliged to admit that he was as astonishing a husband as he was a warrior and a statesman.

There remains but one point to be considered, whether any of the women with whom Napoleon was closely related ever swayed him sufficiently to affect his political views and moves; it does not appear that any woman, either wife or mistress, directly influenced him, but doubtless the impressions received from both, the ideas they advanced and the circumstances accompanying certain of his *liaisons* gave rise to new ideas in his brain and modified old ones.

Dearly loved as Josephine was, she was not among those who were the primary cause of certain political moves. It has been affirmed that it was her influence which surrounded him with people of noble birth and led him, at times, to sacrifice the spirit of the revolution to the traditions of the old *régime*, but that is an error; Josephine sought to draw the old nobility round Napoleon by his order, and it was at his command that she protected them. An insight into the various gradations of society under the old *régime*, some false impressions, some information, much of which was inexact, was about all he gleaned from her.

The birth of a son to Mlle. Denuelle de la Plaegne doubtless first determined him to divorce Josephine, and that of Mme. Walewska's cemented his resolution, while his political attitude towards Poland is explained if one remembers who was his mistress and close companion from 1807 to 1809, even his long friendship for Bernadotte becomes comprehensible when one recalls his tenderness for Désirée.

When Napoleon married Marie-Louise and became, through her, a member of the house of Austria, he believed the relationship so formed was close and binding, as the tie which bound him to his own family, and his faith in the Austrian emperor's friendship, his confidence in his wife's fidelity and discretion is due to his belief in the strength and indestructibility of ties of blood and his conviction that they alone rendered a political alliance inviolate. Marie-Louise, not because she was unusually intelligent, but because of the role she played in his political combinations and the prestige of her motherhood, exercised an unprecedented influence over him. Napoleon set a high value upon ties of blood and the obligations entailed by kinship; he was a true Corsican in the strength of his attachment and his adherence to family, and it appears as if the very value he placed upon the ties which should be the strongest and most sacred to humanity caused his fall.

If women had played no role in his life, Napoleon would cease to be the amazing example of masculine genius that he is, and would become a sexless being without interest to humanity because not subject to the failings and passions of other men, uninfluenced by the traditions which sway them, possessed of no sentiment common to mankind. As it was, this man, whose genius was astounding, who, served by an unparalleled fortune, accomplished the greatest task that mortal ever undertook, was precisely the man to whom no emotion was a stranger. It is human to be influenced by, to believe in and to love woman, to experience by her and for her all the sensations and emotions which she inspires, and in that respect, as in all others, Napoleon was superior to mankind.

www.ingramcontent.com/pod-product-compliance
Lightning Source LLC
Chambersburg PA
CBHW021959160426
43197CB00007B/189